Tort

CORE TEXT SERIES

Tort

Seventh Edition

STEVE HEDLEY MA, LLB, BSc
Professor of Law, University College, Cork

Series Editor
NICOLA PADFIELD
Fitzwilliam College, Cambridge

OXFORD
UNIVERSITY PRESS

OXFORD
UNIVERSITY PRESS

Great Clarendon Street, Oxford OX2 6DP

Oxford University Press is a department of the University of Oxford.
It furthers the University's objective of excellence in research, scholarship,
and education by publishing worldwide in

Oxford New York

Auckland Cape Town Dar es Salaam Hong Kong Karachi
Kuala Lumpur Madrid Melbourne Mexico City Nairobi
New Delhi Shanghai Taipei Toronto

With offices in

Argentina Austria Brazil Chile Czech Republic France Greece
Guatemala Hungary Italy Japan Poland Portugal Singapore
South Korea Switzerland Thailand Turkey Ukraine Vietnam

Oxford is a registered trade mark of Oxford University Press
in the UK and in certain other countries

Published in the United States
by Oxford University Press Inc., New York

© Oxford University Press, 2011

Fourth edition 2004
Fifth edition 2006
Sixth edition 2008

British Library Cataloguing in Publication Data
Data available

Library of Congress Cataloging in Publication Data
Data available

Typeset by Newgen Imaging Systems (P) Ltd, Chennai, India
Printed in Great Britain
on acid-free paper by
Clays Ltd, St Ives Plc

ISBN 978–0–19–958656–1

1 3 5 7 9 10 8 6 4 2

This book is dedicated to the memory of my grandfather, Wilfrid Joyce.

Preface

This book provides a brief summary of the principles of Tort, with proper attention also to the policy basis of the law. Inevitably, I have simplified somewhat; a book of this size cannot be a substitute for a full treatise. Nonetheless, I hope that it will be of some use to students of the area. Overall, I have done my best not simply to state what the law is, but to give some sense of *why* it is, what its significance is, and how it might be improved.

Cases added since the last edition include: *Alexis v Newham London Borough Council* (liability for criminal acts of others); *Bhamra v Dubb t/a Lucky Caterers* (breach and foresight); *British Chiropractic Association v Singh* (defamation); *Ferguson v British Gas Trading* (harassment); *Iqbal v Prison Officers Association* (false imprisonment); *Jain v Trent Strategic Health Authority* (statutory powers and economic loss); *Kaschke v Gray* (defamation); *Maga v Trustees of the Birmingham Archdiocese of the Roman Catholic Church* (vicarious liability); *McKenny v Foster* (animals); *Mitchell v Glasgow City Council* (right to life); *Orchard v Lee* (standard of care); *Patchett v Swimming Pool and Allied Trades Association Ltd* (negligent misstatement); *Savage v South Essex Partnership NHS Foundation Trust* (right to life); *Singh v Eastern Media Group* (defamation); *Total Network SL v Revenue and Customs Commissioners* (conspiracy); *Van Colle v Chief Constable of Hertfordshire Police* (right to life); and *Watson v Croft Promosport Ltd* (injunctions).

The law is generally stated as at 1 August 2010. Thanks are due to Matt Dyson for pointing out an error in the previous edition.

I would be delighted to hear of any comments, suggestions or criticisms that others have of this book.

Steve Hedley
15 August 2010

Contents

Table of cases

Table of statutes

Table of statutory instruments

What is tort?

SUMMARY

The law of tort provides remedies in a wide variety of situations. Overall it has a rather tangled appearance. But there is some underlying order. This chapter explains some of that order. It also reviews the main functions of the law of tort. These include deterring unsafe behaviour, giving a just response to wrongdoing, and spreading the cost of accidents broadly. The chapter then introduces two major institutions within the law of tort: the tort of negligence and the role played by statute law.

Tort: part of the law of civil wrongs

1.1 Where the claimant sues the defendant for a tort, the claimant is complaining of a wrong suffered at the defendant's hands. The remedy claimed is usually a money payment. So proceedings in tort are different from criminal proceedings: in a criminal court, typically, it is not the *victim* of the wrong who starts the proceedings, but some official prosecutor. The remedy will also be different. A criminal court *may* decide that the defendant should pay a sum of money, but if it does, the money will usually be forfeited to the state, rather than to the claimant. (For this reason, some say that tort is about *compensating* the claimant, whereas the criminal law is about *punishing* the defendant. But as you will see, this begs various questions about what 'punishment' means; I will soon return to this issue (**1.12**).)

This is the most basic defining feature of tort. It is a civil, not a criminal, action. The claim is pursued in a civil court, and civil procedure is very different from criminal procedure. The initiative in beginning the action, and many decisions as to the conduct of the action, lie with the claimant; whereas in criminal proceedings, the claimant's role is at most that of a mere witness.

(It is not *quite* that simple. Criminal courts can sometimes award compensation to the victims of crime—about 100,000 compensation orders are made in any one year. And in theory, though only very rarely in practice, the victim of a crime may prosecute, rather than leave it up to officials. But as a broad picture this is substantially accurate. Very often, civil and criminal proceedings are taken over the same wrong.)

Tort is not the whole of the law of civil wrongs

1.2 The remedies available in tort are only part of the large array of remedies available in different situations. Tort represents a diverse and (at first sight) almost random selection of this wider whole. The complaint may be that the defendant injured the claimant's reputation ('defamation', **8.1**). Or the claimant may be complaining about trespass to the claimant's land (**7.2**), or interference with the claimant's enjoyment of it ('nuisance', **7.11**). A variety of careless behaviour threatening the claimant's interests is caught by the tort of 'negligence' (**1.26**). And the defendant may be liable for some source of danger over which the defendant has, or ought to have, some control, such as the defendant's animals (**7.44**). Or the defendant may be held responsible for the acts of others, particularly the defendant's own employees (**9.2**).

Tort is, then, a radically miscellaneous subject. Can we impose some sort of order on this jumble?

> *Q.* Are there common themes running through all the various torts?
>
> *A.* Yes, and they are sufficiently coherent to give an overall picture of the way tort works. But these themes cannot be pushed too far, and certainly cannot be used to resolve problems in concrete situations.

A whole view of tort

Types of misconduct

1.3 In all tort cases, the claimant is making some sort of complaint about misconduct, either the defendant's misconduct, or misconduct for which the defendant is responsible in law. But the type of misconduct varies. In some situations, the defendant must have had an *intention* to harm the claimant before liability can be established. In others, it is enough if the defendant was *negligent* (roughly, careless). In others still, the defendant is subject to *strict liability*, which means that the criterion for liability is harsher than negligence. (Some writers use 'strict liability' to mean that the standard by which the defendant is judged is harsher than 'negligence' but still recognizably a fault criterion, and 'absolute liability' to refer to standards which have nothing to do with fault. But this distinction is very hard to apply in practice.)

So there is a range of different types of wrongdoing, and which type is relevant must depend on the context. However, it is also important to remember that these various types of fault represent a smooth continuum, rather than entirely separate entities.

- 'Intention' is defined differently in different contexts. So a mugger who injures his victims certainly 'intends' harm, for the purposes of the tort of battery (**2.1**). But it is more difficult to say whether an entrepreneur who sets out to ruin a competitor 'intends' harm for the purposes of the economic torts—even though the loss is equally deliberate (**6.18**).

- The courts sometimes talk of a requirement of 'malice' in relation to some torts. This sometimes means 'intent to harm', but sometimes something narrower (such as personal spite against the victim), and sometimes something broader (see **8.30**). *In legal contexts, it is wise never to use the word 'malice' unless you can say precisely what you mean by the expression.*

- 'Negligence' is a useful word, and means (roughly) that the defendant has been clumsy in such a way as to threaten the claimant's legitimate interests. But it is a word to be used carefully, for it runs together two different questions: *(i)* whether the defendant needs to look out for the claimant's interests *at all* and, *(ii)* if so, *how* careful the defendant must be. The first question is often rephrased as asking whether the defendant owes the claimant a *duty of care*, and the second as to the *standard of care* required (**1.36**). It often happens that the defendant owes a similar duty to two claimants, but that the standard is quite different. For example, if the defendant conducts dangerous activities on his or her premises and injures the claimant as a result, the level of duty depends on whether the claimant was on the premises or off and, if on, whether the claimant was a trespasser or a lawful visitor (**4.15**).

- 'Strict liability' can arise in a variety of circumstances, each with their own peculiarities. It is, however, very rare indeed to find an example of strict liability which has no element of 'negligence' in it somewhere. For example, liability for defective products is in theory strict, but a manufacturer is often able to escape liability by proving that all due care was taken (**4.11**).

This classification by type of wrongdoing has its uses, particularly in emphasizing the range of different types of conduct with which we are concerned. But in itself it only begins to unlock the secrets of the area.

Types of injury

1.4 Can we get any further by asking about the injury to the claimant? The injury can take many forms: injury to, or interference with, the claimant's property or body; injury to the claimant's economic interests; or injury to the claimant's reputation. This is a useful approach, though following it through brings to the fore the patchwork nature of tort, and how little some parts of it have in common with others:

- *Interests in land* are well protected by the law of tort, whether against deliberate intrusions ('trespass', **7.2**), careless damage ('negligence', **5.1**) or interference with the claimant's right to enjoy the land ('nuisance', **7.11**). The law of real property is of course a distinct subject in itself, and very often it is purely arbitrary which doctrines are treated as part of tort, and which as part of property.

- *Interests in other forms of property* are protected up to a point by the law of tort. So deliberate taking of tangible property is caught by the tort of 'conversion', and careless damage by the tort of negligence (**5.1**). But the law of tort has far more to say on some forms of property than others. It has next to nothing to say on (for example) shares or financial assets. This makes little 21st-century sense, given the importance of these financial assets; the reasons are historical.

- *The claimant's interest in his or her own bodily integrity* is well protected by the law of tort, and accounts for the overwhelming majority of actions actually brought. The claimant is protected from deliberate injury by the torts of assault and battery (**2.1**), from careless injury by the tort of negligence (**3.1**), and from many other dangers by the tort of breach of statutory duty (**1.46**). But the system of liability in tort makes little sense on its own. It can only be properly assessed in the context of health and safety law, pensions and social security law, and the various ways in which tort liability in this area has been encouraged. The explosion of liability in this area, so surprising in historical terms, was no accident, but a deliberate object of official policy (**3.14**).

  Bodily injury is usually painful, and damages for the injury almost invariably include a sum for pain and suffering (**10.58**). To that extent, 'distress' is not obviously separable from 'bodily injury'. However, a case can be made that the claimant's interest in not being subjected to mental distress is a distinct interest protected by the law (Giliker 'A "new" head of damages: Damages for mental distress in the English law of torts' (2000) 20 LS 19).

• *Economic interests*, by contrast, are only patchily protected by tort law. The protection, such as it is, is against either deliberate harm (**6.1**) or negligent harm (**5.1**). This is a confused and rapidly developing area.

• *Reputation* is protected by the tort of 'defamation' (**8.1**). This is one of the more ancient torts, and the manner in which it protects reputation, and the associated costs, ensures that it is a matter of repeated and bitter controversy (**8.43**).

Combining the approaches

1.5 These approaches to tort may be combined in a single diagram, giving a map of most of tort (see **Table 1.1**).

How useful is such a diagram? That rather depends what problem you are trying to solve. As a way of seeing, roughly, what sort of topics tort covers, it has its uses. Again, if you are trying to answer a practical problem in tort, you can use it to work out, roughly, which area of tort law you should be considering. But it would be hopeless as, say, a guide to how the courts or Parliament are likely to develop the law in the future. If, for example, a right to privacy were introduced, with breach of privacy being a new tort (see **2.16**), where would *that* fit? It would have elements of protection of property, also of reputation, also of protection of bodily integrity. Or again, it is clear that the tort of negligence extends across many of the different boxes of the diagram. So, when is it appropriate to speak of 'negligence' as a single entity, and when is it best to divide it up by context? You should be in a position to answer that question for yourself by the end of your tort course, but there is no very neat answer that can be given at the beginning.

Does tort form a unity?

1.6 As the various torts are all so very different, so much so that it requires considerable mental effort to see any kind of overall pattern at all, why is tort regarded as a subject at all? Certainly the fact that the universities require entrants to study 'tort', and the general conservatism that makes lawyers stick with the concepts they are familiar with, do much to maintain 'tort' as it is. But is that all? If a cynic were to say that 'tort' only exists because examination regulations say that it does, would this be right? There is, after all, no such creature as a 'tort practitioner'. There are general civil practitioners and there are personal injury specialists, and many others who use particular torts on a regular basis. But 'tort' itself seems to make little sense in legal professional terms. Does it make sense in teaching terms, or theoretical terms?

Table 1.1 Tort, ordered by type of misconduct and type of injury

	Intention to harm (or 'malice')	Lack of care	Strict liability
Land	Trespass to land (7.2)	Negligence / Private nuisance (7.11)	*Rylands v Fletcher* (7.35) and liability for fire (7.42)
Chattels	Trespass to goods, Conversion	Negligence (5.1)	Specific statutes e.g. Animals Act (7.44)
Bodily safety and security	Assault and battery (2.1), False imprisonment (2.11)	Negligence (3.1, 4.1)	'Breach of statutory duty' (1.46)
Economic interests generally	Economic torts (6.1)	Negligence (5.1), Public nuisance (7.30)	Specific statutes
Reputation	Defamation in cases of qualified privilege (8.30), Malicious falsehood (8.42)	'Unintentional defamation' (8.25), Negligence (8.42)	Defamation (8.1)

The idea that there is a coherent law of tort, based on a single principle of liability for loss wrongfully caused, was first taken seriously in academic writings in the interwar period, especially in Winfield's *Tort* (1937). This text did much to promote the ideas that tort (not 'torts') was a real subject, rather than a mixture of legal odds and ends. Winfield's view was controversial, and even he does not seem to have thought that tort approached the internal rigour achieved by the law of contract. But by building a model into which all the case law fitted, but which was never meant to include much statute, the eventual obsolescence of his scheme was assured. To ignore statute today is to confine yourself to marginalia.

Much that has happened since 1960 has complicated Winfield's neat picture of a unified law of tort. The growth of the tort of negligence, very much along the unitary lines which Winfield envisaged, has come to dominate the textbooks and (by its sheer bulk and practical importance) to force the other torts into relative obscurity. The student's study of negligence alone now accounts for easily half of the tort course, and whatever may be said of the other torts' internal coherence, the tort of negligence is at least fairly easy to treat systematically. Further, the courts are beginning to come to terms with the relationship between statute and tort, and this too brings in a unifying element. All in all, the cause of tort as a tolerably coherent discipline is stronger today than it has been for the past 50 years.

In any event, while 'tort' up to a point consists of odds and ends, they are for the most part *useful* odds and ends. This is no backwater of the law. Tort, then, seems in no immediate danger of extinction, its ramshackle nature notwithstanding.

How uncertain is tort?

1.7 It is easy to imagine the frustration of many students with tort, on finding many seemingly fundamental questions answered with a 'Don't know', or given different answers by different writers. This is understandable, but must be kept in perspective. Many questions in the law of tort have not received a firm answer precisely because they are *un*important. The question of whether breach of confidence is 'really' a tort, for example, hardly matters to practitioners; so long as the subject is written up in some readily accessible text, it hardly matters whether that text has 'tort' on its spine, or not.

There is a certain amount of looseness in the law of tort—given the wide variety of situations it applies to, this can hardly be avoided. But there is sufficient practical certainty for practitioners to settle nearly all cases by agreement, only a tiny proportion being sent to trial for a judge to decide on. There are certainly some areas of fundamental obscurity and hideous complexity—recovery of purely economic losses (**5.7**) being the most obvious example—but that very obscurity reflects the rarity of such cases. Marginality breeds doubt. So while student confusion at many aspects of tort is understandable, it does not point to a legal system in chaos. At most, it indicates that academic concerns are not always identical with professional concerns—which should not surprise or worry anyone. Many view the loose and open-ended nature of tort as a strength rather than a weakness: it permits the law to adapt to new needs without excessive strain. At least by the end of your course, and possibly before, I imagine that you will have a view on whether this is plausible or not!

Overlap with other heads of civil liability

1.8 This book has no systematic treatment of the other heads of liability which run parallel with tort, but there will be many references to them throughout. It was at one time thought that tort could be rigorously separated from *breach of contract*, but while academics are still divided on how far it is still possible to do so, a complete division is hard to maintain. Indeed, the impossibility of doing so absolutely is almost a cliché in modern legal writing. Tort has traditionally been wary of imposing a duty in areas where contract usually governs, but this tradition appears to be on its last legs; it will later be necessary to ask whether there is any life left in it at all (**5.47**). What of other areas of the civil law? The only cast-iron distinction that can be made between tortious duties of care and *fiduciary duties* is a historical one: before 1875, these duties were applied by quite different courts, applying very different principles. Over a century on, however, it may perhaps make sense to amalgamate the two (**5.46**). The difference between tort and *restitution* is rather more obvious, but even there there is a certain area of overlap (**10.12, 10.20**). Some writers would amalgamate all these various heads of liability, including tort, into a single unitary '*law of obligations*', though it has to be said that this monster unit would be a little inconvenient for teaching purposes.

This book, then, will consider tort alone: but there will be constant references to tort's neighbours.

The law of tort: what is it for, and who pays for it?

1.9 It is said that in some Victorian households, piano legs were covered in drapes, as they otherwise seemed too indecently suggestive. Until very recently, a similar reticence hung about the financing of tort. Issues such as insurance and funding of tort actions were rarely discussed publicly, either in the law reports or in academic articles. Academics and judges pretended that the law of tort floated freely, with no need for support. This was always nonsense, of course, and is today acknowledged as such. It is obvious that running the tort system involves substantial costs. Further, the law itself is profoundly influenced by the way those costs are distributed. And arguments about how these costs should be distributed cannot be separated from arguments over what the law should be. It is no longer possible to have an adequate knowledge of tort law, then, without some understanding of what tort law is for, and how the cost of the system is met.

The need for a substantial defendant

1.10 There is usually little point in securing a legal judgment against the defendant unless he or she has the means to meet it. Yet whether the claimant's injuries were inflicted by someone rich or someone poor will often be a matter of chance. The claimant may often get help from the doctrine of *vicarious liability*, under which the defendant's employer may be liable for torts which the defendant committed in the course of his or her employment (**9.2**), so the real defendant in that case may be a substantial company. Or again, the claimant may find that the defendant has taken out *liability insurance*, that is, the defendant has paid premiums to an insurance company, so that the insurers will themselves fight any action brought against the defendant, and pay the damages if they lose.

It might be asked why anyone would ever take out liability insurance, given that without it the prospect of legal action may be remote. The answer is partly that many people insure against remote risks; also that liability insurance sometimes comes as an incidental part of a wider package (as part of a mortgage arrangement, for example); and finally (most importantly in practice) the law often *requires* the defendant to have such insurance. So both in the case of drivers (**4.12**) and employers (**4.32**), the law insists not only that those who create dangers must be responsible for them in tort, but also that they pay premiums to ensure that they can meet those liabilities if they materialize.

Consider every possible claimant and defendant

In many tort exam problems, it may seem that the defendant either is unlikely to have money, or the claimant is unlikely to sue. You might find yourself saying, for example, 'Surely a two-year-old girl wouldn't sue her own parents? And anyway, how would she instruct a solicitor?' This shows commendable attention to practicalities, but the examiner is testing your knowledge of *tort*, not of the legal system generally. Perhaps the parents are insured. Perhaps they have just won the lottery. Perhaps demonstrating that they are liable is a step on the way to showing that *someone else* is liable. And it most certainly *is* possible for a two-year-old to start a legal action, though for the detail you should study civil procedure rather than tort. Besides, the claimant may be a good deal older by the time the proceedings are started (e.g. *Surtees v Kingston-on-Thames Borough Council* [1991] 2 FLR 559, CA). As a general rule *assume that any individual named in a tort problem can sue and be sued, however implausible this may seem to you now.*

The need for a claimant

1.11 It cannot be assumed that every potential claimant is aware of the possibility of legal action, or that they would want to sue if they knew they could. Very often the claimant has access to alternative remedies or benefits, such as insurance, that lessen the incentive to sue. The costs of litigation are unpredictable, and can be quite large, thus deterring possible claimants.

Civil legal aid, introduced in 1948, made the legal system accessible to many, but was a victim of its own success. The high take-up rate increased the cost to government, which initially responded by reducing availability and eventually abolished it in nearly all personal injury cases. Some claimants have a private entitlement to legal advice: for example, many trade unions offer free legal advice as one benefit to their members, and some forms of insurance carry similar benefits. But for many, legal action remains either unavailable or uncongenial. It remains to be seen what impact the new conditional fee ('no win, no fee') arrangements will have on accessibility of remedies.

The purposes of tort

1.12 Not everyone is agreed on the precise purpose of tort law, or indeed that every part of it *does* serve a useful purpose. But there seems to be virtual unanimity on the sorts of objects such a system must serve if it is to be useful (though terminology and emphasis vary considerably). First, the fact that injured people may sue can *deter* people from harming one another in the first place. Second, it can serve as a *fair and just response* to the infliction of harm: justice may demand that if the defendant injures the claimant, then he or she should pay compensation. Third, it can provide a means of *loss-spreading*: regardless of the rights and wrongs of the injury, tort might provide a conduit for distributing the claimant's loss over the entire community, rather than making the claimant bear the whole. From this third point of view, the objectives of the tort system are not so very different from those of (say) pensions law or social security law.

It should be clear now why I hesitated above (**1.1**) to distinguish tort from crime by saying that the law *punishes* crimes, whereas it *compensates for* torts. The objects of the law of tort are not so very different from those of the criminal law, and handing the defendant a large bill as a result of the defendant's own wrongful behaviour *is* a punishment in one sense, whatever else it may be. But there is always controversy over what the objects of tort should be, and over how closely the actual law complies with them. Moreover, the three broad goals (deterrence, just response, loss-spreading) are not always compatible with one another. It would be very much a mistake to assume that there is unanimity on these questions—or even that most of the contributors to the debate are clear in their own minds what they want from the law.

Deterrence: general considerations

1.13 It is obvious that tort often has a deterrent effect. It is not merely that individual awards make defendants anxious not to repeat the experience. It is also that a general awareness that awards are possible encourages care to avoid injuring potential claimants. Awareness amongst publishers of defamation law (**8.1**), and amongst unions of the economic torts (**6.1**) is high; and, up to a point, this is true of occupiers of premises, and employers, in respect of the law of negligence (**4.15, 4.32**). But arguments as to the size of the deterrent effect, or as to whether it is too small or too great, quickly run into impossible questions of quantification. Does the law on employers' liability really make employers more careful, or is the legal system too slow and too random to drive home the connection between employer carelessness and awards against them? Does the law *over*-deter surgeons, leading to 'defensive medicine', or is 'defensive medicine' a myth? There are no simple or uncontroversial answers to these questions.

1.14 There are a number of questions we need to ask before we can hope to determine how great the deterrent effect of tort is in any one situation:

• *Is it clear what the defendant is being deterred from?* For example, is the tort of negligence's general command to be 'reasonably careful' sufficiently definite? Or should it be more specific?

• *Are victims of the defendant's actions able and willing to sue?* Or can the major perpetrators only be caught by establishing a central agency to conduct prosecutions where necessary? Clearly, a system of deterrence based on tort alone is biased towards the interests of the rich and knowledgeable, who are best able to set the law of tort in motion.

• *Does the defendant have liability insurance?* In this respect, the 'deterrence' objective is straightforwardly opposed to the 'loss-spreading' objective: the defendant may be powerfully deterred by the prospect of a liability greater than the defendant's assets, but if that liability materializes then the defendant will be unable to compensate the claimant fully. Of course, the defendant's insurer may in some cases pressure the defendant to act more carefully, but this effect is in most situations rather a weak one.

The law-and-economics approach

1.15 The proponents of law-and-economics push the deterrence approach to its greatest level of sophistication. They assume that economic actors themselves weigh up the costs and benefits of their possible actions, and choose the course of action which brings the maximum aggregate benefit. The lawyer-economists argue that it is unnecessary for the law to do so as well. Rather, the law should make sure that the full costs and benefits to society are reflected in the decisions of certain crucial economic actors. We cannot, for example, turn manufacturers into altruists, but by ensuring that the costs resulting from unsafe products fall on them, we give them an incentive in that direction.

Absolute safety is not the lawyer-economists' aim. Rather, they aim for *efficiency* in spending on safety. That is, if spending £1 more on safety would produce more than £1 in benefits for society, then the law should give incentives to spend that £1—but not if the benefits would be less. A full survey of the various different approaches within law-and-economics would take far more space than is available here, and there are many different views. Like the language of tort, the language of law-and-economics is a medium for arguing, not a determinate set of clear prescriptions.

1.16 Criticisms of the law-and-economics approach have been many, some attempting to modify it, others to dismiss it outright. The assumption that economic actors are motivated solely by a wish to boost their wealth (even if including their 'psychic wealth', however defined), is at best a loose approximation to reality. There is much debate about how useful an approximation it is. It is hard to put a value on human health and safety; arguments over this are necessarily imprecise, and may be incapable of practical resolution. The viability of tort as a means for bringing all societal costs to bear on those who create them must be doubted, given the many barriers between a claimant and a court which can adjudicate the issue. In any event, the incentive so created is an incentive to reduce the costs involved in litigation, and so involves an incentive to hide information and to delay and frustrate awards.

Do we really *want* to encourage cost-benefit calculations by potential defendants? Suppose a company which makes cars notices a fundamental design defect in their new model, which gives the fuel tank a high propensity to explode in certain sorts of accidents. Calculating that the total cost of a redesign would exceed their total legal costs if sued over the inevitable deaths, they deliberately leave the design untouched. Many would think this disgraceful, and it is certainly enough to justify an award of exemplary damages (**10.10**). Yet is this not precisely the sort of calculation the lawyer-economists seek to encourage? We can hardly complain merely if a decision on the costs and benefits of safety is actually made. Someone has to make it. And if the company's assessment of the costs was wrong, that may only emphasize what a feeble reed the economists' assumption of economic rationality is. Right or wrong, the economic approach to law certainly brings to the fore some awkward questions.

Tort as a just response to wrongdoing

1.17 On this view, the defendant must compensate the claimant because that is what justice demands. This is the traditional justification of tort. While it is often sidelined in academic discussions, it is probably what the courts think they are doing most of the time, and certainly what the press think they ought to be doing. Yet many features of tort jar with this conception:

• *Tort ignores many factors crucial to a moral view of whether the defendant should compensate the claimant.* A notable example is in respect of partial liability: generally speaking, the defendant is either liable or not, with only the occasional concessions to degrees of fault (see **9.26, 11.17**). The defendant's ability to pay is similarly irrelevant.

• *Assessment of damages does not depend on moral fault.* The defendant tortiously injures two claimants, in both cases severely. The first is a retired 70-year-old, the second an employed 30-year-old with excellent promotion prospects. Morally, the first claimant's case against the defendant is no different from the second's. Yet the second's damages will almost certainly dwarf the first's, because the second claimant's loss of income will be higher, and he or she will also need medical care for more years than the first. The second claimant may get millions where the first only gets thousands. Does this disparity accord with morality? Not everyone thinks so.

• *Some of the duties imposed by tort are in fact **impossible** to comply with*—and this is so not merely in the case of the stricter forms of liability (e.g. **4.2**), but even sometimes in the tort of negligence (e.g. **3.9**). Can we really say that the defendant is guilty of 'wrongdoing' when he could not in fact have done anything else? Some cases can be explained by a more sophisticated conception of wrongdoing—perhaps the 'wrongdoing' consisted of the defendant's placing himself or herself in a position where he or she would inevitably harm someone. But such refinements can take us very far indeed from any recognizable form of morality.

• *The identity of the defendant.* Having brought its vast resources and sophistication to bear on the question whether the defendant was morally to blame, the law of tort then proceeds to impose liability on...someone else, usually. It is rare that the person actually at fault pays the bill. The liability is paid for either by insurance, or by someone responsible for the defendant under the doctrine of vicarious liability. Again, this is not *impossible* to justify in moral terms, but the arguments necessary to do so open up wide vistas of moral argument, without a conclusion in sight.

So attempts to explain tort in terms of morality achieve little in themselves. No doubt we should correct a tort system which actively does injustice; but it is another question how much tort is improved by reflections on the meaning of justice. Moreover, on no view can tort be more than a small part of the law's response to injustice. Whatever it does only reveals its true significance when seen in the light of what else the law does in that area.

Tort as a device for loss-spreading

1.18 This final purpose seeks to ignore the precise cause of the claimant's loss and to focus more on the claimant's need which has resulted. The philosophy is that the moral rights and wrongs of the defendant's infliction of the loss are beside the point—either way, the claimant has suffered a loss which demands compensation of some kind—or that any retribution for the defendant's wrong can be better dealt with by the criminal law. The person or organization made to bear liability will therefore be the one best suited to pass on the loss to the wider community. Liability for defective products, for example, might be placed with the manufacturers (**4.2**), who can increase their prices if the losses prove great.

This approach is plainly of more help in some areas than others. It would be vacuous in relation to (say) nuisance, where the 'harm' for which the claimant seeks a remedy is his or her loss of the right to use land when the defendant uses land as he or she wishes. Generally, in relation to property, there are immense practical difficulties in the way of anything which would amount to a centrally organized insurance scheme. In relation to personal injury, the idea has more to be said for it. But it has to be said that, considered as a system of insurance, tort is exceedingly inefficient. In the order of 50 per cent of the sums circulating in the tort system end up paying for lawyers' fees and other overheads, as contrasted with perhaps 10–15 per cent in insurance schemes proper. If the law of tort is a loss-spreading device, then it is an expensive and inefficient one.

Tort at war with itself

1.19 It will be obvious that no one policy objective explains the whole of tort. Consider the way the law of tort deals with road accidents (**4.12**). This has elements of a 'just response' solution: drivers are made liable for their negligence. However, it is, as you will see, a fairly strange version of negligence: even learner drivers are considered to be 'negligent' for not having a depth of experience they cannot possibly yet have acquired (**4.14**). There are elements of deterrence, too, but they are very indirect: the more dangerous drivers may perhaps have to pay higher premiums, the safer drivers may perhaps earn a no-claims bonus. But these seem feeble spurs indeed to safer driving. There are also aspects of loss-spreading: all drivers are compelled to contribute, via their insurance premiums, to a system of compensation for all victims of poor driving. But if that is the rationale of the system, do we really need the time-consuming and expensive enquiry into the cause of the accident? What purpose does it serve, from a loss-spreading point of view?

'The floodgates of litigation'

1.20 Up to a point, then, we can debate what purpose tort should rationally serve, and how its rules might be modified to achieve useful ends. But individual lawyers and their clients make most of the important decisions in tort cases, with their own purposes in mind. These decisions are hard to predict in advance, either individually or wholesale. It is common, for example, to argue for or against suggested changes on the ground that they will reduce or increase the amount of litigation. But such claims are very hard to substantiate, even in retrospect. No-one really knows, for example, how much effect on the legal system the relatively new system of 'conditional fees' is having. How broadly will the government permit the use of 'conditional fees', and on what terms? Within the constraints set by government, by the Bar and by insurers, what terms will solicitors be able to offer potential clients? How many of those clients will find those terms preferable to their other alternatives? And if more litigation *does* result, what will be the effect of *that*—on government, on lawyers, on insurers? It is a mistake to assume that the tort system is rationally planned and systematically ordered. Many individuals, with vastly differing motives, each have an influence on it.

The role of the higher courts

1.21 Fashions and styles of judicial action change with bewildering rapidity. It is trite to say that the courts are only subordinate policy-makers, and should have respect for Parliament's superior authority. Some deduce from this that the courts should do as little as possible that is innovative, leaving all major changes to Parliament's initiative. Others conclude the reverse, reasoning that *because* Parliament can put the judges right if they err, the courts should therefore be bold where it seems that the law is improved by doing so. Willingness to refer to policy varies from time to time, and from judge to judge. At the time of writing, the judges are pretty willing, by the standards of earlier decades, to innovate. Yet they still pay respect to parliamentary policy. Yet respect for Parliament means checking that the innovation gels with whatever else Parliament has done in the area; it does *not* mean waiting for Parliament's explicit permission before doing anything at all. As for Parliament itself, reform of tort law is usually a highly technical matter, which does not usually arouse great passions, or command much parliamentary time. There is currently a great deal of parliamentary anxiety over the extent of liability, particularly in relation to personal injuries; but this is the product of broad public concerns which have little to do with the detail of the law, and it remains to be seen whether it will lead to technical tort reform.

Human Rights Act 1998

1.22 The UK has been legally committed to uphold human rights since 1951, on assenting to the terms of the European Convention on Human Rights. However, it has been a long and tortuous journey towards allowing aggrieved individuals to rely on Convention rights in the courts. At first, the Convention only gave rights *to other states* to complain of infractions. A right of *individuals* to petition the European Court of Human Rights was not conceded until the 1960s. And while the courts in the 1990s increasingly began to refer to the Convention, nonetheless the position remained that contravention of the Convention, while it put the UK in breach of its international obligations, nonetheless was not a ground of challenge in the UK's own courts.

With the passage of the Human Rights Act 1998, this is now past history. As from October 2000, litigants can and do rely on the terms of the Convention itself in the course of arguing for their legal rights. Various Convention articles are directly relevant in tort cases, and especially:

- the right to 'liberty and security of person' (Art 5);
- the right to a fair trial (Art 6);
- the right of everyone to 'respect for his private and family life, his home and his correspondence' (Art 8); and
- the right to freedom of expression (Art 10).

It is obvious that human rights, as defined in the Convention, overlap somewhat with the types of interest protected by the law of tort (above, **1.4**). For example, the Convention's requirement that everyone is entitled to 'peaceful enjoyment of his possessions' (1st Protocol, Art 1) bears an obvious similarity to tort's protection of claimants' property interests. However, while this connection is real not accidental, nonetheless it is misleading if too much attention is paid to it, for at least three reasons:

- The Convention has many concerns which extend well outside tort. For example, the right to freedom of thought (Art 9) is only very tenuously connected to anything in the law of tort.

- Defendants as well as claimants have rights. For example, the right to freedom of expression (Art 10) now places distinct limits on the tort of defamation (**8.1**).

- Even where tort and the Convention confront similar problems, they may do so in very different ways. For example, while the law of tort protects the privacy of claimants in various ways, it recognizes no express concept of 'respect for privacy', unlike the Convention (Art 8). This has various implications for the extent of the protection given (**2.17**).

We can expect to see more and more case law applying these provisions to problems in tort. The courts must take into account the Convention in applying the law, whether statute or common law. Statutes must, where possible, be construed so as to avoid infringing Convention rights. Where there is an unavoidable conflict between statute and the Convention, the courts do not have power to override the statute, but may nonetheless make a 'declaration of incompatibility' calling attention to the problem.

The 'vertical effect'

1.23 The European Convention is most obviously relevant when an individual is litigating with a public authority, whether the UK Government itself, or some local or special authority. The Human Rights Act opens the way for arguments that the public authority cannot be allowed to infringe a Convention right. The Act's notion of a 'public authority' seems to be a wide one, and includes 'any person certain of whose functions are functions of a public nature' (s 6(3)(b)). So, for example, it has been assumed that those who operate sewage works are a 'public authority' for this purpose (*Marcic v Thames Water Utilities* [2003] UKHL 66, discussed below, **7.21**). However, a private residential home is not within the Act even when providing services on behalf of a local authority (*YL v Birmingham City Council* [2007]

UKHL 27). The test is not whether the authority in question is 'public', but whether the function under scrutiny is a public function.

> **R (on the application of Weaver) v London and Quadrant Housing Trust [2009] EWCA 587:** London and Quadrant were a charitable housing association, providing affordable housing for those who could not acquire it in the market. They initially provided accommodation for the claimant but later sought to evict her. The issue arose whether the human rights legislation was relevant. Held: the provision of social housing was a public function, managed in close co-operation with government. While some actions of the trust might be 'private', their decisions in relation to provision of housing were public acts and so subject to the human rights legislation.

Arguments of this sort must now be taken into account whenever a public authority is engaged in litigation. Particularly significant for tort lawyers is that the right to a fair trial (Art 6) has been interpreted to mean that the state must deal even-handedly with litigants, and cannot grant itself special exemptions which it does not allow to defendants generally. Again, the right to life (Art 2) has been held to impose a duty on NHS hospitals to guard those unable to fend for themselves, such as a paranoid schizophrenic patient who escaped from a hospital and threw herself under a train (*Savage v South Essex Partnership NHS Foundation Trust* [2008] UKHL 74; breach of duty ultimately established, [2010] EWHC 865 (QBD)). In principle the same duty to protect life applies to the police, but claimants have had little success in establishing liability: the police are not under a duty to protect witnesses from those they testify against unless there is 'a real and immediate risk to life', and the danger of 'defensive policing' rules out any general duty to protect members of the public from criminal activity (*Van Colle v Chief Constable of the Hertfordshire Police* [2008] UKHL 50; and for a refusal on very similar grounds to say that housing authorities must control their more dangerous tenants see *Mitchell v Glasgow City Council* [2009] UKHL 11).

1.24 Where a public authority is found to have infringed a Convention right, then a court which has the appropriate jurisdiction can award a remedy, including damages (s 8). However, no award of damages can be made unless the court is satisfied that it 'is necessary to afford just satisfaction' to the claimant (s 8(3)); they are not available as of right (*Anufrijeva v Southwark London Borough Council* [2003] EWCA Civ 1406). Further, the court is directed to have regard to the case law of the European Court of Human Rights itself when awarding damages (s 8(4)). This case law emphasizes that an award of damages is by no means an inevitable consequence of an infringement of human rights—in many cases a mere declaration that the claimant's rights have been infringed is enough. Further, there is no scope for granting punitive or exemplary damages: all damages in this context are compensatory, whether for financial or other losses (compare **10.11**). While the case law is still developing, nonetheless it is clear that the courts are often far from generous: the House of Lords has indicated that in relation to Art 6 (right to a fair trial) an award of damages will be very much the exception (*R (on the application of Greenfield) v Secretary of State for the Home Department* [2005] UKHL 14). However, where UK law is more generous than the European Court's approach, the UK measure will be used; there is no justification for treating breaches of Convention rights less seriously than comparable torts (*R (on the application of KB) v Mental Health Review Tribunal* [2003] EWHC 193 (Admin)).

The 'horizontal effect'

1.25 The aim of the Convention is to compel the state to respect the rights of individuals, and so it is not at first sight obvious how it can affect a dispute between two or more private individuals. Or (in the jargon usually used here) it is obvious that the Convention has a 'vertical effect', protecting the individual from the state, but it is not so obvious that it has a 'horizontal effect' on the rights of individuals against one another.

The key to this is that the rights of individuals are enforced through the courts, and the courts are part of the state. In deciding cases between individuals, the court is carrying out a state function, and must respect the litigants' human rights while doing so. So the Convention is relevant even when the case does not affect the rights of the state in any way. The court which decides the case is still a 'public authority' (Human Rights Act 1998, s 6(3)(a)), and so must respect the Convention. The implications of this are uncertain, but likely to prove profound. However, it is much too early to say what they are, or how important they will be in practice.

Negligence: an introduction

1.26 Much of this book is concerned with variations on the tort of negligence. How coherent is it? The tort of negligence covers a wide variety of situations. It is (perhaps inevitably) somewhat uneven as a result. But there is certainly a unitary *terminology*, and certain problems which crop up again and again in different contexts.

In general, if the claimant wishes to establish negligence against the defendant, the claimant must demonstrate the following: *(i)* that the defendant owed the claimant a duty of care; *(ii)* that the defendant broke this duty; and *(iii)* that this breach of duty caused loss to the claimant. Further, *(iv)* there are various possible defences open to the defendant. At this stage, I give a brief description of the law in general. The function of the following paragraphs is not so much to tell you what the law is, as to teach you the language you will need before you can understand an explanation of what the law is. The details of the law will appear in later chapters.

Vagueness

A common complaint about texts on the tort of negligence is that the terminology used is too vague. One answer is that the texts are at least telling it like it is. The law *is* vague, and more precise renditions would be misleading. Indeed, the startling growth of the tort over the last few decades would have been difficult if the courts had been made to express themselves in a more limited and precise way. But it is *also* true that knowledge of how the law of negligence impacts on a particular situation involves not only general concepts, but also the case law for that particular area. This chapter should therefore be treated as introductory, before we come on to how the law applies in particular situations.

Duty

1.27 The most famous statement about duty was made by Lord Atkin. This was in a case where the claimant was seeking to show that the defendant, the manufacturer of a soft drink, owed her a duty to make the drink reasonably safe. The drink had been bought for her by a friend in a restaurant. On pouring out the drink, her nostrils had been assaulted by a decaying snail in the drink bottle and (she alleged) she became ill as a result. In finding that a duty was owed, Lord Atkin said:

> The [Biblical] rule that you are to love your neighbour becomes in law, you must not injure your neighbour; and the lawyer's question, 'Who is my neighbour?' receives a restricted reply. You must take reasonable care to avoid acts or omissions which you can reasonably foresee would be likely to injure your neighbour. Who then, in law, is my neighbour? The answer seems to be—persons who are so closely and directly affected by my act that I ought reasonably to have them in contemplation as being so affected when I am directing my mind to the acts or omissions which are called in question (*Donoghue v Stevenson* [1932] AC 562, 580, Lord Atkin).

This is one of the most quoted passages of the whole law of tort. Its influence is not diminished merely because the facts of the case are obscure and unusual, and the result overtaken by legislation (**4.2**). The idea that a duty is owed to those in the defendant's 'reasonable contemplation' is a powerful one. Nonetheless, the whole of the tort of negligence cannot be reduced to this one judicial *bon mot*. This is for a number of reasons:

- In any common situation, there will usually be far more precise rules, and the 'neighbour' principle is of no real help. It would be a mistake to cite the 'neighbour' *dictum* to support such settled duties as (for example) that owed by one road-user to another. It is only on novel questions that Atkin's *dictum* comes into its own.

- On no view did Atkin mention every relevant matter for determining a negligence claim. Some suggest that it is a strongly suggestive principle: that once the claimant has shown that the 'neighbour' criterion is satisfied, it is for the defendant to suggest reasons why it should not be applied (e.g. *Anns v London Borough of Merton* [1978] AC 728, 751–2; this is sometimes called Lord Wilberforce's 'two-stage' test). Yet even this is far too enthusiastic an approach for others. Reasonable foresight is a necessary part of the test, but not nearly enough in itself (*Yuen Kun Yeu v A-G for Hong Kong* [1987] 2 All ER 705, 710, Lord Keith). Others still deny that any general principle can resolve individual cases (*Caparo Industries v Dickman* [1990] 2 AC 605, 618, Lord Bridge). The differences here are really only differences of emphasis, but they are nonetheless profound for that.

- Negligence is not the whole of the law of tort. For example, if the defendant openly vilifies the claimant, very often the defendant will foresee that the claimant will come to harm through injury to reputation. Yet we would expect most such cases to be dealt with through the tort of defamation, not negligence. To what extent negligence will be allowed to intrude into other areas of law, be it other torts or entirely distinct areas, is often a controversial question. In *Donoghue v Stevenson*, the argument against liability (which convinced several judges, though not a majority), was precisely that the claimant's claim intruded too much into the sphere of contract. It is never enough in those circumstances to stress that the defendant and the claimant are 'neighbours'; much more is required.

- 'Reasonable contemplation' is really a question of values rather than a factual question. There is no such individual as 'the reasonable person', and no-one pretends otherwise. Atkin's *dictum* is not so much about what the courts will do, as the language they use in justifying what they do.

The type of loss

1.28 Atkin's 'neighbour *dictum*' does not seem to distinguish between the various different types of loss the claimant might suffer at the defendant's hands. Yet the law of negligence undoubtedly does distinguish. For example, if it was foreseeable that Donoghue's health would suffer through the unwanted intrusion of a snail from Stevenson's factory, then surely it was equally or more foreseeable that she would lose a perfectly good ginger beer from it. So she might claim that, but for Stevenson's behaviour, she would have received good and wholesome ginger beer, whereas as it was she got a nauseous mess. Yet a claim for the cost of a replacement ginger beer would almost certainly fail. Most negligence claims are either for *personal injury* or for *damage to property*. A claim for a *pure economic loss*—that is, an economic loss other than personal injury or property damage—only rarely succeeds (**5.7**). Other forms of loss may simply not be recognized at all; for example, in many situations the claimant cannot recover for grief or mental distress caused by the defendant (though see **3.18, 10.58**).

'Proximity' and 'remoteness'

1.29 Sometimes duty is discussed in terms of 'proximity'. This is a metaphor, but a simple one. If the defendant wields an axe or some other dangerous tool, the people who are potentially in danger are those who are close by ('proximate'). People who are a long way away ('remote') are not in danger. So if a duty is owed by the defendant, it is to people who are 'proximate' and not to those who are 'remote'. However, the case of the axe is a special case. The danger posed to Donoghue was nothing to do with her being *physically* proximate to Stevenson's factory; what put her in danger was, first, her taste for ginger beer and, second, Stevenson's opaque bottles, which prevented inspection of the ginger beer before it reached her. These factors put her in *causal* proximity to Stevenson. The physical distance between them was irrelevant.

'Proximity' is therefore a rather ambiguous term. It can mean closeness ('physical proximity'). It can mean causal closeness ('causal proximity'). Or it simply denotes legal duty: asking whether there is 'proximity' between the claimant and the defendant might simply be a way of asking whether the defendant owes the claimant a duty ('legal proximity'). Statements about 'proximity' can therefore usually be resolved into statements about foresight, or duty, or both. If 'proximity' means anything else, that additional sense seems hard to define, and is therefore best avoided.

No liability for omissions?

1.30 Atkin's 'neighbour *dictum*' includes not simply acts of the defendant which might injure the claimant, but also omissions. Yet other authorities are keen to insist that there is no general liability for omissions: if the defendant sees the claimant drowning, the defendant is usually under no legal duty to help the claimant, however easy it would be to do so. Which view is right? There is truth in both viewpoints. It is certainly true that *once a duty has been established*, it makes no difference whether the defendant breaks it by acts or by omissions. If the defendant drives carelessly and injures the claimant, it makes no difference whether the defendant's mistake was over-enthusiasm with the accelerator, or reluctance to use the brake. Both negligent acts and negligent omissions attract liability. But if the claimant is still seeking to establish that the defendant owes a duty, the defendant is usually in a strong position if his or her activities do not in themselves pose a danger to the claimant, and the claimant is complaining that the defendant did not *prevent someone or something else* from harming the claimant. Compelling facts are needed if the claimant is to hold the defendant responsible for another's misbehaviour, or for natural processes. The claimant can usually establish a positive duty to act only for very specific reasons, such as:

- The defendant controls premises, the condition of which endangers the claimant (**4.15**).

- The claimant is a child and the defendant has undertaken responsibility for his or her safety (e.g. *Carmarthenshire County Council v Lewis* [1955] AC 549).

- An animal over which the defendant has control, or ought to have control, endangers the claimant (**7.44**).

- The defendant creates a situation on the road where others are likely to come to harm (e.g. *Haley v London Electricity Board* [1965] AC 778).

- The defendant promises the claimant that he or she will take due care.

There will be much more to say about this below, but it will have to be said in individual contexts. In some contexts the judges do indeed say that there is no liability for omissions. In a spate of recent cases on the liability of fire services, the courts have said precisely that. Fire services are liable if they increased the risk of fire by turning off a sprinkler system (*Capital and Counties v Hampshire County Council* [1997] QB 1004), but they are not liable for omissions, such as failing to spot smouldering debris (*John Munroe (Acrylics) v London Fire and Civil Defence Authority* [1997] QB 1004) or failing to maintain fire hydrants (*Church of Jesus Christ of Latter Day Saints (Great Britain) v West Yorkshire Fire and Civil Defence Authority* [1997] QB 1004). A similar rule applies to the coastguard: there is no positive duty to rescue anyone, but there is liability for misconduct which worsens the situation of those at sea (*OLL Ltd v Secretary of State for Transport* [1997] 3 All ER 897). But in other contexts, the courts say that if the defendant had (or should have had) control over some dangerous thing, then the defendant has a positive duty to prevent it doing harm to the claimant (**3.4**). In yet others, the courts say that if statute imposes a positive duty on the defendant, then the claimant may sue in negligence for breach of it (**1.54**). And in yet others they say that the defendant will be under a positive duty to act if he or she promised to act responsibly: defendants are only under a duty if they positively assumed that duty (**5.37**).

So, overall, the position is very mixed. The courts are frequently cautious in imposing liability on those who have not done any positive wrongful act. But in some situations this is not an overriding consideration. (Some judges express this truth by saying that the defendant is not liable for 'pure' omissions, but that a breach of a pre-existing legal duty prevents the defendant from saying that the omission is 'pure'.)

No liability for others?

1.31 It is very often said that the defendant is responsible only for what he or she has done, and not for what others do. There is a kernel of truth in this, but it is a very small part of the truth. The doctrine of vicarious liability and other related notions (**9.1**) often make the defendant liable for the wrongdoing of others. And where both the defendant and some other party share responsibility for the claimant's injury, the claimant may sue either of those responsible. It is no answer to the claimant's action against the defendant that the claimant *could* have sued someone else—although sometimes the defendant may be able to claim a contribution from other guilty parties (**9.26**).

The kernel of truth in the 'no liability for others' rule is this: where all that the defendant has done is to create a dangerous situation, the courts are very reluctant to make the defendant liable when the harm is the direct result of someone else's misbehaviour. This reluctance sometimes manifests itself through a denial of duty, and sometimes through the idea that the loss is 'too remote'. But it would be misleading to suggest that there is a blanket denial of liability whenever the conduct of others outside than the defendant has intervened. Some examples may help.

The claimant's own conduct

1.32 It is a rare case where the claimant successfully sues the defendant for an injury which the claimant did to himself or herself. It will usually involve a demonstration that the claimant was incapable of looking after himself or herself, and some particular reason why the defendant was under a duty to guard the claimant. Typically the claimant will be a child and the defendant an adult with a duty to care for the claimant. But action has occasionally succeeded even where the claimant is an adult.

> ***Kirkham v Chief Constable of Greater Manchester* [1990] 3 All ER 246:** Kirkham,
> a depressed alcoholic with suicidal tendencies, committed suicide while being held on

remand for criminal damage. The arresting officer had not passed on a warning of his dangerous condition, with the result that no special precautions had been taken, and he was treated as an ordinary prisoner. It was held that the police were liable to Kirkham's widow for this failure.

A class of case where even fully responsible adults can recover is where the claimant is a rescuer, who suffers injuries while rescuing others from a source of danger for which the defendant is responsible. The courts tend to assume that 'danger invites rescue', and that it is no answer to the claim that the claimant could very easily have avoided injury by declining to attempt a rescue (**3.31**).

Conduct of third parties

1.33 The courts have always been exceedingly reluctant to hold the defendant liable for the bad behaviour of others, no matter how foreseeable. A highly significant ruling, which broke with this stance, was the path-breaking case of *Home Office v Dorset Yacht Co* [1970] AC 1004. Here, prisoners escaping from borstal destroyed the claimant's property, and the claimant sued the Home Office, on the ground that but for their negligence there would have been no escape, and no injury to the claimant's interests. A majority of the House of Lords was prepared to find that the claimant could sue. But it was made clear that liability was restricted to incidents which took place near the borstal itself. And later cases have not been eager to extend liability.

> *Smith v Littlewoods Organization* **[1987] AC 241:** Littlewoods bought a disused cinema, intending to redevelop the site as a supermarket. Vandals broke into the site and started a fire, which spread to neighbouring properties, including Smith's. Held: Smith could not sue Littlewoods for failing to prevent this injury.

However, while the Lords in *Smith v Littlewoods* gave different reasons, all were clear that there was no absolute ban on liability, and that the defendant might sometimes come under a duty to guard against injury to the claimant from third parties. For example, Lord Goff suggested that the case might have been different if Littlewoods had knowledge (or even *means* of knowledge) of the threat, or if it had created some unusual source of danger to others ([1987] AC 241, 278).

No liability for statements?

1.34 It is simply untrue that there is no liability in negligence for statements, despite many *dicta* to the contrary. Words can and do cause a great deal of harm, and there is no particular reason why the courts should look on this harm with indifference. Moreover, it is often hard to draw the line between statements and acts. Nonetheless, it is understandable that liability for statements is restricted, for two reasons. First, in most cases the loss that is caused is a purely economic loss—and, as you shall see, the courts tend to take a restrictive attitude to losses of that sort (**5.7**). Second, where the claimant suffers loss as a result of the defendant's statement, we run into the courts' reluctance to make defendants liable for the independent actions of others (**1.32**). So if the defendant gives the claimant bad investment advice, on which the claimant relies and suffers loss, the courts are likely to say that investment is a risky business anyway, and the claimant should carry the loss resulting from his or her own investment decisions. So if the claimant's case is that he or she suffered loss in relying on the defendant's advice, the claimant must be prepared for a rough ride from the courts, and must be ready to meet the argument that they should take full responsibility for their own decisions (**5.14**). Again, courts are reluctant to impose liability where others were responsible for the claimant's situation, even if those others may have been influenced by the defendant's statement: so lack of care in analysing water from the well in the claimant's village did not lead to liability when it turned out to be poisonous (*Sutradhar v Natural Environment Research Council* [2006] UKHL 33).

Is 'duty' a necessary concept?

1.35 Not all writers in this area agree that it is useful to talk of 'duties of care'. After all, a 'duty of care' has no legal consequences until it is broken, and it seems a fiction to say that a duty hangs over the defendant's relations with others, waiting to turn into some type of legal liability. On this view, a judge who says that the defendant owed the claimant no duty at all must mean something like 'the defendant is not liable here, nor would he ever be liable on facts like these'. And a judge who says that the defendant owed the claimant a duty but had not broken it must mean 'the defendant is not liable here, but might have been if the facts had been slightly different'.

Nonetheless, 'duty' is a common enough notion, and not everyone agrees it is dispensable in this context. There is no fiction involved in advising potential defendants before the event that they need to take care to avoid liability; nor is there anything unreal about the insurance policies many defendants take out against this risk. It is *also* true, however, that the courts sometimes find 'duties' after the fact, where one would hardly have suspected their existence before it.

Breach of duty

1.36 Assuming that a duty is established, the next question is whether the defendant has broken it. In other words, whether the defendant has failed to come up to the standard required by the law for fulfilment of the duty, and is in that sense at fault. Perfection is not required, only reasonable behaviour. It is commonly said that the standard of care required is an 'objective' one; and this is certainly true in one sense: the question is whether the *court* considers that the defendant was at fault, not whether the defendant personally considered his or her behaviour reasonable. But there are other notions buried in this idea of an 'objective' standard, and there will be more to say on this below (**3.9**).

Particularity of the defendant's situation

1.37 The enquiry is into the reasonableness of the defendant's behaviour *in the particular circumstances in which the defendant was placed*. Accordingly, the court may be required to conduct an elaborate investigation into those precise circumstances. So while past precedents have considerable value as containing general principles, there will always be *some* differences between any two cases, and there is usually little to be gained from discussions of differences and similarities. Individual cases should therefore not be treated as laying down precise rules for the level of duty in concrete situations, even if they claim to. A judge who has adhered to proper general principles will not be reversed on appeal simply for failure to follow apparently similar cases (*Qualcast (Wolverhampton) v Haynes* [1959] AC 743). A potential defendant who wishes to be told precisely what he or she must do to avoid the possibility of liability in the future is unlikely to receive a satisfactory answer.

Burden of proof

1.38 It is for the claimant to prove that the defendant broke the duty of care. The standard of proof is that of the balance of probabilities. That is, the claimant must show that it is more likely than not that the defendant was in breach. However, there is no rule that the claimant must demonstrate *how* the accident happened, so long as the claimant satisfies the burden of proof. Accordingly, the claimant can sometimes argue that 'the facts speak for themselves' (*res ipsa loquitur*). This argument is that a mere recital of the facts so strongly suggests negligence that it is for the defendant to suggest some alternative explanation. For example, if the claimant is admitted to the defendant's hospital for ingrown toenails, but is discharged with an amputated arm, the court will probably hold that (practically if not technically) the burden of proof has shifted to the defendant. And if the claimant is hurt by a machine which was wholly under the defendant's control, again it would be for the defendant to explain what went wrong (e.g. *George v Eagle Air Services Ltd* [2009] UKPC 21—light aircraft crashing without explanation). However, the maxim *res ipsa loquitur* has never developed into a doctrine of law, unlike the experience of other jurisdictions: it is an example of the application of normal principle, not an exception to it.

Relevant factors

1.39 Various factors are consistently mentioned as relevant to the question of whether the defendant was in breach of duty:

• *Size of the risk and size of the threatened harm.* The greater the risk of injury to the claimant, the more likely is the court to find the defendant's conduct to be a breach of duty. Similarly, the greater the possible harm to the claimant (and to others) from the defendant's behaviour, the greater the chances of establishing liability.

• *Cost and practicability of precautions.* Even if the risk was obvious and preventable, the defendant may argue that it was nonetheless unreasonable to expect the defendant to avoid it. This may be on grounds of cost or other practical considerations. So a factory owner, whose factory is in a dangerous condition due to flooding, is not necessarily bound to shut it down until it is safe again (*Latimer v AEC* [1953] AC 643).

• *Utility of the defendant's behaviour.* There is no blanket defence of public benefit. Nonetheless, the value to society of the defendant's activities is a factor in determining their reasonableness. So those who needlessly pollute public waterways are liable for quite unlikely results of it (*Overseas Tankship (UK) v Miller Steamship Co Pty, The Wagon Mound (No 2)* [1967] 1 AC 617). But those who play cricket are not liable for unlikely, though entirely foreseeable, results of their activities (*Bolton v Stone* [1951] AC 850). And those engaged in valuable contributions to the wartime economy can neglect even quite sizeable risks (*Daborn v Bath Tramways Motor Co* [1946] 2 All ER 333).

• *General practice.* There is no absolute defence of common practice, and the courts have on occasion even ruled that the *universal* practice of particular professions is negligent (e.g. *Edward Wong Finance Co v Johnson Stokes & Master* [1984] AC 296). Nonetheless, it is relevant to enquire whether the claimant is demanding a common precaution, or an exceptional one.

A common complaint is that too little weight is given to the deterrent effect of negligence liability: so it is said that in asking whether the defendant acted reasonably, more stress should be placed on general social needs, even though those needs inevitably create risk of injury. So, in a case where the claimant had fallen down a hole left by the erection of a maypole at a village fête, Scott-Baker LJ commented that 'Accidents happen, and sometimes they are what can be described as pure accidents in the sense that the victim cannot recover damages for the resulting injury because fault cannot be established. If the law were to set a higher standard of care than that which is reasonable in cases such as the present, the consequences would quickly become inhibited. There would be no fêtes, no maypole dancing and none of the activities that have come to be associated with the English village green for fear of what might conceivably go wrong' (*Cole v Davies-Gilbert* [2007] EWCA Civ 396, para 36). Similar concerns motivated a recent statutory provision, to the effect that the courts may take into account (presumably, as a point against the claimant) that a finding of liability might deter desirable activities (Compensation Act 2006, s 1).

It was once suggested that the test for breach of duty can be expressed in mathematical terms: the defendant will be found negligent if and only if (cost of precautions) is less than (probability of loss) × (extent of loss). This is the so-called 'Learned Hand' formula, named after its inventor: see *United States v Carroll Towing Co* 159 F 2d 169 (2nd Circ, 1947), Learned Hand J. So put, this test is misleadingly precise, even in a case where the factors mentioned can be precisely quantified, and it is unduly narrow in ignoring other relevant facts. Nonetheless, it is a good general indicator, in cases where it can be applied.

Very small risks

1.40 The smaller the risk, the less likely the defendant is to be held responsible for it. And so if the risk is very small indeed, it is most unlikely that the defendant will be held liable. There are, however, two quite separate arguments the defendant can make in that situation, which need to be carefully distinguished.

- First, the defendant might argue that a particular risk appeared to be so small that it was in fact quite imperceptible: it would not have occurred to a reasonable person that that sort of accident might happen, and so the accident was unforeseeable.

- Second, the defendant might concede that the risk was perceptible, but might argue that reasonable people would decide it was not worth the effort of eliminating it. So it is not that reasonable people would not appreciate the risk, but that, having appreciated it, they would see no point in doing anything about it.

Either argument defeats the claimant's claim if the court accepts it, but different evidence is appropriate in respect of each. The first is simply a matter of showing that the event was extremely unlikely, and so reasonable people would have dismissed the possibility as absurd. The second involves a much broader enquiry, for the defendant's argument is that there was nothing reasonable that could be done about the risk—usually on the ground that any effective precautions would have been too costly. The appeal is not simply to the smallness of the risk, but also to the cost of precautions.

> **Bolton v Stone [1951] AC 850:** A cricket ball was hit for six out of Stone's ground. It flew over 100 yards and hit Bolton, who was standing in the street just outside her house. Balls had been driven out of the ground on average about once every five years. Held: no negligence was established.

> **Overseas Tankship (UK) v Miller Steamship Co Pty, The Wagon Mound (No 2) [1967] 1 AC 617:** Furnace oil was spilled in Sydney Harbour from Miller's ship. The flashpoint of the oil was very high, so reasonable engineers would have considered a fire possible but highly unlikely. However, a fire started in consequence of welding operations carried on by the wharf owner. Held: Miller was liable to the owners of ships damaged by the fire.

It is very hard to distinguish these cases from one another merely on grounds of the apparent degree of risk. In both cases the risk was very small. In neither case did the court make an attempt to estimate it numerically. *Bolton* involved personal injury and *The Wagon Mound* property damage; but that only intensifies the puzzle, because the courts usually treat personal injury *more* generously than property damage. The difference between the cases emerges more clearly when we consider the cost of precautions. In *Bolton*, the risk could only have been avoided either by building some (very high and very expensive) extra netting, or by ceasing altogether to play cricket at the ground. Whereas in *The Wagon Mound*, not only would it have been very easy to avoid spilling the oil, it would even have saved Miller money, as the furnace oil was far from worthless.

A deeper difference between the cases lies in the value of the activity pursued by the defendant. Deliberate pollution of harbours is an activity with rather obvious social costs, and no obvious benefits; whereas cricket, whatever one thinks of it, is (at worst) neutral on that score. Of course, if the risk of harm increases, even cricket may attract liability: so in a case where about eight or nine balls a year flew out of the defendant's ground, liability was established for damage caused (*Miller v Jackson* [1977] QB 966 (**7.16**)).

The 'objectivity' of the test

1.41 It is often stressed that the test of negligence is an 'objective' one. One of the things this entails is that the defendant's own view of the reasonableness of his or her conduct is irrelevant. But it also seems to entail that the court should ignore certain characteristics of the defendant, and of the situation the defendant is in:

• The defendant cannot always plead his or her own personal characteristics. Certainly the defendant cannot plead an impulsive or careless disposition. It seems that the defendant can demand to be judged by the standard of a reasonable person of the defendant's own age, at least if the defendant is under 18. So where two 15-year-old girls fought each other with plastic rulers, resulting in one of them losing an eye, the court applied the standard of the reasonable 15-year-old (liability was on that basis refused: *Mullin v Richards* [1998] 1 All ER 920). (Again, a 13-year-old boy who collided with the claimant while playing a game of tag can expect to be judged by the standard of the reasonable 13-year-old, and accordingly is liable only if 'careless to a very high degree': *Orchard v Lee* [2009] EWCA 195.) It has been held that a driver who suffered a stroke at the wheel was still 'objectively' guilty of negligence if he collided with another car, although the court suggested that matters might be different if the stroke had rendered him unconscious (*Roberts v Ramsbottom* [1980] 1 All ER 7 (**4.14**)).

• If the defendant is performing a task requiring some special skill, he or she cannot usually plead amateur status or lack of experience. But the precise level of skill demanded is unclear. It appears that DIY enthusiasts, whose creations endanger their house guests, must reach a certain level of competence, though it need not be that of a paid professional (*Wells v Cooper* [1958] 2 QB 265). It is sometimes suggested that the governing principle is that the defendant must display any skills which the defendant has given others the impression that the defendant has (sometimes called the 'holding-out' principle). But this cannot explain all the cases—in particular, why a learner driver is expected to show all the skill of a reasonably experienced driver no matter how prominently the 'L' plates are displayed (*Nettleship v Weston* [1971] 2 QB 691 (**4.14**)).

• While the defendant can certainly plead the cost of precautions, it appears that the defendant cannot usually plead poverty, or that he or she personally cannot afford the suggested precautions. In other words the amount that better precautions would cost is relevant, but whether the defendant in fact had that much cash to spare is not. The distinction is a subtle one, however, and in one context at least it has been ignored: see *Leakey v National Trust* [1980] QB 485 (liability of owner of land for hazards naturally arising, **7.23**; see also **4.28** for another possible exception). It has also been suggested that where the defendant is a government department, the defendant's level of funding may be relevant to the level of duty (see *Knight v Home Office* [1990] 3 All ER 237), but the limits of this are quite unclear.

The law here is confused. These ideas make major inroads into the principle that the defendant must personally be at fault, without always explaining why this should be so. Some at least of the cases are explicable, if not always defensible, by noting the judicial generosity to those injured in car accidents (on which see below, **4.12**). And others are defensible on the ground that the defendant may bear some responsibility for getting into a situation that he or she was incapable of handling. It is frequently unclear, however, what policy is served by holding the defendant to a standard which he or she cannot possibly meet.

Quantification of loss, and defences

1.42 Assuming that the claimant has managed to establish both the existence of duty and its breach, a few hurdles yet remain. The claimant must demonstrate that a loss has been suffered and must quantify it (**10.18**); must show that there is a sufficient causal link between the defendant's conduct and the loss the claimant suffers (**10.21**); and must show that the loss is not too 'remote'—roughly, that it was not too freakish a consequence of the defendant's conduct (**10.28**). There are also various defences which may go to reduce or entirely eliminate the claim (**11.1**).

Conclusion: negligence as personal fault

1.43 In summary, then, any brief description of the law of negligence is likely to give the impression that it is an enquiry into whether the defendant is personally at fault for the claimant's loss. Yet there are several factors at work which look a little odd from that perspective. The level of fault is often high, sometimes inhumanly so. The courts' commitment to examining each case on its merits, after the event, is quite incompatible with laying down firm rules in advance. And despite the apparently stern message of personal responsibility the law embodies, in most cases no-one supposes that the defendant will personally bear the loss. Rather, it is borne by the defendant's insurer, or the defendant's employer. It seems futile to debate whether negligence 'really' involves an enquiry into fault, or whether this enquiry is a sham; rather, the tort confronts a wildly diverse array of circumstances, and pursues a variety of policies in relation to each.

Tort and statute

1.44 The growth of tort over the 20th century was truly remarkable. But it is dwarfed by the growth of statute law over the same period. Many statutes modify tort liability, whether by expanding it or contracting it. Today, it makes no great sense to discriminate between 'common law torts' and 'statutory torts', because most torts are influenced by both. However, there are recurrent problems where a statute places the defendant under an obligation, but fails to spell out whether the defendant can be sued for breach of that obligation by those affected.

1.45 There are three main ways in which the infringement of a statute may result in an action in tort, and it is important to keep them distinct. First, there are some torts where it is necessary for the claimant to show that the defendant's conduct was in some sense 'unlawful', and breach of a statute may supply this missing element **(6.27)**. Second, there is a distinct tort of breach of statutory duty, under which those who suffer from the defendant's breach of statute may sometimes recover damages **(1.46)**. And third, a statutory duty may form part of a case that the defendant was under a duty in the tort of negligence to look after the claimant's interests **(1.53)**. These torts are all distinct from one another.

It has frequently been suggested that this arrangement of the law is over-elaborate, especially since all three of the torts concerned are rather uncertain in their application. Nonetheless, the courts have to date resisted attempts to amalgamate them into a single entity.

> **Chipchase v British Titan Products Co [1956] 1 QB 545:** Chipchase was injured at work when he fell from a ledge six feet from the ground. If the ledge had been six inches higher, his employers would have been in breach of statutory obligations as to safe working conditions. Chipchase argued that facts so close to being in breach of safety regulations constituted evidence of negligence. Held: there was no evidence of negligence.

It is possible for the same facts to give rise to action under more than one of the torts. In some contexts (and particularly that of industrial accidents) it is common for the claimant to combine action for negligence with action for breach of statutory duty **(4.32)**.

The tort of breach of statutory duty

1.46 The tort of breach of statutory duty consists of breaking the provisions of a statute, in such a way as to cause loss to the claimant. Sometimes the statute itself says whether a civil action lies for a breach. A notable example is the duty of local authorities to maintain the highway, where the statute (Highways Act 1980, ss 41 and 58) explains precisely when liability is available (see discussion in *Cross v Kirklees Metropolitan Borough Council* [1998] 1 All ER 564). But what if the statute does not say whether action lies? How the court resolves that matter is the subject of this section.

While not as ancient as some torts—it is barely a century and a half old—nonetheless it is showing its age. Methods of statutory drafting have altered considerably over that time, yet this has not made much difference to the doctrine. In practice, the tort is little used, because the judges have consistently refused to find it applicable to most statutes. The major area where it applies is industrial safety legislation. Here, infringements of the law not only lead to criminal penalties, but also to private action in tort by injured workers. However, the doctrine has never, in theory, been confined to that situation, and it makes occasional appearances outside it (e.g. *Monk v Warbey* [1935] 1 KB 75, below **1.48**).

'Parliamentary intention'

1.47 The orthodox view is that no action lies for breach of statutory duty unless Parliament intended that it should. The statute must therefore be scanned in detail for indications of intention on the matter. Yet while this enquiry might have had some purpose when the doctrine was in its infancy, in the early Victorian period, given the modern style of drafting statutes, it seems futile. If Parliament had intended action to lie, in modern circumstances we would expect the statute to say so expressly: and this is very frequently the conclusion to which the courts come in individual cases. Very occasionally, statutes state expressly that no action lies (e.g. Health and Safety at Work etc Act 1974, s 47(1)). In general, however, statutes contain no indication either way. So there is a farcical evasion of responsibility, under which Parliament leaves the matter to the courts, who themselves pretend to defer to 'Parliament's intention'. A Law Commission Proposal for a statutory presumption of liability (*The Interpretation of Statutes*, Law Com 21, 1969) found no favour in Parliament, and has never been acted on.

'Parliament's intention' is here largely fictitious. The real question is therefore what the courts do under cover of interpreting Parliament's intention. Unfortunately, this is very unclear. In practice, the courts rely on a few general presumptions about what Parliament is likely to have meant. The House of Lords (e.g. *Lonrho v Shell Petroleum Co (No 2)* [1982] AC 173) has approved the use of these presumptions, which I now describe.

Legislation meant to protect specific groups

1.48 There is a presumption that a statute intended to protect a specific group of people gives a right to those people to sue.

> **Monk v Warbey [1935] 1 KB 75:** Warbey lent his car to a friend, without arranging for third party insurance. The friend's poor driving injured Monk. Monk successfully sued Warbey for failing to arrange for insurance to ensure compensation in these circumstances.

> **Todd v Adam [2002] EWCA Civ 509:** A fishing trawler sank off Cornwall with all hands. It was held that if the accident could be traced to the owner's breach of the relevant safety legislation, then the owner could be sued by the estates of the drowned deckhands.

Conversely, the defendant may defeat an action by pointing out that the claimant is not a member of the class meant to be protected.

> **Cutler v Wandsworth Stadium [1933] 2 KB 297:** Cutler, a bookmaker, argued that Wandsworth Stadium had caused him loss of business by failing to make space available for him, contrary to the legislation on betting then in force. Held: that Act was passed to benefit Cutler's potential customers rather than Cutler himself, and accordingly no action lay.

The presumption has been criticized, most famously by Atkin LJ. He pointed out that it is odd that a duty owed to everyone is not thought to merit legal action, whereas a duty to a narrow class is (*Phillips v Britannia Hygienic Laundry Co* [1923] 2 KB 832, 841). And the criterion is often difficult to apply. Nonetheless, the presumption is well established, though judges differ in how much weight they give to it. There will also often be scope for argument over the precise purpose of legislation. So, for example, while *one* purpose of the prison rules on segregation of prisoners was to protect especially vulnerable prisoners, it was not their *only* purpose, and accordingly no action lay by a prisoner under them (*R v Deputy Governor of Parkhurst Prison, ex p Hague* [1992] 1 AC 58). Or again, the homeless persons legislation has been held to be for the public benefit generally, rather than particularly for the benefit of homeless persons (*O'Rourke v Camden London Borough Council* [1998] AC 188). By contrast, where injuries were caused by a breach of statutory rules on the laying of tram rails, the Court of Appeal were happy to allow a claim; the rules were evidently meant to protect road users, and this was enough to satisfy the 'somewhat nebulous requirement for a limited class' (*Roe v Sheffield City Council* [2003] EWCA Civ 1). This approach comes close to making the requirement meaningless.

The type of loss

1.49 Where the claimant suffers loss as a result of the defendant's breach of statutory duty, the defendant has a defence if the claimant's loss was of a different sort from that which the statute was meant to prevent.

> **Gorris v Scott (1874) LR 9 Exch 125:** Sheep belonging to Gorris were lost overboard, as a result of Scott's breach of provisions of the Contagious Diseases (Animals) Act 1869. Held: as the purpose of that Act was to safeguard public health rather than to prevent damage to property, Gorris's claim was outside the statute.

> **Vibixa v Kumori [2006] EWCA Civ 536:** Kumori sold printing equipment to Vibixa. The equipment was defective, resulting in a fire and damage to Vibixa's property. Held: while Kumori were in breach of industrial safety legislation, the purpose of that legislation was to protect health and safety rather than to guard against other losses. Accordingly, no action could be based on it.

This apparently straightforward rule allows for many differences in approach. It has sometimes been used with nit-picking exactness.

> **Nicholls v F Austin (Leyton) [1946] AC 493:** Nicholls was injured when the circular saw he was using threw out a sharp piece of wood. This would not have happened if his employers had fenced the saw, as statute required. Held: the object of the fencing obligation was to keep workers' fingers out, not pieces of wood in, so Nicholls's claim under the statute was not admissible.

Adequacy of other remedies

1.50 All agree that it is highly relevant what other remedies are available. But there are important differences of emphasis. Some judges say that if the statute provides its own remedy, then it is not for the courts to add others. If right, that would effectively mean that the doctrine should *never* apply, except in the rare case where Parliament specifies a duty but says nothing about the consequences of failure to carry it out (as in *Dawson & Co v Bingley UDC* [1911] 2 KB 149). This approach would mean that the tort of breach of statutory duty would hardly ever apply in modern conditions. Another approach is more lenient: an apparently complete code of enforcement is taken only as a *strong indication* that additional remedies are not called for.

> **X v Bedfordshire County Council [1995] 2 AC 633:** Children who claimed to have suffered injury as a result of breaches of the Children Act 1989 by their local authority, sued the authority. Held: in the light of the elaborate range of remedies available under

that Act, it was inconceivable that Parliament intended an additional right of action for breach of statutory duty.

> **Feakins v Dover Harbour Board [1998] 36 LS Gaz R 31:** Sheep exporters were not allowed to export their sheep to France, as a result of the activities of animal rights protestors. Held: assuming that the Harbour Board was in breach of its duties, nonetheless no action lay. Public law remedies were available for breach of the statutory duties, and these duties were imposed for the public benefit, not for the benefit of a particular class of persons.

A subtly different approach is to look at the claimant's legal rights and remedies in the round, and to ask whether other statutory or common law remedies are adequate, or whether justice demands a remedy for breach of the statute.

> **McCall v Abelesz [1976] QB 585:** McCall, the tenant of property, sued his landlord, for breach of the statutory duty not to harass tenants. Held: McCall and others in his position had adequate common law remedies for breach of contract and for trespass, and the action for breach of statutory duty did not lie.

Whatever we may make of individual decisions, there is a lot to be said for this approach generally. It allows the court to argue openly about whether liability should be imposed, in the light of the provision the law makes in that area generally. However, there can be no pretence that all the case law is reconcilable with it.

If in doubt, refuse to find liability?

1.51 It is tempting today, in the light of frequent refusals to find liability, to postulate a final presumption: that unless there is strong reason to the contrary, either in the form of earlier cases favouring liability or indications in the statute itself, liability will be refused. It is always open to Parliament to impose liability expressly, and if it has not done so it is usually hopeless to argue that it nonetheless intended so to do. Certainly there is a huge reluctance to imply a liability to compensate where none has been provided by Parliament, even if that means that some statutory requirements can be infringed without any consequences for the infringer (e.g. *Trustee in Bankruptcy of St John Poulton v Ministry of Justice* [2010] EWCA Civ 392). The tort is considered by many to be a historical relic, and there is little enthusiasm for extending it.

No defence of due diligence

1.52 If liability is found, there is no defence of due diligence or lack of care. Of course, a statutory duty may be expressed as a duty to take due care, or words may be used which have a similar effect, such as by providing a defence where it is 'impracticable' to act in a safe way (Mines and Quarries Act 1954, s 157). But there is no presumption that common law negligence is the standard imposed by any regulatory act. If a breach is established, it is no defence that compliance is difficult—or even that it is impossible.

> **John Summers & Sons v Frost [1955] AC 740:** Frost was injured as a result of his employers not having securely fenced the machine on which he was working. The employers argued that the machine could not be used if it were fenced as the Act required. Held: the employers were nonetheless liable for breach of statutory duty.

Statutory powers and negligence

1.53 Where the defendant is a public authority with statutory powers, the claimant may claim that those powers should not be used in ways which injure the claimant. So the claimant may sue in negligence, alleging misuse of the defendant's statutory powers. It was at one time thought that a statutory power could not be the foundation of an action in negligence. It was said that there was a world of difference between a statutory *duty*, which was mandatory, and a statutory *power*, which was not. Most famously in *East Suffolk Rivers Catchment Board v Kent* [1941] AC 74, where a statutory body ineptly failed to prevent flooding to the claimant's land, it was thought crucial that the body was under no duty to act. And so a majority of the House of Lords considered that no action lay for its failure to do the work to a satisfactory standard.

However, that approach was disapproved in *Home Office v Dorset Yacht Co* [1970] AC 1004. That case involved mismanagement of a borstal, with the result that some of the inmates escaped and destroyed the claimant's property. Liability was established. The distinction between the authority's powers and its duties was not thought particularly helpful. It was suggested that the true distinction was between *policy decisions*, which could not be questioned in an action for negligence, and merely *operational decisions*, which could. But this distinction has in its turn been subjected to criticism, and is in any event a very hard line to draw (**1.56**).

1.54 Liability in this area goes backwards and forwards with alarming speed. In *X v Bedfordshire County Council* [1995] 2 AC 633 the House of Lords was prepared to find that powers to provide for special educational needs could in certain circumstances be made the basis of action by those whose needs were unmet, even though there was no indication that Parliament had intended this. However, the Lords refused to find that an action lay for misuse of local authority powers to prevent child abuse. And in *Stovin v Wise* [1996] AC 923 a differently constituted House of Lords held, by a majority, that no action lay for motorists injured by negligent exercise of powers to improve highways, seemingly on the ground that there was no reason to suppose that Parliament intended an action to lie. These relatively recent cases show great reluctance to impose a negligence liability on local authorities.

Yet already the tide seems to have turned again. A denial of liability in respect of child abuse in *X* has been found to contravene the European Convention on Human Rights (*Z v United Kingdom* [2001] ECHR 333), both under Art 3 (prohibition of inhuman treatment) and Art 13 (need for an effective remedy). It follows that there can be liability in a claim brought by a child, though not by the child's parent (*D v East Berkshire Community Health NHS Trust* [2005] UKHL 23). And recent cases have shown a greater willingness to find liability than was apparent before.

> ***Barrett v Enfield London Borough Council* [2001] 2 AC 550:** Barrett, who had been in local authority care from age 10 months until age 17, argued that his profound psychiatric problems could be traced to poor decisions by the council. These decisions included inappropriate foster placements and frequent moves between different residential homes. Held: it could not be said that all of those decisions were non-justiciable. The case must proceed to trial so that more detailed findings could be made.

> ***W v Essex County Council* [2001] 2 AC 592:** Before a 15-year-old boy was placed with foster carers, the carers asked for a specific assurance that he had no history of child abuse. Wrongly, they were given this assurance. The boy went on to abuse the foster carers' own children. Held: the risk from the boy should have been obvious, and the claim could not be struck out as unarguable.

> ***Phelps v Hillingdon London Borough Council* [2001] 2 AC 619:** A number of test cases were brought against education authorities, for failing to make adequate diagnosis of or provision for learning difficulties resulting from dyslexia and muscular dystrophy. Held: the education authorities owed duties of care to their pupils in respect of their education.

> ***Kane v New Forest District Council* [2001] EWCA Civ 878:** A local planning authority approved a development which included a new footpath, ending on the inside bend of a road. It was appreciated that access to the road was unsuitable because of the absence of sightlines from the road. However, nothing had been done about this five months after the footpath opened, when Kane, 24 years old, stepped from the path into the road and was injured by a car. Kane sued the planning authority, who applied to have the claim struck out, on the authority of *Stovin v Wise* (above). Held: the claim was a strong one, which could not be struck out. This was a case of the authority's

standing by and failing to deal with a known hazard, and so was easily distinguishable from *Stovin*.

The more recent cases are not, however, all one way.

Gorringe v Calderdale Metropolitan Borough Council **[2004] UKHL 15:** Driving over a sharp crest in a road, Gorringe suddenly saw a bus and slammed on her brakes. The brakes locked, the car skidded and collided with the bus, which was being driven perfectly properly. Gorringe argued that the highway authority were liable for her injuries, by failing to paint 'SLOW' at some point on the road. Held: the claim would be dismissed on the authority of *Stovin v Wise* (above).

Rowley v Secretary of State for Work and Pensions **[2007] EWCA Civ 598:** Claimants dissatisfied with the way their family's claims had been dealt with by the Child Support Agency sued the relevant Secretary of State for negligence, alleging economic and psychological harm of various sorts. Held: given the elaborate statutory scheme under which the Agency did its work, which included a right of appeal against incorrect assessments and a right to interest on arrears in certain circumstances, it would not be fair, just or reasonable to impose negligence liability as well.

Jain v Trent Strategic Health Authority **[2009] UKHL 4:** Trent SHA applied to a magistrate for the removal of the claimants' nursing home from the national register, effectively closing it. The claimants successfully appealed the magistrate's order, but considerable damage was suffered by their business before they could resume operations. Held: the statutory duties imposed on health authorities in respect of nursing homes were for the benefit of the residents of those homes, and it would not be appropriate to limit those duties by allowing action by others affected, such as the owners of the homes. Accordingly, no action lay.

This whole area is therefore in flux, and will probably continue to be so, at least until the courts have become comfortable with the Human Rights Act 1998 (**1.22**), which is potentially relevant in any case where the defendant is a public body. One area of confusion has already been cleared up. In *Osman v United Kingdom* (1998) 29 EHRR 245, where a victim of a mentally unstable attacker sued the police for failing to take action sooner than they did, the European Court held that a denial of liability was an infringement of Art 6. To refuse to find liability was equivalent to granting a special immunity to the police, which was incompatible with the claimant's right to bring his grievance before an impartial tribunal. However, in *Z v United Kingdom* [2001] ECHR 333 the court backtracked somewhat. It could not be said that the courts were granting the police an 'immunity' merely because they had refused to extend liability into a novel and contentious area. Certainly such cases raised human rights issues—and breaches of the Convention were established in the case, as noted above (**1.54**)—but the blanket approach in *Osman* was misconceived.

What factors seem relevant to the existence of a duty of care, on top of the usual questions asked in all negligence cases?

Consistency with parliamentary intention

1.55 The courts will scrutinize the statute itself, and will not find liability if that would conflict with the policy embodied in the statute. So if the statute provides its own regime of rights and procedures for challenging decisions made under it, the courts will avoid creating additional rights under the tort of negligence (e.g. *Jones v Department of Employment* [1989] QB 1, social security tribunals). Or again, the courts may refuse to allow the claimant an action on the ground that the claimant was not the sort of person the Act was meant to benefit (*Caparo Industries v Dickman* [1990] 2 AC 605).

This is not quite the same thing as asking whether Parliament meant there to be liability; that would be to ask the unanswerable question of what Parliament meant, whereas the question the courts ask—whether the imposition of liability sabotages what Parliament expressly provided—seems at least in principle capable of sensible answer. An added twist is that, in deciding what Parliament's intention is, the courts might decide that this is compatible with some types of negligence claims but not others. So, for example, the statutory scheme for the inspection of civil aircraft is thought compatible with a claim by a passenger injured by a defective aircraft (*Perrett v Collins* [1999] PNLR 77), but not with a claim by the owner of the aircraft (*Philcox v Civil Aviation Authority* [1995] 27 LS Gaz R 33). A similar result holds in relation to inspection of fishing vessels, where negligent errors by officials can lead to actions to redress physical damage, but not pure economic loss (*Reeman v Department of Transport* [1997] 2 Lloyd's Rep 648).

The policy/operation distinction

1.56 It is often said that the courts will not allow the claimant to challenge 'policy' decisions, but only 'operational' ones. Matters of policy are for democratically accountable public officials, and not the courts, but incompetence in everyday operational matters should be open to correction by the courts. But this distinction, while easy to state, is clearly no magic key to the area. It 'does not provide a touchstone of liability' (*Rowling v Takaro Properties* [1988] 1 All ER 163, 172, Lord Keith). It is still, however, of some importance. There is a great difference between suggesting that a mistake was made in matters of policy formation, on the one hand, and suggesting that there was incompetence in carrying out a settled policy, the merits of which are not in issue, on the other. In the former case, opinions can reasonably differ, and democracy requires judges to leave certain decisions to other public officials, whereas there is no democratic mandate for everyday incompetence.

> **Kent v Griffiths [2001] QB 36:** A doctor attending a patient experiencing an asthmatic attack ordered an ambulance to take her to hospital, but there was then a delay. It was later found that the ambulance arrived 14 minutes later than it should have done. This delay, coupled with poor care on the journey to hospital, led to respiratory failure and consequent brain damage. Held: while the courts might not be prepared to find liability where the ambulance service could plead lack of resources or conflicting priorities, here there was no such excuse, and the service would be liable if fault on its part was demonstrated.

The policy/operation distinction is therefore of considerable utility. It is another question, however, whether individual administrative decisions can be mechanically classified as 'policy' or 'operational' decisions, or whether a finding that a decision is a 'policy' matter precludes legal challenge entirely.

Must the issue be justiciable?

1.57 It is also said that the issue must be 'justiciable', that is, suitable for resolution in a law court; and this point has recently been reiterated by the House of Lords in the *Barrett* case (**1.54**). But which issues are suitable for the courts, and which not? To many, this just looks like the policy/operational distinction in disguise: 'policy' is not for the courts but for the wider political process, which is why it is 'non-justiciable'. And certainly the Lords in *Barrett* thought the two concepts related (though they did not say they were the same). It seems that the courts are groping for a way of saying that only some types of local authority decisions can be questioned in an action for negligence, but that they have not yet agreed how precisely to formulate this.

FURTHER READING

Beyleveld and Pattinson 'Horizontal applicability and horizontal effect' (2002) 118 LQR 623.

Fairgrieve 'The Human Rights Act 1998, damages and tort law' [2001] PL 695.

Fairgrieve 'Pushing back the boundaries of public authority liability: Tort law enters the classroom' [2002] PL 288.

Gearty '*Osman* unravels' (2002) 65 MLR 87.

Hepple 'Negligence: The search for coherence' (1997) 50 CLP 69.

Hickman 'Negligence and article 6: The great escape?' (2002) 61 CLJ 1.

Howes 'Liability for breach of statutory duty—Is there a coherent approach?' (2007) 1 JPIL 1.

Morgan 'Questioning the "true effect" of the Human Rights Act' (2002) 22 LS 259.

Steele 'Damages in tort and under the Human Rights Act' (2008) 67 CLJ 606.

Varuhas 'A tort-based approach to damages under the Human Rights Act 1998' (2009) 75 MLR 750.

Wade 'Horizons of horizontality' (2000) 116 LQR 217.

Wexler 'Do we really need the Hand formula?' (2001) 9 Tort Law Rev 81.

SELF-TEST QUESTIONS

1 Given that having liability insurance greatly increases the chances of being sued, why does any rational person ever take it out (**1.10**)?

2 Is it true that there is no liability in negligence for:
   (a) omissions (**1.30**)?
   (b) statements (**1.34**)?
   (c) policy decisions of a public authority (**1.56**)?

3 What interests are protected by the law of tort (**1.4**)?

4 How accurate is Atkin's 'neighbour *dictum*' as a statement of the modern law of negligence (**1.27**)?

5 Would it be more accurate to call this subject 'tort' or 'torts' (**1.6**)?

6 Is there a defence of 'public benefit' in negligence (**1.39**)?

7 How effective is tort as a method of deterring harmful behaviour (**1.13–1.16**)?

8 The European Convention binds 'public authorities', not private individuals. Does it therefore follow that the Convention is irrelevant in a case where none of the parties is a 'public authority' (**1.25**)?

Deliberate harm to the person

SUMMARY

Certain types of harm to the claimant are tortious if they are deliberate:

- Assault
- Battery
- False imprisonment
- Unlawful harassment
- Invasion of privacy (possibly)

Tort here plays second fiddle to the criminal law. But it has an important role where substantial compensation is demanded. It may also be useful if the victim wants to retain control of the conduct of proceedings, rather than appearing as a mere witness.

Assault and battery

2.1 If the defendant deliberately inflicts force on the claimant, the defendant commits the tort of *battery*, unless there is some defence. To threaten immediate force constitutes the tort of *assault*. Both torts are actionable without proof that any financial loss resulted from the defendant's activities ('actionable without proof of special damage'). There can be assault without battery (e.g. the defendant threatens to hit the claimant but does not), and battery without assault (e.g. the defendant creeps up behind the claimant and hits her). The distinction between the two torts is clear enough in theory, but is in many situations unimportant. In practice it is common, if not entirely accurate, to refer to instances of assault and of battery as 'assault'.

Deliberate, not negligent, harm

2.2 Assault and battery are different species of the tort of trespass to the person. (The third species, false imprisonment, is dealt with below, **2.11**.) Whatever may have been the position historically, it is now clear that merely careless harm is actionable only if negligence is proved.

> **Fowler v Lanning [1959] 1 QB 426:** While on a hunting expedition, Fowler was injured by a bullet from Lanning's gun. Fowler argued that Lanning was guilty of trespass to the person, unless he could prove that it was a non-negligent accident. Held: Lanning would be liable if intent to wound or negligence could be shown, but in either case the burden of proof was on Fowler.

Assault: definition

2.3 The defendant commits assault if he or she causes the claimant to fear immediate personal violence. The threat to the claimant must be immediate; mere hostility is not enough, unless the claimant apprehends violence then and there.

> **Tubervell v Savage (1669) 1 Mod Rep 3:** In the course of a furious argument, Tubervell put his hand on his sword and said to Savage 'If it were not assize time, I would not take such language from you'. Held: this did not amount to an assault.

Tubervell v Savage was at one time thought to mean that words alone cannot constitute an assault. But that is not what the report says, and it would be a strange rule—why shouldn't the defendant's words be an indication of whether he or she is likely to be violent? In any event it does not explain the decision, as Tubervell had used a gesture to his sword as well as threatening words. And it is certainly not true that there can be no assault if the defendant makes qualifications to his hostile intent.

> **Read v Coker (1853) 13 CB 850:** Coker demanded that Read leave the premises where he was, saying that he would break Read's neck if he did not go. Held: this constituted assault against Read.

The claimant's fear of violence must be reasonable. There is no liability for assault if the defendant makes a threat which the claimant knows the defendant cannot carry out, or where the defendant points a gun at the claimant which the claimant knows is not loaded.

> **Thomas v National Union of Mineworkers (South Wales Area) [1986] Ch 20:** Mineworkers were bussed into work, passing through considerable numbers of

pickets urging a strike and making violent threats and gestures. Held: this could not be assault, as there was no way in which the pickets could reach those in the bus.

Battery: definition

2.4 The defendant is liable for battery if he or she inflicts force on the claimant. The degree of force does not matter: 'the least touching of another in anger is a battery' (*Cole v Turner* (1704) 6 Mod Rep 149). Presumably an unwelcome kiss is a battery as well, though there is no authority on the point. The force can be transmitted indirectly, as for example where:

- Horn threw a bucket of boiling water over Pursell (*Pursell v Horn* (1838) 8 Ad & El 602).

- Reeve deliberately drove his gig at a carriage, which overturned; Hopper, inside, was hurt (*Hopper v Reeve* (1817) 7 Taunt 698).

- Burford hit Dodwell's horse, which ran off and threw Dodwell down (*Dodwell v Burford* (1669) 1 Mod Rep 24).

- Fagan accidentally drove his car onto a policeman's foot. He then refused to reverse, and switched the engine off. Held: Fagan was guilty of assault on a constable (*Fagan v Metropolitan Police Commissioner* [1969] 1 QB 439). (*Fagan* was a criminal case, and there is a closely reasoned dissent by Bridge J; it is therefore a weak authority, and it is uncertain whether it is correct as to the tort of battery.)

Assault and battery: the mental element

2.5 It is usually stated that intention on the defendant's part is necessary if the claimant's action is to succeed. This is broadly true, but certain qualifications must be made. First, there is clear criminal law authority that 'subjective recklessness' (conscious risk-taking) is sufficient. So the defendant is guilty of battery if he kicks out at random and happens to connect with the claimant (*R v Venna* [1976] QB 421). Presumably this is true of the tort of assault as well. Second, if the defendant intended to batter *someone*, it seems not to matter if he accidentally hits the claimant, rather than the person he intended to hit. Third, one modern case casts considerable doubt on the whole matter, by suggesting an additional requirement of 'hostile intent'.

> **Wilson v Pringle [1987] QB 237:** Wilson and Pringle were both schoolboys. Pringle kicked Wilson, causing him to fall over and injure himself. Was there any possible defence to an action of battery? Held: the kicking was intentional and it was no defence that the consequential injury was not. However, Wilson must also prove that Pringle acted with hostility, and there was a triable issue whether that was so.

This suggested additional element of 'hostility' is vague, particularly as the court insisted that it did not mean malevolence or ill will. The meaning is unclear. If there is such a requirement, it is likely to lead to confusion in sexual harassment cases, where the defendant and the claimant are likely to disagree on whether the defendant's behaviour can be styled 'hostile'. The notion was disapproved by Lord Goff in *Re F* [1990] 2 AC 1, though he added that the defendant's behaviour would not constitute battery where it was merely 'physical contact which is generally acceptable in the ordinary conduct of everyday life' ([1990] 2 AC 1, 73).

Impact of the criminal law

2.6 Both assault and battery are crimes as well as torts. A court which has just convicted the defendant may order the defendant to pay compensation to the claimant for personal injuries or property damage. However, these powers are limited, and in deciding whether to make an order, the court must take into account the defendant's ability to pay—which would be irrelevant if the claimant were suing the defendant in a civil court. In practice, the powers are little used for victims of personal injury, though much used in cases of property damage.

Under the Criminal Injuries Compensation Scheme, the victims of violent crimes may recover benefits from public funds. Under the original scheme, as established in 1964, these benefits were the same as would have been available against the criminal in tort, had the criminal been able to pay. However, these benefits have now been reduced, and under the Criminal Injuries Compensation Act 1995 the victims of crimes receive sums set by a fixed statutory tariff, which is unrelated to (but generally lower than) tort damages. The amount received may also be reduced, perhaps to zero, for matters which would be irrelevant in a tort action, such as the claimant's bad record.

Harassment and other deliberate harm

Beyond assault and battery

2.7 It has long been recognized that the defendant should be responsible for deliberate physical harm to the claimant, even where it would be difficult to describe the defendant's conduct as battery.

> **Wilkinson v Downton [1897] 2 QB 57:** As a practical joke, Downton told Wilkinson that her husband had been injured in a road accident and was in hospital. Wilkinson suffered

nervous shock and was sick for some weeks before she recovered. Held: she could sue Downton for the consequences of his unlawful and unjustifiable conduct, even though there was no evidence that he intended her illness.

The case is a strong one, particularly as it was decided before general tortious recovery for nervous shock (**3.18**) was recognized in law. Cases are rare, but any doubts that the liability is still part of the law have recently been put to rest.

C v D [2006] EWHC 166 (QB): Under cover of supervising C at school, D performed various acts of abuse, including deliberately exposing C's genitals and staring at them. C later suffered various psychiatric problems which could be traced to this abuse. Held: D was liable for this harm even though not everything he did could be regarded as an assault. It was not necessary to prove that he intended harm; it was enough that harm was very likely to occur, or that D was reckless as to whether it occurred.

Nonetheless, the liability is fairly narrow, because the claimant may not be able to prove nervous shock, which will usually be regarded as an essential element of the action. ('Nervous shock' must consist of a recognizable medical condition with physical symptoms, not merely 'shock' as ordinary people would use the term, see **3.19**.)

2.8 Various attempts have been made to extend *Wilkinson v Downton* to establish tort liability for something akin to unlawful harassment or deliberate humiliation of the claimant, initially with some success.

Khorasandjian v Bush **[1993] QB 727:** Bush stalked Khorasandjian, by following her around, sending her unwanted messages, and telephoning her and her relatives. Bush admitted he could be restrained from using violent threats and acts, but argued that he committed no tort by mere harassment. Held: harassment was a tort whether or not it involved violence or the threat of violence.

However, the enactment of the new *statutory* tort of harassment (**2.10**) has discouraged this development; there is no obvious need for the common law to add to the statutory solution. In *Wainwright v Home Office* [2003] UKHL 53, where a mother and son visiting prison were subjected to an unnecessarily embarrassing strip-search in breach of the Prison Rules 1964, the House of Lords refused to allow a remedy in tort. Lord Hoffmann criticized the reasoning in *Wilkinson v Downton*, suggesting that the case should today be treated as one of the negligent infliction of nervous shock (on which see **3.18**). He was unconvinced that there was a tort of deliberate infliction of mental distress falling short of shock, or that the harm inflicted in *Wilkinson v Downton* was deliberate. (Note however a subsequent ruling by the European Court of Human Rights in *Wainwright v United Kingdom* [2006] ECHR 807, that the Home Office was in breach of Art 8 of the

Convention (privacy and family life) though not Art 3 (inhuman or degrading treatment).)

Sexual harassment

2.9 It is sometimes argued that the courts pay insufficient attention to issues of gender relations, and are too ready to accept the defendant's story that his harassment was (at worst) a joke and (at best) secretly welcomed by the claimant, rather than the claimant's story that it was unlawful aggression against her. However, there is a problem here, that the law of tort is usually an awkward method for controlling sexual harassment, and is therefore little used for that purpose. In practice, issues of sexual harassment usually surface either as issues in employment law (with the employer being accused of exercising insufficient control over male employees who harass female employees) or, in extreme cases, in the criminal courts. (The law has recently been restated: see the Employment Equality (Sex Discrimination) Regulations 2005.) Suing in tort is costly. This ensures that it is very much a weapon of last resort in the armoury of the victim of assault—even though it can occasionally be used with devastating effect.

Harassment: legislation

2.10 Under the Protection from Harassment Act 1997, a course of conduct amounting to deliberate or negligent harassment of the claimant is forbidden (s 1). 'Harassment' is not defined, but includes alarming the claimant or causing him or her distress, whether by speech or by other conduct (s 7(2) and (4)). The definition has also been expanded to include harassing conduct designed to make two or more people behave in a particular way (Serious Organised Crime and Police Act 2005, s 125). The Act requires that any alleged course of conduct amounting to harassment involve at least two distinct incidents (s 7(3)). There is a defence if it can be shown that the defendant's conduct was reasonable, or was designed to comply with some rule of law, or was for the prevention or detection of crime (s 1(3)). Harassment is both a crime (under s 2) and a tort (under s 3). If the claimant treats it as a tort, he or she may obtain an order restraining the defendant from further harassment, as well as damages, which may include an element for 'any anxiety caused by the harassment' (s 3(2)).

The Act was passed in response to cases of obsessive men following and harassing particular women. But the Act is not only gender-blind, but also is drafted in very broad terms. For example, it has been used against animal rights protesters targeting particular companies; the company itself cannot be 'harassed', but its employees can, and the company can take action on their behalf (*Daiichi UK Ltd v Stop Huntingdon Animal Cruelty* [2003] EWHC 2337 (QB)). It has also been thought arguable that the Act can be invoked against a newspaper, by the claimant who was the target of a series of racist stories (*Thomas v News Group Newspapers* [2001] EWCA Civ 1233). Perhaps most striking of all, it has been held that the Act applies to a gas supply company seeking payment from a former customer (with threats of disconnection, court proceedings and reports to credit agencies) while ignoring her attempts to demonstrate that the amounts claimed were not in fact owing (*Ferguson v British Gas Trading Ltd* [2009] EWCA 46). It also applies to employers who harass their employees, though the indications are that the claimant will have to meet a high threshold before liability will be established (*Sunderland County Council v Conn* [2007] EWCA 1492). It remains to be seen whether the Act's broad impact will be significantly limited by the Human Rights Act 1998 (**1.22**), which might be invoked by those who argue that it restricts their liberty (Art 5) or their freedom of expression (Art 10); though in the more serious cases at least the courts are likely to place as much emphasis on the claimant's rights as the defendant's.

False imprisonment

2.11 The defendant is liable for false imprisonment where the defendant deprived the claimant of the liberty to go where he or she wished. No special damage need be proved before the claimant may recover damages for this tort, and in an appropriate case aggravated damages may be awarded (**10.16**).

Completeness of the restraint

2.12 The tort consists of depriving the claimant of his or her liberty. It is not committed by mere obstruction of *one* route the claimant could have followed, so long as others are reasonably open to the claimant.

> **Bird v Jones (1845) 7 QB 742:** Part of a bridge was unlawfully fenced off, for watching a boat race. Bird climbed over the fence, following his normal route, but was prevented from following the path he wished, being told to go back and cross outside the fence. Held: Bird had not been falsely imprisoned.

However, if there was a clear intention to restrain the claimant, it seems to be irrelevant how the defendant proposed to enforce this, or what would have been the likely outcome if the claimant had resisted the restraint. If the defendant says to the claimant 'you are under arrest', it appears to be irrelevant whether the defendant was in a position to restrain the claimant. Conversely, if the claimant is *in fact* under restraint, it appears to be irrelevant whether the claimant knows this. So in *Murray v Ministry of Defence* [1988] 2 All ER 521 the House of Lords would have been prepared to hold that false imprisonment is committed where soldiers would have refused to release the claimant had she demanded it, whether or not she realized that this was the case. (On the facts, however, the restraint was held to have been authorized by statute.) Of course, whether the claimant knows about the restraint will affect the degree of humiliation suffered, and consequently the level of damages the claimant can expect if liability is established.

Entry subject to conditions

2.13   Some authorities suggest that if the claimant enters the defendant's premises, knowing that the defendant intends to impose conditions, then the claimant cannot later complain when the defendant insists on compliance with the conditions, at least if the court considers the conditions to be reasonable ones.

> **Robinson v Balmain New Ferry Co [1910] AC 295:** A ferry company ran ferries from its wharf across a river. It charged one penny to enter or to leave the wharf. Robinson paid one penny to enter the wharf and then changed his mind and tried to leave, but refused to pay another penny. Held: the ferry company did not commit false imprisonment by refusing to let him pass.

> **Herd v Weardale Steel, Coal and Coke Co [1915] AC 67:** Herd, a coal miner, decided that conditions in the pit were unsafe, and demanded that he be allowed to return to the surface immediately. His employers refused, returning him only at the end of his shift. It would certainly have been possible to return him before. Held: Herd had not been falsely imprisoned down the pit.

Considerable stress was placed on the point that Herd was in breach of his employment contract. Today, the courts would be unlikely to hold that anyone had contracted out of their right to reasonably safe employment, even if it is lawfully possible to do so (on which see *Johnstone v Bloomsbury Health Authority* [1992] QB 333).

The defendant's responsibility

2.14   Probably the defendant can only be liable for *deliberately* imprisoning the claimant. However, this is not beyond all doubt; when the question whether negligence was enough came up in *Weldon v Home Office*, Gibson LJ left it open ([1990] 3 WLR 465, 470). (A remedy is available in the tort of negligence in that situation, see **5.41** below.) Where someone else, acting on the defendant's instigation, unlawfully detains the claimant, it is sometimes possible to make the defendant liable, but the defendant's responsibility for the actions of the imprisoner must be clear.

> **Prison Officers Association v Iqbal [2009] EWCA Civ 1312:** A strike of prison offic-
> ers was called by the Prison Officers' Association, and very few of them appeared for
> work on the day in question. The prison governor decided that prisoners should remain
> locked in their cells for that day. Iqbal, one of the affected prisoners, sued the Association
> for this deprivation of his liberty. Held: even though the strike was in breach of contract,
> nonetheless the deprivation of liberty was not the responsibility of the Association or the
> officers in question, but of the governor, who was clearly acting lawfully.

> **Davidson v Chief Constable of North Wales [1994] 2 All ER 597:** Yates, a store
> detective, observed Davidson in a shop and formed the inaccurate impression that
> Davidson had stolen a tape cassette. She passed this information on to the local police,
> who arrested Davidson. Held: Yates was under no liability for false imprisonment, as she
> had merely passed on information to the police, rather than providing encouragement to
> them to commit unlawful acts.

The reasoning in *Davidson* seems unsatisfactory. Yates could surely guess what the police would do with her information. It was perfectly true that the police did not take orders from Yates, but it seems strange to deny that she encouraged them to make an arrest. The difficulty was that the police had a defence to any action (as they had acted on reasonable suspicion), whereas Yates, not being a police officer, would not have been able to take advantage of that defence, even if her belief had been reasonable. Can Davidson's arrest be 'lawful' when she sued the police, but 'unlawful' when she sued Yates? Sir Thomas Bingham MR thought it would be 'somewhat anomalous' if it were so ([1994] 2 All ER 597, 601), yet this may be the result of the case.

Defences

2.15   General defences are dealt with below (**11.1**), but there are several defences pecu-
liarly relevant to false imprisonment. Powers of arrest are governed by the Police
and Criminal Evidence Act 1984, as amended: extensive powers are given to the
police, including powers of search, and much more limited powers of 'citizen's
arrest' to persons generally. Restraint in prison is authorized by comprehensive legislation. In the light of that, the House of Lords has ruled that there is no 'residual
liberty' left to prisoners. Accordingly, no rights are infringed by keeping them in
one part of the prison, rather than another where they would prefer to be (*R v
Deputy Governor of Parkhurst Prison, ex p Hague* [1992] 1 AC 58).

Invasion of privacy

2.16 The orthodox view is that there is no tort of invasion of privacy at common law.

> **Kaye v Robertson [1991] FSR 62:** Kaye, a famous comedy actor, was in hospital after a road accident. A journalist and a photographer, acting on Robertson's instructions, entered the private ward where Kaye was. They interviewed Kaye (or so they later claimed), and took a number of photos before being evicted. Held: no tort had been committed against Kaye, nor could they be restrained from printing the photographs, so long as they made it clear that they were taken without Kaye's consent.

This approach was confirmed by the House of Lords in *Wainwright v Home Office* (above, **2.8**), where Lord Hoffmann considered that respect for privacy was a value to be found in the common law rather than the name for a distinct tort. *Wainwright* does not definitively rule out the development of a right based on Art 8 of the European Convention (respect for privacy and family life), but does nothing to encourage it. Some recent actions have been based on Art 8, including a (successful) action in respect of clandestine recording of the claimant's sexual activities (*Mosley v News Group Newspapers Ltd* [2008] EWHC 1777 (QB), and an (unsuccessful) action against the police for photographing those engaged in peaceful demonstrations (*R (Wood) v Commissioner of Police of the Metropolis* [2009] EWCA Civ 414).

Particular examples

2.17 Nonetheless, it has sometimes proved possible for the claimant to use other torts or legal doctrines to remedy what amounts to an invasion of the claimant's privacy.

• Where the defendant publishes photographs of the claimant or the claimant's family, the claimant may sometimes be able to assert breach of copyright (*Williams v Settle* [1960] 2 All ER 806). This doctrine has also been used when the defendant published the claimant's confidential papers, the court being extremely unsympathetic to an attempt to invoke the defendant's right to freedom of expression (*Ashdown v Telegraph Group* [2001] Ch 685).

• Surveillance of the claimant or the claimant's property may sometimes amount to trespass (**7.2**) or nuisance (**7.11**).

• The claimant's privacy may sometimes be protected by the statutory tort of harassment (**2.10**) or of unlawful interception of a communication on a private telecommunication system (Regulation of Investigatory Powers Act 2000, s 1(3)).

- Unwelcome phone calls may sometimes constitute a public nuisance (**7.30**).

- 'Personal data', as defined by the Data Protection Act 1998, s 2, is protected in a number of ways. The data subject may object to data processing 'causing or...likely to cause substantial damage or substantial distress' (s 10), and may sue for damages (s 13). However, the Act contains a generous exemption for press activities (s 32).

- The publication of private information may sometimes be restrained as being a breach of the claimant's confidence. The model Naomi Campbell was recently awarded damages for revelations about her private life. Campbell admitted that the bare bones of the stories—that she was receiving treatment for drug addiction—were true, but nonetheless successfully argued that the particularly damaging and hurtful way in which the story was reported amounted to a breach of confidence (*Campbell v Mirror Group Newspapers* [2004] UKHL 22). There have been a number of further examples in recent years, actionable breach of confidence being found where:

— A former friend of a famous folk singer published a book revealing many personal matters about her (*McKennitt v Ash* [2006] EWCA Civ 1714).

— A husband whose wife had an affair sought to publish the details, in an attempt to embarrass the other man. Eady J refused to accept the argument that adulterous conduct did not deserve protection from the courts (doubting that there was any moral consensus he could resort to), and noting that the husband's conduct was apparently motivated by spite and a desire to make money (*CC v AB* [2006] EWHC 3083 (QB)).

— A newspaper published photographs surreptitiously taken at a wedding, knowing that the celebrity couple had already sold the publicity rights to a rival newspaper. The rival successfully sued for the commercial value of what was taken (*Douglas and Zeta-Jones v Hello!* [2007] UKHL 21).

While the law is currently expanding, the limits are controversial. Where the popular author JK Rowling was photographed walking in a public street with her husband and young son, it has been held to be at least arguable that the son was entitled to protection in respect of his privacy (*Murray v Express Newspapers* [2008] EWCA Civ 446). By contrast it has been held that an anonymous blogger had no reasonable expectation of confidentiality as to his identity (*Author of a Blog v Times Newspapers Ltd* [2009] EWHC 1358 (QB)), and a solicitor found by a Law Society adjudicator to be in breach of his duties had no reasonable expectation of confidence in respect of that finding (*Napier v Pressdram Ltd* [2009] EWCA Civ 443). This is a developing area.

A vital question is the remedy claimed. An injunction to prevent public disclosures about the claimant's private life is a far superior remedy to an action for damages after disclosure has taken place. But attempts to restrain the defendant prior to publication also raise substantial human rights concerns. The claimant's right to privacy will be balanced against the defendant's right to publish, with the balance heavily in the defendant's favour (see particularly Human Rights Act 1998, s 12; *Cream Holdings Ltd v Banerjee* [2004] UKHL 44; *Browne v Associated Newspapers* [2007] EWCA Civ 295). So in several recent cases, celebrities have failed to prevent publication of details of their private lives *even though* the court thought the publication might well be a breach of the claimant's confidence. (See especially *Douglas and Zeta-Jones v Hello!* [2001] QB 967; *A v B (a company)* [2002] EWCA Civ 337.)

Reform? Waiting for developments

2.18   Whether the law should be reformed, by introducing a tort of invasion of privacy, is a matter of some debate. Considerable judicial distaste at intrusive press behaviour has become apparent, particularly in *Kaye v Robertson* (**2.16**) and later cases. It is clear that certain judges at least would welcome the creation of a tort of invasion of privacy, and might apply it with some enthusiasm. And while the impact of the Protection from Harassment Act 1997 is as yet unclear (**2.10**), it is plainly capable of applying in some instances of invasion of privacy.

'Everyone has the right to respect for his private and family life, his home and his correspondence' (European Convention on Human Rights, Art 8.1). And it is clear that this right not only requires the state to respect privacy but also to enact strong laws requiring the press to do so as well (*von Hannover v Germany* [2004] ECHR 294). However, defendants have rights too, in particular the right to freedom of expression (Art 10). The Human Rights Act 1998 therefore requires the courts to engage in a balancing exercise, which they have done on several occasions (e.g. *Campbell*, **2.17**). So far, the effect of the Act has merely been interstitial: the courts have simply borne the Convention in mind in their development of the law. It is an open question whether they can or should go further, and hold that the Convention requires the existence of a right of privacy. A straw in the wind is *Wainwright v United Kingdom* [2006] ECHR 807, where the House of Lords' refusal to grant a remedy for an intrusive strip-search was held to violate Art 8 (privacy and family life). This is one aspect of the broader question whether the Act has a substantive 'horizontal' effect, as well as a 'vertical' effect against public authorities (see **1.25**). The courts can expect to be faced with many questions of this sort over the early years of the 21st century.

FURTHER READING

Buxton 'Private life and the English judges' (2009) 29 OJLS 413.

Conaghan 'Tort litigation in the context of intra-family abuse' (1998) 61 MLR 132.

von Heussen 'The law and "social problems": The case of Britain's Protection from Harassment Act 1997' [2000] Web JCLI (<http://webjcli.ncl.ac.uk/2000/issue1/vonheussen1.html>).

Lunney 'Practical joking and its penalty: *Wilkinson v Downton* in context' (2002) 10 Tort Law Rev 168.

Moreham '*Douglas and others v Hello! Ltd*—The protection of privacy in English private law' (2001) 64 MLR 767.

Moreham 'Privacy in the common law: A doctrinal and theoretical analysis' (2005) 121 LQR 629.

Morgan 'Privacy, confidence and horizontal effect; "Hello" trouble' (2003) 62 CLJ 444.

Mulheron 'A potential framework for privacy? A reply to *Hello!*' (2006) 69 MLR 679.

Phillipson 'Transforming breach of confidence? Towards a common law right of privacy under the Human Rights Act' (2003) 66 MLR 726.

Seymour 'Who can be harassed? Claims against animal rights protestors under s 3 of the Protection from Harassment Act 1997' (2005) 64 CLJ 57.

Witzleb 'Monetary remedies for breach of confidence in privacy cases' (2007) 27 LS 430.

Young 'Remedial and substantive horizontality: The common law and *Douglas v Hello! Ltd*' [2002] PL 232.

SELF-TEST QUESTIONS

1   If the claimant complains of invasion of his or her privacy, which torts, if any, are likely to be applicable (**2.17**)?

2   Why might the claimant be interested in establishing that the defendant was liable for battery, even if the defendant is entirely without funds (**2.6**)?

3   What is the mental element of assault (**2.5**)?

4   Is it possible to falsely imprison the claimant without the claimant's being aware of it (**2.12**)?

5   What are the requirements of the statutory tort of harassment (**2.10**)?

Negligent harm to the person: general considerations

SUMMARY

Redressing personal injury is the most important application of negligence law. This chapter describes the general rules on establishing duty and breach of duty. It then describes the system of recovery for injuries in negligence. It then covers certain special categories of claimant: those who suffer nervous shock, those complaining of negligence in relation to birth, and rescuers.

Negligence: the scope of the following chapters

3.1 In **Chapter 1**, the basic concepts of negligence law were reviewed: existence of duty, breach of duty, causation, defences (**1.27**). But some areas of the law are better worked out than others. So it is necessary to discuss both general principles, and their application to particular areas. To put some flesh on the bones, we have to start distinguishing between different classes of case. This chapter and the following one deal with negligence as it relates to claimants who have suffered personal injury. Property and economic losses are left to a later chapter (**5.1**), and damages and defences to still later ones (**10.1, 11.1**).

This chapter deals with general principles of recovery for personal injury; the following chapter deals with the most common duty situations. The law is a lot clearer in some areas of this than others. Very roughly, the better worked-out areas are so because most of the litigation occurs there. It is *because* there is so much litigation relating to road accidents that it is possible to be fairly precise about how the courts react to them (**4.12**); similarly with claims by employees against their employers (**4.32**). The general principles of negligence, by contrast, are most useful when the court is in unfamiliar territory.

Duty

Foresight of the particular claimant

3.2 The claimant can only sue for personal injury in negligence if he or she was a foreseeable victim of the defendant's activities (**1.27**). In many situations, it is enough simply to ask whether the defendant was careless: Did the defendant's behaviour create unreasonably large risks for others, or not? Yet while adequate for most purposes, the question is often insufficient. A more focused one must be asked: Was it foreseeable that the defendant's behaviour would injure the claimant? By asking specifically whether the defendant's behaviour threatened the claimant in this way, we focus on the legal relation between those two individuals. This is sometimes more generous to the claimant than simply asking whether the defendant was 'careless', sometimes less so.

> *Wright v Lodge* **[1993] 4 All ER 299:** Shepherd's car ground to a halt on a busy A-road, due to mechanical failure. Rather than push her car onto the hard shoulder, which she could easily have done with her passengers' help, she simply sat in it. Lodge, a lorry driver who was going much too fast for the foggy conditions, swerved to avoid Shepherd's car, skidded across the central reservation and collided with other cars, including Wright's. Held: Wright was not a foreseeable victim of Shepherd's misconduct.

The question is therefore whether the defendant ought to have foreseen danger *to the claimant*. So even though the defendant's behaviour is plainly careless, and in fact causes the claimant's injury, nonetheless a court may refuse to compensate the claimant, on the ground that the claimant was an unforeseeable claimant, so that the defendant owed the claimant no duty. But equally, focusing attention on the relation between the claimant and the defendant may allow the claimant to recover even where people generally cannot.

> *Haley v London Electricity Board* **[1965] AC 778:** Manual workers excavating an electricity cable made a sizeable hole in the road, which they indicated to passers-by by leaving a long-handled hammer in front of it. Haley, who was blind, did not realize that there was a hole, and walked into it. Held: even though the precautions taken were adequate to warn sighted people of the danger, they were inadequate to protect Haley and others like him. Blind people were not so rare as to be unforeseeable.

So duty is owed to each possible claimant individually. This is nonetheless so because the court discusses the claimant as part of a class or group of people. Of course, what it is reasonable to expect of the defendant is limited by human capabilities. If no reasonable person would have thought of the claimant or of the claimant's special needs, then a court is unlikely to find liability.

Adequacy of the 'foresight' criterion

3.3 The notion of 'reasonable foresight' has been much criticized, particularly on the ground that it is very loose, so loose that it enables the courts to do whatever they want with it. This is absolutely true. But it entirely misses the point. It is not a mechanical formula leading to definite results in each case. Indeed, it is a little hard to see how a liability as broad as negligence *could* be regulated by mechanical formulae. It is pointless to criticize the looseness of the criterion in the abstract; we must first see how the judges have *in fact* used the considerable discretion it gives them.

You have already seen a great deal of how the judges use their power to declare events to be 'foreseeable' or 'unforeseeable' (**1.27**), and it is clear that in personal injury matters at least they take a very broad view. It is always easy to be wise after the event, and so to say that the defendant 'should have foreseen' events which must have seemed very unlikely to someone thinking about matters before the event. This is quite different from the position as to pure economic loss, for example (**5.7**). So it is often said that the courts take an unrealistic view of what the defendant can be expected to foresee before the event, and are much too demanding in the level of care the defendant is expected to give. But the law of negligence serves many purposes (**1.12**). It is not a case of the judges being 'unrealistic', but of their making a particular value-judgement about the availability of liability. Of course, the standard of care prescribed by the tort of negligence is far higher than anything most defendants are in fact likely to achieve, and indeed in some cases the law's prescribed level of care is actually *impossible* to achieve (**1.41**). It is not hard to see that a finding of 'negligence' is nonsense as a comment on what the defendant 'should have done'. The challenge is to think of something that would be less ridiculous!

Omissions

3.4 As already explained (**1.30**), it is a complete misconception to say that negligence law imposes no duty in respect of omissions. *Once it is established that the defendant owes the claimant a duty*, then the duty may be broken by omission as much as by action. So once we have concluded that manufacturers of ginger beer owe a duty not to include snails in their product, it hardly matters whether snails get there by omission (the manufacturer fails to stop snails slithering in) or by action (the manufacturer carelessly inserts them into the bottle). Unreasonable omissions are as culpable as unreasonable actions, and just as likely to lead to legal action by the victim.

However, there is a kernel of truth in the 'no liability for omissions' rule. If the defendant's behaviour has in no way added to the dangers which the claimant faces, then prima facie the defendant is under no duty at all. If the claimant argues that the defendant is under a positive duty to save the claimant from dangers created by others, then the claimant must give a very specific reason for this. It is not enough that the defendant could easily have helped the claimant. If a duty is found, it will usually be because the defendant had control over the source of danger to which the claimant succumbed, or should have had control of it. Many examples can be given:

• Where the defendant carelessly abandons his horse and it runs off, the defendant owes a duty to those who make reasonable attempts to recapture it (*Haynes v Harwood* [1935] 1 KB 146).

• Where children at the defendant's primary school escape and run across roads, causing the claimant's lorry to swerve and crash, the defendant owes a duty to the claimant to prevent his injuries (*Carmarthenshire County Council v Lewis* [1955] AC 549).

• Where the claimant seeks a divorce from her violent husband and the defendant, her husband's solicitor, gives undertakings as to matters relating to her personal safety, breach of those undertakings may constitute actionable negligence (*Al-Kandari v JR Brown & Co* [1987] QB 514).

• Where the condition of the defendant's football ground is poor, with pieces of concrete left around, and hooligans admitted to a game start throwing them, injured spectators may sue the defendant (*Cunningham v Reading Football Club* (1991) 157 LG Rev 481).

• Where an ambulance is sent to collect the claimant but fails to do so, the ambulance service may be liable in damages if the failure occurred 'for no good reason' (*Kent v Griffiths* [2001] QB 36).

• Where the claimant is a mentally unstable prisoner lawfully in the defendant's custody, the defendant may owe the claimant a duty to prevent him from injuring himself (*Kirkham v Chief Constable of Greater Manchester* [1990] 3 All ER 246). Again, where a prisoner known to be a suicide risk is put in the same cell as the claimant, the prison authorities may owe a duty to the claimant to guard against psychological harm should suicide occur (*Butchart v Home Office* [2006] EWCA Civ 239). However, while there is a duty to assess whether the claimant is a suicide risk, a reasonable decision that he or she is not removes any further duty to guard against suicide (*Orange v Chief Constable of West Yorkshire Police* [2001] EWCA Civ 611).

• Where the claimant is a player at a rugby match and the defendant a referee, the defendant owes a duty to the claimant to act carefully in relation to particularly dangerous situations, such as by taking reasonable precautions to avoid the collapsing of scrums (*Smoldon v Whitworth* [1997] ELR 249; *Vowles v Evans* [2003] EWCA Civ 318). Again, a regulatory body in charge of a particularly dangerous sport may be liable to those injured as a result of inadequate rules or enforcement of rules (*Watson v British Boxing Board of Control* [2001] QB 1134 (boxing)) or poor safety advice (*Wattleworth v Goodwood Road Racing Co* [2004] EWHC 140 (QB) (vintage car racing)).

• Where the defendant, a non-profit-making body concerned with the advancement of amateur flying, negligently issues a safety certificate in respect of a light aircraft, the claimant, who is injured in the subsequent crash, may argue that a duty was owed (*Perrett v Collins* [1999] PNLR 77).

However, the limits are quite unclear. Suppose a bus company carelessly leaves its bus in a public street, with the doors unlocked and the keys still in the ignition. If a joyrider seizes this opportunity and drives off, running over the claimant, may the claimant sue the bus company? The Court of Appeal initially thought that the claimant could (*Hayman v London Transport Executive* [1981] CLY 1834), but has now definitively reversed this (*Topp v London Country Bus (South West)* [1993] 3 All ER 448). Again, where a man with a dangerous psychopathic disorder escapes from the custody of the defendant health authority, and attacks the claimant, then the defendant is not usually held liable (*Palmer v Tees Health Authority* [2000] PIQR P1), unless the claimant can show that something amounting to a 'special relationship' existed between her and the defendant. Again, it is usually assumed that the defendant will not be liable for a failure to rescue the claimant from danger. In *The Ogopogo* [1971] 2 Lloyd's Rep 410, the Canadian Supreme Court was prepared to hold that a duty arose. It held that the host of a boating expedition was under a duty to rescue guests who fell in the water—though on the facts it held that the host had done all that could reasonably have been expected of him, and so was not in fact liable for the guests' deaths. It is quite unclear whether the English courts would follow this ruling.

Alexis v Newham London Borough Council [2009] EWHC 1323 (QB): Alexis, a teacher, drank from a bottle of water she kept in her classroom, and became violently ill. It emerged that the water had been adulterated by two students with whiteboard cleaner fluid. She sued the education authority for allowing this to happen. Held: while it was recognized as good practice at the school that students should not be allowed unsupervised access to classrooms, it was not an invariable rule. In the absence of evidence of a specific threat, allowing these students access could not be regarded as a breach of duty to the claimant.

In many of these cases, it is obvious that the main cause of the harm the claimant suffers is because of criminal action by some third party. So if the first defendant stabs the claimant, who is taken to hospital and treated negligently by the health authority, then the claimant is much more likely to sue the health authority (which has money) rather than the first defendant (who may not). It is important to realize that in the eyes of the law of tort, both defendants are wrongdoers. It is therefore no answer to the claim against a second defendant that the claimant's injuries are in a sense the first defendant's fault. If proper care on the second defendant's part would have led to a speedy recovery, whereas in fact the claimant suffers over a long period, then to that extent the claimant's injuries are the second defendant's fault as well. It may be that if the first defendant turns out to have money, then the second defendant can recover from the first (see **9.26**). But it is no answer to the claim against the second defendant that the first defendant was primarily responsible for the claimant's injuries.

Statutory authorities

3.5 The courts are usually reluctant to impose liability on public authorities for misuse of statutory powers. They are reluctant to put broad duties on public authorities, or to allow particular individuals to skew broad questions of governmental policy round to the question whether they, personally, have done well out of them.

> *M v Newham Borough Council* **[1995] 2 AC 633:** Children complained that their special educational needs had initially not been diagnosed by their local authority, and that when ultimately diagnosed they had wrongly been told that their existing schools were adequate. They sued in negligence. Held: a duty of care by the authority was owed to the children.

> *Stovin v Wise (Norfolk County Council, third party)* **[1996] AC 923:** Wise negligently drove out from a side-road onto the main road, causing injury to Stovin who was carefully driving down it. Wise sought to join the local transport authority as co-defendant, arguing that the poor road design had significantly contributed to the accident. Held: the highway authority did not owe a duty, or if it had, it had not broken it.

> *K v Secretary of State for the Home Department* **[2002] EWCA Civ 775:** A foreign citizen with limited leave to remain in the UK committed a string of violent offences. He was detained under a deportation order, but then released. He committed further serious offences. One of his victims sued the Secretary of State for failure to deport him. Held: there was no private right of action.

The law is confused, however, and each regime of statutory powers and duties requires separate consideration (**1.53** above).

The police

3.6 One particular set of public authorities treated with special generosity by the courts is the police authorities.

> **Hill v Chief Constable of West Yorkshire [1989] AC 53:** A serial killer, the 'Yorkshire Ripper', murdered a number of women in the Leeds area before being caught. The estate of his last victim sued the police authority, arguing that, with the exercise of reasonable care, he would have been caught earlier. Held: the police owed no legal duty to individual members of the public who might be affected by their failure to apprehend the killer.

> **Ancell v McDermott [1993] 4 All ER 355:** Ancell was involved in a road accident caused by a leaking oil tank. The accident would have been avoided if certain police officers had acted more promptly in reporting the patch of oil. Held: the duty of the police to road users did not extend to a tortious right of action by injured parties.

Various factors were suggested in these cases, as tending towards a finding that there was no enforceable duty. It was said that there was a risk of 'defensive policing', the police being more concerned with warding off legal action than with doing their proper duties. It was also said that there was no need for tort liability as a spur to make the police do their job, as they were already adequately motivated in that regard. Finally, it was suggested that the appropriate bodies to monitor police efficiency were the bodies appointed for that purpose, rather than the courts. However, none of this has convinced very many legal commentators, who cannot see why any of it is true of police authorities, when it could equally be said of many other tort defendants. Are the police really so different from other major classes of defendants, such as employers (**4.32**)? If the police are different, this should be a matter of evidence, rather than of *ex cathedra* pronouncements from the bench. Does 'defensive policing' exist? Can the incentives on the police be improved? These are not purely legal questions.

An important, though somewhat ambiguous, ruling is that in *Osman v United Kingdom* (1998) 29 EHRR 245. In this case a teacher developed a sexual fixation on one of his students; dangerously mentally unstable, he showed increasingly bizarre behaviour, which culminated in his shooting members of the student's family with a sawn-off shotgun. An action in tort was mounted against the police, suggesting that they should have apprehended the teacher before he could do damage. This action was rejected by the Court of Appeal, on the basis of a blanket police immunity. The European Court of Human Rights held that this was impermissible: a rule forbidding action against the police regardless of the circumstances was contrary to Art 6. However, as discussed above (**1.54**), the European Court in *Z v United Kingdom* [2001] ECHR 333 has somewhat retreated from this position. The objection to *Hill* is not to the result in the case, which may well be correct, but to a blanket police immunity, applying regardless of all other considerations. So the courts are entitled to have regard to a general policy against such actions, so long as they allow claimants who were especially at risk to explain why they should be exceptions. This general policy remains in force, and has subsequently been used to justify a ruling that the police do not in general owe duties of care to victims and witnesses in criminal cases (*Brooks v Metropolitan Police Commissioner* [2005] UKHL 24).

A clear line needs to be drawn between cases like *Osman*, where the claimant was particularly at risk from the police's failure to act, and cases like *Hill*, where the claimant was only at risk in the same sense that a great number of other people were as well.

> **Swinney v Chief Constable of the Northumbria Police [1997] QB 464:** Swinney passed on to the police information about a man who had killed a police officer. Relevant documents were left in a police car, in an area notorious for theft. The documents were stolen, and found their way into the hands of the killer, who terrorised Swinney and her husband. Could Swinney sue the police? Held: her case was arguable and should be allowed to proceed to trial. (However, at trial it was found on the facts that the duty was not broken: *Swinney v Chief Constable of the Northumbria Police (No 2)* (1999) Times, 25 May.)

> **Waters v Metropolitan Police Commissioner [2000] 4 All ER 934:** Waters, a police officer, was the victim of a serious sexual assault by another officer. Her complaint about this made her the target of harassment and victimization by other officers. She sued the Commissioner for negligent handling of her complaint. The Commissioner applied to strike out her claim, on the authority of *Hill*. Held: her complaint was in essence no different from a complaint of an employee against an employer, and so was very different from a claim by a member of the public, as in *Hill*. The action could not be struck out, and must proceed to trial.

(As an alternative, a claimant in this class of case might consider an action under the Human Rights Act 1998 (**1.22**), though the test applied there seems to be similar, as is the vocal judicial insistence on the dangers of 'defensive policing' (see e.g. *Van Colle v Chief Constable of Hertfordshire Police* [2008] UKHL 50).)

Concurrent liability

3.7 Liability here may overlap with that in other areas of law. So, private medical patients whose doctors are guilty of extreme carelessness may sue in breach of contract or in negligence, entirely as they wish. Care is sometimes needed, however, in distinguishing a personal injury claim from a pure economic loss claim, where concurrence of contract and tort is still viewed with suspicion.

> **Van Oppen v Clerk to the Bedford Charity Trustees [1989] 3 All ER 389:** Van Oppen, a pupil at Bedford school, was injured in the course of a rugby game. No negligence in the running of the game was alleged on appeal, but Van Oppen claimed that the school should have insured its pupils against injury. Held: such a duty could only arise, if at all, under a contract with the school, not in tort.

Claims for purely economic losses, then, are treated with much less generosity than are claims for personal injury. The matter is dealt with in more detail in a later chapter, at **5.1**.

Breach of duty

Duty is owed to each individual claimant

3.8 While it is often enough simply to ask whether the defendant was 'negligent' or 'careless', strictly speaking the question is whether the defendant was negligent *in relation to a particular claimant* (**3.2**). It follows that each claimant's case is different, even where the same 'negligence' is in issue.

> **Paris v Stepney Borough Council [1951] AC 367:** A garage hand lost the sight of one eye when a metal chip flew off the axle he was hammering. His employers had not provided him with safety goggles. His other eye, as his employers knew, was not good. Held: his employers' knowledge that one eye was bad placed them under a higher duty than they owed to their other employees, and they were liable.

Again, in *Excelsior Wire Rope Co v Callan* [1930] AC 404, children playing on the defendant's machinery were injured when it was unexpectedly turned on. The risk of injury was the same to both adults and children; but the House of Lords held that the children's propensity to fool around near machinery meant that the duty owed to them was greater. Accordingly, the children recovered damages in circumstances where adults certainly would not. This principle can work either for or against the claimant: the question is whether the defendant broke the duty owed to the claimant, and it is irrelevant whether the duty owed to others is higher, lower or merely different.

> **Bourhill v Young [1943] AC 92:** Young drove his motorcycle recklessly, causing a collision from which he died. Bourhill, who was eight months pregnant, was some way away at the time of the accident, but saw the aftermath, including large quantities of blood. She suffered nervous shock and miscarried. Held: she was not a foreseeable victim of Young's negligence, and so could not recover.

The standard of care: 'subjective' or 'objective'?

3.9 The standard of care is that of the reasonably experienced person in the defendant's position (**1.41**). The duty is 'subjective' in the sense that it relates to the reasonable person *in the defendant's position*. So if the defendant has to make a decision on the spur of the moment, this will not be regarded as negligent merely because a reasonable person with more time to consider the matter would probably have done something different.

> ***Watt v Hertfordshire County Council* [1954] 2 All ER 368:** A firefighter was injured when a heavy jack loaded into the fire engine moved and fell on him. He sued the fire authority, arguing that a different engine, which was designed to transport the jack in safety, should have been used for this job. Held: the decision on which engine to use had not been unreasonable, in the light of the short time in which a decision had had to be made.

However, the duty is 'objective' in the sense that the defendant's own character and dispositions are irrelevant. If reasonable people would regard the defendant's conduct as rash and dangerous, it is no defence that the defendant was a rash person and that, by his own lights, what he did was rather restrained. And if the defendant undertakes a job requiring professional skill, the defendant will be judged by the standard of the reasonably competent professional, whether or not the defendant in fact has that level of skill. So each patient is entitled to expect professional competence from a surgeon, even if this is the surgeon's first ever operation. The courts are very reluctant to dilute this rule in major areas of liability: they even hold learner drivers to the standards of experienced professionals (**4.14**). However, in more marginal situations they are more generous, demanding only that the defendant come up to the level of expertise that an impartial observer would have assumed that the defendant had.

> ***Wells v Cooper* [1958] 2 QB 265:** Wells was injured when a door handle in Cooper's house came away from the door. Cooper had fitted it himself. Held: Cooper need not attain the standard of a reasonably competent carpenter doing the work for another, but only the standard of a reasonably competent DIY enthusiast, which he had.

> ***Philips v William Whiteley* [1938] 1 All ER 566:** Philips arranged for her ears to be pierced by Whiteley's staff. The jeweller concerned sterilized his needle by putting it in a flame and in disinfectant, but did not take the precautions which a surgeon conducting a similar minor operation would have done. Held: Whiteley were not liable when Philip's ear became inflamed, as they had never claimed to reach the standard which a surgeon would have done.

Magnitude of risk versus cost of precaution

3.10 The most important factors in determining whether there has been a breach are those suggested by the 'Learned Hand' formula (**1.39**). The claimant must establish that there is some precaution against harm which the defendant should have taken, and which would have prevented the harm the claimant suffered. In considering whether the defendant should have taken any particular precaution, the court will weigh up the cost of doing this, and assess the degree of protection it would have given. This will be a function both of the risk of harm, and of the degree of harm if it eventuates: '... the law in all cases exacts a degree of care commensurate with the risk created' (*Read v J Lyons & Co* [1947] AC 156, 173, Lord Macmillan). Where it is clear that *no* precaution would have avoided the risk flowing from the defendant's activities, which are therefore *intrinsically* dangerous, then the question is whether the reasonable person in the defendant's position would have carried out the activity at all, bearing in mind the degree of danger to others. In other words, the question is the same, but the 'precaution' in issue is the complete abandonment of the defendant's activity—and the cost to the defendant of abandoning it is a factor against liability.

The system generally

[*Warning: The figures in this section are very rough. They are derived from a number of surveys which were a good deal more precise, but which often give conflicting accounts. A full discussion of which surveys are to be preferred would be a very substantial enterprise indeed!*]

Numbers of victims

3.11 It is difficult to give a precise picture of the pattern of accidents and of how the legal system deals with them. Patterns of reporting vary; there is no obvious, precise definition of 'serious' injury; different bodies collect statistics for different reasons, and with different definitions.

A very vague picture is as follows. The number of accidental injuries in Britain each year, serious enough to merit a few days off work, is in the millions, though not the tens of millions. Perhaps one-fifth is the result of industrial accidents and perhaps one-tenth is the result of road accidents; a very large proportion, perhaps one-quarter, occur in the home or in residential institutions. The bulk of the accidents are at the more trivial end of the scale, with the result that numbers of accidents drop sharply as we raise the severity of accident we are interested in. Only about

1–2 per cent of victims of accidents still suffer from the effects after six months. 'For every person who is off work for months, hundreds are off work for weeks; and for everyone off for weeks, scores are off for days' (Cane *Atiyah's Accidents Compensation and the Law* (6th edn, 1999) 18). At the extreme end of seriousness, perhaps 14,000 people die in accidents each year: maybe one-third in road accidents, one-third at home or in residential establishments, and one-tenth in industrial accidents. Slightly over 1,000 are either homicides or deaths caused by dangerous driving.

At all levels of seriousness, injuries in accidents are far outnumbered by injuries due to disease. Perhaps 20 working days are lost through disease for every one through accident. Cigarette smoking alone accounts for more than 100,000 deaths a year.

Willingness to sue

3.12 There are a number of reasons why injured people may not sue, if indeed they realize that they might be able to. There is a huge reluctance to sue family or friends; understandably so, though sometimes this may indicate lack of understanding of the workings of liability insurance. There are noticeable differences between different classes of claimants: men are more likely to sue than women; those of working age are more likely to sue than are children or the old; the poor are more likely to sue than the rich. Levels of claims also vary with the context of the injury. Road accident and work accident victims are relatively ready to consider legal action: one in three road accident victims, and one in four work accident victims, go so far as to consult a solicitor. Others who are injured are much less likely to consider legal action. It is not entirely clear why this is, unless it is simply a self-perpetuating fashion: 'everyone knows' that you can't sue for accidents in the home (even though perhaps one-fifth of home accidents are the fault of someone other than the victim). No doubt, without social security benefits, sick pay and the NHS, minor injuries would do more harm to people's pockets, and so would be more likely to prompt litigation. Numbers of participants in legal actions can be greatly raised by publicity, as those promoting mass actions over specific incidents or products have found. A leading example is the Dalkon Shield action, which attracted an estimated 250,000 claimants worldwide.

Numbers who sue and who receive compensation

3.13 Perhaps 200,000 people per year receive compensation for torts, which is in the order of 5 per cent of all those injured. It is not usually necessary to go to court to secure an award. Legal proceedings are started in perhaps less than one-third of those cases, and very few of those proceed to trial: perhaps 10 per cent of cases where proceedings are started end up in a full trial. Of all claimants who seriously pursue a claim, whether they start legal proceedings or not, about 90 per cent secure some sort of settlement or award.

So, roughly 5 per cent of all those injured receive tort damages, but the total amount paid out by defendants is about half the total social security injury benefits paid to *all* those injured! Thus we see a clear (and rather controversial) value-judgement effected through our system: that those injured by someone's fault deserve to recover more than victims of misfortune alone. The vast bulk of successful claims are for relatively small amounts, in the hundreds and low thousands of pounds. However, there is a 'long tail' of massive claims for permanent disablement: the top 1 per cent of tort claims account for about one-quarter of the total amounts awarded. Road accident and employment-related claims account for over 90 per cent of the total.

Defendants

3.14 There is rarely any point in pursuing a claim in tort unless it is absolutely clear that the defendant can meet it if it is established. Accordingly, the overwhelming bulk of tort claims are (as a matter of financial reality, if not strict law) against insurance companies. Nearly all of the others are against substantial companies, organs of government, or others with substantial wealth. Both employers and drivers are required by law to carry liability insurance, and an insurance industry body, the Motor Insurers' Bureau (MIB), acts as defendant in cases where the driver concerned was uninsured. Perhaps 90 per cent of tort claims are covered by liability insurance, nearly all of the remainder being against firms wealthy enough to carry the financial risk themselves. Probably less than 1 per cent of tort claims are against private individuals.

The reality of most tort litigation, therefore, is that it usually involves the claimant's solicitor negotiating with a solicitor acting for an insurance company. This reality is not usually mirrored in tort textbooks. From the textbook point of view, tort often seems like an exercise in determining whether the defendant was at fault, and who is to meet the claim is a mere peripheral detail. From an insurance perspective, the defendant's fault has very little to do with it—indeed, the defendant has very little to do with the claim, which is dealt with between the claimant and the defendant's insurer. What the court is really discussing is not 'the extent of the defendant's liability'—the defendant will not be paying a penny, whatever happens—but rather the extent of the *insurance company's* liability. Which perspective is the better one is a matter of opinion, but it is certainly true that the elaborate system of fault-finding that is modern tort law would not exist in its current form without the laws which require compulsory liability insurance.

Claimants

3.15 Claimants are typically less well organized than defendants. Very possibly the claimant had no particular interest in legal matters before the accident, unlike most insurance companies. Until recently, it would have been fair comment that solicitors acting for claimants would typically be less experienced than solicitors acting for defendants—though as a result of various pressures towards specialization, this is less true today, if it is true at all.

Financing an action is a hurdle many claimants are unable to get over. Some claimants negotiate with the insurance company directly, in some cases with success. There are also a number of 'claims assessors' who will act for a claimant, but as these assessors may have no formal legal qualification and therefore cannot lawfully start legal proceedings on their clients' behalf, their negotiating strength is limited. Some claimants turn out already to have bought the right to legal services. It is comparatively rare to buy 'legal expenses insurance' for its own sake, but it often comes as part of wider insurance cover, or as part of a package of services offered by membership organizations, and especially by trade unions. Indeed, unions provide legal advice in a large proportion of work-related claims and a significant number of road accident claims, acting on behalf of their members. An uncomfortable illustration of this is in relation to the Hillsborough Stadium disaster, where claims were brought both by injured fans and by injured police officers. The Police Federation is a well-organized body, entirely familiar with the procedures for establishing legal rights on its members' behalf; whereas the fans are not normally organized for that sort of task at all. The greater success of actions by police claimants is therefore no surprise.

These cases apart, the claimant is liable to pay the costs personally. Most such work is done at an hourly charging rate for the solicitor's time. It has recently become possible for solicitors to charge on a 'conditional fee' basis, under which they charge nothing for their time unless they secure an award or a sum in settlement, in which case they charge rather more than their normal hourly rate. The scheme is still effectively experimental, and operates within financial limits, in that there is a maximum 'uplift' of 100 per cent—in other words, the solicitor cannot charge a successful client more than double what they would have charged if working for their normal hourly rates. A claimant who sues but fails is liable for the defendant's legal costs, whether the claimant's own solicitor is working on a 'conditional fee' basis or not. In practice, therefore, 'no win, no fee' is a risky business for the claimant unless the solicitor with whom the claimant deals can procure insurance against the risk that the claimant will lose.

The settlement process

3.16 Personal injury claims typically take months or even years to resolve. A certain amount of delay is inevitable, unless (unusually) the claimant's prognosis is clear from the outset. Delay may be increased by a wait for other legal processes to run their course, such as criminal proceedings arising out of the accident. Negotiations typically start with a standard letter from the claimant's solicitor claiming damages, which receives a standard reply from the defendant's solicitor denying liability, and asking for details of the alleged negligence. Collection of evidence is often a slow and expensive process, and neither side will be willing to reveal the complete picture to the other even when they know it themselves. Accordingly, there is usually a significant element of bluff and counter-bluff involved in the negotiations, though there are attempts in recent reforms of the civil justice system to reduce the importance of this. As a rule, delay favours the defendant rather than the claimant, because the claimant needs the money more than the defendant needs to close the file. It seems that entirely hopeless claims are usually recognized as such at an early stage, which may explain why about 90 per cent of cases actually proceeded with result in some sort of settlement. However, the costs involved even in a quick settlement are large. The total amounts received by successful claimants are only slightly more than the amounts paid to the firms representing them. If tort is contrasted with other mechanisms under which accident victims may receive cash payments, such as private insurance and social security, the relative inefficiency of tort is very apparent.

The future of the system

3.17 The increase in the number of legal claims for personal injury over the last half-century proved an increasing drain on the legal aid fund, leading to their eventual removal from legal aid. Various reforms for personal injury recovery have been mooted. It remains to be seen how many firms of solicitors will be prepared to take on significant numbers of conditional fee cases, given that they expose solicitors to substantial financial risk. Risk management of that type and severity will be new to many practices, and will require a cultural sea-change in the attitude of the legal professions.

In the following sections, I consider some special categories of personal injury claimants.

Nervous shock

3.18 It is common to say of someone hurt in an accident that they were 'shocked' or 'in shock'. This is a vague usage, though the medical reality to which it points is definite enough. However, these cases do not pose particular problems for the personal injury lawyer: the 'shock' is compensatable as part of the action for the injury itself, probably as part of the claim for pain and suffering (**10.58**). Where personal injury lawyers talk of 'nervous shock', they have a more precisely defined problem in mind. In some cases, the claimant does not suffer any physical injury at all, but nonetheless emerges from the accident with psychiatric injuries of some gravity. Liability sometimes arises in this situation, but the law is not as generous to the claimant as in cases of actual physical injury.

The need for a distinct psychiatric illness

3.19 The claimant's case has to involve proof that the claimant was mentally ill as a result of the shock, and it is axiomatic that pain, grief or distress are not enough in themselves to constitute 'nervous shock'. Currently, the lawyers' 'nervous shock' is roughly equivalent to the doctors' 'post-traumatic stress disorder' (PTSD), though any recognized psychiatric illness should usually be enough to establish action. The diagnosis of PTSD involves three major symptoms:

- persistent flashbacks or intrusive recollection of the traumatic incident, perhaps involving a re-experiencing of emotions felt at the time, or even a feeling that the trauma is recurring; and

- avoidance of people, places or activities which remind the claimant of the traumatic events; and

- increased psychological arousal, possibly manifested in sleep disorder, irritability, poor concentration.

The claim to suffer from PTSD is likely to be examined by the courts in considerable detail if it is disputed, and the law is no longer open to the criticism (if it ever was) that it allows a legal action to lie merely for grief, sadness, or anxiety.

> *Rothwell v Chemical and Insulating Co* **[2007] UKHL 39:** The claimants sued their employers after they developed pleural plaques. These plaques (areas of thickness on the membranes surrounding the lungs) were themselves harmless, but indicated exposure to asbestos, which might independently cause life-threatening diseases. Held: no action lay. The plaques themselves did not constitute injury, neither did the risk of developing a disease, nor did the anxiety that disease might occur. One of the claimants was in fact psychiatrically ill as a result of the anxiety—while *this* claimant had suffered compensatable damage, it was not a foreseeable consequence of anything his employer had done, and so it was not actionable.

(This proved controversial, and attempts were made to reverse the decision by statute. In the event, the UK Parliament refused to do so, but the Scottish Parliament enacted the Damages (Asbestos-related Conditions) (Scotland) Act 2009, declaring asbestos-related pleural plaques to be an actionable injury. A no-fault compensation scheme was subsequently introduced for England and Wales.)

Two major problems persist.

First, there are many possibilities for fraud and for 'functional overlay' (unconscious exaggeration of symptoms). This is also true in other areas of personal injury law, but is particularly acute here. Sometimes the claimant's illness can be shown to be a 'litigation neurosis' which will dissipate once the action is over. This is no bar to the claimant's claim, though in those circumstances the claimant's damages will certainly be reduced if any significant delay in the litigation can be laid at the claimant's door.

Second, the courts, in their anxiety to avoid the charge that they are treating mere sorrow as if it were an illness, have drawn a sharp distinction between 'abnormal' mental diseases and 'normal' emotional reactions to distressing circumstances. But this distinction is in many contexts increasingly implausible. So the courts have refused the claim of a couple trapped in a hospital lift, on the ground that it was 'merely' claustrophobia complicated by anxiety connected to the heart condition from which one of them suffered (*Reilly v Merseyside Health Authority* [1995] 6 Med LR 246). Yet the distress involved was as traumatic and as prolonged as many 'nervous shock' cases. And the Court of Appeal has been faced with the unedifying task of determining whether the claimant's condition amounted to PTSD or 'merely' to a severe grief reaction at the drowning of his daughters (*Vernon v Bosley* [1997] 1 All ER 577). The doctors are becoming less and less of a help in maintaining the distinction been 'normal' and 'abnormal' conditions. Perhaps the courts will soon be forced either to abandon the distinction, or to admit that it is legal and conventional, rather than rooted in any medical reality.

Liability: basic principles

3.20 Until quite recently, the courts treated nervous shock as a distinct type of damage, quite distinct from other types of personal injury. Accordingly, it was said that 'the test of liability for shock is forseeability of injury by shock' (*King v Phillips* [1953] 1 QB 429, 441, Denning LJ). However, the courts now recognize that this is unrealistic. The cases now distinguish between cases where the defendant ought to have foreseen physical injury to the claimant (where the claimant is accordingly a 'primary victim') and cases where the claimant can only say that the defendant ought to have foreseen shock (where the claimant is a 'secondary victim').

'Primary victims'

3.21 Where the defendant's activities posed a foreseeable risk of physical injury to the claimant, so that if the claimant had been physically injured the claimant could have maintained an action for those injuries, then the claimant may sue for any proven psychiatric harm. In other words, if it was foreseeable that the claimant would be injured, it is no defence that the claimant's injury happens to take a psychiatric rather than a physical form.

> **Page v Smith [1996] AC 155:** Page and Smith collided in a car accident which was wholly Smith's fault. Page was physically unharmed, but subsequently suffered a recurrence of a pre-existing condition of myalgic encephalomyelitis (ME) as a result of the trauma of the incident. Held: Smith must take his victim as he found him, and was accordingly liable for Page's condition.

It follows that where physical injury would have been a foreseeable consequence of the defendant's negligence, there is liability for any nervous shock regardless of whether there is physical injury (*Simmons v British Steel plc* [2004] UKHL 20). This principle has also been applied in a case where the defendant's carelessness resulted in the claimant's shock because of the operation of the legal system.

> **McLoughlin v Jones [2001] EWCA Civ 1743:** McLoughlin was charged with robbery, and convicted despite the efforts of his solicitor, Jones. He spent 3½ months in prison, a traumatic experience as a result of which he became a depressive. His conviction was quashed when new evidence became available. He sued Jones for negligence in the conduct of his defence; Jones argued that he owed no duty to guard against threats to McLoughlin's mental health. Held: a duty was owed to McLoughlin, as a primary victim.

It follows that where the defendant's negligence creates a risk of physical injury to a group of people, then the main question for a claimant suffering nervous shock is whether he or she was within the 'zone of danger' which represents the limits of the defendant's reasonable foresight. The claimant can recover if within the zone, but otherwise not.

> **McFarlane v EE Caledonia [1994] 2 All ER 1:** McFarlane witnessed the fire at the Piper Alpha oil rig, being about 100 metres away at the time. He felt considerable anxiety for his own personal safety, and later experienced psychiatric illness. Held: his fear for his own safety was unreasonable, and his condition was not actionable.

However, while many cases are clearly one side of the line or the other, this doctrine still leaves a considerable grey area. Take the old case of *Bourhill v Young* [1943] AC 92, where the defendant's poor driving on his motorcycle led to an accident from which he died. The claimant, who was eight months pregnant, was some way away at the time of the accident, but saw the rather gory aftermath. This had such an effect on her that she miscarried. The House of Lords in 1942 held that she was an unforeseeable claimant. Would the courts say the same today? It would have been very surprising if she had been physically hurt, but if she had been (say by a piece of debris from the collision, thrown on a freak trajectory) the courts would almost certainly have allowed her to recover. Does that put her within the 'zone of danger'? The courts have become much more generous towards 'nervous shock' claimants in the half-decade since *Bourhill*, but it is not entirely clear how far they are now prepared to go.

'Secondary victims'

3.22 Where the claimant was not physically at risk from the defendant's activities, but nonetheless suffers shock on witnessing them, then a duty may in principle be owed. But rather more is required than in cases of 'primary victims'. This usually involves two aspects:

- *A clear emotional connection between the traumatic event and the shock the claimant suffers.* So witnessing injuries to a close relation is more likely to result in a successful claim than witnessing a stranger suffer.

- *Clear perception by the claimant of the traumatic event.* Seeing your parents being crushed to death is more likely to lead to a successful claim than hearing via the radio that this has happened.

However, these are only factors in a larger question, and their relative importance differs from case to case. There is really only one question: ought the defendant to have realized that a person of reasonable psychological firmness in the claimant's position might suffer shock as a result of the defendant's activities? Of course, people differ in their ability to withstand shock. Nonetheless, to ask whether the claimant's firmness was 'reasonable' is rather odd. A claimant who is unusually susceptible to shock can certainly be regarded as *unlucky*, but it is a strong thing to regard such a claimant as *unreasonable*; what was the claimant supposed to do about it? Are we simply asking whether the claimant was average in this regard? Much is unclear here.

However, it is also clear that if the court considers that a reasonable person in the claimant's position might have suffered shock, then it makes no difference that the claimant's reaction is more severe than the defendant might reasonably have expected. Once liability is established, defendants must take their victims as they find them.

> *Brice v Brown* **[1984] 1 All ER 997:** Brice and her daughter were involved in a road accident which was wholly the fault of Brown. Brice already had a mild hysterical personality

disorder. As a result of the injuries to herself and her daughter, Brice's psychological condition worsened considerably, involving her in bizarre and unsocial behaviour, and a number of suicide attempts. Held: once liability for her nervous shock was established, damages were not to be reduced merely because the claimant's behaviour was of an unforeseen type. It was enough that it was the direct effect of the psychiatric injury done to her.

Close emotional link with traumatic event

3.23 The archetypal 'secondary victim' is the claimant who sees a close relative suffer injury or death. The closer the emotional tie between the claimant and the 'primary victim' of the accident, the more foreseeable is shock as a result.

> **Alcock v Chief Constable of the South Yorkshire Police [1992] 1 AC 310:** Ten claimants alleging nervous shock arising out of the Hillsborough Stadium disaster sued the police authority in charge of the incident. Nine were relatives of primary victims, one the fiancée of a primary victim. None of the claimants were spouses or parents of primary victims. Held: no duty was owed to any of the claimants.

In *Alcock* the House of Lords seemed happy to endorse the result of the earlier case of *McLoughlin v O'Brian* [1983] 1 AC 410. There the Lords had granted a remedy to a woman who suffered nervous shock on the injury of her husband and three children. She had heard the news of the accident at her home, but when driven to the hospital was told that one of her children had died and saw those who had survived, still injured and in great distress. However, *Alcock* is plainly a retreat from the position of Lord Scarman in *McLoughlin*, who was happy to declare that foresight should be the sole criterion, 'untrammelled by spatial, physical or temporal limits' ([1982] 2 All ER 310, 311). It is clear that there is no fixed rule: the closeness of the relationship is only one factor, and the Lords in *Alcock* did not rule out the possibility of recovering for the effects of injury to a complete stranger, if it occurred in sufficiently disturbing circumstances. In some cases, such as brother and sister, the court is unlikely to be happy with a bare statement of the relationship, but will want some evidence of its closeness in fact. In other cases, special factors may intervene.

> **Leach v Chief Constable of Gloucestershire Constabulary [1999] 1 All ER 215:** The police decided to interview a mentally disordered murder suspect. Leach, a voluntary worker, attended as statutory independent 'appropriate adult'. As a result of the suspect's horrifying confession, of which Leach had no advance warning, she suffered nervous shock. The police argued that they owed her no duty, as her position was by definition independent of the police. They therefore applied to strike out her action against them. Held: on the assumption that the police had complied with relevant codes

of conduct, they owed Leach no duty in respect of the interview, though arguably there was a duty owed to provide her with post-interview counselling.

There is obviously an element of arbitrariness in the test applied here, even if it is founded on straightforward, and apparently accurate, notions about when claimants are likely to suffer shock. The Law Commission has mooted the idea of a fixed statutory list of relationships which are considered likely to give rise to shock; only if the relationship fell outside the statutory list would the claimant have to prove the emotional closeness of the relationship. This would have the merit of clarity, and is no more obviously arbitrary than current arrangements.

Perception of the traumatic event

3.24 The claimant's chances of establishing liability improve with the clarity with which the claimant was able to perceive the traumatic event. So shock occasioned by seeing a traumatic event at close hand may give rise to liability, even though hearing of the same incident by word of mouth may not. So in the *Alcock* case (**3.23**), it was made clear that claimants who had seen the Hillsborough disaster on a TV screen, but not in person, could not possibly recover. However, it was also made clear that this was not a rule about TV transmission as such, but only because the images in the case had been censored. TV broadcasters are subject to a code which forbids (amongst other things) close-ups of people being crushed to death. Lord Ackner at least was clear that TV images might in appropriate cases give rise to claims in nervous shock, as where a balloon trip is filmed on live TV, and a sudden catastrophe entails that parents watch their children plummeting to their deaths ([1991] 4 All ER 907, 921).

This criterion of the claimant's depth of perception is vague. It also reflects what is probably a psychological misconception. At least in the case of close relatives, it does not appear to be true that a better chance to view their injury results in an increased risk of shock. To be blunt about it, there is *no* pleasant or unstressful way to hear that your spouse or your child has been mangled to death. And it does not appear to be true that those who hear about it on the radio find the blow less severe than those who are on the scene to see it. Certainly where a mother suffers shock on hearing that her four-year-old daughter has been abducted, sexually assaulted and murdered, it seems harsh to deny liability because she did not actually see these events taking place (as occurred in *Palmer v Tees Health Authority* [2000] PIQR P1 though there were other reasons for denying liability as well).

Varieties of traumatic event

3.25 Most cases of 'secondary victimhood' involve injuries to relatives, but there is no rule of law restricting liability to such cases. All that is required is that the event has such a direct and obvious effect on the claimant that any reasonable person in the defendant's position must have foreseen shock.

> **Attia v British Gas [1988] QB 304:** Due to the negligence of British Gas employees, a fire started in Attia's house. She arrived home to see it engulfed in flames. Held: her nervous shock was a foreseeable consequence of British Gas's negligence and she could recover damages accordingly.

In *AB v Tameside and Glossop Health Authority* [1997] 8 Med LR 91, the defendant health authority discovered that one of their health workers was HIV positive. They decided to inform those he had treated of the (very slight) risk of infection, inviting them for tests. Some of the recipients of the letters sued for shock. In the event, the health authority admitted the existence of a duty, but successfully argued that they had acted reasonably in the circumstances. Obviously a court will be reluctant to find a breach of duty in that situation—what was the authority supposed to do?—but the existence of a duty is plain. Liability is rather more obvious where the information communicated—that the claimant's baby was dead—was inaccurate as a result of the defendant health authority's negligence. Breach of duty was found, even though the officer who passed the information on had shown adequate sensitivity (*Allin v City and Hackney Health Authority* [1996] 7 Med LR 167).

It is clear that while the idea of a 'traumatic event' usually signifies immediacy, nonetheless the claimant can equally recover for an 'event' which occurs over a period. So where the claimant is present while her 10-month-old son suffers liver failure due to the defendant's negligence, starting a train of events which ends 36 hours later with her son dead in her arms, liability was established (*Walters v North Glamorgan NHS Trust* [2002] EWCA Civ 1792). Further, when the claimant is told that her 16-year-old daughter has been run down by the defendant, and then sees her corpse in the mortuary, this may be a sufficiently clear perception of the accident or its immediate aftermath so as to establish liability (*Atkinson v Seghal* [2003] EWCA Civ 697).

It has been held that there can be no liability for nervous shock where the primary victim is actually the defendant (*Greatorex v Greatorex* [2000] 4 All ER 769). In other words, it is not enough to witness even the most severe injuries to a close relative, if that close relative was responsible for their own injuries. Cazalet J argued that this was required by the need to avoid undesirable intra-family litigation. This seems a rather arbitrary limitation, however.

Reform

3.26 With every advance of medical knowledge in this area, the line between physical injury and 'nervous shock' has become harder to draw, as has the line between 'normal' and 'abnormal' reactions to disturbing circumstances. The drastic limitations on the foreseeability of 'secondary' shock are not based on a realistic assessment of who is likely to suffer shock and who is not, but are the product of extreme judicial caution. Such caution is perhaps justified on questions where medical knowledge is far from complete, but is hard to justify in areas where it is more definite. Several legal commentators have urged that no firm line can be drawn between physical and mental trauma, and that they should be dealt with by the same rules.

However, even assuming that this is the right attitude to take (the matter is far from certain), it is another question whether the courts should say so all at once, or whether they are not doing claimants a service by only slowly assimilating 'nervous shock' cases to liability generally. Can the courts' current approach be regarded as a process of slow assimilation? If so, the pace is truly glacial. At the current rate of progress, we will be well into the 21st century before assimilation is complete.

Negligence and the unborn child

3.27 Where, as result of the defendant's activities, a developing foetus suffers an injury, can legal action be taken? Legal personality is not acquired until live birth; there is no such thing as an unborn claimant. In the early 1970s it was unclear whether or not a legal action vested in the claimant on birth, in respect of matters occurring before it. Parliament therefore intervened to establish liability, by the Congenital Disabilities (Civil Liability) Act 1976, vesting a right of action in any child born alive for injuries suffered in the womb. It was later held that this was also the position at common law (*Burton v Islington Health Authority* [1993] QB 204), and accordingly a remedy is available whether the defendant's negligence took place before or after the Act came into force.

The statutory right of action is derivative from the rights of the parents: the defendant is liable for conduct which affected the ability of either parent to have a normal healthy child, or affected the mother during her pregnancy, and which resulted in disability to the child. The rule is, in effect, that if the parent could have sued had he or she suffered injury, then the child can sue. It is no defence that, in the event, the parent suffered no injury (s 1(3)). This derivative liability, in the Act as originally drafted, did not catch the case where the defendant damaged gametes or eggs held in a laboratory, and which were subsequently implanted and grew to form the child. This case is provided for expressly by the Human Fertilisation and Embryology Act 1990, s 44, which introduces a new s 1A to the 1976 Act. An exception clause which would have barred action by the parent concerned also bars a claim by the child (s 1(6)). If the parent concerned was partly responsible for the damage, then the amount of the claim is reduced by whatever share the court thinks just and equitable (s 1(7)). No action lies if the defendant's misconduct occurred before conception and at least one parent knew of the risk (s 1(4)).

Claims against the parents

3.28 It is clear from the 1976 Act that the father may be liable for injuries to the child. Where the father's breach of duty occurred before conception, the mother's awareness of the risk of disability is a defence (s 1(4)). The mother, by contrast, is liable in only one case: where, when she knew or ought to have known that she was pregnant, she drives a motor vehicle in a manner threatening the safety of the foetus. (In that situation she will probably have liability insurance and so will not pay the damages personally (**4.13**).) In this case, she owes a duty directly to the foetus, though it is actionable only in the event of a live birth (s 2).

'Wrongful life'

3.29 Suppose that, but for the defendant's negligence, the child would never have been conceived at all. Action by the child in those circumstances seems unlikely to succeed, but actions by the parents were at one time common. Initially, after some confusion, the courts were inclined to accept these actions.

> **Emeh v Kensington and Chelsea and Westminster Area Health Authority [1985] QB 1012:** In consequence of a negligent sterilization by the health authority, Emeh had an unplanned daughter. Held: she was entitled to damages for *(i)* the pain, suffering and 'general wear and tear' involved in birth and parenthood, though with a deduction for the more positive aspects of the experience, and *(ii)* the financial cost of bringing up the unplanned child. Emeh's refusal to have an abortion was not considered a ground for reducing her damages.

Emeh was an example of a negligent failure to sterilize the mother; other cases involved negligent failure of a vasectomy on the father, and poor advice on how soon it is safe to have unprotected sex after a well-performed operation. The latter occurred in *McFarlane v Tayside Health Board* [1999] UKHL 50, where the House of Lords (in its capacity as a Scottish court) reconsidered the matter. The approach taken by the Lords was, however, more restrictive than that in *Emeh*. While allowing the parents an action for the mother's pain and suffering during pregnancy, childbirth, and the immediate aftermath, and any expenses incurred during pregnancy, nonetheless the Lords laid down that there could be no action for the economic cost of bringing up a healthy child. This result was justified by some of their Lordships on the (curious) ground that the doctors had not assumed liability for these costs, and by others on the (more plausible) ground that it is unreasonable to place this burden on hospitals.

This much more restrictive approach was reconsidered by a seven-strong bench of law lords in *Rees v Darlington Memorial Hospital NHS Trust* [2003] UKHL 52. By a majority, the main point in *McFarlane* was upheld: there could be no award for damages for the birth of a healthy child. However (and to some minds inconsistently), they added that as the claimant in such cases was undeniably the victim of a legal wrong, a 'conventional' award of £15,000 should be made for the injury and loss represented by the birth. *Rees* leaves open the question whether the birth of a sick or disabled child might lead to an action for economic loss. Such an award was made in *Parkinson v St James and Seacroft University Hospital NHS Trust* [2001] EWCA Civ 530. The Lords in *Rees* were clear that the mother's own disability was irrelevant, even where (as in *Rees* itself) it had given her a powerful reason to avoid having a child of her own. But whether *Parkinson* was rightly decided, and (if so) whether the 'conventional' award should be made in such a case, is at present an open question.

Deprivation of chance to abort

3.30 A rather different claim, more relevant where the foetus has severe abnormalities, is that while the foetus's disabilities are not the defendant's fault, nonetheless if the defendant had acted properly then the parents would have appreciated the position and arranged for an abortion. Such claims may in principle be brought by either of the parents, or by the child, or by all three. Claims by parents have occasionally succeeded.

> **Thake v Maurice [1986] QB 644:** On carrying out a vasectomy, Maurice negligently failed to warn Thake of the small risk of spontaneous natural reversal of the process. It was found that if Thake had been aware of this risk, he and his wife would have recognized her pregnancy earlier and would have been able to abort. Held: action lay in negligence.

However, while the principle of the case is still good, the courts are reluctant to find a breach of duty in this situation. In *Gold v Haringey Health Authority* [1988] QB 481 a similar claim by a woman whose sterilization reversed itself failed, because there was no unanimity amongst doctors that a warning was necessary in her case, and so it was impossible to prove breach of duty. And in *Rance v Mid-Downs Health*

Authority [1991] 1 QB 587 further doubt was cast on this type of claim, the court suggesting that the mother might not be entitled to an abortion in those circumstances at all. Claims by the child have also received short shrift.

> **McKay v Essex Area Health Authority [1982] QB 1166:** McKay, who was pregnant, suspected that she had contracted rubella, but was wrongly assured by her health authority, after negligently conducted tests, that she had not. Her child was born with deformities. Held: neither mother nor child could sue the health authority.

Assuming that it is clear, as it was in *McKay*, both that the defendants were negligent and that the mother would have had an abortion had she known the truth, then the normal elements of a negligence claim are all present. Nonetheless, both claims were rejected in *McKay*, on the rather dubious ground that the loss in question is incapable of measurement. In other words, even though the law in other contexts accepts that it may sometimes be better to die than to live (e.g. *Re J* [1991] Fam 33), nonetheless some difficulty was felt in putting a price tag on this. Yet the law of tort seems capable of putting a value on life in other contexts (see **10.66**), and it is not clear why the task should be any more difficult here. So the reason given in the case is weak; which is not to deny that better reasons might be found.

Rescuers

'Danger invites rescue'

3.31 Where the defendant's negligence puts someone in danger, and the claimant attempts a rescue, but is injured in the process, the claimant may be able to sue the defendant. If the creation of the danger was foreseeable, then equally it should be foreseeable that someone will try to save others from it.

The principle is obvious enough. But it reverses the value-judgement normally made about people who deliberately go towards a source of danger. Normally, we would expect to say that it is not foreseeable that someone would deliberately increase the risks they were running; or that the defendant cannot reasonably be expected to provide for such a person; or that the claimant can be met by a defence, such as the *novus actus interveniens* principle (**10.41**), or the defences of contributory negligence (**11.17**) or consent (**11.2**). So if the defendant is responsible for the occurrence of an accident, very probably the defendant will also be responsible for the fate of those who rush in to alleviate the consequences, and will not be able to plead that these rescuers are the authors of their own misfortune.

Defendants who endanger themselves

3.32 Sometimes the claimant sets out to rescue the defendant, and then sues the defendant for injuries received, on the ground that the entire incident was the defendant's fault. While defendants cannot be said to owe duties to themselves, they may nonetheless be said to owe a duty to those who seek to rescue them.

> **Harrison v British Railways Board [1981] 3 All ER 679:** Howard, a British Rail employee, attempted to board a train just as it was leaving the station. Harrison, the guard, made an ineffective attempt to stop the train, then tried to pull Howard on board. They both fell off onto the track. Held: Harrison could sue Howard for his injuries, though with a 20 per cent reduction for contributory negligence.

Defendant endangers X, claimant rescues X, claimant sues defendant

3.33 A more common situation is where the claimant is hurt attempting to rescue a third party, from a danger created by the defendant. Generally speaking, in this situation the defendant has broken a duty to X, and what the courts are doing is effectively extending the benefit of that duty of care to the claimant as well. If the defendant is responsible for the injury to X, the defendant is also responsible for the claimant's response to it.

> **Baker v TE Hopkins & Son [1959] 3 All ER 225:** Employees of Hopkins were overcome by noxious carbon monoxide fumes while at work, in circumstances which were held to be the result of negligence by Hopkins. Baker, a doctor, tried to rescue them, but was himself overcome by fumes, and died. Held: Baker's widow could sue Hopkins.

Very occasionally, the possibility of a rescue, or of its precise mode of execution, has been considered unforeseeable.

> **Crossley v Rawlinson [1982] 1 WLR 369:** A lorry burst into flames due to the negligence of Rawlinson. Crossley rushed towards it with a fire extinguisher, but tripped over a concealed hole and injured himself. Held: this injury was an unforeseeable consequence of Rawlinson's conduct and there was no liability.

The decision is an unusual one, and is out of line with most authorities. If injury of some sort to the claimant is foreseeable, generally speaking it is no defence that the claimant suffers a different sort of injury (**10.32**).

Nervous shock

3.34 Suppose the defendant creates a source of physical danger. The claimant is well outside the 'danger zone' at the time, and so if the claimant suffers nervous shock we would expect the claimant only to recover damages if the claimant satisfies the strict rules for 'secondary victims' (**3.22**). However, if the claimant attempts a rescue of the primary victims and suffers shock, it seems that the claimant is entitled to be regarded as a 'primary victim' as well. It is no defence that it was the claimant's own decision which brought the claimant into the 'zone of danger'.

> *Chadwick v British Transport Commission* **[1967] 2 All ER 945:** Chadwick took part in rescue operations following a rail crash near his home, where 90 people were killed and many more were trapped and injured. He subsequently suffered a recurrence of psychoneurotic symptoms from which he had suffered when younger, but which would not have been expected to recur under the ordinary stresses of life. Held: the British Transport Commission, who were responsible for the crash, were liable to Chadwick also.

The rule is well established, but it leaves difficult questions of who is a 'rescuer', and who is merely someone who arrives in the aftermath of the tragedy. At present, a narrow view is being taken of the concept of 'rescuer'.

> *White v Chief Constable of the South Yorkshire Police* **[1999] 2 AC 455:** A group of six police officers involved in the disaster at the Hillsborough football ground sued their Chief Constable for their nervous shock arising out of their work on that day. Some had attempted resuscitation at the ground, moved bodies there, and dealt with the crowd-control problems in the immediate aftermath of the disaster; others moved bodies and attempted to revive bodies; another had stripped and labelled bodies and dealt with distraught relatives. Held: all of these claimants were dealing with the 'aftermath' of the incident, not the incident itself, so none could recover.

> *Duncan v British Coal Corpn* **[1997] 1 All ER 540:** Duncan, a pit deputy, rushed to help a colleague trapped in a conveyor machine. The incident occurred while he was 275 metres away. The victim was dead by the time Duncan arrived, though this did not become apparent for a while. Held: Duncan was not a 'rescuer' and could only recover if he satisfied the tests for secondary victims.

> *Hunter v British Coal Corpn* **[1999] QB 140:** In another mine accident, Hunter was only 30 metres from the scene of the accident, when a hydrant burst. Feelings of responsibility for this accident led him to suffer shock on seeing, 15 minutes later, what looked like a co-worker being carried away dead. Held: Hunter had not been present at a shocking incident, and so could not recover.

It now seems to be accepted that rescuers who were never themselves in danger cannot recover, at least if their belief that they were in danger was unreasonable (*Monk v Harrington* [2008] EWHC 1879 (QB)).

Duty owed individually to the rescuer

3.35 In a sense, the duty just described is 'derivative', in the sense that the claimant will usually prove that a duty was owed *to someone else* and that it was foreseeable that the claimant would then help that someone. Usually this is an adequate description. However, it is not complete. Cases where the claimant rescues the very person responsible for the danger (**3.32**) cannot be analysed this way: it is impossible to owe a duty to yourself. More generally, the claimant is allowed to plead a duty arising on ordinary principles, and this may mean that the claimant can recover *even though the endangered person cannot*.

> **Videan v British Transport Commission [1963] 2 QB 650:** Videan, a station-master, rushed onto the railway line in an attempt to save his two-year-old son who had wandered onto it. Both were crushed to death by a negligently driven motorized trolley. The son was an unforeseeable trespasser and so could not recover; it was argued that if the son was unforeseeable, then logically an attempt to rescue him was unforeseeable too. Held: the father was lawfully on the line and thus a foreseeable victim of bad driving. Accordingly, liability was established.

The law on trespassers has changed since the time of *Videan*: the fact that the son was a trespasser might not doom his claim today (**4.26**). But the main point is that the father could rely on his status as employee and lawful visitor on the premises of the main defendant. In that limited sense, the case was (as Pearson LJ said, [1963] 2 QB 650, 682–3) not really a 'rescuer' case at all: the father could prove that a duty was owed to him and was broken, without adverting to the fact that he was engaged in a rescue.

It is sometimes suggested that 'professional' rescuers should be placed in a special position, though whether that position would be better or worse than that of others is not always clear. But certainly the House of Lords would have no truck with this idea in *White v Chief Constable of the South Yorkshire Police* [1999] 2 AC 455. Here, police officers at the Hillsborough Stadium disaster argued that a greater duty was owed to them than to the injured fans, as the defendant was their employer. The Lords pointed out that while there might be two sources for the duty owed, the question was whether the *content* of the duty was any different from that owed to the fans, and it seemed that it was not. The existence of two reasons why a duty was owed did not establish that the duty was any more demanding.

Action against the rescuer

3.36 Rescuers are usually thought of as a class on whom the law of negligence looks with favour. To a certain extent this is still true, as the preceding paragraphs show. However, the climate is becoming more chilly. The courts have on a number of occasions been prepared to hold the emergency services liable for failing to do their jobs, though they have been rather cautious in so doing (see **1.30** and **1.56** above). Voluntary rescue by someone who was entitled to walk away from the scene is still praiseworthy, but professional incompetence is not. In some jurisdictions, it has proved necessary to pass 'Good Samaritan' statutes, exempting rescuers from legal action for the results of their work, at least unless a quite staggering degree of incompetence is shown. The English legal system has so far not enacted any such rule, but if liability is extended much further, doctors and others may begin to clamour for it.

FURTHER READING

Chamberlain 'Alcohol provider liability in Canada and the UK' (2004) 33 CLWR 103.

Chico 'Wrongful conception: Policy, inconsistency and the conventional award' (2007) 8 MLI 139.

Dingwall, Durkin, Pleasence, Felstiner and Bowles 'Firm handling: The litigation strategies of defence lawyers in personal injury cases' (2000) 20 LS 1.

Handford 'Psychiatric injury in breach of a relationship' (2007) 27 LS 26.

Mason 'Wrongful pregnancy, wrongful birth and wrongful terminology' (2002) 6 ELR 46.

McIvor 'Getting defensive about police negligence' (2010) 69 CLJ 133.

Morgan 'Tort, insurance and incoherence' (2004) 67 MLR 384.

Mullender and Speirs 'Negligence, psychiatric injury, and the altruism principle' (2000) 20 OJLS 645.

Nolan 'New forms of damage in negligence' (2007) 70 MLR 59.

Turton 'Defining damage in the House of Lords' (2008) 71 MLR 987.

Wheat 'Proximity and nervous shock' (2003) 32 CLWR 313.

Williams 'State of fear: Britain's "compensation culture" reviewed' (2005) 25 LS 499.

SELF-TEST QUESTIONS

1 Why do so few victims of personal injuries sue those who injured them (**3.12**)?

2 Is it possible to sue for nervous shock consequential on what the claimant has seen on a TV screen (**3.24**)?

3 In the wake of the Hillsborough disaster, many claimants sued for nervous shock. Why should you expect police claimants to have a much better chance of recovery than spectator claimants (**3.15, 3.35**)?

4 In what circumstances may the claimant sue his or her mother for injuries inflicted while she was pregnant with the claimant (**3.28**)?

5 Give examples of defendants who have been held liable for inflicting harm on others by omissions rather than acts (**3.4**).

4

Negligent harm to the person: special duties

SUMMARY

Litigation over personal injuries is much more common in some areas than others. The principles in the case law are correspondingly more detailed in some areas than others.

The areas considered in this chapter are:

- Products liability
- Road accidents
- Occupiers' liability
- Employers' liability
- Medical care

Between them, these heads account for nearly all personal injury litigation in tort.

4.1 This chapter considers a number of special cases of negligence liability. The basic principles have already been explained. The areas considered here include the major areas where litigation actually occurs. Nearly all of the cases considered here are concerned with personal injury, though they may sometimes involve property damage instead, or in addition. So a car accident typically includes both personal injury and property damage.

While most of the chapter concerns negligence, there are various statutory liabilities which it is convenient to treat here, even though the liability is sometimes strict.

Products liability

4.2 One of the most famous and influential cases in the whole of the law of tort, *Donoghue v Stevenson* [1932] AC 562, was a products liability case. That case is the foundation of much of what is now understood about the law of negligence. Ironically, the context in which this leading case occurred was a highly atypical one. Defective products cases are only rarely brought before the courts: barely 1 per cent of all injuries are caused by defective products, and perhaps only 5 per cent of people so injured are successful in claiming any compensation. So despite the importance of *Donoghue* to the way lawyers approach the whole area of negligence liability, products liability cases are of relatively little importance when considering tort generally.

Now that we are more than 75 years away from the seminal ruling in *Donoghue*, the legal system has outgrown it in a number of ways. You have already seen how it is misleading as a general indication of the scope of liability in negligence (**1.27**). There is now extensive legislation on product safety, but it does not give rise to civil liability (the law is now in the General Product Safety Regulations 2005). For those seeking to establish civil liability, *Donoghue* has been superseded by an EU directive, which provides for a broader liability for injuries caused by defective products, generally removing the need for the claimant to establish fault (**4.6**). Nonetheless, there are cases which the directive does not reach, or where it makes sense to claim under the common law as well as the legislation (e.g. the *Bogle* case, **4.10** below). And so the discussion will start with the law of negligence, before moving on to the somewhat stricter duty which is in some cases prescribed by legislation.

Common law

Who owes the duty?

4.3 *Donoghue* itself involved the liability of the manufacturer of the defective product. But there is nothing in the reasoning to confine it to the manufacturer, and subsequent cases have allowed action against others with some influence on the state of the product when it ultimately reached the consumer. So those who assemble goods (*Howard v Furness Houlder Argentine Lines* [1936] 2 All ER 781) or repair them (*Haseldine v CA Daw & Son* [1941] 2 KB 343) owe a similar duty to the ultimate consumer. Even those who merely distribute goods owe a duty to the consumer, if in the circumstances they should have made a safety check—although of course the consumer's action will ultimately fail if the safety check would not have prevented the claimant's injuries. There is no general duty on distributors to make a check, but the following special circumstances have been held to lead to a duty:

- where the goods came from another supplier with a dubious reputation (*Watson v Buckley, Osborne, Garrett & Co* [1940] 1 All ER 174);
- where the manufacturer's instructions are that there should be a check (*Holmes v Ashford* [1950] 2 All ER 76).

It even seems that sellers of second-hand cars generally may be under a duty to make at least a superficial check by a competent mechanic on cars before they sell them (*Andrews v Hopkinson* [1957] 1 QB 229).

Content of the duty

4.4 In *Donoghue*, great stress was placed on the fact that the product in question (a bottle of defective ginger beer) was sealed in the defendant's factory. The bottle was opaque, and so there was no realistic prospect of intermediate examination before the product arrived in front of the claimant. The point is a vital one, for the manufacturers will rarely have control over what is done to the product after it leaves their hands, and so can only be blamed for the most obviously foreseeable happenings thereafter. So if intermediate examination of the product seems probable, the manufacturer is not liable for any injuries which this examination would have prevented. Contrary to *dicta* in *Donoghue* itself, it is not enough that intermediate examination is merely *possible*, if it was most unlikely (*Griffiths v Arch Engineering (Newport) Co* [1968] 3 All ER 217). However, even when intervening conduct does not remove the duty, it may nonetheless make it harder for the claimant to establish a claim.

> **Evans v Triplex Safety Glass Co [1936] 1 All ER 283:** The windscreen of a car shattered for no apparent reason, injuring the occupants of the car. They sued the manufacturer. Held: the claim failed. There were various opportunities for intermediate examination after the car left the factory, and no evidence that the defect was caused by poor manufacture, as distinct from poor fitting of the windscreen.

Again, if the manufacturer issues a warning about the product's safety, which ought reasonably to have put consumers on their guard, then there would be no liability for injuries which the reasonable claimant would then have avoided.

> **Hurley v Dyke [1979] RTR 265:** Dyke sold a second-hand car to Hurley, the car being sold as seen and with all its faults. Hurley was then severely injured and rendered a paraplegic, after the car went out of control on the road. Held: the warning that the car came with all faults discharged the seller's duty, and subsequent injury to the buyer of the car did not give rise to an action in negligence.

Cases where liability will be found are likely to be ones where the consumer has been injured despite using the product in a reasonable and foreseeable way.

Grant v Australian Knitting Mills [1936] AC 85: Grant bought underwear in a shop, and soon afterwards began to suffer from skin irritation, which was caused by chemicals on the underwear, left over from the manufacturing process. It was shown that there would have been no problem if Grant had washed the underwear once before wearing it. Held: as there was no warning, when the product was sold, that initial washing would be necessary, liability in negligence was found.

What claims can be made

4.5 Any foreseeable victim of the defective product is within the scope of the duty, and may accordingly sue for personal injuries suffered. It is irrelevant whether that consumer bought the product in person, or was given it by a relative or friend (*Donoghue v Stevenson* [1932] AC 562). Products such as cars obviously carry risks not only to their users, but also to others on the scene when they are used. So if the claimant is injured in a car accident which can be traced to the poor state of another driver's car, the claimant may be able to sue the repairer of that car (*Stennett v Hancock* [1939] 2 All ER 578). Or if a poorly made tyre blows out while the car is going, all those injured as a result may sue (*Carroll v Fearon* [1999] ECC 73—a case where the accident occurred six years after the tyre was fitted!).

Haseldine v CA Daw & Son [1941] 2 KB 343: Haseldine was injured when a lift in which he was riding fell. The defect in the lift was traced to poor repair work done the day before. Held: the repairers owed a duty to all who used the defective lift.

An interesting case, on which differing opinions are held, pushes concepts of foresight to their limits.

Bhamra v Dubb t/a Lucky Caterers [2010] EWCA Civ 13: Dubb supplied food for a Sikh wedding. For ritual reasons, such food is forbidden to contain meat, fish or egg. Bhamra, a guest at the wedding, suffered an allergic reaction to some of the food served, and as a result died from anaphylactic shock; it emerged that this was the result of some egg having been included, and that this was the result of lack of care on Dubb's part. Bhamra was well aware of the risks his allergy posed, but had assumed that this food would be egg-free. Liability was established.

So those who suffer personal injury are well protected. However, the claim does not usually extend to cover purely economic losses (**5.7**).

Muirhead v Industrial Tank Specialities [1986] QB 507: Industrial Tank supplied Muirhead with electrical pumps, which he used for a tank containing lobsters. The pumps supplied were however designed to run at the wrong voltage. They cut out, and the lobsters died. Held: Muirhead could recover for loss of the lobsters (property damage) and loss of profit on them (economic loss consequential on property damage), but not for the cost of replacing the pumps (purely economic loss).

The line is sometimes hard to draw. In *M/S Aswan Engineering Establishment Co v Lupdine* [1987] 1 All ER 135 buckets supplied for carrying waterproofing compound overseas melted when left on a quayside in Kuwait, spilling their contents. For various reasons, it was held that the buckets could not be considered defective. If they had been, could their owner have recovered for the lost compound? The issue did not directly arise; there are *dicta* both ways ([1987] 1 WLR 1, 21, Lloyd LJ; 29, Nicholls LJ).

If the claimant notices the defect in the product before it has the chance to do anyone any harm, the claimant has no claim in tort. The loss suffered by that stage is purely economic (the product the claimant owns is less valuable than it would have been had the manufacturer acted carefully). If the claimant then proceeds to use the product anyway, a defence of *novus actus interveniens* (**10.36**) or contributory negligence (**11.17**) will meet any claim for later personal injury. If the claimant has a remedy at all in that situation, it will be by a contractual claim against whoever sold the claimant the goods.

Statute

4.6 Attempts to harmonize the law of products liability across the EU led in 1985 to a directive, requiring member states to enact a new regime of liability (Council Directive (EEC) 85/37 on liability for defective products). The directive was made part of UK law by the Consumer Protection Act 1987.

The Act is more technical than the directive, and rather restrictive in some of its provisions. Indeed, it has been suggested that the Act may put the UK in breach of its obligations under EU law, in not giving to consumers all the rights the directive intended them to receive. To date, however, the European Court of Justice has accepted no such argument. It has ruled in particular that the UK Government was entitled to introduce the 'development risk' defence protecting manufacturers who have complied with the best technical standards current at the time they made the product (see *EC Commission v United Kingdom*, **4.11** below). The Consumer Protection Act 1987 can therefore be taken as definitive for the present, although the directive can certainly be used as a guide to the Act's interpretation (see s 1(1)). As will become apparent, the Act does not cover all possible cases, and so the common law is not fully superseded in this area.

The main feature of the new regime is strict liability. The Mrs Donoghues of the 21st century may sue the manufacturer without having to prove either the existence of a duty or negligent behaviour. However, this principle is hedged around with various qualifications and defences, and considered overall, the new regime is not noticeably more generous than the old. In particular, the problems faced by the claimant in proving that a product is 'defective' seem remarkably like the difficulties the claimant would earlier have had in establishing that the manufacturer was negligent (**4.10**).

What claims may be made

4.7 The law under the 1987 Act is essentially concerned with consumer safety, and as such the main type of claim envisaged is a claim for personal injury. Claims for property damage are permitted within limits, but the limits are narrower than those of the common law, thus preserving a role for the law of negligence in this area. The limits are designed to exclude both trivial claims and claims for injury to business property, while preserving the right for consumers to complain about property damage. Claims for property damage are barred unless they exceed £275 (s 5(4)). Further, the property concerned must both be 'ordinarily intended for private use, occupation or consumption' and 'intended by the person suffering the loss or damage mainly for his own private use, occupation or consumption' (s 5(3)). Claims for damage to the product itself, or to articles supplied along with the product, or claims for purely economic loss, are not recoverable at all (s 5(1), (2)).

Against whom may claims be made

4.8 The strict liability in the Act is aimed principally at the producer or manufacturer of the goods in question, rather than at intermediaries such as suppliers. However, there are often difficulties in establishing precisely who the producer is, or in taking legal action against them if they are not based within the EU. Accordingly, the Act casts the net wider. In addition to the producer, the following are also liable for defects in the products:

- Anyone who holds themselves out as the producer (s 2(2)(b)). So if a supermarket sells 'own brand' goods, they are liable for defects, whether or not they produced the goods themselves.

- Anyone who imports the goods into the EU (s 2(2)(c)). However, if the goods were merely imported from one EU country to another, only the manufacturer is liable, not the importer.

- Anyone who manufactures a defective component which is incorporated into the product; though the component manufacturer is responsible only for its own component, not the whole product into which it was incorporated (s 4(1)(f)).

A mere supplier of goods is not usually liable under the Act. However, suppliers are bound by the Act to keep records of the producers of goods they supply, and if they fail to hand over this information to the victim of a defective product when requested, they are themselves liable as producer (s 2(3)).

What is a 'product'

4.9 'Product' is defined broadly as including all goods (s 1(2)). 'Goods' may include 'substances, growing crops and things comprised in land by virtue of being attached to it' and 'any ship, aircraft or vehicle' (s 45(1)). It is not restricted to manufactured goods, but also includes goods produced by mining or quarrying (s 1(2)(b)). It also includes electricity (s 1(2)). Certain products are exempted from the scope of the Act:

• *Buildings* are 'goods' within the meaning of the Act, but nonetheless someone who does building work is only caught by the Act in so far as the work 'involves the provision of any goods to any person by means of their incorporation into the building' (s 46(3)). Cases where the supply involved 'the creation or disposal of an interest in...land' are excluded (s 46(4)). The overall effect of these provisions is that consumers can complain that individual items incorporated into a building (such as doors or windows) are defective, but the Act cannot be used to complain that an entire building is a 'defective product'. In such a case the claimant would have to invoke the law of contract, or possibly the Defective Premises Act 1972 (**5.39**).

• *Books* are undoubtedly 'products', and presumably *computer programs* are too, at least if they are supplied on physical media such as a floppy disk or CD. It is, however, not clear at all whether damage caused by either is recoverable under the Act. Is information a 'product'? The issue has yet to be decided.

What is a 'defective' product

4.10 A product is defective 'if the safety of the product is not such as persons generally are entitled to expect' (s 3(1)). Matters stated in the Act to be relevant include:

• the way the product has been marketed, including 'its get-up' (s 3(2)(a));

• any instructions or warnings supplied with the goods (s 3(2)(a)); and

• 'what might reasonably be expected to be done with or in relation to the product' (s 3(2)(b)).

The burden of proof is on the claimant.

Foster v Biosil (2000) 59 BMLR 178: Foster received breast implants after a mastectomy. However, within seven months both implants had to be removed, one having ruptured and the other having started to leak silicone. It was never established how this happened, though the court was able to rule out negligence by the surgeon. Foster invited the court to infer that the implants were defective. Held: it was for the claimant to prove both that there was a defect and that it caused her injury, on the balance of probabilities. She had not done so, and accordingly her claim failed.

Plainly the Act does not mean that products must be *absolutely* safe, but only that they are as safe as reasonable people would expect. The test is designed to do many things at once. In particular, it seeks to encourage manufacturers to make goods safer, and accordingly provides that subsequent improvements to safety should not lead to the inference that the product was formerly unsafe (s 3(2)). And presumably, though the Act does not say so expressly, the cost of making the product safer is relevant.

In most situations, there does not appear to be a huge difference between asking whether a product is 'defective' under the Act, and asking whether the manufacturer was negligent at common law. However, the test is not what the manufacturer can reasonably do, but what the consumer can reasonably expect. In cases where the relevant risks should be well understood by the public, this comes to much the same thing.

> **Bogle v McDonald's Restaurants [2002] EWHC 490 (QB):** Bogle and others suffered serious injuries through spillages of hot coffee purchased at McDonald's. Held: it is common knowledge that hot drinks are dangerous if spilled. The public reasonably expect that precautions will be taken against this (by providing adequate cups and lids, as well as adequate staff training), but they do not expect to be guaranteed against any possibility of an accident. Claims under the Act and for negligence were accordingly rejected.

> **Tesco Stores v Pollard [2006] EWCA Civ 393:** A 13-month-old boy ingested dishwasher powder from a plastic bottle. It was alleged that the child-resistant closure cap on the bottle was not adequate. Held: people in general are entitled to expect that a child-resistant closure cap will be more difficult to open than an ordinary screw top, but the law goes no further. The bottle in question complied with that standard, and so no action lay.

But where the public are unaware of the risk, the difference between what the manufacturer can reasonably do, and what the consumer can reasonably expect, becomes more prominent.

> **A v National Blood Authority [2001] 3 All ER 289:** The claimants were infected with Hepatitis C as a result of transfusions of blood from donors who already had the virus. As was well known in medical circles, but was not then public knowledge, this risk was impossible to avoid, as the virus was undetectable in blood. Held: the infected blood was a 'defective product' under the Act.

Defences

4.11 Various matters amount to defences. Some arise under the general law. If the matter is in dispute, it would be for the claimant to prove a causal connection between the defect and the loss suffered (**10.21**). It is not clear whether remoteness is a defence under the Act. Contributory negligence by the claimant may lead to a reduction in damages (**11.17**). It is no defence that others contributed to the claimant's damage, though this might enable the defendant to claim contribution from those others (**9.26**). In addition, there are various special defences mentioned specifically in the Act:

- that the defect was attributable to the defendant's compliance with some requirement of the law (s 4(1)(a));
- that the defendant never in fact 'supplied' the product at all (s 4(1)(b)) (for example where it was stolen from the defendant);
- that the supply was not in the course of a business, and was not done with a view to profit (s 4(1)(c));
- that the defect did not exist at the time of the supply (s 4(1)(d));
- that the defect was effectively undiscoverable by producers of the type of goods concerned given 'the state of scientific and technical knowledge at the relevant time' (the 'development risk' defence) (s 4(1)(e)).

It is the last defence that is the most controversial. It is effectively a plea of lack of negligence at the design stage, so that the much-vaunted 'strict' liability under the Act is strict only as regards *production* defects, not *design* defects. In cases of design defects, then, the only difference effected by the Act has been to put the burden of proof onto the producer of the dangerous goods rather than the injured consumer. Yet the main economic justification of the Act was to place both the costs and the benefits of technical innovation on the shoulders of the manufacturers, whereas the 'development risk' defence seems to leave them with the benefits while placing the risks on the consumers of their products.

Many commentators have suggested that the 'development risk' defence enacted in the 1987 Act is broader than that contained in the directive it is meant to implement. The Act talks about the knowledge available *to manufacturers*, whereas the directive talks rather of the state of scientific and technical knowledge *generally*. The European Court of Justice has, however, now rejected this argument, while emphasizing that the UK courts will need to refer to the directive in deciding precisely how the Act should be interpreted (*EC Commission v United Kingdom* [1997] All ER (EC) 481). And the defence has been given a narrow interpretation in the UK courts. It was rejected in the *National Blood Authority* case (**4.10** above), as the risk of a defect was well known to the defendant. It was no answer to this that the risk could only be avoided by the (obviously impossible) strategy of refusing to supply any more blood to anyone until a test to detect the defect was available.

Road accidents

4.12 The roads are a major source of accidents. Indeed, they always were, even before the invention of the motor car. Under modern conditions they are all the more dangerous. And these accidents are very much the concern of tort law. Perhaps a quarter of a million people are injured on the roads each year, though most of these injuries are trivial. Perhaps one-quarter of all those injured in road traffic accidents take legal action. Nearly all of those who start a claim obtain damages of some sort. This suggests that the law is in practice highly predictable, with lawyers on both sides being able to tell with high reliability which claims have some prospect of success, and which ones are bound to fail.

There is surprisingly little to say about road traffic cases that is not true of negligence claims generally. They are simply the application of general principles to this one special, if rather common, case. Reported cases concentrate on the novel and the marginal. In particular, the courts are very reluctant to lay down precise rules as to the standards applicable to drivers. Indeed, judges who think that they have identified a hard rule are probably slipping to error.

> *Worsfold v Howe* **[1980] 1 All ER 1028:** Howe was attempting to turn right out of a minor road onto a major road; a petrol tanker which had stopped just to his right obscured his view. Inching his car forward, Howe collided with Worsfold's motorcycle, which was passing the tanker at an excessive speed. The trial judge considered both parties equally at fault, but thought himself bound by a rule that all someone in Howe's position is bound to do is to inch forward with all due care. Held: no such rule was apparent in the authorities, and so the judge should have found the parties equally liable.

It is significant that the Court of Appeal in the case was anxious not to retry it. 'I am not saying for a moment that if I myself had been trying this case I should have apportioned the responsibility fifty-fifty, but it is not possible for this court to go into the question of apportionment or alter the judge's view about that' ([1980] 1 All ER 1028, 1033, Browne LJ). There is little to say about these cases in very general terms; everything turns on the precise facts and circumstances, which are not very reportable. So this very major class of negligence litigation in fact appears in the law reports much less often than its importance suggests it should.

Emphasis on compensation, not deterrence

4.13 Ever since the Road Traffic Act 1930, car drivers have been required to be insured against possible tort claims that might result from poor driving on their part. Compulsory insurance for the population generally is therefore achieved, not by first party insurance (making pedestrians and drivers insure against possibility of injury to themselves), but by third party insurance (making wrongdoers insure so that they can pay damages to their victims). When compared to other areas of tort, the function of tort as insurance system is very much to the fore. Indeed, it is even proposed (under the fifth motor insurance directive (Directive (EC) 2005/14)) that drivers should be liable to cyclists involved in collisions with them, *even where* it is clear that the car driver was not at fault! The courts are noticeably more generous to claimants than they are in other areas, perhaps because they are far more concerned with the claimant's need for compensation than with determining whether to punish the defendant by imposing liability. As the claim will be met by the defendant's insurers, an order to pay damages is not much of a punishment; and if the defendant has behaved in a way meriting punishment, this can be done through the criminal law, and need not concern tort lawyers. Nonetheless, if tort law here operates as a system of insurance alone, it is a very imperfect system. The claim is still nominally based on the defendant's fault, and so if the claimant cannot prove fault in some shape or form the claimant will receive no compensation.

What of the claimant who cannot prove which driver inflicted the injuries, or where the driver at fault failed to purchase insurance? Before 1946, the claimant would have been without a remedy, but now under the Motor Insurers' Bureau (MIB) scheme, the claimant has a right to receive compensation from a fund established by the major insurance companies to cover this gap in insurance provision.

Application of negligence law

4.14 With the need to compensate the claimant very much to the fore, and questions of whether the defendant was morally to blame largely irrelevant, the courts apply ordinary negligence rules in a very generous spirit indeed. Many rulings are hard to make sense of as a moral judgement on the defendant's behaviour; making this sort of judgement does not seem to be what the court is about.

> *Roberts v Ramsbottom* **[1980] 1 All ER 7:** Ramsbottom suffered a stroke while at the wheel of his car. Out of control, the car crashed into another, injuring Roberts and others. Held: from an objective standpoint Ramsbottom's behaviour amounted to negligence, and accordingly he was liable for Roberts' injuries.

The court indicated that the case might have been different if Ramsbottom had become unconscious through his injuries. He would then have been in a state of 'automatism', and not responsible for his actions. But as he was in fact unable to control the car, it is not clear why it matters whether he was conscious or unconscious throughout. *Roberts* has been doubted, at least in cases where drivers are not aware of the disabilities that they are under (*Mansfield v Weetabix Ltd* [1998] 1 WLR 1263). But a similarly pro-claimant approach has been taken in other cases:

> **Nettleship v Weston [1971] 2 QB 691:** Nettleship, an experienced driver, was giving driving lessons to his friend Weston, a learner. On the third lesson, Weston failed to straighten out after turning left, mounted the curb and collided with a lamppost. Held: Nettleship could recover in negligence from Weston for his injuries, as she had failed to attain the standard to be expected of a reasonably experienced driver.

The latter result is surprising, as learner drivers can hardly be accused of concealing their lack of skill; the function of 'L'-plates is precisely to warn other road users that they are not reasonably skilled drivers. Ironically, the law insists that they advertise to the world that they do not have ordinary driving skills, yet regards them as negligent if they do not display those skills anyway! However, despite the marked generosity of the courts to claimants, the basic test is still whether negligence can be found. The courts have applied the negligence standard generously towards claimants, but it is still the negligence standard, and the claimant cannot recover unless the defendant was in some sense at fault.

Liability of occupiers to those on their land

4.15 The following sections deal with the liability of occupiers to those who suffer injury while on their land. The main focus is on personal injury, though many of the same principles apply to injury to property, as where a visitor tears her coat on a dangerously placed nail on the defendant's premises.

In the 19th century, the common law developed an elaborate scheme of different classes of entrants, the duty varying with each class. Modern cases and statutes have amalgamated several of these classes. The result is a simpler and rather more pro-claimant set of rules. It is still necessary, however, to distinguish between three classes of entrants:

- those to whom the defendant has given permission to enter the land ('visitors') (**4.16**);

- those who have a legal right to be on the land, regardless of the defendant's permission (**4.21**); and

- those who entered with neither permission nor a legal right to enter ('trespassers') (**4.26**).

Liability of occupiers to their visitors

4.16 The law here was much simplified by the Occupiers' Liability Act 1957. This Act provides that the occupier of premises owes a 'common duty of care' to all visitors. This duty is stated in terms which are very similar to the common law negligence duty. The duty applies quite generally, in contrast to the earlier law, which distinguished different categories of visitors. The duty arises in tort even when there is a contract between the defendant and the claimant relating to the claimant's admission to the premises. Indeed, it has been held (controversially) that the tortious duty in that situation is quite independent from any contractual duty of care (*Sole v WJ Hallt* [1973] QB 574). The pre-1957 law distinguished not only between different classes of visitors, but also between the 'occupancy duty' relating to the state of the premises and the 'activity duty' relating to what the defendant did there. Most commentators now agree that all of this has been swept away, as indeed the wording of the Act suggests: the Act governs in its entirety.

'Premises'

4.17 The duty is imposed on the occupier of 'premises'. This word includes everything which is within the ordinary meaning of the expression, and more. It seems that any piece of real property is caught. The Act itself says that it applies to 'any fixed or moveable structure, including any vessel, vehicle or aircraft' (s 1(3)(a)); so the duty that car drivers owe to their passengers could technically be described as an occupier's duty. More generally, it seems to be a matter of degree what can be regarded as 'premises'. A tunnel-cutting machine has been so regarded (*Bunker v Charles Brand & Sons* [1969] 2 QB 480). The state of 'premises' may include the state of articles on it, such as a ladder (*Wheeler v Copas* [1981] 3 All ER 405); though the court doubted whether a ladder could itself constitute 'premises'.

'Occupier'

4.18 The 'occupier' of premises is the person who has the legal right of control over it. This is logical enough: the Act imposes the duty on the person legally entitled to do something about the state of the premises and the activities carried on there.

> ***Wheat v E Lacon & Co* [1966] AC 552:** Lacon & Co owned a pub, which they hired a manager to run. The premises included a private flat, which the manager was entitled to occupy and to use for paying guests. One such guest fell down an unlit defective staircase in the flat. Held: as Lacon & Co had the legal right to control the flat, they were its occupier, and so were liable in respect of the state of the premises.

The emphasis here is on the *legal right* of control, rather than actual control. Lacon & Co were held responsible because they had retained the legal right to do repairs on the flat. It might have been different if they had leased the flat to the manager and entirely relinquished legal control over it. So it is perfectly possible for the defendant to be held to be 'in control' of premises, on the ground that he *ought* to be in control, even though in fact no-one is in control. Abandoned premises may therefore still have an 'occupier' for this purpose.

> ***Harris v Birkenhead Corpn* [1976] 1 All ER 341:** As part of a slum-clearance scheme, Birkenhead Corporation served a notice on a house, requiring the tenant to vacate the property. The tenant did so; however, the corporation did not follow its usual policy of bricking up such premises. Harris, 4½, entered the premises and fell out of a top-story window. Acting through her mother, she sued the tenant, the landlord and the corporation. Held: only the corporation was 'occupier' and therefore liable to Harris.

However, there is no rule that only one person may be occupier at any one time; indeed, a majority of the House of Lords in *Lacon* considered that the manager of the pub was also 'occupier' for the purposes of the Act. Where occupancy is shared in this way, the rule seems to be that each occupier is under a duty, though the duty is not necessarily the same: the greater the degree of *actual* control, the higher the duty (*AMF International v Magnet Bowling* [1968] 2 All ER 789). Or again, if there is a clear division of labour between occupiers as to responsibility for different aspects of the premises, the duty may be split in the same way.

> ***Collier v Anglian Water Authority* (1983) Times, 26 March:** Collier was injured while walking along a seaside promenade, the injury being attributable to the state of repair of the promenade. The promenade was controlled jointly by the water authority, as it formed part of the area's sea defences, and the local authority, who swept up accumulated rubbish. Held: as Collier's injuries were attributable to the state of the promenade rather than to rubbish, it was the water authority which was liable, and not the local authority.

'Visitors'

Persons with express permission to enter

4.19 The most obvious members of the class of 'visitors' are those who have been given express permission to come onto the land. It does not matter today whether this permission was granted as part of a contract with the occupier; the duty is the same either way (s 5(1)). Where the occupier places some limit on the permission, the entrant becomes a trespasser when the limit is exceeded. So permission to enter for a short time does not justify an indefinite stay. 'When you invite a person into your house to use the staircase, you do not invite him to slide down the banisters, you invite him to use the staircase in the ordinary way in which it is used' (*The Calgarth* [1927] P 93, 110, Scrutton LJ).

Persons with implied permission to enter

4.20 Permission to enter the land need not be given in any particular form. So if it is clear that the occupier is extending permission to the claimant to enter, the claimant will be a visitor when he or she enters, whatever the occupier may or may not have said. In particular, it will usually be assumed that anyone who wishes to talk to the occupier has implied permission to come onto the land to call on him. If in fact certain types of enquiries are not welcome, the occupier must make this clear in advance (e.g. by posting a notice saying 'No Canvassers').

Difficult questions can arise where the occupier knows that the claimant has entered or plans to enter, but says nothing. Cases early in the 20th century seem very willing to infer that permission has been given, even where the occupier had earlier made determined but futile attempts to keep people out (e.g. *Lowery v Walker* [1911] AC 10). The courts seemed particularly anxious to hold that children entering the land had implied permission, especially where there was some sort of 'allurement' which children found particularly attractive (e.g. poisonous berries, *Glasgow Corporation v Taylor* [1922] 1 AC 44). No doubt this attitude of the courts had much to do with the fact that trespassers could not sue the occupier no matter how shocking the latter's neglect of their safety. Now that trespassers have a right to sue (**4.26**), we can expect that the courts will not strain to find an implied permission where none is very obvious. Nonetheless, the courts still show some generosity here. So, for example, if the defendant hands over the management of land to X, who then lets in the claimant, it may be held that the claimant has the defendant's implied permission to be there—even if the defendant made it clear to X that the claimant was not to be let in (*Ferguson v Welsh* [1987] 3 All ER 777, 785, Lord Goff).

Persons with a right to enter

4.21 What if the claimant has a right to enter the land, but nonetheless does not have the occupier's permission? The Occupiers' Liability Act 1957 itself states that anyone who enters land under a right conferred by law is to be treated as a visitor (s 2(6)). So if the defendant carelessly starts a fire on his land and the claimant, a firefighter, is burned while putting it out, the defendant is liable for the claimant's injuries

(*Ogwo v Taylor* [1988] AC 431). This is the general rule. But a few cases fall outside the scope of the Act. Users of rights of way across the land are not 'visitors', whether the right of way is private (*Holden v White* [1982] QB 679) or public (*Greenhalgh v British Railways Board* [1969] 2 QB 286). And by s 1(4), the Act does not apply in favour of those who enter the land under an access agreement or by virtue of an order under the National Parks and Access to the Countryside Act 1949. (See also Countryside and Rights of Way Act 2000, s 13.) The precise duty that is owed at common law under these circumstances is not entirely clear. What little case law there is suggests that the occupier of the land is bound to abstain from positive, dangerous acts, but is not liable for failure to act. In other words, the occupier is liable for 'misfeasance' but not for 'nonfeasance'. So if the claimant is injured on a public right of way going across the defendant's land, the claimant has no right to complain that the defendant should have maintained the right of way (*McGeown v Northern Ireland Housing Executive* [1995] 1 AC 233). In some of these cases, the duty is the same as that owed to trespassers (**4.26**); but the limits of this are unclear, and certainly those using the highway are not so protected (Occupiers' Liability Act 1984, s 1(7)).

The standard of care

4.22 The occupier of premises owes visitors the 'common duty of care' (Occupiers' Liability Act 1957, s 2(1)). This is a duty 'to take such care as in all the circumstances of the case is reasonable to see that the visitor will be reasonably safe in using the premises for the purposes for which he is invited or permitted by the occupier to be there' (s 2(2)). The burden of proof is on the claimant to demonstrate that the duty has been broken. The test is the same as in negligence generally (**3.8**). Relevant factors include the size of the risk, and the cost and practicability of taking precautions against it.

> **Simms v Leigh Rugby Football Club [1969] 2 All ER 923:** In the course of a rugby game, Simms was tackled, breaking his leg, allegedly after coming into contact with a concrete wall slightly over seven feet from the touchline. Held: even if he in fact hit the wall, this was such an unlikely event as to be unforeseeable by the occupier of the ground, and so it was not liable to him.

This does not mean, however, that the claimant must necessarily show precisely how the accident happened; it is enough that the defendant was probably to blame.

> **Ward v Tesco Stores [1976] 1 All ER 219:** Ward was injured when she slipped on some yoghurt spilled on the floor of Tesco, where she was shopping. Tesco gave evidence that the floor was generally brushed six times a day, and that staff were instructed

to deal with spillages if they saw them. Held (by a majority): there was sufficient evidence of negligence, and in the absence of explanation Tesco would be held liable.

Compare:

Tedstone v Bourne Leisure Ltd [2008] EWCA Civ 654: Tedstone was injured when she slipped on a puddle of water near a jacuzzi on Bourne's premises. There was evidence that Bourne knew that some areas held water and needed repair. Held: it was clear that the water came from an unusual spillage which could only have happened one or two minutes before Tedstone's accident. No conceivable reasonable system could have dealt with the spillage in the time available, and accordingly there was no liability.

Care expected from visitors

4.23 The occupier is bound to take due care for the visitor, but the visitor too is expected to exercise due care. Accordingly, in assessing the steps the owner is bound to take, the court will have regard to what visitors should reasonably be expected to do for themselves. So the content of the duty depends on 'the degree of care, and of want of care, which would ordinarily be looked for in such a visitor' (s 2(3)).

This is a principle of general application. (For an example see the 'Bouncy Castle' case, *Harris v Perry* [2008] EWCA Civ 907.) The Act mentions two special cases by way of example.

• *Children*. The occupier 'must be prepared for children to be less careful than adults' (s 2(3)(a)). So the occupier must make allowances for behaviour which would be unreasonable in adults. In particular, the defendant must make allowances for so-called 'allurements', which might attract children but not adults; poisonous berries are an obvious example (*Glasgow Corpn v Taylor* [1922] 1 AC 44). Nonetheless, the courts are reluctant to put the onus for children's safety entirely onto the occupiers of land they happen to wander onto. 'It would not be socially desirable if parents were, as a matter of course, able to shift the burden of looking after their children from their own shoulders to those of persons who happen to have accessible bits of land' (*Phipps v Rochester Corpn* [1955] 1 QB 450, 472, Devlin J). Note, however, that in *Phipps* Devlin J nonetheless found liability, in a case where the claimant fell into a trench on the defendant's land. The existence of the trench would have been obvious to an adult, but Devlin J held that the occupier owed a duty to the five-year-old claimant to guard him against it. Where dangers should have been obvious to the defendants but also to the children's parents, the courts are reluctant to find liability (see e.g. *Bourne Leisure Ltd v Marsden* [2009] EWCA 671).

• *Workers*. Conversely, those who come on to the premises to do a job of some sort are expected to know the risks, and how to minimize them. The occupier 'may expect that a person, in the exercise of his calling, will appreciate and guard against any special risks ordinarily incident to it, so far as the occupier leaves him free to do so' (s 2(3)(b)). So it has been held that a claim by chimney sweeps against a householder for dangers arising from fumes was not available (*Roles v Nathan* [1963] 2 All ER 908). Likewise, we would not expect electricians to have much success in suing for injuries caused by bare live wires. However, this is not a blanket defence to all risks which the claimant ought to anticipate, if in fact there is little the claimant can do about them. So where the defendant carelessly starts a fire on its premises and the claimant is injured fighting the fire, the defendant cannot defeat the claim merely by saying that the risk is inherent in the job of a firefighter (*Salmon v Seafarer Restaurants* [1983] 3 All ER 729).

So the safety of visitors is, in fact, the joint responsibility of the occupier and of the visitors themselves. The precise balance between the two can only be settled by looking at all relevant circumstances. In cases where the balance is nearly even, the court can resolve the matter by means of the defence of contributory negligence, which allows the court to reduce the damages by whatever amount seems fair in the light of the visitor's own responsibility for the accident (see **11.17** below).

> **Brannan v Airtours** (1999) **Times, 1 February:** While at a party on a package tour organized by Airtours, Brannan suffered injuries after standing on a table and colliding with a fan 7½ feet above the floor. The organizers had earlier warned guests not to stand on the tables. Held: given the nature of the event (a dinner disco with unlimited free wine), and given that the organizers had made no attempt to prevent other guests from climbing on the tables, a breach of duty was found. However, damages would be reduced by 50 per cent for Brannan's own contributory negligence.

Liability for misconduct by others

4.24 The duty owed by the occupier to the visitor is non-delegable. That is to say, if no due care was in fact taken of the claimant, it is no defence that the defendant had done his best to make sure that care would be provided. Suppose that a court holds that the claimant, who is 10 years old, would only have been reasonably safe on the defendant's land if the defendant had provided some sort of supervision. If the defendant did not in fact provide supervision, it is no defence that the defendant had made reasonable efforts to hire a supervisor, or that the supervisor failed to turn up at work through no fault of the defendant's. This matter is dealt with in greater detail below (**9.24**); it is important, because many occupiers are companies, which cannot 'personally' look after the claimant's safety, but must necessarily act through others. In addition, an occupier may be vicariously liable for misconduct by one of its own employees (**9.2**). What if the danger to the claimant arose from misconduct of some independent contractor? In that situation, the defendant is not directly liable for the contractor's misbehaviour; however, the defendant cannot wash their hands of the matter simply by entrusting it to a contractor. The defendant is expected to use all due care in selecting an appropriate contractor; the defendant is also expected to make reasonable checks that the work has been done properly (s 2(4)(b)). Accordingly, if the claimant is injured as a result of poor workmanship by an independent contractor, the claimant may sometimes be able to sue the occupiers as well as the contractor, but only by showing that the occupiers were themselves at fault.

> ***Gwilliam v West Hertfordshire Hospitals NHS Trust* [2002] EWCA Civ 1041:** A hospital trust running a fund-raising fair hired an independent contractor to organize a 'splat-wall', by which participants would bounce from a trampoline and adhere to a wall by Velcro. The contractor assured the hospital that it was properly insured. Injuries resulted from the contractor's poor arrangement of the trampoline. However, the contractor's public liability insurance had expired four days before the accident. Held: the hospital's duty to its visitors included a duty to enquire into the insurance position, so that its interests would be safeguarded in the event of an accident. However, it was unreasonable to expect the hospital to have checked the actual policy document. The duty was not broken, and the claim failed.

Warnings and exclusions

4.25 The basic principle is that if the defendant gives the claimant a warning of the danger, which gives the claimant a fair chance to escape it, then the defendant will not be liable. However, there are actually quite a number of different legal rules at work here, and it is important not to confuse them. Suppose the defendant warns the claimant of a danger, to which the claimant subsequently succumbs. What defences will the defendant raise?

• *Satisfaction of duty.* The defendant may argue that the only thing the reasonable occupier could be expected to do in that situation was to give a warning, and so, having given that warning, the defendant has done everything the duty requires (e.g. *Titchener v British Railways Board* [1983] 3 All ER 770). The Act itself makes it clear that this is a perfectly good argument, provided that the warning was 'in all the circumstances... enough to enable the visitor to be reasonably safe' (s 2(4)(a)). Where the defendant provides facilities for the claimant to engage in obviously risky activities, difficult questions can arise as to the extent of the defendant's duty to advise and to supervise, though it is clear that the defendant will not be held liable in respect of risks of which the claimant was entirely aware (*Poppleton v Trustees of the Portsmouth Youth Activities Committee* [2008] EWCA Civ 646).

• *Consent.* The defendant may argue that the claimant agreed to run the risk (s 2(5)). Agreements of that sort usually have to be express, though in extreme cases the claimant may be held to have agreed impliedly to run a risk which was very obvious (**11.6**).

• *Causation or remoteness.* The defendant may argue that the claimant's decision to ignore the risk was unforeseeable, or at least broke the chain of causation and relieved the defendant of responsibility for the consequences which followed (**10.35**). This argument is unlikely to succeed unless the claimant's conduct was irrational and reckless in the extreme.

> **Sayers v Harlow UDC [1958] 1 WLR 623:** Sayers became trapped in a public lavatory because the cubicle's lock was defective. After shouting for help for 10 or 15 minutes, she attempted to climb out, and injured herself in the process. Held: the occupiers of the premises were liable for her injuries, though the damages would be reduced by 25 per cent for contributory negligence. 'I do not think that the plaintiff should be adjudged in all the circumstances to have acted unreasonably or rashly or stupidly...Indeed, she showed a very considerable measure of self-control' ([1958] 1 WLR 623, 631–2, Morris LJ).

• *Contributory negligence.* The defendant may argue that the claimant is partly to blame for the accident, through the failure to heed the warning. The effect of this argument is only to reduce the claimant's damages, not eliminate the claim entirely, and so does not take extraordinarily strong facts to back it up (**11.17**).

• *Exclusion of liability.* The defendant may argue that a warning of danger constituted an exclusion of the defendant's liability. The relevant principles are discussed below (**11.2**); where the premises are business premises, the argument is almost certain to fail.

The law is rather elaborate here, arguably too elaborate; it is trying to achieve a number of different objectives. The main point is perhaps that warnings can take many forms. At one extreme, the defendant may warn the claimant of the precise danger to which the claimant ultimately fell victim; in a case like that, the defendant will have a serious argument that the injuries are the claimant's own fault. At the other, the defendant has simply posted a notice disclaiming all responsibility for the state of the premises. Notices of that sort, which are of no help at all in enabling the claimant to avoid the danger, are generally ineffective today.

Liability of occupiers to trespassers

4.26 Until recent years, the general position was that no duty was owed to trespassers, unless the occupiers recklessly injured a trespasser they knew to be present (*Robert Addie & Sons (Collieries) v Dumbreck* [1929] AC 358). Some particularly deserving claimants had a remedy found for them by devious means: so, for example, the courts were very willing to find that young children were not trespassers at all, even in cases where the defendant had expressly prohibited them from coming onto the land.

The decisive break came in 1972, when the House of Lords held that there *was* a duty owed to trespassers. This was not the 'common duty of care' in the Occupiers' Liability Act 1957, but a 'duty of common humanity' which provided for a bare minimum of care (*British Railways Board v Herrington* [1972] AC 877). This duty was restated and extended in the Occupiers' Liability Act 1984, which is now the governing legislation.

The duty is somewhat similar to the duty owed to visitors. Nonetheless, much less care is owed. Injuries caused to adult trespassers who well knew that they had no business to be on the defendant's land are likely to receive little sympathy; though even there, liability may be found if the facts are strong enough. The duty does not extend to protect the trespasser's property (s 1(8)); so while an injured trespasser may possibly have an action against the occupier on the principles discussed in this section, there can be no action for a trespasser's ripped or damaged clothing.

Duty

4.27 Rather than the general duty owed to visitors under the 1957 Act, the duty under the 1984 Act is more narrowly focused. It is not a general duty to look after the trespasser's safety, but a duty in respect of particular dangers. The duty is owed to a trespasser only if three conditions are satisfied (s 1(3)):

    (a) the occupier knows of the danger, or has reasonable grounds to know it exists;

    (b) the occupier knows the trespasser is, or may in the future, come into the vicinity of the danger, or has reasonable grounds to know it; and

    (c) it is reasonable to expect the occupier to offer some protection to the trespasser against the risk.

The general lines of this are clear: the duty is a duty to act reasonably in the light of what the occupier knows. It seems that a restrictive scope will be given to the duty.

So where on 27 December the claimant dives off a slipway and into a harbour, it was held that the harbour owner owed no duty: it was unforeseeable that anyone would trespass this way, even though similar conduct in summer might be entirely fore-seeable (*Donoghue v Folkestone Properties Ltd* [2003] EWCA Civ 231). And even in the case of child claimants, the courts have been unresponsive: so in a case where the defendant occupiers knew that children played on their premises, an action by an 11-year-old boy failed, the court arguing that any danger to the boy was caused by his own actions rather than by anything to do with the state of the premises (*Keown v Coventry Healthcare NHS Trust* [2006] EWCA Civ 39).

No doubt in time the bare bones of the statute will be fleshed out by case law. One issue which will need to be resolved is the scope of *(a)*: in particular, to what extent it imposes a duty on the occupier to check the premises for dangers. Or (to put it the other way around), to what extent does the statute allow the occupier to leave his own land well alone, at least if he has no lawful visitors? Proving that the occupier is, or should be, aware of trespassers (requirement *(b)*) is usually difficult. The Court of Appeal has refused to assume that an occupier who took steps to keep out tres-passers necessarily fell within requirement *(b)*. Whether the requirement is satisfied 'had to be answered by looking at the actual state of affairs on the ground when the injury was met with' (*White v St Albans City and District Council* (1990) Times, 12 March, Neill LJ).

(On the special situation where a trespasser is injured by an animal on the defend-ant's land, see below, **7.47**.)

Standard of care

4.28 Unlike the general duty owed to visitors, the duty owed to trespassers is specific to the danger. The claimant will only have been able to establish a duty *in respect of a particular danger* (**4.27**). But if the claimant has done this, then the content of the duty is straightforward: it is 'to take such care as is reasonable in all the circum-stances of the case to see that [the trespasser] does not suffer injury on the premises by reason of the danger concerned' (s 1(4)). This is obviously in many respects simi-lar to the duty owed to visitors. Much that is stated in the 1957 Act is left unstated in the 1984 Act, though probably the courts will imply it anyway. In particular, presumably they will hold that the occupier 'must be prepared for children to be less careful than adults', just as under the 1957 Act (**4.23**).

> ***Ratcliff v McConnell* [1999] 1 WLR 670:** Ratcliff and friends, all students at the defend-ant college, decided after a night of drinking to dive into the college's (locked) swimming pool. Ratcliff dived into the shallow end, hit the bottom, and suffered injuries leading to tetraplegia. Held: the danger should have been apparent to any adult, drunk or sober.

There was no breach of duty and, even if there had been, Ratcliff had consented to run the risk involved.

As is always the case in negligence, the claimant can only establish liability by showing both that there is something the defendant should have done *and* that it would have made a difference (the requirement of causation, on which see in detail **10.21** below).

> **Tomlinson v Congleton Borough Council [2003] UKHL 47:** The occupiers of a disused quarry, known to attract many visitors in hot weather, erected prominent notices saying 'Dangerous water: No swimming' next to a lake in the quarry. Tomlinson, aged 18, dived from a standing position, struck his head on the sandy bottom, and was rendered tetraplegic. Held: Tomlinson's injuries were not caused by the state of the premises or by any conduct of the occupiers, but by his own misjudgement. There was no liability, and indeed there might not have been liability even had he been a lawful visitor in the lake.

An important unanswered question is whether the occupier can plead lack of resources as an answer to the claim. Before the Act, it was thought that lack of resources would be a defence here (*British Railways Board v Herrington* [1972] AC 877, 899, Lord Reid), even though it is not usually a defence in negligence (**1.41**). The matter is not addressed in the Act.

Warning and exclusions

4.29 Just as for the case of visitors, the law here is complex, though most of the complexities are the same as those for visitors (**4.25**). A warning alone may be sufficient to discharge the defendant's duty of care, if that is all that a reasonable person in the occupier's position would do (s 1(5)). In appropriate cases, the claim may be defeated by defences of consent (s 1(6)) (**11.2**) or contributory negligence (**11.17**), or by the doctrines of causation or remoteness (**10.35**). A difficult question is whether it is possible to apply the principles of exclusion (**11.13**), so that an occupier may avoid the duty entirely by posting a prominent notice denying the duty. The Act itself does not say either way. It would be very surprising if the duty could be excluded in this way, as by definition the defendant has already made it clear that the claimant should keep out. If posting a notice saying 'No Trespassers!' does not exclude the duty, why should a notice saying 'No Trespassers and No Civil Actions either!'? Yet there are still cases where it is possible to exclude the duty owed to lawful visitors (**11.14**), so why not to trespassers as well? The neatest solution, from a logical point of view, would be that the duty to trespassers is not excludable, and it applies *also* in favour of visitors against whom the normal duty is excluded—so the higher duty owed to visitors is sometimes excludable, the lower duty never. However, there is absolutely no warrant for this solution in the Acts themselves, and the matter remains shrouded in mystery.

Liability of non-occupiers to those on the land

4.30 Suppose the claimant is injured while lawfully on land, and wishes to sue the defendant, who is not the occupier, but is in some respect responsible for the state of the premises. Most of the law applicable in that situation has already been described. So if the claimant is injured by the activities of an independent contractor on the land, the claimant's action against the contractor is the standard negligence action against those who engage in dangerous activities. In the early 20th century, judges were reluctant to allow action against builders and others whose carelessness had injured those other than the current occupier (e.g. *Bottomley v Bannister* [1932] 1 KB 458), but any immunity they may have had is now abolished by statute. The careless builder is liable for negligence even if the premises have since changed hands (Defective Premises Act 1972, s 3(1)).

> ***Rimmer v Liverpool City Council* [1985] QB 1:** Shortly after moving into his new council flat, the tenant complained of a particularly dangerous panel of breakable glass, which he argued was a danger to his young son. He was told that it was a standard installation, and could not be changed. Nineteen months later, his son was injured by putting his hand through it. Held: the council was liable for negligence, in its capacity as designer and builder of the flats.

However, there is still a reluctance to allow action against builders for purely economic losses; after the *Murphy* decision (**5.4**), action lies under statute, if at all.

Landlords

4.31 At common law, it was almost impossible to sue landlords in tort for injuries to those on the premises (e.g. *Cavalier v Pope* [1906] AC 428). Today, action can be maintained in two situations.

- *Landlord created the danger* (e.g. *Rimmer v Liverpool City Council* (**4.30**)).

- *Landlord under a duty to repair.* By statute, a landlord who is bound to repair owes a duty to all who might reasonably be expected to be affected by defects in the premises (Defective Premises Act 1972, s 4(1)). The duty applies in all cases where the landlord knew of the defect, or ought to have known of it (s 4(2)). Note that in the case of residential leases of less than seven years, there is a statutory obligation on the landlord to repair (Landlord and Tenant Act 1985, ss 11, 12;

and see Housing Act 1988, s 16), and so the negligence duty applies. Even if the landlord is not bound to repair, nonetheless if the landlord has power to enter and repair, a duty of care is owed to everyone except the tenant (s 4(4)). However, the duty is only a duty of reasonable care. In particular, where landlords are accused of performing repairs in an unsafe way, they are entitled to be judged by standards of safety applicable at the time they did the work, not by hindsight (*Adams v Rhymney Valley District Council* (2000) 33 HLR 446). Further, the duty does not extend to design defects in the property: if the property is in good repair, the landlord is not required to correct items not in disrepair, even if a good case can be made that they are unsafe.

> **Alker v Collingwood Housing Association [2007] EWCA Civ 343:** Alker was badly injured when she accidentally put her hand through a glass panel in her front door. The panel consisted of ordinary glass only; however, it was undamaged before the accident, and compliant with building regulations at the time the house was built. Held: the door was not defective in any relevant sense, and so no action lay for leaving it in that condition.

Employers' liability

4.32 The liability of employers to their employees is ancient. But for most of its history, the potential of the law of negligence to protect employees from workplace accidents was held back by the existence of very broad defences. Since the 1940s, the defences have been considerably narrowed, and in some instances abolished. Liability insurance, already very common, was made compulsory by the Employers' Liability (Compulsory Insurance) Act 1969. (The governing legislation is now the Employers' Liability (Compulsory Insurance) Regulations 1998.)

Employers' liability is now one of the most important heads of negligence liability. The total number of work injuries in any one year is probably about 500,000. Perhaps 10 per cent of those injured at work obtain tort-based compensation for it; the more serious the injury, the more likely is the victim to consider legal action.

The privileged position of employees

4.33 The liability described in this section is in favour of employees only, not other grades of workers. (For the precise distinction between 'employees' and other workers, see **9.4**.) The protection afforded to other workers is distinctly less generous, though far from useless in all situations. Some, but by no means all, of the industrial safety legislation applies to other workers as well as to employees. The negligence duty discussed in this section does not apply, but in the case of an injury on work premises, a similar duty will be owed under the law of occupiers' liability (**4.16**). In other areas, the courts have sometimes drawn analogies with the employer–employee relation to describe similar duties (e.g. *Beasley v Buckinghamshire County Council* [1997] PIQR P473, local authority–foster parent).

The duty generally

4.34 Employees are entitled to expect from their employer that reasonable care will be taken to ensure their safety. The duty is imposed by the law of negligence and is not absolute; the general principles of negligence liability need to be borne in mind. It is usual today to consider the employer's duty under four heads:

- the duty to provide safe premises;
- the duty to provide safe plant, materials and equipment;
- the duty to provide competent staff; and
- the duty to institute safe work practices.

These are not, however, distinct duties, but rather different aspects of the same duty. 'They lie within, and exemplify, the broader duty of taking reasonable care for the safety of his workmen which rests on every employer' (*Winter v Cardiff RDC* [1950] 1 All ER 819, 823, Lord MacDermott). Very often, what is in essence the same complaint can be raised under various different heads. So a complaint by the claimant that she suffers from Repetitive Strain Injury (RSI) as a result of using machines in the defendant's office can be put in various ways. It may sometimes be put as a complaint that the equipment provided is not reasonably safe. In other cases it may be better to plead it as a case about poor work practices, as where the defendant did not provide proper breaks from using the machine, or proper training or medical care. *There is only one duty, namely to take reasonable precautions to ensure the claimant's safety.*

The duty is quite independent of statutory duties on the employer. If the employer is in breach of the common law duty, it is no answer that the employer has done everything that statute requires in the matter, even if the statute addresses the very danger to which the claimant succumbed (*Bux v Slough Metals* [1974] 1 All ER 262).

The duty cannot be delegated

4.35 The claimant is entitled only to a reasonably safe working environment, not an absolutely safe one. However, if the environment is not reasonably safe, it is no defence that this was the fault of someone other than the claimant's employer. This is sometimes summed up by saying that the duty is non-delegable (**9.22**). So if the claimant is injured by the acts of a fellow employee, it is usually possible to argue that the employer is liable directly, without having to argue that the employer is vicariously liable for the other employee's behaviour. The principle is most important in the case where the employer temporarily posts an employee to another firm. Assuming that the relationship of employer and employee continues, then so does the duty, even though the employer may have no control over the employee's work environment.

> ***McDermid v Nash Dredging and Reclamation Co* [1987] AC 906:** McDermid was injured when the tug on which he was working as a deckhand started unexpectedly. He was pulled into the water, suffering a serious leg injury as a result. The accident was the fault of the tug's master, who was employed not by McDermid's employer but by the employer's parent company. Held: McDermid's employers were liable for his injury.

The result in *McDermid* is unsurprising. The claimant and the man who injured him were part of the same small work team, and to refuse the claimant a remedy merely because they have different employers sounds like a rather undeserving technicality, given that both employers were part of the same group. However, the reason given for imposing liability—that the employer's duty is not delegable—is plainly capable of applying in other cases, and it is not clear to what extent it will be applied. In the earlier case of *Davie v New Merton Board Mills* [1959] AC 604, the claimant was injured by defective equipment while at work; the equipment had been negligently made, but it was not reasonably possible for the claimant's employer to spot the defect. On those facts, the House of Lords refused to find the claimant's employers in breach of their obligations. This approach clearly conflicts with that taken in *McDermid*; it was not commented on by the Lords in *McDermid*, perhaps because it has been reversed on its facts by statute (**4.38**). It is an open question how far each approach will be taken. The signs are that the courts are very reluctant to find employers liable in a case where in reality they have no control at all over the claimant's safety (e.g. *Square D v Cook* [1992] IRLR 34).

Safety in all respects?

4.36 Nearly all of the cases involve threats to employees' health through physical impact of some kind, as whether the claimant accidentally comes into contact with dangerous machinery. In principle, however, any threat to the claimant's physical health is within the law. Claims for illness caused by work conditions are perfectly standard, though they are usually hard to prove. Claims for nervous shock (**3.18**) may also be brought. In exceptional circumstances, it is even possible to sue for the consequences of extreme stress due to work conditions.

> **Walker v Northumberland County Council [1995] 1 All ER 737:** Walker, a social services manager, suffered a nervous breakdown through overwork. He returned to work after his employers gave him specific promises of extra assistance. The promises were broken, and six months after his return he suffered a second breakdown which permanently disabled him from working. Held: his employers were liable for the consequences of the second breakdown.

Now that claims of this sort are becoming more common, the Court of Appeal has attempted to lay down general guidelines (in *Hatton v Sutherland* [2002] EWCA Civ 76). The court stressed that the ordinary principles of employers' liability applied. Employers were entitled to assume that employees could withstand the ordinary pressures of the job, but could be liable if they knew or should have known of a particular problem or vulnerability; and the courts have not been very receptive when employers argue that while extreme stress was foreseeable, illness resulting from stress was not (*Dickins v O2 plc* [2008] EWCA Civ 1144). Capacity to resist stress varies, and employers must heed warning signs from those who are less able (*Barber v Somerset County Council* [2004] UKHL 13). Whether the action then taken in response to warning signs is reasonable will depend on all the circumstances of the case.

> **Daw v Intel Corporation (UK) [2007] EWCA Civ 70:** After a period of heavy overload at work, Daw discussed her situation with one of her managers. Extra help was promised, and the company provided a confidential counselling service for its employees. Daw nonetheless suffered depression, leading to a suicide attempt. Held: Intel was liable. While earlier cases had stressed that provision of counselling services might be a reasonable response in such cases, there was no magic formula, and each case must be judged on its merits. Here the danger to Daw's health was obvious, and the company's response clearly inadequate—the promise of extra help was never honoured.

However, there is no claim for purely economic loss based on the employer–employee duty (*Reid v Rush & Tompkins Group* [1989] 3 All ER 228). Such a claim is only justified either on normal principles (**5.1**; e.g. *Lennon v Metropolitan Police Commissioner* [2004] EWCA Civ 130, **5.22**), or through the law of contract (e.g. *Scally v Southern Health and Social Services Board* [1992] 1 AC 294).

The duty in detail

Safe premises

4.37 The place of work must be maintained in a reasonably safe condition. In many respects this aspect of the employer's duty is no different from that of an occupier to his or her visitors generally (**4.16**). But the fact that the claimant is there to work is of course one factor in what it is reasonable to expect by way of provision for safety. Where there is a known source of danger, the employer is required to act reasonably in the face of it, and the court will pay attention to the practicality of the various options available.

> **Latimer v AEC [1953] AC 643:** The floor of a factory became wet and slippery through flooding. The owner put down sawdust, but did not have enough to cover the entire floor. Latimer, an employee, slipped on a wet patch and injured himself. Held: the employer had done everything possible short of temporarily shutting the factory, which in the circumstances would have been an overreaction. Accordingly, Latimer could not sue for his injuries.

It has even been held that the employer may be under a duty to dismiss the claimant employee, if the risk to the employee's health is substantial and cannot otherwise be avoided (*Coxall v Goodyear Great Britain Ltd* [2002] EWCA Civ 1010).

Very often, the nature of the job requires the claimant to work in an inherently unsafe position. In cases of that sort, the duty is likely to require that the employer provide instruction and safety equipment. Where the danger is obvious and easy to avoid, it is possible that a court might be persuaded that any accident to the claimant was the claimant's own fault. But it would be unwise for an employer to rely on that.

> **General Cleaning Contractors v Christmas [1953] AC 180:** Christmas, an experienced window cleaner, was injured when the window he was cleaning suddenly and unexpectedly moved. He was not wearing a safety harness, because there was nowhere to which it could be attached at that location. Various precautions his employers could have taken to prevent such an accident were suggested. Held: failure to attach to the building hooks for a safety harness was not a breach of duty. However, his employers were in breach for (i) failure to warn their employees to test windows before cleaning them and (ii) failure to provide wedges to keep windows still.

Recall that the duty in negligence is owed to each individual claimant (*Paris v Stepney Borough Council* [1951] AC 367) (**3.8**), and accordingly the duty to relatively inexperienced employees may be higher than that owed to the experienced.

Safe plant, materials and equipment

4.38 Reasonable steps must also be taken to ensure that plant, materials and equipment also are reasonably safe for those working in their vicinity. The common law is here enhanced by the Employers' Liability (Defective Equipment) Act 1969, which provides (reversing *Davie v New Merton Board Mills* [1959] AC 604) that the employer is liable for equipment which is defective through the negligence of third parties. 'Equipment' is broadly defined in the Act as including 'any plant and machinery, vehicle, aircraft and clothing' (s 1(3)). The equipment must be 'provided by [the] employer for the purposes of the employer's business' (s 1(1)(a)). Case law has taken a broad view of the provision, making it clear that it covers not simply the tools the claimant uses, but also whatever the claimant was working on.

> ***Knowles v Liverpool City Council* [1994] 1 Lloyd's Rep 11:** Knowles, a labourer involved in repairing pavements, was manhandling a flagstone into the shovel of a JCB mechanical digger. The flagstone broke, injuring Knowles. The cause was a negligent defect in the manufacturing process, which Knowles' employers could not reasonably have discovered beforehand. Held: the flagstone was 'defective equipment' and so his employers were liable for his injuries. (Note also the possibility of an action against the manufacturers of the flagstone (**4.2**).)

It has also been held that a ship can be 'defective equipment' under the Act (*Coltman v Bibby Tankers* [1988] AC 276).

Difficult questions sometimes arise here where the equipment the claimant uses cannot do the job, because the claimant is using it for a job it was not designed to do. The court would have to ask whether the equipment was in any real sense 'defective', and if so whether that led to liability. The courts will not find liability if the main cause of the accident was the claimant's own foolish selection of the wrong tool for the job (*Leach v British Oxygen Co* (1965) 109 Sol Jo 157).

An interesting, if not particularly realistic, hypothetical (suggested in Dias (ed) *Clerk and Lindsell on Torts* (16th edn, 1989)) is as follows. Suppose two employees on a factory floor quarrel. One attempts to hit the other with a hammer. He misses and the hammer hits the wall; because of a defect due to negligent manufacture, the hammer splinters, and the fragments injure a third employee. Can the injured employee sue the employers? On the literal wording of the 1969 Act, it appears that he can. Whether there is any escape from this rather surprising conclusion must be in the realms of speculation, but none is very obvious. (Of course, if the employers are liable they will be able to claim contribution from the hammer-wielding employee, and possibly from the manufacturer of the hammer too.)

Competent staff

4.39 Each employee is entitled to expect that reasonable care will have been taken in the selection and training of other employees. Where the claimant is injured by the misbehaviour of a fellow employee, very often the claimant may sue the employer on the basis of vicarious liability for the other employee's tort (**9.2**). But, where necessary, the claimant can plead that poor selection or control of the other employee constituted a breach of duty, quite regardless of any vicarious liability.

> **Hudson v Ridge Manufacturing Co [1957] 2 QB 348:** Hudson was injured while fending off a mock attack by Chadwick, another employee. Chadwick's propensity for practical jokes was well known, but his employers had taken no steps to discipline him. Held: Hudson's employers were liable for his injuries.

However, isolated instances of misconduct by a particular employee will probably not be enough to lead to this result (*Smith v Crossley Bros* (1951) 95 SJ 655).

Safe work practices

4.40 The final respect in which employers are bound to provide a reasonable level of safety is in the work practices they maintain. This is traditionally called the duty to maintain a 'safe system of work', although that phrase is also used to sum up the entire duty on the employer. The content of the duty varies considerably with the type of work. It will include a duty to issue standing orders in safety matters, and to supervise employees to prevent dangerous situations from developing. There is no conclusive rule, but a number of considerations are relevant on a routine basis.

- Where there is an obvious risk to the safety of employees, much will turn on whether it is reasonable to leave avoidance of the risk to the employees themselves.

> **Nolan v Dental Manufacturing Co [1958] 2 All ER 449:** Nolan was sharpening a tool on a grinder. A splinter of metal flew out and entered his eye. Nolan's employers never issued goggles to workers in his position. Held: the employers should have issued goggles and enforced strict orders to wear them, and were accordingly in breach of duty.

(Compare *McWilliams v Sir William Arrol & Co* [1962] 1 All ER 623, a case on similar facts which has often been criticized precisely because the House of Lords seemed to conclude too hastily that the claimant would never have used the safety equipment provided, and so there was no causal connection between his employer's breach of duty and the claimant's death (**10.25**). Right or wrong, the case is certainly unusually generous to employers.)

- 'Workmen are not in the position of employers. Their duties are not performed in the calm atmosphere of a boardroom with the advice of experts. They have to make their decisions on narrow window sills and other places of danger and in circumstances in which the dangers are obscured by repetition' (*General Cleaning Contractors v Christmas* [1953] AC 180, 190, Lord Oaksey).

- Standard practice in the industry concerned is a weighty, though not a conclusive, factor. If the danger to the claimant could only be avoided by taking precautions which few or no employers actually do, then a court will hesitate long before deciding that this particular employer should have done it. Nonetheless, the courts are prepared to hold even well-established industry practices to be negligent, if the facts justify this (*Brown v John Mills & Co (Llanidloes)* (1970) 8 KIR 702).

Newly emerging dangers to employees

4.41 The employers' duty includes a duty to keep abreast of new developments and knowledge which may reveal new threats to their workers, or improved ways of combating old threats. Where a danger has only recently emerged, it may sometimes be necessary for a court to identify the precise point at which the reasonable employer ought to have realized the problem and done something about it. Prominent examples of this type of litigation in recent years have included repetitive strain injury (RSI) (e.g. *Pickford v Imperial Chemical Industries* [1998] 3 All ER 462), vibration white finger (VWF) (e.g. *Bowman v Harland and Wolff* [1992] IRLR 349) and the effects of noise on ship-building workers (*Thompson v Smiths Shiprepairers (North Shields)* [1984] 1 All ER 881):

> The employer is not liable for the consequences of [apparently inescapable] risks, although subsequent changes in social awareness, or improvements in knowledge and technology, may transfer the risk into the category of those against which the employer can and should take care. It is unnecessary, and perhaps impossible, to give a comprehensive formula for identifying the line between the acceptable and the unacceptable. Nonetheless, the line does exist...(*Thompson v Smiths Shiprepairers (North Shields)* [1984] 1 All ER 881, 889, Mustill J).

The armed services

4.42 Until quite recently, a common law immunity barred action by active service personnel for injuries suffered. This immunity was, however, removed by the Crown Proceedings (Armed Forces) Act 1987. It was recently argued that the same result could be achieved under the Human Rights Act 1998, with the effect that claims arising *before* 1987 are now actionable. That argument succeeded at first instance, but has now been rejected by the House of Lords (*Matthews v Ministry of Defence* [2003] UKHL 4).

The quantity of litigation unleashed as a result has surprised many observers, and is certainly by any standard large. This new head of liability has involved the courts being invited to apply concepts of employers' liability to rather non-standard situations.

> **Mulcahy v Ministry of Defence [1996] QB 732:** While Mulcahy was engaged in cleaning a howitzer with a mop and bucket, the gun commander ordered it to be fired at Iraqi troops. Mulcahy suffered various injuries, including substantial damage to his hearing. Held: the duty of an employer to provide a safe system of work did not extend to cover soldiers in the course of hostilities.

This immunity for the battlefield itself has been confirmed in subsequent decision (e.g. *Multiple claimants v Ministry of Defence* [2003] EWHC 1134 (QB)). But outside it, liability is easier to establish.

> **Jebson v Ministry of Defence [2000] 1 WLR 2055:** After a recreational evening in Portsmouth, Jebson was one of a group of soldiers driven back to camp in an army lorry. Jebson injured himself during an attempt to climb from the tailgate onto the canvass roof of the lorry while it was moving. Held, exploits such as Jebson's were within the scope of the foreseeable drunken behaviour which his employers should have taken precautions against, such as by providing supervision. Liability was established, but reduced by three-quarters for Jebson's own contributory negligence.

This area of the law is very much in its infancy. It would of course be very strange if an army fighting a war were to be subject to the same duties as a peacetime employer. But equally it is not obvious that there should be no liability at all, no matter how clear the evidence of guilt in the way the claimant's injuries happened.

Defences

4.43 Defences to negligence actions generally are discussed below (**11.1**). In theory, an employer can plead either consent or contributory negligence wherever the worker knew of the risk concerned. In practice, successful pleas of consent are virtually unheard of today (**11.2**), and while the 'contributory negligence' plea tries to strike a rough balance between the defendant's lack of care and the claimant's lack of care, the scales are heavily, and intentionally, weighted in the claimant's favour (**11.17**).

Statutory duties

4.44 Alongside the general common law duty to take care is a wide array of statutory duties in relation to health and safety of employees. The principles under which these statutory duties can sometimes give rise to a civil right of action have been discussed above (**1.46**). The specific duties set out in the legislation vary considerably, some of them being framed in terms of negligence, others in absolute terms, and yet others in an intermediate style, such as by requiring an employer to achieve a certain result 'so far as is reasonably practicable'. The entire area is currently in transition, with the gradual implementation of the Framework Directive on health and safety (Directive (EC) 89/391), which should eventually lead to a general code of rules applicable to all workplaces, as well as specific regulations on particular industries.

Medical care

4.45 Actions for medical negligence form a substantial part of the overall total of tort claims. Significant amounts are paid out by the NHS every year as compensation for clinical negligence, and legal and other related costs push the total bill much higher (the NHS Litigation Authority paid out £826m in 2009/10).

Injuries induced by medical care are as old as medicine itself. Nonetheless, the current relatively high level of litigation has only been reached over the past half-century. At the start of the 20th century, many factors inhibited litigation. Key factors were difficulty in finding funds to sue; also social deference to doctors, which made claimants reluctant to sue and courts reluctant to find doctors liable. Courts were also unhappy at making large damages awards against charity hospitals, then very common institutions. The introduction of both civil legal aid and a National Health Service in the late 1940s transformed the area. And ironically, advances in medicine mean *more* dissatisfaction with medical care. Expectations are higher, and with better tests available it may be easier to demonstrate what has gone wrong, and whose fault it was.

Hospitals and their staff accordingly protest that there has been a massive increase in their legal liabilities, which has nothing to do with any rise in injuries suffered. Lawyers retort that the low level of litigation in earlier years was not an indication that all was well in medical circles, but demonstrated rather the huge difficulties facing anyone who wished to sue. Meanwhile, medical negligence is probably the least efficiently run of all areas of negligence law. Barely 10 per cent of claimants who start proceedings obtain any kind of compensation, which suggests that their lawyers are remarkably bad at spotting which cases have a real chance of success and which do not.

Generally speaking, the remedy in these cases is sought by the immediate victim of poor health care. Several claimants have recently sought to push back the boundaries of liability further here, and it is undeniably true that a failure of proper health care will often have financial implications for many in addition to the immediate victim. So far, however, the courts have resisted the temptation to expand the range of possible claimants.

> **Islington LBC v University College London Hospital NHS Trust [2005] EWCA Civ 596:** On postponing an operation at their hospital, UCLH negligently failed to advise their patient to continue to take the anticoagulant Warfarin. As a result she suffered a stroke, resulting in a need for long-term care which was paid for by her local authority, Islington. Islington sued UCLH. Held: it was not for the judiciary to extend liability to cover this case. 'As between these different authorities, it may be the case that the obligation that rests on Islington in relation to impecunious persons in need of care has arisen by statutory accident; and it is very doubtful whether it has arisen in pursuit of any desire to aid the tortfeasor. But the sorting out of the present position, accidental or not, would seem to be essentially a matter for Parliament, or at least for political decision, rather than for a court deciding a particular case' ([2005] EWCA Civ 596, para 38, Buxton LJ).

> **West Bromwich Albion FC v El-Safty [2006] EWCA Civ 1299:** Appleton, a footballer hired by WBA, suffered an injury to his right knee. WBA's doctor referred Appleton to El-Safty, a specialist in this type of injury. As a result of El-Safty's negligent decision to operate, Appleton never recovered and had to retire from professional football; with proper treatment, the injury should have healed in four months without surgery. WBA sued El-Safty but were unable to establish that they had a contract with him. Held: there was no duty in tort either.

Breach of duty

The *Bolam* test

4.46　The level of duty owed by doctors, surgeons and other health professionals is in many respects unremarkable. Any health professional must act as the reasonable health professional would act in that situation. What is reasonable is judged by the standards current at the time, not later knowledge and understanding (*Roe v Minister of Health* [1954] 2 QB 66). All of this is what one would expect from general principle (**3.8**). The level of duty has, however, a peculiarity, normally known as the *Bolam* test (after *Bolam v Friern Hospital Management Committee* [1957] 2 All ER 118). The test is not whether *all* health professionals would approve of what this particular health professional did. It is a defence if what they did was thought adequate by a significant number, *even if most competent professionals would disapprove*. Or as it was put in the *Bolam* case itself, a doctor

> ...is not guilty of negligence if he has acted in accordance with a practice accepted as proper by a responsible body of medical men skilled in that particular art...Putting it the

other way round, a man is not negligent if he is acting in accordance with such a practice, merely because there is a body of opinion which would take a contrary view ([1957] 1 WLR 582, 587, McNair J).

Subsequent cases have not only endorsed this but have gone further, saying that it is not enough that some sort of error can be shown, if it is not of the requisite seriousness. A 'mere error of judgement' is not necessarily negligence, even if its consequences are gruesome (*Whitehouse v Jordan* [1981] 1 All ER 267). The level of duty owed is therefore in practice rather low by the standards of negligence law generally.

Will the *Bolam* test survive?

4.47 Until recently, the courts stoutly resisted attempts to water down the *Bolam* test. The test was endorsed and extended by the House of Lords in *Whitehouse v Jordan* [1981] 1 All ER 267. The same thing happened in *Sidaway v Board of Governors of the Bethlem Royal Hospital* [1985] AC 871, where the claimant's argument that her rights as a patient included a right to be informed of the risks of treatment was defeated on proof that current medical practice was the contrary. There were some discordant notes in the case—a strong dissent ([1985] AC 871, 876, Lord Scarman) and a recognition that steps would sometimes be 'so obviously necessary' that a court would require them no matter what clinical practice prevailed ([1985] AC 871, 900, Lord Bridge). But overall the case was yet another endorsement of the *Bolam* approach.

Nonetheless, the principle is subject to obvious criticisms. The courts do not allow such a high degree of autonomy to other professions, and give no very clear reason why the medical professions should be special in this respect. By treating medical judgement as a black box which the courts will decline to open, they effectively allow doctors to continue to use outdated notions, so long as they can find others who have not updated their knowledge either. In recent years, the courts have shown increasing dissatisfaction with the *Bolam* test, though equally they are reluctant to set the law on a collision course with medical practice generally. In *Newell v Goldenberg* [1995] 6 Med LR 371 Mantell J noted that 'the *Bolam* principle provides a defence for those who lag behind the times' ([1995] 6 Med LR 371, 374). He refused to allow the doctor in the case to rely on the principle, the doctor having admitted that he followed an older practice not through intellectual adherence to it, but simply by accident. In *Bolitho v City and Hackney Health Authority* [1998] AC 232, the House of Lords denied that professional opinion would always be conclusive:

> . . . if, in a rare case, it can be demonstrated that the professional opinion is not capable of withstanding logical analysis, the judge is entitled to hold that the body of opinion is not reasonable or responsible ([1997] 4 All ER 771, 779, Lord Browne-Wilkinson).

Important though this statement is, Browne-Wilkinson stressed that it would only be rarely that a court would go so far as to override professional opinion in this way. Whether this new way of thinking will turn out to be significantly different from the old remains to be seen. It has already been employed in a few cases as one factor in holding a health authority liable (e.g. *Penney v East Kent Health Authority* (1999) 55 BMLR 63, which concerned the adequacy of cervical smear test procedures); but it has yet to form the sole ground for a decision of that sort. It has also been discussed in relation to the standard of care to which alternative medical practitioners should be held (*Shakoor v Situ* [2000] 4 All ER 181).

Alternatives

4.48 Dissatisfaction with the law on medical negligence is nearly universal. Much can be done to improve the working of the law, even on the assumption that the main principles are to remain as they are. In particular, there seems to be plenty of scope for encouraging more co-operative pre-trial procedures, the better to identify which cases have a real chance of success and which must ultimately fail. It remains to be seen whether the new protocols for the conduct of litigation, introduced as part of the Woolf reforms, will have that effect. Whether the standard of care needs attention from reformers is not so obvious. Even if hospitals were made strictly liable, so that injured patients could recover merely by showing that the care they received caused their injuries, without proving fault, this would still be a complicated and expensive area for litigation. In practice, proof of causation in this area is far more time-consuming and wasteful of resources than proving fault.

There seems to be a high, though admittedly not universal, level of agreement that providing monetary compensation for claimants is much lower down the scale of desirable objectives here than it is in other areas. There are certainly cases where the claimant's desperate need, after incompetent care, is for money, as where the defendant's lack of care severely damaged the claimant's earning power, or created the need for long-term treatment, or both. But in most cases, money does not seem the right remedy. On the defendant's side, the money must come out of their resources generally, and so ultimately from the same pot as that for money for the care of other patients. If the claimant succeeds, this success is at the expense of other patients. And on the claimant's side, all the claimant is likely to get from a legal action is money; whereas what many claimants say they want is rather an explanation of what happened, and perhaps an apology. If claimants in these cases often seem too eager for money, it should be remembered that nothing else is on offer.

What direction reforms should take, therefore, depends on what we are trying to achieve. If the object is to provide compensation for injured patients, the system is a very bad one, for few patients receive compensation; but are we prepared to pay the bill for greater compensation? Alternatively, if the object of damages awards is to provide pressure towards greater safety, the criticism would be that it is a rather indirect way of doing that, and alternatives need to be considered. In particular, legislation has only recently permitted the disciplining of doctors for 'seriously deficient performance' (see Medical (Professional Performance) Act 1995), and an improved NHS complaints process is in its infancy (see especially the NHS Redress Act 2006). Perhaps experience of the operation of the new law will show whether this is a better route for the control of dangerous medical practices.

FURTHER READING

Brazier and Miola 'Bye-bye *Bolam*: A medical litigation revolution?' (2000) 8 Med Law Rev 85.

Brodie 'Hospitals and non-delegable duties' (2009) 4 JR 235.

Buckley 'Occupiers' liability in England and Canada' (2006) 35 CLWR 197.

Deards and Twigg-Flesner 'The Consumer Protection Act 1987: Proof at last that it is protecting consumers?' (2001) 10 Notts LJ 1.

Elvin 'How should the law respond to stress-related claims?' (2010) 21 KLJ 41.

Farrell and Devaney 'Making amends or making things worse? Clinical negligence reform and patient redress in England' (2007) 27 LS 630.

Howells and Mildred 'Infected blood: A first exposition of the EC Product Liability Directive' (2002) 65 MLR 95.

Middlemiss 'Employers liability for death by suicide or stress and overwork in the workplace' (2009) 4 JR 245.

de Prez 'Something "old", something "new", something "borrowed" . . . The continued evolution of *Bolam*' (2001) 17 Prof Neg 75.

Shears 'The EU Product Liability Directive—Twenty years on' (2007) JBL 884.

Williamson 'Compensation for infected blood products' (2003) 7 Electronic Jour Comp Law (5) (<http://www.ejcl.org/75/art75–5.html>).

Lord Woolf 'Are the courts excessively deferential to the medical profession?' (2001) 9 Med Law Rev 1.

SELF-TEST QUESTIONS

1   If the facts of *Donoghue v Stevenson* were to recur, what defences would potentially be open to Stevenson (**4.11**)?

2 In what circumstances is an employer liable to the employee for the fault of others (**4.35**)?

3 In what circumstances is a landlord liable for injuries to the tenant's guests (**4.31**)?

4 Can the driver of a car be said to 'occupy' it for the purposes of the Occupiers' Liability Acts (**4.17**)?

5 Why may an occupier's warning of danger be held to defeat an action by a visitor who falls a victim to that danger (**4.25**)?

5

Negligence: property and economic losses

SUMMARY

A duty in negligence will usually exist where the claimant can show that:

- the defendant injured the claimant's property; or
- there was a sufficiently close relationship ('special relationship') between the claimant and the defendant.

Liability will not always be refused in cases falling outside those two categories, but the law is in an advanced state of confusion from which it currently shows no sign of recovering.

The outward drift of the law

5.1 From *Donoghue v Stevenson* [1932] AC 562 onwards, the tort of negligence has expanded greatly. However, that development has never been smooth. There have been many judicial disagreements over how, or whether, to expand it in particular areas, or indeed whether particular bold decisions of earlier years should not be reversed by later, more cautious judges.

This is not a legal history text. Nonetheless, some understanding of the key decisions of the last few decades is necessary for understanding where the law has got to, and how it might progress in the future.

5.2 *Spartan Steel and Alloys v Martin & Co (Contractors)* [1973] QB 27. In this case, electrical contractors carelessly cut through a power cable, with the expensive consequence that the claimant's foundry was deprived of power. The claimant's molten metal cooled and solidified where it was. An expensive clean-up operation was necessary after power was restored. Profit was lost on these melts; and yet further profit was lost on melts which could have been performed but for the power cut. How much of this was recoverable in a legal action against the contractors? To award nothing, and therefore to put the whole cost of the accident onto the claimant even though it was the defendant's fault, seemed unpalatable. But equally it seemed excessive to put the entire cost on the defendant, leaving the defendant with a huge bill for a relatively small error. In the event, the Court of Appeal in effect imposed a compromise. The physical mess left by the accident was chargeable to the defendant; and all economic costs which flowed directly from that physical situation could also be recovered. But purely economic losses—losses which neither consisted of property damage nor flowed directly from it—were held irrecoverable.

The arbitrariness of the line being drawn was obvious enough. The reasons given for the result hardly suggest a great degree of judicial unanimity. Lawton LJ relied heavily on the absence of precedent:

> Water conduits have been with us for centuries; gas mains for nearly a century and a half; electricity supply cables for about three-quarters of a century; but there is not a single case in the English law reports which is an authority for the proposition that mere financial loss resulting from negligent interruption of such services is recoverable ([1973] QB 27, 47).

Lord Denning MR preferred to stress policy considerations. He noted that the power might have been cut for many reasons, and that there was a risk of a large number of relatively small claims. These claims, he thought, could better be met by letting the loss lie where it fell, rather than by concentrating it on a single individual, who might not be able to bear it ([1973] QB 27, 37–9). Edmund-Davies LJ dissented, arguing that Martin & Co should be liable for all the loss they had caused:

> ... if economic loss of itself confers a right of action this may spell disaster for the negligent party. But this may equally be the outcome where physical damage alone is suffered, or where physical damage leads directly to economic loss ([1973] QB 27, 40).

The distinction between physical damage and purely economic loss has a certain attraction on the facts of *Spartan Steel* itself. But it is another question whether it should have wider application. Nonetheless, the case played an important part in establishing the modern orthodoxy that *foreseeable injury to property is usually recoverable, whereas foreseeable injury to purely economic interests is not*. The first part of the proposition is as important as the second, and is now very well established. And in many contexts it seems to fit with the court's view of the proper policy basis for liability. The controversies in the following years have been over the second limb: when and how the courts will allow a remedy for purely economic losses.

5.3 *Hedley Byrne & Co v Heller & Partners* [1964] AC 465. If *Spartan Steel* is now the general rule, then the earlier decision of the House of Lords in *Hedley Byrne* can only represent a major exception to it. The claimant had doubts about the creditworthiness of one of its clients and, through an intermediary, asked the defendants for a credit reference. The defendants responded that 'We believe that the company would not undertake any commitments they were unable to fulfil', though they added that 'Your figures are larger than we are accustomed to see'. They added that their reference was 'For your own private use and without responsibility on [our] part...' The claimant lost significant sums when its client went into liquidation, which it sought to recoup by action against the defendants. The action failed, largely because of the way in which the defendants had qualified their reference, but a majority of the House made it clear that negligent misstatements of this sort could give rise to liability in tort. The defendants had only narrowly escaped liability. The Lords tried to meet the danger of an indeterminate liability to a wide class of potential claimants by stress on the close association ('special relationship') which must have existed between the defendants and the claimant if action were to be possible.

There have been many later controversies over the limits of this liability. One open question, indeed, is whether the same result would today be reached on those facts, or whether it would be held that the defendant had in fact assumed responsibility to the claimant (**5.15**). But the basic principle has not been doubted, and is the starting point for modern discussions of the recovery of purely economic losses.

5.4 *Anns v Merton London Borough Council* [1978] AC 728. This case represented a serious, if slightly indirect, challenge to the line drawn in the *Spartan Steel* case. The claimant bought a flat, but later realized that its foundations were utterly ruined: the builders had not dug deep enough for such soil, and the local planning authority had not checked up on the builders. The claimant sued both the builder and the planning authority, and succeeded. Lord Wilberforce, who delivered the leading judgment in the House of Lords, declared that the claimant's loss was in fact physical rather than purely economic, but that it did not matter either way ([1978] AC 728, 759). He proposed a two-stage test for duty, under which the main question was whether loss to the claimant was a foreseeable consequence of the defendant's action, but under which liability could then be limited if there was something in the situation to require it. Whether the claimant's loss was physical or purely economic was not, for him, a matter of great importance.

Anns was initially followed with enthusiasm, notably in *Junior Books v Veitchi Co* [1983] 1 AC 520, which concerned the owner of premises suing sub-contractors for defective building work. Nonetheless, there was a strong dissent by Lord Brandon in that case, and later cases showed increasing dissatisfaction with it. These cases culminated in *Murphy v Brentwood District Council* [1991] 1 AC 398, when *Anns* was definitively overruled. The division between property damage and purely economic loss was reasserted as fundamental. However careless the defendants, no duty was owed in relation to purely economic loss.

There is a certain irony in the reasoning in *Murphy*. The opinions place much stress on the need for certainty in the law—a strange point to emphasize when overruling a decision which had stood for 13 years. They also stress the desirability of the 'incrementalist' approach of building on past precedents—again not what we would expect when overruling one of the most significant holdings of recent years. The opinions also stressed the need for orderly development of the law and respect for what Parliament had laid down. Yet legislation had already been passed which plainly assumed that *Anns* was law (Latent Damage Act 1986); and the distinction between property damage and economic loss is the courts' creation, not the legislature's! Whatever the Lords were paying respect to, it does not appear to be anything of parliamentary origin. Moreover, the Privy Council (in its capacity as court of final appeal in the New Zealand legal system) has rejected the *Murphy* decision (*Invercargill City Council v Hamlin* [1996] AC 624).

5.5   *White v Jones* [1995] 2 AC 207. Here, the defendant acted as solicitors for the claimant's father, and showed gross negligence by failing to carry out his instructions to draw up a will for him. The father died before the will was drawn up and the claimant, who would have benefited from a legacy in it, sued the defendant for negligence. The father's estate could not sue the defendant, as it was no worse off than if the defendant had acted carefully; but a majority of the House of Lords was prepared to compensate the claimant.

The opinions are notable for their close concentration on the defendant's legal situation, which is analysed in considerable detail. The major point of disagreement between the Lords was whether a duty to someone other than the defendant's client was compatible with proper execution of the duty to the client, which all agreed was primary. Nonetheless, the case plainly indicates a willingness to extend liability to fresh situations, even where the loss is plainly economic rather than physical. The years following the case have seen plenty of litigation in this area, and the precise terms of the liability have been spelled out in greater detail:

• The precise circumstances in which the lack of care occurred is immaterial, so long as breach of the defendant's professional duty can be shown. *White v Jones* itself involved failure to draw up a will as instructed, but the same principle applies where the defendant drew up a will but misunderstood the nature of the property, so that the will did not have the intended effect (*Carr-Glynn v Frearsons* [1999] Ch 326). It also applies where the client drew up a home-made will and then retained the defendant to check it (*Gray v Buss Murton* [1999] PNLR 882).

• The duty does not extend to looking after the beneficiary's interests where they are not identical with the testator's. So advice to a client on making a charitable gift need not include information on how the charity may reduce its tax liability (*Cancer Research Campaign v Ernest Brown & Co* [1998] PNLR 592).

• The existence of other possible remedies does not necessarily rule out the remedy in tort. So the possibility of a contract action by the estate of the dead person against the solicitors does not prevent the intended beneficiaries from suing in tort (*Carr-Glynn v Frearsons* [1999] Ch 326); though the courts will presumably stop the beneficiaries from recovering their loss twice over by this means. Where the beneficiaries can undo the effects of the defendant's negligence by an action against the dead person's estate, perhaps by an action to rectify a will or by an action under the Inheritance (Provision for Family and Dependants) Act 1975, then they are expected to do that. They cannot opt to sue the solicitor without good reason (*Walker v Geo H Medlicott & Son* [1999] 1 All ER 685). However, the claimant's duty is only to act reasonably, and if those other remedies seem doubtful or for some other reason undesirable, then they may sue the defendant (*Horsfall v Haywards* [1999] 1 FLR 1182). (This is an example of the principle of mitigation of loss, which is explained further at **10.36** below.)

The position today

5.6 These famous decisions form the backdrop to any discussion of the modern law, and they establish many important points. Negligence liability for physical loss or damage will be easy to establish, and so will liability where the claimant suffers loss after a defendant with whom the claimant is in a 'special relationship' negligently misrepresents the truth. But how much wider can liability stretch? Would a court today refuse liability on the facts of *Hedley Byrne* (**5.15**)? Was it right for the Lords in *Murphy* to overrule *Anns*, or might not the 'two-stage' test of duty be superior to anything *Murphy* sought to replace it with (**5.34**)? And was *Junior Books* not perfectly right, on its facts if not in its reasoning (**5.4**)? These are all open questions under the current law, which is characterized by a high degree of doubt and uncertainty. In the sections which follow, I will review the more established areas of doctrine, before proceeding to the wilder regions at the edge of the modern law.

The distinction between property damage and pure economic loss

Definition and terminology

5.7 'Purely economic' losses are economic losses which cannot be traced to physical damage to the person or to property. In other words, all economic losses either result from personal injury or from property damage, or are *purely* economic losses. Economic loss consequential on physical damage is not caught by the restriction here described: so if the claimant is injured in the leg and has to take a less well-paid job as a result, the claimant need not fear that this loss of wages will be thought 'purely economic'. It results from a physical injury, and the damages for the injury will include it (**10.59**). (It is usually obvious which of the three categories—personal injury, property damage or purely economic loss—is in issue. For a rare case where this was in dispute, see *Yearworth v North Bristol NHS Trust* [2009] EWCA Civ 37, which concerned sperm which the male claimants had left with the defendants for storage. The sperm was treated as the men's personal property.)

Confusion is sometimes caused by shorthand references to 'economic loss', meaning *pure* economic loss. This is obviously a misleading usage. If the claimant's car, worth £1,000, is destroyed, then obviously the claimant has suffered an economic loss. The car cost money to buy, and will cost money to replace. (Indeed, most of the losses for which the law of tort allows compensation are economic, in this sense only.) But it is not a *purely* economic loss, but rather damage to the claimant's property. The precise terminology is perhaps not important; what is important is to remember that the objection is not to losses which are economic, but to losses which do *not* constitute either personal injury or damage to property, and are not losses consequential on such damage.

A restriction on recovery?

5.8 At this stage, I will simply discuss whether particular situations are regarded as examples of purely economic losses, or whether they will be placed in another category. But it would be quite wrong to suggest that, having classified a particular loss as purely economic, the court will *always* go on to deny liability. On the contrary, several judges have in particular contexts denied that it is of any significance at all whether the loss is purely economic. Whether liability will be allowed despite this is discussed below (**5.33**).

Contractual rights are not 'property'

5.9 The rule requires not merely damage to property, but that the property must have belonged to the claimant at the time when it was damaged. It seems not to matter that the property was at the claimant's risk, so that the claimant must bear the loss if it is damaged, if the claimant was not its owner.

> **Leigh & Sillavan v Aliakmon Shipping Co [1986] AC 785:** Aliakmon Shipping damaged a cargo of steel which they were carrying. The steel was at Leigh's risk, though ownership had not passed to them at the time of the damage. Held: Leigh's loss was a purely economic loss, and accordingly irrecoverable from Aliakmon.

This principle sometimes entails a minute analysis of the nature of the claimant's interest in some property which has been damaged.

> **Candlewood Navigation Corporation v Mitsui OSK Lines [1986] AC 1:** Mitsui owned a ship, which they chartered (by demise charter) to Matsuoka; Matsuoka immediately chartered it back (by time charter) to Mitsui. The ship was then damaged through the negligence of Candlewood. Held: as a time charter, unlike a demise charter, did not give a property right to the charterer, Mitsui's claim was for a purely economic loss and therefore could not succeed.

These decisions show the rule against pure economic loss at its most technical and arbitrary. If in fact the cost of certain property damage is borne by the claimant and the (technical) owner does not suffer any financial loss at all, then a refusal of compensation is impossible to defend on grounds of over-broad liability, and very hard to defend on any other ground. Lord Goff, who in the Court of Appeal had argued for liability in the *Aliakmon* case (see [1985] 2 All ER 44), subsequently promoted legislation which has the practical effect of reversing it on its facts (see Carriage of Goods by Sea Act 1992).

Failure to provide proper services

5.10 It is at first sight strange that Anns and other claimants, who find their houses crumbling about their ears, are refused a claim in tort because their loss is purely economic, rather than an injury to property. Indeed, some judges in earlier decades were prepared to regard this sort of loss as physical. The orthodox reasoning today is, however, that the loss is not physical, but rather a complaint of the lack of proper professional service by the defendant. *Anns* would have been quite different if the claimant had at one time owned good foundations, which the defendant ruined. Rather, there never was a good set of foundations. Whether the claimant's claim is good or not, it is not a claim for damage to property, for there never was a good piece of property which the defendant injured. When the defendant supplies a defective article which ends up with the claimant, we must therefore ask whether the defendant's negligence damaged the claimant's property, or whether the claimant is simply complaining of the low value of the article the claimant now has.

> **Muirhead v Industrial Tank Specialities [1986] QB 507:** Muirhead bought pumps as part of his system for storing live lobsters in an aquarium, for later sale. The pumps failed and the lobsters died. Muirhead sued Industrial Tank, the manufacturers, who were found to have been negligent. Held: Muirhead could recover the value of the dead lobsters, but not the purely economic loss of having to repair or replace the defective pumps.

> **Hamble Fisheries v Gardner and Sons [1999] 2 Lloyd's Rep 1:** Manufacturers sold defective pistons, some of which were ultimately incorporated into the engine of a fishing vessel sold to Hamble. Gardner subsequently acquired the manufacturers' business. Held: Gardner were under no duty to warn Hamble, nor were they liable to replace the pistons. Such a liability would only be imposed if some very high degree of proximity was shown between the two companies.

Possible exceptions

'Complex structures'

5.11 If we consider Anns to own a single structure—a house with foundations—then clearly he suffered no property damage, for he never had a house with good foundations. If, however, we say he owned two things—bad foundations, with a perfectly good house sitting on top of them—then the case is altered, for while Anns cannot argue that his foundations were damaged, he can argue that the house was. Accordingly, by the mental device of separating the good from the bad, what was apparently a purely economic loss can be converted, at least in part, into property damage for which a claim can be made. This line of argument has received some support from the House of Lords (e.g. *D & F Estates v Church Commissioners for England* [1989] AC 177). However, it obviously subverts the approach the House of Lords sought to establish in *Murphy*, where Lord Bridge disapproved it, at least in so far as it gave any support to *Anns* ([1990] 2 All ER 908, 928). Yet he and his colleagues stopped short of condemning it outright, and its status today is somewhat obscure. Probably the idea will be of most value in cases where different firms built different parts of the structure; certainly the courts seem to have shown little enthusiasm for it in other contexts.

> **Tunnel Refineries v Byran Donkin [1998] CILL 1382:** Donkin sold an 8-tonne compressor to Tunnel Refineries. Subsequently, a fan which was an integral component of the

compressor failed, damaging the rest of the machine. A claim was made in tort. Held: the rest of the machine could not be regarded as 'other property', and accordingly the claim was for purely economic loss and so must fail.

Bellefield Computer Services v E Turner & Sons [2000] BLR 97: Turners constructed a new dairy processing plant, with an internal fire-stop wall between the storage area and the rest of the building. However, in breach of contract, they did not build the fire-stop wall to its full height. Twelve years later, by which time Bellefield had acquired the building, a fire started in the storage area and, because of the low wall, it spread to the whole building. Held: Turners were not liable for any of the damage to the building, though they were liable for equipment and other chattels damaged outside the storage area.

'Pre-emptive damages'

5.12 If the claimant, the owner of defective premises, allows them to crumble, and rubble falls onto the claimant's car, then certainly the claimant has suffered physical damage. If the rubble falls on the claimant personally, he or she has suffered personal injury, and so again may recover damages. It seems strange to hold that if the claimant acts to obviate this threat of physical injury, this money is irrecoverable as being a purely economic loss. Accordingly, money spent in this pre-emptive way is treated by some judges as recoverable, as if it represented a physical loss. This was one strand of Lord Wilberforce's reasoning in *Anns*: Anns was paying to clear up a danger to his own and his family's health and safety (see *Anns* [1977] 2 All ER 492, 505). In *Murphy*, the Lords were obviously not anxious to lend any credence to *Anns*, and would not accept that the claimant could recover if the danger were merely to the claimant personally. Nonetheless, Lord Bridge at least seemed to accept that there might be something in the argument, in some circumstances at least:

> [I]f a building stands so close to the boundary of the building owner's land that after discovery of the dangerous defect it remains a potential source of injury to persons or property on neighbouring land or on the highway, the building owner ought, in principle, to be entitled to recover in tort from the negligent builder the cost of obviating the danger, whether by repair or by demolition, so far as that cost is necessarily incurred in order to protect himself from potential liability to third parties ([1990] 2 All ER 908, 926).

Conclusion

5.13 The line between property damage, on the one hand, and purely economic losses, on the other, is sometimes difficult to draw, and hard to justify once drawn. It is in some respects surprising that the more conservative judges have not allowed a looser definition of 'physical' damage, the better to reconcile the more radical judges to the continued existence of the distinction. As will be seen (**5.33**), it has proved impossible to hold the line.

'Special relationships' and negligent misstatement

5.14 Where the relationship between the claimant and the defendant is such that the claimant reasonably reposes a high degree of trust in the defendant's advice, then bad advice to the claimant, resulting in loss, may lead to an action in negligence against the defendant. It seems to be irrelevant that the loss the claimant suffers is usually purely economic. At this stage, the discussion will be confined to the case where the defendant misadvises the claimant, rather than the case where the claimant suffers because of bad advice the defendant gave *to someone else* (that case will be considered below, **5.35**). It may also be assumed that the cases mentioned will concern purely economic loss, for while statements can certainly lead to physical damage, it does not appear that such cases are treated any differently from cases of physical damage caused by actions.

> **Clayton v Woodman & Sons (Builders) [1962] 2 All ER 33:** Clayton, a building worker, injured himself as a result of careless instructions from the architects of the building project. Held: the architects were liable for these injuries.

'Special relationship' or 'reasonable foresight'?

5.15 Even in the *Hedley Byrne* case itself, which first recognized this head of liability, there were considerable disagreements as to its nature, quite apart from disagreements about its limits.

• Lord Reid preferred to talk of a *special relationship* between the claimant and the defendant. The characteristics of this relationship are that the claimant reasonably placed reliance on what the defendant said, and the defendant knew or ought to have known that that was so ([1964] AC 465, 486).

• Lord Devlin said that the liability attached to relationships which were *equivalent to contract* ([1964] AC 465, 529). It is unclear which relationships will be so regarded. It is obviously not enough to say that this means relationships which would be contracts but for the fact that they aren't. If Lord Devlin meant relationships of close trust and confidence, then his *dictum* seems confused. Contracts are not necessarily relationships of trust and confidence—it may, indeed, be the parties' *lack* of mutual trust that led them to try to tie each other down by contract in the first place.

- Various *dicta* in the case tie the liability to an *assumption of liability*. The defendant is liable not because the law seeks to impose a duty, but because the defendant made it clear to the claimant that the defendant was *undertaking* a duty (e.g. [1964] AC 465, 486, Lord Reid). It is very unclear what this means, or how we are to recognize such an 'assumption' when it is present. The 'assumption of responsibility' approach was rejected as not 'a helpful or realistic test in most cases' by Lord Griffiths in *Smith v Eric S Bush* [1990] 1 AC 831, 864.

- Lord Morris said that the true principle is simply *reasonable foresight* that the claimant will rely on what the defendant says ([1964] AC 465, 503). Yet plainly liability is narrower than liability for negligent acts, which is also usually described in those terms. Yet again, we see that the range of foresight depends at least partly on policy considerations. Economic losses are treated as less foreseeable than personal injury.

It is impossible to reduce liability to a simple formula. The various theories mentioned are very little different in their practical effects. It is well to bear in mind that, quite apart from the general caution the courts exercise in relation to claims for purely economic losses, there are specific reasons for restricting liability in these cases. Words are easily passed on, and can have far greater consequences than individual acts. And while the claimant presents the case as being that the defendant did the claimant harm, it would often be fairer to say that the claimant did himself or herself harm by taking a bad decision (in which the defendant's advice was merely one contributing factor), or that others harmed the claimant (in a way which the claimant might have been able to avoid if the defendant had given better advice). If claimants are to be treated as responsible for their own actions, the liability of defendants in negligent misstatement must be narrow. The real question is as to the reasonableness of the claimant's reliance on the statement.

> **Law Society v KPMG Peat Marwick [2000] 4 All ER 540:** KPMG prepared the annual report of a firm of solicitors for submission to the Law Society. The firm subsequently went bankrupt, leading to successful claims totalling £8½m against the Law Society's compensation fund. Held: the purpose of such reports was precisely to alert the Law Society to possible financial difficulties in solicitors' firms, and so a duty of care was owed them by KPMG.

The statement: addressed to whom?

5.16 In principle, the question should be whether *the claimant* was entitled to rely on the defendant's statement, and it is not obviously relevant whether anyone else can. In practice, the more generally the defendant's statement is broadcast, the less likely is the court to hold that there is a 'special relationship' between the defendant and any one person who heard it and relied on it. Sometimes this can be justified on the ground that a statement addressed to many people will obviously not be tailored to any one person's individual needs. In most cases it would be more realistic to say that the courts are scared of imposing too broad a liability. But there is no ban on liability merely because the claimant is not the person at whom the statement is primarily aimed.

> **Smith v Eric S Bush [1990] 1 AC 831:** Smith sought a loan on mortgage, to enable her to buy a house. Bush surveyed the house on behalf of the mortgage company, failing to notice fundamental structural defects. As Bush must have known was likely, Smith obtained a copy of the survey, and relied on it instead of paying for one of her own. Held: Smith's reliance was reasonable, and Bush was liable to her.

However, it is important not to lose sight of the defendant's position. The surveyor was paid to produce a report for the mortgage company, on whether the house was good security for the amount they sought to lend. If that task had been done reasonably well, the claimant would have had no case that she had been poorly advised on how comfortable or otherwise desirable the house was likely to be for her. The defendant was only bound to do the job he had said he would do, not some more extensive one that the claimant would have liked him to do.

Widely disseminated statements

5.17 Only rarely will information, released to the public generally, successfully be made the subject of an action in negligence. However, where the defendant has compiled an apparently authoritative report on some matter, it may be reasonable for the claimant to rely on it. In those circumstances, the courts in recent years have tended to ask themselves whether the claimant is the sort of person the report was prepared for.

> **Caparo Industries v Dickman [1990] 2 AC 605:** Caparo mounted a takeover of a firm, Fidelity, in which they already held shares. In their financial calculations, Caparo relied on Fidelity's statutory accounts as giving an accurate picture. On discovering that the accounts were in fact highly inaccurate, they sued Touche Ross, the firm's auditors, who had certified the accounts as being a true and fair view of Fidelity's position. Held: statutory accounts were produced to enable existing shareholders to safeguard their position, not to facilitate takeovers, and accordingly Caparo had no claim.

> **Mariola Marine Corpn v Lloyd's Register of Shipping [1990] 1 Lloyd's Rep 547:** Mariola purchased *The Morning Watch*, a motor yacht, relying in part on its having received a glowing report from Lloyds' Register. The yacht turned out to be seriously

corroded. Held: the purpose of Lloyds' surveys was to protect life and property when vessels were at sea, rather than to protect the economic interest of purchasers.

The principle is not an obvious one. If the claimant's use of the circulated report is foreseeable, why should it matter that the original purpose of preparing such reports was different? Yet, even taking the principle of those decisions as a given, nonetheless its application to their facts is disputable. In particular, the view of statutory accounts taken in *Caparo* has been described by one commentator as 'an artificial interpretation which takes no account of commercial reality', especially since audited accounts are one of the few reliable ways by which outsiders may determine how well the company is being run (Percival 'After *Caparo*—Liability in business transactions revisited' (1991) 54 MLR 739, 742). The Court of Appeal subsequently distinguished the case on very similar facts:

> **Morgan Crucible Co v Hill Samuel & Co [1991] Ch 295:** Morgan Crucible made a takeover bid for FCE, an electronics firm. The directors and auditors of FCE released a 'defence document' advising rejection of the bid, and including various pieces of account information about FCE. Morgan Crucible increased its bid, and completed the takeover. It later sued the directors and auditors, having discovered the account information to be inaccurate. Held: the case was distinguishable from *Caparo* and so need not be struck out.

The case suggests a rather different criterion, for which there is also support in the opinions in *Caparo:* that the defendant will be liable to the claimant where the defendant has actual knowledge of the claimant's plans. A similar criterion was also used when auditors failed to detect fraud in a subsidiary company's accounts; the subsidiary was then sold, and the purchasers (on discovering the fraud) sued the parent company. It was held that the parent company could not sue the auditors, for while it was obvious that the parent would read and rely on the accounts, nonetheless the auditors had not assumed any responsibility to them for this use of the accounts (*MAN Nutzfahrzeuge AG v Freightliner Ltd* [2007] EWCA Civ 910).

A final case of note involves information disseminated on the internet.

> **Patchett v Swimming Pool and Allied Trades Association Ltd [2009] EWCA Civ 717:** SPATA's website offered a 'member finder' to enable visitors to the site to find SPATA members close to them; the site also included details of SPATA's Bond and Warranty scheme, guaranteeing proper execution of work by SPATA members. The Patchetts hired Crown Pools from firms listed on the site, but that firm became insolvent before finishing the work. A very careful examination of the site would have revealed to the Patchetts that Crown were not members of SPATA but only associate members, not covered by the scheme. Held: the information on the website was to be taken as a whole, and when so read could not reasonably have been relied on in the way the Patchetts did.

Is a statement necessary at all?

5.18 If a sufficiently strong 'special relationship' is demonstrated, it might be thought that the defendant could break the duty this relationship produces as much by silence as by bad advice. Liability for a failure to speak in pre-contractual negotiations was refused in *Banque Keyser Ullman (UK) Insurance Co v Skandia* [1991] 2 AC 249. This was, however, on the ground that it would unsettle what had long been understood to be the law on silence in negotiations; the case is no authority against liability for silence in other contexts. However, it has been said that there will only be liability if the defendant has a duty to speak (e.g. *Tai Hing Cotton Mill v Liu Chong Hing Bank* [1986] AC 80, 110, Lord Scarman). It is entirely unclear when such a duty will arise, and despite occasional *dicta* in favour of such liability, there appears to be no clear example of it in this jurisdiction.

The 'special relationship'

The nature of the relationship

5.19 It is difficult to generalize on the nature of the relationship necessary to give rise to liability. The extent to which the claimant relies, the reasonableness of so relying, and the defendant's actual or reasonably attainable knowledge of this, are all relevant factors. But there is no simple formula to apply. Two sample cases where the claimant relied on the defendant, who was a solicitor acting for someone else, may be contrasted.

> ***Gran Gelato v Richcliff (Group)* [1992] Ch 560:** Gran Gelato took a sub-lease of premises, its landlord's solicitor having carelessly assured it that its head lease was good for ten years. After five years, the freehold owner unexpectedly but lawfully terminated the head lease. Held: Gran Gelato had no action against its landlord's solicitors.

> ***Edwards v Lee* [1991] NLJR 1517:** Lee, a solicitor, gave Edwards a reference for Hawkes, his client, on the strength of which Edwards allowed Hawkes to take away a Mercedes car on credit. Hawkes subsequently absconded; as Lee knew, he was on bail pending trial for criminal dishonesty. Held: even though legal professional privilege would not have permitted Lee to mention the charges against Hawkes, nonetheless the reference was misleading, and Edwards could recover damages. They would, however, be reduced by 50 per cent for contributory negligence.

In *Gran Gelato*, Nicholls V-C made much of the point that the client, rather than the solicitor, was the obvious person to sue. The same of course is equally true of *Edwards*, though possibly the case is different; Edwards had asked for the reference precisely because the client's reliability was doubtful.

Merely social relationships

5.20 If the relationship between the claimant and the defendant is purely social, then it is usually unreasonable to place much reliance on anything the defendant may say, and accordingly no duty is owed. There will not be many cases where the claimant can place much weight on what the defendant may have told the claimant off-the-cuff at a party. But there is no firm rule, except that the claimant cannot sue unless the claimant's reliance was, in all the circumstances, reasonable.

> *Chaudhry v Prabhakar* **[1988] 3 All ER 718:** Chaudhry, who had just passed her driving test and knew little about cars, sought the advice of Prabhakar, a close friend with some knowledge of cars. Prabhakar subsequently recommended a particular Volkswagen Golf, making a number of careless statements about it. The Golf turned out to be unroadworthy and worthless. Held: a duty was owed to Chaudhry, and was broken.

The case has been doubted, not least because counsel for Prabhakar appears to have *conceded* that some sort of duty was owed to Chaudhry. It remains the case that strong facts must be shown before any such claimant is likely to succeed.

Potentially contractual relationships

5.21 For some years after *Hedley Byrne* it was thought that parties negotiating for the formation of a contract could not be in a 'special relationship'. It was thought that someone who shows enough self-reliance to negotiate terms with the defendant is plainly *not* relying on the defendant very much, if at all. There was also at that time a general wariness at letting tort slip into contractual contexts. However, this attitude oversimplified a number of issues, and it was eventually established that one negotiating party can owe a duty to another.

> *Esso Petroleum v Mardon* **[1976] QB 801:** Mardon sought the advice of an expert of Esso as to the likely sales at a particular filling station, on which Mardon was considering purchasing the franchise. On the strength of the expert's over-optimistic and careless prediction, Mardon took the franchise and subsequently made large losses. Held: Esso owed a duty to Mardon, which had been broken by its expert's poor advice.

It has even been held that the defendant might be in breach of duty for failing to advise the claimant to enter into a contract with the defendant:

> *Crossan v Ward Bracewell* **[1986] NLJ Rep 849:** Crossan consulted a solicitor for advice whether he should pursue a claim arising out of a road accident. After hearing the financial implications, Crossan decided that he could not afford to pursue the claim. The solicitor had, however, carelessly failed to appreciate that Crossan would have been entitled to have his legal expenses met from insurance. Held: the solicitor was liable to an action in negligence.

Relationships which later become contractual

5.22 It is no longer the law that the existence of contractual duties automatically excludes liability in tort in the context of the same relationship. So, for example, while it was held in *Groom v Crocker* [1939] 1 KB 194 that the duty owed by solicitors to their clients is contractual only, in *Midland Bank Trust Co v Hett, Stubbs & Kemp* [1979] Ch 384 this approach was repudiated. So there is no longer a general rule excluding tort liability. Nonetheless, in economic loss cases generally, and especially cases connected with construction work, the courts are acutely conscious that parties may have intended that their written contracts should be the definitive statement of their obligations. Accordingly, they may refuse to add fresh obligations via the law of tort (**5.50**); and this may prevent the claimant recovering damages.

> **Pacific Associates Inc v Baxter [1989] 2 All ER 159:** Pacific Associates undertook dredging work in Dubai. Their employer hired a consultant engineer to supervise the work. Finding the work unexpectedly difficult, Pacific sought to sue the engineer for providing them with misleading geological data. There was no contract between Pacific and the engineer. Held: no duty was owed in tort either.

It was relevant that the engineer had disclaimed all liability for this sort of loss under his contract with his employer (see [1989] 2 All ER 159, 179), but very probably the case would have gone the same way in any event.

Where the defendant's poor advice results in the claimant's forming a contract with the defendant, there is a statutory remedy under the Misrepresentation Act 1967, s 2(1). If this remedy applies, the claimant is almost certain to use it in preference to the remedy under *Hedley Byrne*. Under the statute, there is no need to establish a duty; lack of care is for the defendant to disprove, rather than for the claimant to prove; and damages are assessed on a more generous basis, as if the claim were one for deceit (see **6.2**; *Royscot Trust v Rogerson* [1991] 2 QB 297).

It is even thought that a duty might arise where the relationship between the claimant and the defendant is already contractual, though such cases must be rare.

> **Lennon v Metropolitan Police Commissioner [2004] EWCA Civ 130:** Lennon, a member of the Metropolitan Police, wished to transfer to the Royal Ulster Constabulary. He received detailed advice on the transfer from a personnel executive officer, who encouraged him to leave all the details to her. As a result of her mishandling of the matter, Lennon lost his continuity of service, and with it a substantial housing allowance. Held: even in a situation of employment (or as here, a relationship akin to employment), a voluntary assumption of liability in an important financial matter could be enough to establish a duty. A duty was found.

Law enforcement officials

5.23 Suppose the defendant, a public official, insists that the claimant's business is not in compliance with current regulations, and accordingly demands changes. The claimant makes those changes, but then discovers that the defendant's view of the law was wrong. Can the claimant sue for the money thrown away on the basis of the defendant's instructions? This is obviously not quite a 'relationship of trust and confidence', but nonetheless it is analogous, and the courts have several times been asked to impose liability. The answer seems to be that in principle the claimant may sue, if the defendant gave the claimant no practical alternative to spending the money. But, as with all liability that occurs against the backdrop of statutory powers, the court must ask itself whether the imposition of liability is compatible with the aims of the statute (see generally **1.53** above).

> *Welton v North Cornwall District Council* **[1997] 1 WLR 570:** Welton's guest house was inspected for compliance with food safety legislation. The compliance officer identified 13 changes that should be made to attain compliance, and threatened to close the guest house down if they were not made. Having made the changes (which included major alterations to the kitchen), Welton discovered that many of them were in fact not required by the relevant regulations. Held: the *Hedley Byrne* principle applied, and the council were liable.

> *Harris v Evans* **[1998] 3 All ER 522:** Harris proposed to make bungee-jumping facilities available to the public by the use of a mobile telescopic crane. However, a local HSE officer insisted that the crane required official certification of fitness for that purpose. When Harris objected, a prohibition notice was issued against him. Held: assuming that the notice was wrong and negligently issued, nonetheless Parliament could not have intended action to lie in those circumstances. Prohibition notices almost inevitably resulted in economic loss, and the safety legislation included its own remedies against wrongful notices. However, the Court of Appeal conceded in *Harris* that an HSE inspector whose wrongful advice created a *new* danger might be liable for all of the consequences of that danger, whether physical or economic.

Exclusion of liability

5.24 In the *Hedley Byrne* case itself, the claim failed because the defendant had made it clear that it accepted no liability for its statement. However, in modern conditions, and especially given that not all judges accept that the claimant's claim is based on an 'assumption of responsibility' by the defendant (see **5.37**), this is no longer a very obvious conclusion. If the defendant knows that the claimant will rely on the information, and that it is reasonable to do so (perhaps the defendant is the claimant's best or only source of information), can the defendant escape all liability merely by stating that the information is given without responsibility? This is not obvious even so far as the common law is concerned. Moreover, legislation now forbids the exclusion of 'business liability' for negligence, except where the exclusion is a reasonable one (Unfair Contract Terms Act 1977, ss 1, 2 and 13). The precise effect of this is unclear, however. If the defendant makes it clear that the advice is made without responsibility, is the defendant excluding a duty, contrary to the Unfair Contract Terms Act 1977, or does the notice preclude the claimant from establishing reasonable reliance, so that there is nothing to exclude?

In *Smith v Eric S Bush* (**5.16**), the House of Lords preferred the first interpretation. Lord Griffiths mentioned various factors which needed consideration on whether the clause was unreasonable within the meaning of the Act ([1990] 1 AC 831, 858–9).

- 'Were the parties of equal bargaining power?'
- '[W]ould it have been reasonably practicable to obtain the advice from an alternative source taking into account considerations of costs and time?'
- 'How difficult is the task being undertaken for which liability is being excluded?' and
- 'What are the practical consequences of the decision on the question of reasonableness? This must involve the sums of money potentially at stake and the ability of the parties to bear the loss involved, which, in its turn, raises the question of insurance.'

On the basis of these factors, he held unreasonableness established. The claimant was in no position to object to the clause (first factor); she was relatively impecunious (second factor); the work was straightforward (third factor); and while insurance would undoubtedly raise the defendant's costs somewhat, it should not be by much (fourth factor).

The generosity of the Lords here is an odd contrast to the restrictive attitude in cases like *Caparo* (**5.17**). Conceivably they thought that corporate raiders are less in need of protection than first-time house buyers. *Smith v Bush* was not a case where the warning was very prominent. Possibly the defendant's claim that the duty was excluded might get a better hearing if the defendant made it very obvious that no liability was accepted.

Must the defendant be a professional?

5.25 A few years after the *Hedley Byrne* decision, the Privy Council ruled that the claimant could not rely on any 'special relationship' unless the defendant was some sort of professional person, exercising relevant special professional skills (*Mutual Life and Citizens' Assurance Co v Evatt* [1971] AC 793). Accordingly, it refused to find liability when a life assurance company gave unsound advice to the claimant about the financial standing of an associated company, as the defendant's business was life assurance, not financial advice. However, there were powerfully argued dissents in the case, and the majority's approach has been rejected in England. If the defendant has special knowledge or expertise on which the claimant relies, it does not matter whether the defendant's career consists of utilizing that knowledge or expertise (e.g. *Esso Petroleum Co v Mardon* [1976] QB 801).

Reliance in fact, and causation

5.26 Having established a duty and breach of that duty, the claimant must also demonstrate a loss flowing from the claimant's reliance on the defendant's poor advice. This will be particularly difficult in a case where the claimant takes an independent decision in reliance on a range of information, of which the defendant's input is an important but not all-embracing part. The courts have occasionally reduced the claimant's damages for contributory negligence (e.g. *Edwards v Lee* (**5.19**)), which seems to imply that it is not a complete answer to the claimant's claim that he or she acted unreasonably in following the advice.

The cutting edge of liability

5.27 Despite the confusion, there is a fair degree of certainty about the law of negligence. In many common situations, the existence and the limits of the duty are established with reasonable clarity. It is always true that the higher courts can overrule earlier cases, but for those cases which are not going to end up in the higher courts (the overwhelming majority) this possibility can be neglected. The best guide to what the courts will do in the future is to ask what they have done in the past. Moreover, the degree of confusion that remains is partly illusory: it indicates not an insoluble problem, but only that the higher courts prefer to delegate detailed application of their rules to lower courts. So while there is no denying that portions of the law are in a state of hideous confusion, it is important not to get it out of proportion.

> Your examiners will not expect you to solve problems which have baffled judges and academics alike, and which have regularly led to furious dissension and argument. However, it is not unreasonable to expect you to be familiar with the leading cases, to be able to expound the major schools of thought and to venture a reasoned view of which you think preferable.

Philosophies of legal development

5.28 One major reason for dissension in the higher courts is differences of view over when, and by what methods, it is open to the courts to develop the law. To parody the opposing views (though not really by much), some judges are unimaginative bookworms, who stick closely to the text of past precedents and react with indignation at the idea that the courts might do something for which there was no precedent. Others, we might say, have forgotten that the courts are distinct from the Law Commission, and draw no very sharp distinction between expounding the law and making it afresh. Throughout this area, there is conflict between those judges who wish to develop the law in a relatively 'incrementalist' way, and those who are bolder. Both types appeal to Parliament. The more timid judges insist that development of tort is a matter for the legislature, not the courts, perhaps arguing that legislation can implement detailed restrictions and qualifications on liability which the common law cannot (e.g. *D & F Estates v Church Commissioners for England* [1989] AC 177, 210, Lord Bridge; *London Borough of Islington v University College London Hospital NHS Trust* [2005] EWCA Civ 596, para 38, Buxton LJ). The braver ones regard Parliament as a long-stop if the courts' attempts to develop the law go awry, and even threaten to use their position as law lords to introduce new legislation themselves, if they cannot persuade their colleagues to develop the law through the courts (e.g. *White v Jones* [1995] 2 AC 207, 265, Lord Goff). Short of clear evidence that Parliament has already considered the possibility of negligence liability and rejected it as unsuitable, arguments of this sort cannot conclude the matter either way.

Few fundamental points are established

5.29 The disagreements in this area are not confined to the interpretation of agreed principles, but extend to fundamental disputes over what the relevant principles are. For example, some judges are happy to assert that there is a principle against the recovery of pure economic loss, whereas other judges deny that the distinction is of any importance at all. There is also little unanimity on the *function* of tort law in this area. For judges who stick closely to the precedents, this is perhaps not much of a problem: no policy not already endorsed in earlier cases need be adverted to. For judges who take a broader view of their responsibilities, however, there is a real problem, and no agreed solution.

The leading cases are not final

5.30 The higher courts are frequently asked to pronounce on topical issues in this area, yet their rulings seem to have little finality about them. Indeed, many of the live issues are precisely over whether particular decisions should be overruled. At the time of writing, it is highly debatable (for example) whether *Murphy* was rightly decided, whether it was right to overrule *Anns*, and whether the much-criticized *Junior Books* might not have been right for the wrong reasons. And while no-one supposes that the existence of dissenting judgments in itself calls decisions into question, nonetheless many of them are well worth reading. For example, Lord Mustill's dissent in *White v Jones* seems likely to be highly influential. As he noted, many disagreements in cases of this sort derive from a failure to agree on the justice of the claim itself. Assumptions on questions of that sort, he noted, 'dominate the landscape within which the whole inquiry takes place' ([1995] 2 AC 207, 277).

The fear of indeterminate liability

5.31 Many judges are concerned about over-extension of liability: that 'the floodgates of litigation' will be opened, with dire consequences for all. However, the argument is invoked rather too often to be convincing. Most professions are ready with arguments why the sky would fall if they were held responsible in damages for all of the consequences of their actions. If the argument is to be taken seriously (and sometimes it is), then various different types of cases need to be distinguished.

First, the argument might be an appeal to the consequences *for the legal system* if liability is permitted. The court system would be deluged by claims, clogging up the arteries of justice and ultimately stopping the heart of the system of justice.

This argument can be overstated, and frequently has been. It is only rarely that the courts deal with any one case which in itself would have any significant impact on the total number of cases brought in any one year. No doubt it is true that the gradual broadening of the tort of negligence over the 20th century is a factor in the gradual increase in the numbers of claims. But a problem as large as that requires a solution of more general import. Arguments that allowing a particular claim will lead to an unacceptable number of further claims are rarely supported by evidence of any sort, and are often merely a protest at a claim which is novel. In terms of number of claims, cases of purely economic loss are very much a sideshow to the main business of tort law: personal injury claims arising out of motor collisions and workplace accidents.

5.32 A second, and quite different, argument is that it would be undesirable to make the defendant liable for the large sums which would be assessed *against him or her* if liability were allowed: the classic case here being the *Spartan Steel* case. Here, the *number* of cases is not the point; rather, the argument is that the *total liability* on the defendant will be more than the defendant can pay, or more than he fairly should. The argument is often unattractive morally, as it suggests that the more harm the defendant does, the less likely is the defendant to be held liable. However, it should not be forgotten that the defendant's degree of fault is usually ignored in assessing damages—if the defendant is found negligent, even in some relatively trivial respect, then the defendant is liable for the whole of the loss caused, be it large or small. Arguably, to deny the relevance of degrees of fault is unfair, and so it is not too surprising if, having thrown this principle out of the front door, some judges try to sneak it in through the back.

A related argument is that of the availability of insurance. Many judges would feel uncomfortable in holding the defendant liable in circumstances where liability insurance was unavailable, or was very costly. Courts have, however, not always found it easy to discover whether insurance is available; and of course the courts' decision to impose liability will influence the availability of insurance, being one more circumstance to which insurers must adapt. Nonetheless, the availability of insurance is certainly a factor. It seems that the decision in the *Murphy* case was influenced by the fact that the claimant was insured and the defendant was not ([1991] 1 AC 398, 458, Lord Keith). If the *real* claimant is an insurance company which has already been paid to bear the risk in question, and the *real* defendants are the local tax payers, it is not too surprising if the courts seem sympathetic to the defendants.

Organizing concepts

5.33 No one set of concepts provides a magic key to this area. Certain ideas are, however, encountered again. Some of them concentrate on the relationship itself, asking whether there is *proximity* between the claimant and the defendant, or whether their relationship is a *special* one entailing a high degree of care. Others look at the matter from the claimant's side, asking whether he or she has *reasonably relied* on the assumption that the defendant will behave in a careful way. Or again, looking at it from the defendant's side, some ask whether the defendant has *voluntarily assumed responsibility* for safeguarding the claimant's interests. Sometimes these concepts are used together, in various combinations; sometimes they are used alone. Each concept has its judicial supporters and detractors. Perhaps the truth is that each of them makes sense in some areas but not others.

'Proximity'

5.34 It is on any view relevant how close a connection there was between the defendant's behaviour and the claimant's financial or business well-being. It is also often the most obvious ground for liability, in cases where the claimant's contact with the defendant has been minimal.

> **Ministry of Housing and Local Government v Sharp [1970] 2 QB 223:** Would-be purchasers of land applied to the local land charges registry to see whether any interests were registered against it. Due to the carelessness of a registry clerk, they were not told of the Ministry's planning charge, with the result that the Ministry lost the benefit of this charge. Held: the local registry was liable to the Ministry for this error.

Yet 'proximity' has been over-used. In the *Junior Books* case (**5.4**), a majority of the House of Lords was mightily impressed by the close degree of proximity between the claimant and the defendant. The claimant knew the defendant well and had indeed specifically instructed the head contractor to employ the defendant as sub-contractor. The link between them was 'almost as close a commercial relationship...as it is possible to envisage short of privity of contract' ([1983] 1 AC 520, 542, Lord Roskill). Yet while this feature of the case was real enough, it is by no means apparent why it should make any real difference, or why the claimant's case for compensation was any stronger than that of *any* owner of premises who hires a contractor who the claimant knows will himself hire sub-contractors. A high degree of proximity is necessary but not sufficient, and merely proving an exceptional degree of proximity cannot get around the need for additional factors. Equally, in *Ross v Caunters* [1980] Ch 297, where a solicitor misadvised his client with the effect that a legacy to the claimant failed, Megarry V-C made the high degree of proximity between solicitor and legatee the main point in establishing liability. A subsequent House of Lords found this reasoning hopelessly unenlightened and preferred to ignore Megarry's judgment. 'It is better to start again' (*White v Jones* [1995] 2 AC 207, 283, Lord Mustill).

'Special relationship'

5.35　The typical *Hedley Byrne* case is two-handed: the defendant gives poor advice to the claimant, who acts on it and suffers injury. Sometimes the advice follows a rather tortuous route on its way from the defendant to the claimant (e.g. **5.17**), but nonetheless the basic situation is still a two-handed one. However, the tort has occasionally been used in three-handed situations: the defendant gives poor advice to X, who acts on it in some way which injures the claimant. The analogy between these two situations is, however, somewhat imprecise. Some judges reject it altogether: in *White v Jones* [1995] 2 AC 207, Lord Mustill reasoned that *Hedley Byrne* required some sort of reciprocity or mutuality between the claimant and the defendant, and thus considered it quite different from a three-party situation ([1995] 2 AC 207, 287). The point of the analogy is unclear as well: is the 'special relationship' between the claimant and the defendant? Or is the relationship between the defendant and

X regarded as 'special', inasmuch as it has the capacity to harm others? The phrase 'special relationship' perhaps trips too easily off the judicial tongue. No doubt every relationship is special in some respect. It is very hard to understand the repeated suggestion that *Junior Books* may really be explained as a 'special relationship' case (e.g. *Murphy v Brentwood District Council* [1991] 1 AC 398, 466, Lord Keith). The relationship there was indeed close and special, but it is quite unclear why that should lead to the imposition of liability.

'Reliance'

5.36 Again, the idea of 'reliance' makes a certain amount of sense in the two-handed *Hedley Byrne* situation: the claimant relies on the defendant's poor advice and thereby suffers harm. It also makes a certain amount of sense in cases where the defendant is doing work which is meant to benefit the claimant, and for which the claimant ultimately pays. Yet on that basis it is unclear why liability is sometimes established (e.g. *Henderson v Merrett Syndicates* [1995] 2 AC 145) yet sometimes refused (e.g. *Leigh & Sillavan v Aliakmon Shipping Co* [1986] AC 785). It makes less sense in other cases, including some where liability has been established. For example, in what sense does a would-be legatee 'rely' on the testator's solicitor, given that the legatee has no legal right to check up on how the work has gone, and has no legal rights if the testator has a change of heart? It is true that *after* the decision in *White v Jones* [1995] 2 AC 207 legatees are legally entitled to rely on the testator's solicitor, but to use that argument as a reason for establishing liability in the first place seems to be arguing in a circle.

'Voluntary assumption of responsibility'

5.37 This has proved to be one of the more fertile ideas in this area, but perhaps this is because of its inherent vagueness. Nearly all tort liability is 'voluntarily assumed', in the sense that the defendant did not *have* to engage in the conduct of which the claimant is now complaining. Nobody *forced* Stevenson to manufacture and market ginger beer (*Donoghue v Stevenson* [1932] AC 562). But equally, that observation is not enough in itself to justify a finding of liability, and presumably something more is meant by the phrase, though it is not always clear what. This explanation is at its strongest where the defendant undertakes some professional task, in the knowledge that it is the claimant who is really paying for it (albeit indirectly), and the claimant who will suffer if it is done poorly.

Henderson v Merrett Syndicates [1995] 2 AC 145: Henderson, as a 'name' at Lloyd's, entrusted considerable assets to his underwriting agent, who in turn entrusted them to Merrett for investment. Held: Merrett had undertaken responsibility to Henderson and the absence of a contract between Henderson and Merrett was no bar to action in negligence for mismanaging Henderson's assets.

Bailey v HSS Alarms (2000) Times, 20 June: Burglars entered the Baileys' premises and stole property. A burglar alarm system was installed by D&K Electronics, but D&K had sub-contracted the monitoring work to HSS, through whose negligence the police were not informed until some time had passed. D&K were insolvent. Held: HSS owed a duty directly to the Baileys, in respect of both property damage and pure economic loss.

It has also been suggested that this is the true explanation of the *Junior Books* case: the defendant's communications with the claimant arguably added up to an undertaking that the work would be done with reasonable care. Nonetheless, the notion plainly cannot explain all cases—where, for example, was the 'assumption of responsibility' in cases like *Smith v Eric S Bush* (**5.16**)?—and there are also recurrent problems with this notion.

- *Precisely what responsibility is assumed?* The test of 'assumption of responsibility' is vague in its details. For example, are employers under a duty to their employees if they send them on foreign assignments, yet neither insure them against personal injury nor advise their employees to insure themselves? There might be arguments both ways, but it seems inadequate simply to say that this duty was not within the scope of the duty assumed by the employer (*Reid v Rush & Tompkins Group* [1989] 3 All ER 228, 239, Ralph Gibson LJ; similarly *Van Oppen v Clerk to the Bedford Charity Trustees* [1989] 3 All ER 389, where the court denied that schools must insure their students against injuries in games. In both cases the court gave other reasons as well).

- *To whom is responsibility assumed?* The defendant might admit that responsibility for a particular task was assumed, but deny that it was assumed *to the claimant*. Sometimes this argument has been accepted, as where the claimant asks X to sell his car and X delegates the task to the defendant; if the defendant loses the money, the claimant cannot sue the defendant, because the defendant owed a duty to X only (*Balsamo v Medici* [1984] 2 All ER 304). Yet why was this argument rejected in *White v Jones* [1995] 2 AC 207, where equally the defendant solicitor could say that the duty he assumed was not a duty to the testator's daughters, but to the testator himself? Lord Mustill, dissenting, took precisely this point: the duty 'is between himself and his client' ([1995] 2 AC 207, 281). Lord Nolan observed the solicitor had talked to the daughters and said that it would be 'astonishing' if the family solicitor owed a duty only to the head of the family and not to all members of it ([1995] 2 AC 207, 295). Lord Goff side-stepped the issue, admitting that it was hard to see how there could be any assumption of responsibility here; but '[e]ven so it seems to me that it is open to your Lordships' House ... to fashion a remedy to fill a lacuna in the law and so prevent the injustice which would otherwise occur on the facts of cases such as the present' ([1995] 2 AC 207, 268).

> To explain why none of these notions can be the complete explanation of the law of pure economic loss is rather easy. What is less easy to get over is how these concepts are actually used in judicial reasoning and how they are combined with one another to justify concrete results. There is no substitute for a close reading of the leading cases.

The influence of surrounding areas of law

The expanding tort of negligence

5.38 As the tort of negligence has expanded, it has repeatedly encountered questions of liability which are dealt with by other torts or other heads of the law. Negligence has raced ahead, while other areas have stayed still. Whether negligence should be allowed into these other areas is not an easy question. Opposition is not necessarily based on blind conservatism. The intrusion of negligence law should be seen not necessarily as an opportunity for conflict, but rather an opportunity for reflecting what negligence law is for, and what it can add. It is of course equally true that a willingness to let in negligence principles may well be a covert admission that the existing rules in an area are inadequate, or at least would benefit from being supplemented through negligence.

A thorough survey of all the areas on which negligence might have some influence would be beyond the scope of this book. I will review those areas where the possibility for conflict with other areas has been most obvious. I have dealt above with the general question of tort and the liability of statutory authorities (**1.53**).

Defective Premises Act 1972

5.39 This Act gives a remedy to any person acquiring an interest in a 'dwelling' who then finds that the defendant undertook building work on it, but did not do so 'in a workmanlike or, as the case may be, professional manner, with proper materials and so that as regards that work the dwelling will be fit for habitation when completed' (s 1(1)). The duty is similar to a duty in negligence, but there are various limits on liability. It only applies to 'dwellings', not premises generally. It only applies to those who 'take on' building work; it is most unclear to what extent it catches people who arrange for others to do such work, though clearly it does to some extent (see s 1(4)). The limitation period runs from the date of the defective work, not its discovery, and accordingly will often be unrealistically short.

The operation of the Act is wholly excluded if the house is subject to an approved National House Building Council scheme (s 2); compensation is then under the scheme, rather than under the Act. In the early years of the Act, most houses were so covered, making the remedy virtually useless. However, while a revised NHBC scheme for a while remained on the books (approved by SI 1979/381, since revoked), it appears that in the late 1980s the builders privately decided that they would no longer follow the terms of the scheme. So the official approval effectively became a dead letter (see Duncan Wallace, '*Anns* beyond repair' (1991) 107 LQR 228, 243). It appears that the builders do not intend to seek official approval of their current scheme or subsequent modifications to it, and accordingly the Act applies in full force. It makes an occasional appearance in the law reports (e.g. *Andrews v Schooling* [1991] 3 All ER 723).

Was the 1972 Act a factor in the development of the common law? In *Anns* (**5.4**), neither counsel nor judges referred to the Act at all. In *Murphy*, *Anns* was criticized on that ground, the Lords arguing that it was not for the courts to rush in where Parliament had feared to tread. There was, however, no very full discussion of whether Parliament had intended to exclude a common law remedy, or whether Parliament's intervention in relation to domestic housing should be thought to exclude a remedy in relation to all building work. The Lords also seemed unaware of the builders' decision to dispense with official approval for their schemes.

Hague Rules 1924

5.40 The terms of certain international trade transactions are standardized by treaty. One such treaty embodies the Hague Rules, regulating liability between ship-owners and cargo-owners. A broad view has been taken of the policy of this treaty.

> **Marc Rich & Co AG v Bishop Rock Marine Co [1996] AC 211:** Cargo was lost on the sinking of the bulk carrier *The Nicholas H*, when its hull cracked. Possible cracking had been suspected, but the ship-owner's classification society had surveyed the vessel and agreed it could sail. The cargo-owners claimed from the ship-owners the maximum damages permitted under the Hague Rules, and sued the classification society for the balance. Held: to allow such a claim would subvert the Hague Rules.

The law of negligence is accordingly excluded from the area, because the principles of liability are already settled and it would be undesirable for negligence law to unsettle them again.

The administration of justice

5.41 It would have startling consequences if individuals engaged in the justice system could generally sue one another for paying insufficient attention to one another's interests. The courts have usually refused to find any such liability. So:

- the Crown Prosecution Service does not owe a duty to those it prosecutes (*Elguzouli-Daf v Metropolitan Police Commissioner* [1995] QB 335);

- a police authority owes no duty to officers it investigates for alleged misconduct (*Calveley v Chief Constable of the Merseyside Police* [1989] AC 1228);

- the Home Office owes no liability to an asylum-seeker who, through an administrative error, is detained longer than he should have been (*W v Home Office* [1997] Imm AR 302);

- an official receiver is under no liability for statements made in an official capacity while bankruptcy proceedings are running their course (*Mond v Hyde* [1999] QB 1097);

- a bank which has been served with a freezing order in respect of one of its customers is not liable to those who suffer if it carelessly authorizes payments in breach of the order (*Customs and Excise Commissioners v Barclays Bank* [2006] UKHL 28);

- a statement submitted by a potential expert witness cannot be the basis of an action, whether or not the expert is subsequently called on to testify (*Stanton v Callaghan* [2000] 1 QB 75).

However, this immunity is conferred simply because to do otherwise would make the working of the system impossible. Therefore it does not cover every aspect of the work of every person engaged in legal work. For example, it does not provide a defence if, through an avoidable administrative error, the claimant is detained in prison for longer than he should have been; the authority which caused the error is liable to an action (*Clarke v Chief Constable of Northamptonshire* (1999) Times, 14 June).

A special 'advocates' immunity'?

5.42 Lawyers are certainly liable in general for bad advice to their clients, but whether they are entitled to any immunity on this public policy ground is a much-disputed question. Before the *Hedley Byrne* decision, it was assumed that the absence of a contract between barristers and their clients prevented action for shoddy work. Plainly that explanation would not do after *Hedley Byrne*, but the House of Lords accepted in *Rondel v Worsley* [1969] 1 AC 191 that most such actions would simply be attempts to re-litigate issues which should be regarded as settled, and accordingly denied liability. However, it followed that the true distinction was not between work done by barristers and work done by solicitors, but between court work and other work. It was not a barristers' immunity, but an advocates' immunity (*Saif Ali v Sydney Mitchell & Co* [1980] AC 198).

However, the climate of liability has changed a good deal since that time. The modern approach is that earlier cases were confusing two quite distinct principles.

5.43 The first is a supposed public interest in freeing advocates from the consequences of their own negligence. The merits of this rule seem doubtful, and the House of Lords in *Arthur JS Hall & Co v Simons* [2002] 1 AC 615 has now definitively held that there is no longer any such rule. Most of the traditional reasons put forward to support it, such as the intrinsic difficulty of the advocate's role, and the fact that the advocate owes duties to the tribunal as well as to the client, are not obviously any stronger than they are in relation to other professions. It is certainly not clear what a barrister could say to justify the immunity, that could not equally be said by, say, surgeons.

5.44 A second principle now acknowledged to be at work here, and one which is a great deal easier to defend than the 'advocates' immunity', is the so-called principle against 'collateral challenges'. Suppose that the claimant starts a legal action, which fails. The claimant then argues that this was the fault of the defendant, who was a barrister acting for the claimant. The claimant therefore sues the defendant. Obviously, if the claimant is to receive substantial damages from the defendant, it can only be on the basis that the earlier judgment was wrong. In other words, the claimant's later action is an indirect attempt to reopen the issues settled in the first action. The rule is that the earlier ruling cannot be challenged 'collaterally' in this way. The claimant must either challenge it directly, by appealing the earlier judgment, or not at all. So this rule is not concerned with protecting advocates as such, but with achieving finality in the legal process.

This principle has a much more solid policy foundation than the 'advocates' immunity', and it really is inconceivable that we should be without some such rule. Nonetheless, there are serious divergences of approach over it. A harsh line has been taken in relation to criminal cases: claimants who say that they would not have been convicted but for the defendant's poor advocacy (*Smith v Linskills* [1996] 2 All ER 353) or even that they have been pressurized to plead guilty (*Somasundaram v M Julius Melchior* [1989] 1 All ER 129) have been denied a right of action. But those cases recognize that matters may be different where the claimant is introducing completely new evidence, which through the defendant's negligence was not made available at trial; or where the claimant has already succeeded in having his conviction set aside by the Criminal Division of the Court of Appeal (*Acton v Graham Pearce & Co* [1997] 3 All ER 909). As for the standard of care where a duty exists, there is little case law as yet; indications are that the courts will be reluctant to be too demanding, at least where the view counsel took of the case was defensible, even if not every qualification that might have been present to his or her mind was explained (*Moy v Pettman Smith* [2005] UKHL 7).

Defamation

5.45 The harm that the defendant might do to the claimant by sending out an inaccurate job reference for the claimant is obvious enough. Nonetheless, it is not an obvious subject for a remedy in negligence, as it seems classic defamation territory. Nonetheless, the House of Lords has been prepared to hold that action lies in negligence (*Spring v Guardian Assurance* [1995] 2 AC 296). The decision would be very hard to understand if defamation were an area of law held in high regard by lawyers generally. But in fact the law of defamation is notoriously unsatisfactory (**8.43**), and this may well have been a factor in the Lords' decision. Nonetheless, the decision is a little startling. If the claimant had sued in defamation, he would almost certainly have been met by a defence of qualified privilege, which would have defeated the action (**8.35**). An action for negligence is very different from an action in defamation, in many respects. It is much cheaper to mount; damages will only be for proved financial loss, with no sum for injury to feelings; and the main issue is likely to be whether the defendant was careless, which in an action for defamation is not usually relevant.

Equity and property law

5.46 The divisions between legal subjects are often hard to justify except as the product of a long and complicated history. The notion that there is a very close relationship between the defendant and the claimant, and that it is accordingly reasonable to hold the defendant to be under a duty to look to the claimant's interests, appears under various guises. It appears in tort as the '*special relationship*'; but it also appears in equity as the idea of a '*fiduciary relationship*' between them, entailing a *fiduciary duty* to take due care. Indeed, it seems unlikely that the common law would have waited for so long to recognize a tort of negligent misstatement, had not this gap in the law been partly filled by the fiduciary duty (as recognized in cases such as *Nocton v Lord Ashburton* [1914] AC 932). The tort of negligence has been expanding at the same time as the fiduciary duty has been going through a (noticeable but more modest) period of expansion. In both *White v Jones* (**5.5**) and *Henderson v Merrett Syndicates* (**5.37**) either development could be used to justify liability. Which the individual law lords chose reflected their different legal specialisms (compare, in both cases, the opinions of the common lawyer Lord Goff with the equity specialist Lord Browne-Wilkinson). (See also for example *Medforth v Blake* [2000] Ch 86, where receivers were appointed to run a farm. The farm's owner complained that they were not running it effectively, and it was held that a duty was owed. The duty was said to be equitable, but again it makes very little difference in most cases where it is regarded as equitable or tortious.) There seems in general to be little scope for conflict between the two different areas of the law, and they can exist side by side, or indeed overlap, with no problems.

One interesting puzzle is why no conflict between different areas of law was perceived in *White v Jones* (**5.5**), where the claimant's complaint was that her father's legacy would not reach her as he intended. Yet *why* was the legacy not payable? It is because the doctrines of property law stopped it. The law of tort and the law of property approach the case with quite different presuppositions: the tort lawyers are happy to rely on whatever evidence of intention can be produced, whereas the property lawyers will only act on a testator's supposed intention if it is embodied in a special type of document, namely a will. In other words, the court deciding the tort claim was assuming that the property lawyers got the testator's intention wrong! This is a curious state of affairs indeed, and some have suggested that the defendant solicitors should have a remedy against those who actually received the settlor's money, on the ground that they were unjustly enriched. It is, however, hard to see how this claim can lie under the law as it now stands, unless a case for rectification of the will can be made out. Moreover, while the result is strange, it is by no means indefensible.

Contract

5.47　Whether tort and contract are distinct subjects, and if so, how important the distinction is, are questions which different generations of lawyers have answered in very different ways. At the present day, there would be few who would deny that tort and contract are distinct, but the distinction is accorded less weight than it has been at any point in the last two centuries. Traditionally, it has been thought that unrestricted extension of tort liability undermines fundamental doctrines such as consideration and privity. But those doctrines are themselves distinctly unsatisfactory (as witness the enactment of the Contracts (Rights of Third Parties) Act 1999, which makes a large inroad into the doctrine of privity as traditionally understood). The tort of negligence is very often the simplest vehicle for avoiding the least satisfactory aspects of contract law. Accordingly, the old objections to 'concurrent liability'—that is, to liability in contract and tort on the same facts—have largely fallen away, as has the idea that there might be an 'exclusive contractual zone', where liability must be based on contract if there is to be liability at all.

How might negligence interfere with contract?

5.48 The existence of a possible remedy in contract is still relevant in determining liability in negligence. There seem to be four ways in which the law of contract can still restrict the availability of a remedy in negligence, and the following paragraphs set them out in more detail. First, if there is reason to suppose that any contract between the claimant and the defendant was meant to be a definitive statement of their entitlements as against each other, then the courts will not undermine this by granting additional rights under the tort of negligence. Second, and analogously, if there is no contract between the claimant and the defendant, and there is reason to believe that this is because they meant *not* to have mutual rights, then again the courts will not impose rights despite this. Third, where the task which the defendant is expected to perform is one the defendant contracted to do, then the courts will look to the contract to define the nature and detail of the task. Fourth, where the defendant only agreed to do the task subject to conditions limiting liability, those limitations will probably apply to restrict any tort liability as well.

There are common themes running through all of these cases. The most obvious is that the claimant will not be allowed to go against rules which are agreed, or at least generally accepted, in that particular area of work. Another theme, rather more muted but nonetheless an influence, is that negligence is a relative newcomer to many areas of law, and should only be allowed in where this would improve the law's panoply of remedies.

Contract intended to be definitive

5.49 Where there is a contract between the claimant and the defendant, which was meant to be a complete statement of the parties' entitlements against each other, then the courts will respect that bargain. The courts will assume that no rights were meant to be available beyond those in contract, and accordingly they will not impose additional rights and obligations through the tort of negligence. Nonetheless, contract lawyers have in the past been too ready to assume that the contract was meant to be definitive. This approach seems most likely to succeed today in areas where the case law is of long standing and already denies tortious liability.

> ***Tai Hing Cotton Mill v Liu Chong Hing Bank* [1986] AC 80:** An employee of Tai Hing forged cheques on the company's accounts with its bank. The bank paid on the cheques, and on discovering the truth sued Tai Hing to recover the money. Held: it was settled law that in general banks were responsible for paying out on forged cheques (subject to exceptions irrelevant here) and there was no general duty of care on their clients to prevent this.

The result may be right, though some of the reasoning of the Privy Council seems unacceptably broad. If, for example, it is true that '[t]heir Lordships do not think that there is anything to the advantage of the law's development in searching for a liability in tort where the parties are in a contractual relationship' ([1986] AC 80, 107, Lord Scarman), then they are at odds with a very large number of their colleagues (see, for example, **5.21**). The truth is that it is often very difficult indeed to determine whether or not the parties meant their contract to be the definitive statement of their rights.

Absence of contract as definitive

5.50 It may be that the *absence* of a contract between the claimant and the defendant was also meant to be definitive: in other words, they entered into no contract because they did not wish to have any mutual rights and obligations, and it would therefore be wrong for the courts to imply any. Again, the argument is sometimes plausible, but has been overused. If it deserves to be taken seriously, this will presumably be in a case where it would have been relatively easy for the claimant and the defendant to contact one another and negotiate terms (the case involving low transaction costs).

The argument has been used the most in cases concerning the construction industry, where there is typically a strong chain of command—each contracting party knows to whom they are responsible—and so the absence of a contract between any two parties is probably no accident. This argument was deployed again and again in the cases which came after *Anns* and eventually led to its overthrow: notably *Simaan General Contracting Co v Pilkington Glass (No 2)* [1988] QB 758 (main contractor *vs* supplier of glass to a sub-contractor). The logic of such cases is not compelling. It is one thing to point out that there is a precise chain of command, quite another to deny liability to someone who cannot give orders to the defendant, no matter how obvious it was that he or she will suffer from the defendant's carelessness. The absence of a contract between the defendant and the claimant *may* be because they intended no mutual obligations, but that should not be an obvious inference without more to support it.

Contract defining the defendant's task

5.51 Where the principal reason for supposing that the defendant has undertaken a particular task is that the defendant has entered into a contract to do it, then it will be important to see precisely what that task is. The defendant cannot fairly be blamed for failing to perform a different task from the one the defendant was actually engaged on. Thus in *White v Jones* [1995] 2 AC 207, it was emphasized that all the claimant was demanding was that the defendant do the job for which he had been paid. It would have been quite different if the argument had been that the defendant should respect the claimant's interests where they diverged from his client's.

> **Clarke v Bruce Lance & Co [1988] 1 All ER 364:** Clarke was the beneficiary under a will, under which he was to receive an interest in a petrol service station. The testator later instructed his solicitors to alter his will, to give a third party an option to purchase the service station. After the testator's death, Clarke argued that the solicitors had advised the testator poorly over the change to the will. Held: the solicitors owed Clarke no duty in the matter.

Contract limiting the defendant's liability

5.52 Finally, where the defendant undertook a duty by contracting to do it, then any limitation on liability in the contract will probably be held to limit the duty in tort as well. The argument was accepted by the House of Lords in *Junior Books v Veitchi Co* [1983] 1 AC 520, and even (controversially) in *Norwich City Council v Harvey* [1989] 1 All ER 1180, a case of property damage. Where the defendant's duty is stated in elaborate detail, it can sometimes be a difficult question whether the defendant is protected or not.

> **British Telecommunications v James Thomson [1999] 2 All ER 241:** BT hired a construction company, MDW, to repair a switching station. The contract required BT to purchase insurance to cover the station during the work. MDW hired JT as sub-contractor. Some of JT's employees having negligently started a fire, it was argued that it was not reasonable to impose liability, as BT should have insured and so avoided the loss. However, such insurance normally grants the insurance company the right to sue the party responsible for the fire (under the doctrine of 'subrogation'); BT were obliged to secure a policy without subrogation rights where they nominated the sub-contractors themselves, but not otherwise. Held: as BT would have been within their rights to secure a policy which left JT liable to an action in respect of the fire, JT had no valid cause for complaint.

It is not entirely clear how this doctrine is affected by modern legislation limiting the effect of exemption clauses (e.g. Unfair Contract Terms Act 1977, **11.14**). However, *Smith v Eric S Bush* [1990] 1 AC 831 suggests that exempting conditions which would be struck down in a contract action will also be ignored in tort (**5.24**).

FURTHER READING

Barker 'Wielding Occam's Razor: Pruning strategies for economic loss' (2006) 26 OJLS 289.

Duncan Wallace '*Donoghue v Stevenson* and "complex structure": *Anns* revisited?' (2000) 116 LQR 530.

Katter 'The ambit of duty of care for negligent misstatement in the UK and Australia' (2002) 18 Prof Neg 82.

Markesinis and Deakin 'The random element of their Lordships' infallible judgment: An economic and comparative analysis of the tort of negligence from *Anns* to *Murphy*' (1992) 55 MLR 619.

Mullender 'Negligent misstatement, threats and the scope of the *Hedley Byrne* principle' (1999) 62 MLR 425.

Seneviratne 'The rise and fall of advocates' immunity' (2001) 21 LS 644.

Stapleton 'Duty of care: Peripheral parties and alternative opportunities for deterrence' (1995) 111 LQR 301.

Steele 'Scepticism and the law of negligence' (1993) 52 CLJ 437.

Tettenborn 'Professional negligence: Can you owe a duty to the dead?' [2005] Conv 288.

Weston 'Suing in tort for loss of computer data' (1999) 58 CLJ 67.

Witting 'Justifying liability to third parties for negligent misstatements' (2000) 20 OJLS 615.

Witting 'Physical damage in negligence' (2002) 61 CLJ 189.

SELF-TEST QUESTIONS

1 It seems strange that a house-owner with cracked foundations is not thought of as someone who has suffered property damage, but rather as someone who has suffered a purely economic loss. Why is this (**5.10**)?

2 The 'floodgates argument' is really a number of different arguments run together. Summarize these arguments (**5.31–5.32**).

3 How satisfactory is 'voluntary assumption of liability' as a criterion for liability in negligence (**5.37**)?

4 How was the rule in the *Hedley Byrne* case explained by the judges who decided it (**5.15**)?

5 Is it true that liability for negligent misstatement cannot occur in the context of a purely social relationship between the claimant and the defendant (**5.20**)?

Deliberate infliction of
economic loss

SUMMARY

Various torts protect the claimant's economic interests against deliberate harm. Some are best defined as particular types of forbidden conduct: such as deceit, intimidation and conspiracy. Others are best defined as protecting particular economic interests, particularly the claimant's interest in the performance of contracts to which the claimant is party. It is an open question whether all these various instances of liability could or should be fused into a single 'genus' tort of unlawful interference with the claimant's legitimate interests.

6.1 Tort can be looked at from two quite different points of view. From the defendant's point of view, it can be seen as marking out certain types of *conduct*, forbidden on pain of being held liable to the claimant for the consequences (**1.3**). From the claimant's point of view, tort can be seen as protecting certain *interests* from infringement (**1.4**). The choice between the two perspectives is often arbitrary, and more a matter of educational technique than legal principle. For the torts in this chapter, I have chosen a mixture of techniques. First, some of them are best summarized as defining particular prohibited practices: notably the telling of lies, though also the formation of conspiracies and the practice of intimidation. (Very often these practices constitute crimes as well, though that is not particularly relevant here.) Second, some are best seen as defining particular interests: principally in the due performance of the claimant's contracts. Finally, I consider the 'genus' tort of unlawfully inflicting harm to the claimant's legitimate interests: an attempt to fuse the two perspectives.

Deceit

6.2 Where the defendant dishonestly misinforms the claimant, and the claimant suffers loss through relying on this misinformation, then the claimant may sue the defendant for the loss suffered. The defendant is said to have committed the tort of 'deceit'. The defendant's conduct is also sometimes labelled 'fraud', but 'fraud' has several possible meanings in legal contexts, of which this is only one. ('Fraud' may also refer to crimes, particularly those under the Fraud Act 2006; further, it may refer to equitable wrongs such as undue influence or breach of fiduciary duty. The treatment here is limited to civil law, not criminal law; and to 'common law fraud', not 'equitable fraud'.)

Fraud and other torts involving misrepresentation

6.3 The distinguishing features of the tort of deceit are that *(i)* the defendant has misled the claimant and *(ii)* the defendant's behaviour is dishonest. Where the claimant suffers loss because the defendant has misled others, the claimant may have a remedy in defamation (**8.1**) or malicious falsehood (**8.42**), but not in deceit. Where the defendant's conduct was not dishonest, the claimant's remedy, if any, will be in negligence. (In relation to contracts, there is an exception: careless statements which result in a contract may sometimes be treated *as if* fraudulent, by virtue of the Misrepresentation Act 1967, s 2(1). For a full treatment, see your contract text.)

A misrepresentation of fact or law

6.4 The defendant must have made a misrepresentation. This basic requirement is easy to state, and in many cases easy to apply as well. The defendant is liable for misleading the claimant, but not for failing to correct the claimant's misconceptions—even if the defendant knows of them, and could easily have set the claimant straight. A misrepresentation can be made implicitly, or even by conduct. In one famous old (criminal) case, the defendant orders goods at the claimant's shop dressed in a student cap and gown; as he knows, the claimant is prepared to give credit to students, but not to others. This was a fraud whether or not the defendant *said* he was a student (*R v Barnard* (1837) 7 C & P 784). In general, it makes no difference what form the misrepresentation takes. However, by statute a misrepresentation as to the financial standing of a third party is actionable only if in writing and signed (Statute of Frauds Amendment Act 1828, s 6); oddly, this provision does not bar action in negligence (*WB Anderson & Sons v Rhodes (Liverpool)* [1967] 2 All ER 850). There is occasionally a suggestion that in some circumstances there will be a duty of disclosure, so that the defendant will be treated as deceitful on a failure to volunteer certain facts (e.g. *Conlon v Simms* [2006] EWHC 401 (Ch)), but this is unusual.

Problem cases

6.5 The basic rule is that misrepresentation is actionable, but silence is not. The border-line between the two is vague, however, and many issues are matters of degree. A good rule of thumb is that the defendant is likely to be held liable if the defendant has exploited the claimant's ignorance—but not if the defendant knows no more than the claimant about the matter in question. Certainly if the defendant set out to mislead the claimant and was successful, it will rarely be a defence that what the defendant said was *literally* true.

• *Where the defendant takes active steps to mislead the claimant*, a court is likely to find a misrepresentation. This is so whether the defendant does so by making true but misleading statements, or by actively concealing inconvenient facts (as in *Gordon v Selico Co* (1984) 129 SJ 347, where Selico deliberately hid patches of dry rot in a house to induce Gordon to take a tenancy there).

• *Where the defendant makes ambiguous statements*, then the defendant is liable only if the defendant *meant* to mislead the claimant and the claimant was *in fact* misled (*Smith v Chadwick* (1884) 9 App Cas 187).

• *Where the defendant makes a statement to the claimant and only later discovers that it is false*, the defendant is treated as having made a false representation to the claim-ant *at the time when the defendant could have corrected the claimant's mistake* (*Briess v Woolley* [1954] AC 333). Conversely, if the defendant makes a statement fraudu-lently, but by the time the claimant acts on it circumstances have changed and it is the truth, no fraud is committed (*Ship v Crosskill* (1870) LR 10 Eq 73).

• *Where the defendant makes a false statement of intention*, this is deceit: 'the state of a man's mind is as much a fact as the state of his digestion' (*Edgington v Fitzmaurice* (1885) 29 Ch D 459, 483, Bowen LJ). But if the defendant has merely changed his mind at a later point, this is not deceit, however awkward it is for the claimant, or however weak the defendant's excuse for failing to mention it.

• *Where the defendant makes a promise to the claimant and then breaks it*, generally speaking this is not deceit (though it may be a breach of contract). Deceit will only be established where the defendant can be shown to have misrepresented some fact. This would occur if, for example, the claimant could show that the defendant never intended to keep the promise (e.g. *Re Eastgate* [1905] 1 KB 465).

• *Where the defendant expresses an opinion*, this will not be deceit merely because the opinion is wrong. It will be deceit if the defendant did not in fact hold the opin-ion expressed. It will also be deceit if the defendant deliberately implies something the defendant knows to be untrue, such as that he has solid grounds for what he says (*Brown v Raphael* [1958] Ch 636).

'Dishonesty'

6.6 The requirement that the defendant make the misrepresentation 'dishonestly' involves proof either *(i)* that the defendant knew the representation was false or *(ii)* that the defendant made the statement without belief in its truth. This last case includes the case where the defendant doesn't know, and doesn't care, whether it was true or not. (This is often styled 'recklessness', but that word has too many meanings in law to promote clarity here.) Negligence, even gross negligence, is not enough for liability (*Derry v Peek* (1889) 14 App Cas 337), except where statute makes it so (Misrepresentation Act 1967, s 2(1)).

6.7 The requirement that the defendant make the misrepresentation 'dishonestly' also involves proof that the defendant meant the claimant to act on the statement. This is usually clear, though it is less so where the statement is communicated to the claimant indirectly. There is no additional requirement of intent to *harm* the claimant, or of 'malice', however defined (*Brown Jenkinson & Co v Percy Dalton (London)* [1957] 2 QB 621).

Assessment of the claimant's loss

6.8 The claimant is entitled to recover the amount by which the claimant would have been better off had the defendant not engaged in fraud. The claimant may recover for any form of quantifiable loss caused by fraud, including personal injury, but in practice the loss is almost invariably purely economic. In principle, calculation is straightforward. Difficulties arise in cases where the defendant has fraudulently induced the claimant to invest in a particular business, at least if it is not clear what the claimant would have done with his or her money but for the defendant's inducement.

> ***Smith New Court Securities v Scrimgeour Vickers (Asset Management)* [1996] 4 All ER 769:** Scrimgeour fraudulently induced Smith to buy a large block of shares at 82p per share. The shares were then trading at 78p on the stock market. Soon afterwards, another fraud (not related to Scrimgeour's) was revealed, which took the trading price of the shares down to 44p. Held: Smith could recover for the entire drop in value from 82p to 44p, even though as a general rule it would fall on Smith as owners of the shares.

> ***Downs v Chappell* [1996] 3 All ER 344:** Downs bought a bookshop from Chappell for £120,000, after fraudulent representations as to its turnover. On discovering the truth, Downs tried to sell the business, but refused two offers of £76,000, eventually being

forced to accept an offer of £60,000. Robert Owen QC found that Downs would probably have bought the business anyway had he known the business's true value, and accordingly gave no damages. Held: on appeal, the truth was that the value was unknown at the time Downs bought, so this was not the right approach. Damages were assessed at £44,000 (i.e. £120,000 less £76,000).

Other torts of making false statements

6.9 Where the claimant suffers loss because the defendant has made false statements to others, various torts are potentially relevant, none of which will be treated in detail here. Where the defendant does injury to the claimant's reputation, then the torts of *defamation* (**8.1**) and *malicious falsehood* (**8.42**) may be relevant. If the defendant casts aspersions against the claimant's business or against goods the claimant sells, this will not usually be defamation. It may, however, be malicious falsehood; and there is a distinct but related tort of *slander of title*, which consists of creating doubts whether the claimant has the legal right to sell his goods. Another highly specific tort is *passing off*, where the defendant sets out to confuse his or her own products with the claimant's in the eyes of the public. (See, for example, *Taittinger v Allbev* [1994] 4 All ER 75, where Allbev described its carbonated drink as 'Elderflower Champagne', thus risking confusion with real champagne made by Taittinger and others.)

Intimidation

6.10 Where the defendant makes an unlawful threat which induces someone else to harm the claimant, the defendant has committed the tort of intimidation. Usually the defendant makes the threat to some third party, who then harms the claimant ('three-party intimidation'); occasionally the threat is addressed to the claimant personally, who feels compelled to act contrary to his or her own interests ('two-party intimidation'). It is sometimes said that the action induced by the threat must itself be lawful; but this simply seems to reflect the obvious point that if it is not, the claimant will have a simple and obvious remedy for it without resorting to this rather arcane tort.

The 'unlawfulness' of the threat

6.11 The defendant's threat is not actionable unless it was to do something contrary to law. However, it need not be something in itself actionable by the claimant (and it will rarely be necessary to invoke this tort if it is). It seems that crimes and torts are for this purpose 'unlawful'. A threat to break a contract made with the party threatened will also be sufficient, even though the claimant would have had no legal ground of complaint if the parties to the contract had voluntarily agreed to terminate it.

> **Rookes v Barnard [1964] AC 1129:** Rookes' employer sacked him, to avert a threat of strike action by Barnard and others, officials of a union seeking to impose a closed shop on the firm. Held: the threat of a strike, being a threat to breach an employment contract, was sufficiently unlawful to found an action by Rookes, even though the sacking was itself perfectly lawful.

So the definition of 'unlawfulness' is broad, and while the authorities are unclear, there does not seem any reason in principle why it cannot cover breach of any duty under common law, equity, or statute. But the matter is not so simple. Often it is legitimate to ask, 'How does it happen that the defendant's threat is "unlawful" and yet the claimant has no remedy unless it is for "intimidation" '?

• In the *Rookes v Barnard* type of case, the reason why the claimant has to resort to 'intimidation' is because the doctrine of 'privity of contract' prevents the claimant complaining more directly that the defendant has threatened to break his contract. There is considerable academic debate on the merits of the 'privity' doctrine and whether it should also prevent action in intimidation.

• Where the 'unlawfulness' consists of breach of a duty imposed by statute, the courts often ask whether Parliament also intended to create a private right of action (e.g. *Lonrho v Shell Petroleum Co (No 2)* [1982] AC 173). Simply because Parliament intended a duty, even a duty backed up with criminal sanctions, by no means necessarily implies that a private right to sue was meant as well. But it cannot be pretended that it will always be clear precisely what Parliament intended. This issue has already been discussed above, in connection with the tort of breach of statutory duty (**1.47**).

Intent to injure the claimant

6.12   Action lies only if the defendant intended to injure the claimant. Difficult questions arise where it is clear that the defendant deliberately set out to injure the claimant, but was not motivated by personal spite, but rather by some economic objective. Do we regard the deliberate infliction of *economic* harm as 'intentional injury'? In what little case law there is, it seems to be assumed that pursuit of one's own economic interests is no defence. So in *Rookes v Barnard* [1964] AC 1129 (**6.11**) it was assumed that Barnard and his colleagues meant to injure Rookes, even though it appears that their sole motive was to dispose of an individual inconvenient for their scheme for a closed shop. *Dicta* in *Rookes* and elsewhere suggest that there may sometimes be a defence of justification, excusing quite deliberate harm, perhaps as a response to provocative behaviour by the claimant (compare **6.26**).

The effectiveness of the threat

6.13 It is clear that the defendant's threat must place considerable pressure on the person to whom it is addressed, if it is to be the foundation of an action in intimidation. Mere idle abuse, however humiliating, will not do, unless it is clearly meant to push the victim in the direction of certain conduct. There is no clear test in the authorities, however. Some judges distinguish between a 'threat' and a mere 'warning'. But while the manner in which the defendant expresses himself or herself is a relevant circumstance in assessing the defendant's behaviour, this is hard to apply as a test. A polite threat is still a threat. No doubt a genuine willingness to explore alternatives other than submission to the threat or its execution goes a long way towards minimizing its coercive character.

Is two-party intimidation different?

6.14 Intimidation is usually a three-party affair: the defendant threatens X, inducing X to harm the claimant. But it is clearly stated in *Rookes v Barnard* [1964] AC 1129 and other authorities that an action lies equally in the case where the defendant unlawfully threatens the claimant directly. This is odd, however, because we would naturally expect an unlawful threat against the claimant directly to be actionable in itself, without the need for a distinct tort of 'intimidation'. So if, for example, the defendant threatens some tort against the claimant, we would expect the claimant to be able to claim a *quia timet* injunction against the defendant to prevent the threat becoming an actuality (**10.3**). The 'two-party' version of the tort is hardly ever invoked, and remains highly controversial.

Conspiracy

6.15 Where two or more people agree to act in a way which they know will injure the claimant, then in certain circumstances the claimant may sue any or all of them for the loss caused by this 'conspiracy'. It may fairly be asked why conspiracy should be any concern of the law. If the loss would not have been actionable in itself, why should it matter that there was a 'conspiracy' to do it? There is no very obvious answer to this point. It is sometimes said that two or more people may do more harm than one, and so represent a special danger, to which the law must give particular heed. But this is absurd. If two market stallholders attempt to drive a third out of business, this may be an actionable conspiracy; if a single chain store attempts to do the same, it is not. Yet which situation represents the more serious abuse of economic power?

Agreement

6.16 Whether there was in fact an agreement is usually a purely factual question, and the courts are reluctant to generalize about it. There is no rule that someone who knowingly receives the proceeds of fraud *must* have been part of a conspiracy to injure the victim (*CIBC Mellon Trust Co v Stolzenberg* [2003] EWHC 13 (Ch)). It was at one time thought that an agreement between a wife and her husband could not constitute a 'conspiracy', because of the ancient maxim that husband and wife are one person. But this contention has now been rejected: 'The gravity of the injury sustained does not vary according to whether those who inflict it are casual acquaintances or are indissolubly conjoined in wedded bliss' (*Midland Bank Trust Co v Green (No 3)* [1979] 2 All ER 193, 219, Oliver J).

Can a business be regarded as a conspiracy between the various people who constitute it? Cases on businesses are confused. It is said that the employees of a firm cannot be treated as conspirators in the execution of a business plan (e.g. *Crofter Hand Woven Harris Tweed Co v Veitch* [1942] AC 435, 468, Lord Wright). However, a plan hatched by the directors may constitute a conspiracy between themselves and the company too (*Belmont Finance Corpn v Williams Furniture (No 2)* [1980] 1 All ER 393); though it was also said in that case that the company would *not* be regarded as a conspirator if it was *itself* the intended victim of the conspiracy. It has been held (in a criminal case) that a one-person company cannot be treated as conspiring with the person who controls it, on the ground that it has no independent mind (*R v McDonnell* [1966] 1 QB 233). But this reasoning is unsatisfactory, as contract lawyers have no difficulty with the idea that a one-person company can contract with the person concerned. Cases of this sort emphasize the oddity of the requirement adopted. Why should liability for particular harm vary depending on whether the person inflicting it acted alone?

6.17 There is a division in the law, depending on whether the means adopted by the conspirators were in some sense unlawful.

'Conspiracy to injure'

6.18 Where the predominant purpose of the conspiracy was to injure the claimant, then the conspiracy is actionable *whether or not* unlawful means were employed. The difficult question has always been over the necessary intent. A narrow view was taken in a famous 19th-century case:

> **Mogul Steamship Co v McGregor, Gow & Co [1892] AC 25:** One shipping company, Mogul, was driven out of business by the concerted action of others, including McGregor, Gow. These competitors had used a variety of tactics, including the offering of special rebates to customers not to deal with Mogul, and arranging services and prices in such a way as to deprive Mogul of custom rather than to run at a profit. Held: as no illegal means had been employed, no action lay.

Obviously we cannot explain this result by saying that the conspirators meant their victim no harm (plainly they did), or even that they bore no personal ill will (they may well have done). Rather, it is a defence that they were motivated by self-interest rather than spite, *even though Mogul's ruin was a necessary part of their self-interested plan.* This has obviously gone beyond a proposition about the meaning of 'intent'. What would we make of an argument that a mugger does not 'intend' to harm his victims if he does not hate them personally, and does not care *how* he obtains their money? His indifference to his victim's fate is precisely what makes him dangerous. Yet in the case of *purely economic* harm, a different attitude is taken. Public policy towards competition has changed somewhat since 1892, and we would today expect McGregor, Gow, and their co-conspirators to receive some attention from the competition authorities. But *Mogul* still represents the common law.

'Intent to injure'

6.19 The narrow rule on 'intent' stated in the previous paragraph has had its ups and downs, but represents the current law. *Allen v Flood* [1898] AC 1 was taken to establish that conduct by trade unions that stayed within the law would not be tortious merely on the ground that it was clearly meant to harm the claimant. However, some outrageous bench-packing by the Conservative Lord Chancellor, Lord Halsbury, secured a contrary result in *Quinn v Leathem* [1901] AC 495, where conduct designed to coerce the claimant into accepting a closed shop was held to be an actionable conspiracy. (See Stevens *Law and Politics* (1979) 93–4.) Only by slow stages (culminating in *Crofter Hand Woven Harris Tweed Co v Veitch* [1942] AC 435) were the courts prepared to apply the same rule to trade unions as to others, namely that pursuit of their own economic interests protected them from a charge of 'intent to injure'. But the 'pursuit of economic self-interest' defence does not protect those whose behaviour has no rational economic basis.

> **Gulf Oil (GB) v Page [1987] Ch 327:** Page was involved in a commercial dispute with Gulf, in a case where Gulf was found by a court to be in breach of contract. Page and

others hired a light aircraft to tow a banner saying 'Gulf exposed in fundamental breach' over a race meeting where Gulf was entertaining clients. Held: even though the banner told the truth, nonetheless there was an actionable conspiracy to injure.

However, since that case it has been stressed that action lies only where loss is proved, and so a mere general allegation of 'injury to reputation' will not do (*Lonrho v Fayed (No 5)* [1994] 1 All ER 188). This is one more ad hoc limit on the tort, which is now in practice very hard to establish. Views differ considerably on whether this tort is a useful legal institution unreasonably hedged about with technicalities, or whether it is fundamentally anomalous, and is rightly kept within narrow bounds.

'Unlawful means'

6.20 Liability is easier to establish where the means employed by the conspirators are themselves unlawful. But what is meant by 'unlawful' in this context? Until very recently, the leading cases put strict limits on liability under this variety of the tort.

> **Lonrho v Shell Petroleum (No 2)** [1982] AC 173: Lonrho constructed an oil pipeline running from Rhodesia to Mozambique. However, this pipeline stood idle for many years, as a consequence of international sanctions applied to Rhodesia after its declaration of independence. Lonrho alleged that Shell had illegally supplied oil to Rhodesia, thus prolonging the life of the regime and incidentally lengthening the time for which Lonrho's pipeline lay idle. Held: no action lay, first, because Shell had no intention to harm Lonrho, and second, because breach of the sanctions legislation did not count as 'unlawful means' for this purpose.

On the 'intent' point, this comes close to smuggling the defence of economic self-interest into this variety of the tort too. It is not clear whether the Lords were applying the full rigours of the *Mogul* test, but the fact of the matter is that Shell were not treated as intending harm to Lonrho, even though they appreciated very well the harmful effect of their actions. The Lords have since that time slightly backed away from that conclusion. They have now said that 'when conspirators intentionally injure the claimant and use unlawful means to do so, it is no defence for them to show that their primary purpose was to further or protect their own interests' (*Lonrho v Fayed* [1992] 1 AC 448, 465–6, Lord Bridge; and see to the same effect *Kuwait Oil Tanker Co v Al Bader* [2000] 2 All ER (Comm) 271). But the Lords did not criticize *Lonrho v Shell*, and plainly a strict line is still being taken.

As to 'unlawful means', *Lonrho* required not only that the defendant's conduct must be in some sense illegal, but also that it must be actionable in a civil court. So conspiracy to commit torts would usually be actionable, but conspiracy to commit crimes will not be, unless they are torts as well. But the most recent authority contradicts this, apparently holding that any means involving a breach of statute or regulation will be 'unlawful' for this purpose.

> **Total Network SL v Revenue and Customs Commissioners [2008] EWHL 19:** Total were party to an alleged 'carousel fraud', under which goods were sold and resold amongst conspirators. One of these sales would generate a liability to pay VAT, and a subsequent one would generate a right to reclaim that VAT; the essence of the fraud was that the VAT would never in fact be paid but it would be 'reclaimed' anyway. The Revenue sued for conspiracy, the 'unlawful means' consisting of the breach of revenue law. Held: conduct which was criminal, whether at common law or by statute, was 'unlawful' for this purpose, and an action lay accordingly.

Interference with contractual rights

6.21 This tort is defined as protecting a specific interest—namely, the claimant's interest in the performance of any contract to which the claimant is a party. Where the defendant intentionally interferes with performance, the claimant may have an action for the loss which results. This tort has its origins in the mediaeval law of enticing away the claimant's servant or a member of the claimant's family. In principle today it applies to any type of contract, though the cases are still heavily concentrated in the employment field.

Need the defendant induce a breach of contract?

6.22 This tort is sometimes called 'inducing breach of contract', and the modern position appears to be that a breach of contract must be established before action could proceed (see *OBG v Allan* [2007] UKHL 21, in this respect overruling the earlier case of *Torquay Hotel Co v Cousins* [1969] 2 Ch 106).

The mental element

6.23 It is sometimes said that the interference must be 'intentional', though if so 'intent' is being used in a very broad sense. At minimum, the defendant must know of the contract; it is not enough that the defendant had the means of acquiring that knowledge (*Unique Pub Properties Ltd v Beer Barrels and Minerals (Wales) Ltd* [2004] EWCA Civ 586). There is, however, no additional requirement that the defendant's conduct be 'aimed at' the claimant. It does not matter whether the defendant knows the precise details of the contract concerned (*JT Stratford & Son v Lindley* [1965]

AC 269). It has been stated that 'intention' here is a flexible criterion, and that this criterion and others 'are designed to keep a wide-ranging tort within bounds. It is therefore important that they are not applied mechanically and that regard is had to the balancing demands of moral constraint and economic freedom' (*Stocznia Gdanska SA v Latvian Shipping Co (No 3)* [2002] EWCA Civ 889, para 131).

Direct persuasion inducing breach

6.24 One variety of the tort is where the defendant convinces a contracting party to breach it. It is then irrelevant whether the defendant used unlawful means or not, or whether the defendant's behaviour would more accurately be styled as 'coercion' or 'persuasion'. It is sometimes said that mere advice will not do: 'To induce a breach of contract means to create a reason for breaking it; to advise a breach of contract is to point out the reasons which already exist' (Heuston and Buckley *Salmond and Heuston on the Law of Tort* (20th edn, 1992) 363). This appears to be the law, though it is a difficult distinction to apply.

Inducement by unlawful act

6.25 If there is no persuasion, the claimant may sue the defendant only if the means the defendant employed were 'unlawful'. It was at one time common to distinguish between 'direct inducement', where the defendant gets at the other party to the contract, and 'indirect procurement', where the defendant induces others to thwart the contractual performance. It is sometimes said that the courts will require a higher degree of knowledge in the second class of the case than in the first. There seems little point in such a distinction today, except by way of emphasizing the range of different situations to which the tort is relevant. In any event, it is most unclear what is meant by 'unlawful' here, though it appears that most torts will do (e.g. trespass to goods, *GWK v Dunlop Rubber Co* (1926) 42 TLR 593). It would be surprising if breach of a penal statute which did not itself give rise to civil liability would be sufficient; but in the current state of the authorities it is hard to be very definite on the matter.

A defence of justification

6.26 In certain circumstances, the defendant may be able to argue that the interference was justified. The defence relies on a thorough examination of the precise facts of each case. Numerous attempts by trade unions to argue that individual actions are justified have failed. The one exception was a case where counsel scared the court with the suggestion that the union's members would be forced into prostitution if they could not induce their employers to raise their wages (*Brimelow v Casson* [1924] 1 Ch 302). More successful are defendants who have argued that they were merely seeking to vindicate a legal entitlement of their own (e.g. *Edwin Hill and Partners v First National Finance Corpn* [1989] 1 WLR 225).

This variety of the defence is said to lie where the defendant's right is an 'equal or superior' entitlement to that of the claimant. The range of different circumstances in which the defence might be invoked means that this is a rather opaque phrase. It seems doubtful whether even a *very* superior entitlement could justify the use of unlawful means.

The 'unlawful means' tort

6.27 We have now looked at a number of torts which start from particular types of misconduct by the defendant ('intimidation', 'conspiracy', etc.), and at one which starts from the infringement of the claimant's legitimate interests ('interference with contractual performance'). There is potential for considerable overlap between these torts. It has been suggested that each of these individual torts is merely a 'species of [a] wider genus of tort', that wider genus being interference with the claimant's trade interest by unlawful means (*Merkur Island Shipping Corpn v Laughton* [1983] 2 AC 570, 609–10, Lord Diplock). In time, the 'genus' may come to be stated in sufficiently precise terms for it to swallow up the individual species. However, the House of Lords in *OBG v Allan* [2007] UKHL 21 has for the present rejected the 'genus' tort, insisting that the 'unlawful means' tort is merely one of the economic torts, not to be seen as potentially subsuming them all.

Definition

6.28 The defendant commits this tort by deliberate interference with the claimant's trade or business interests by unlawful means. The defendant's conduct must actually be unlawful, not merely antisocial: 'There is no tort of unfair trading' (*Associated Newspapers v Insert Media* [1990] 1 WLR 900, 909, Mummery J). Despite its uncertainty, the tort plainly has the potential to reach facts that other torts cannot reach.

> **Lonrho v Fayed [1992] 1 AC 448:** Lonrho was in competition with the Fayed brothers to take over House of Fraser. Lonrho's bid was delayed by being referred to the Monopolies and Mergers Commission; the Fayeds avoided this, allegedly as the result of fraudulent misrepresentations, and were therefore able to make a successful bid. On these assumed facts, the Fayeds were liable for unlawful interference with Lonrho's business.

It appears that most torts (such as fraud in *Lonrho v Fayed*) and (probably) breach of contract will constitute 'unlawful means'. There is little to suggest that breach of a statutory duty will do, unless actionable as such. The required degree of intent to harm the claimant is unclear, though manifestly there is no *Mogul*-type defence of pursuit of economic self-interest.

The interest protected

6.29 In many cases, there is no doubt that the defendant's conduct was 'unlawful' under some specific head of the law (such as a definite statutory provision), or that the harm it caused the claimant was deliberate. There are, however, two obstacles to the claimant's case, one being that it is unclear whether there is the right sort of 'unlawfulness', the other being lack of clarity whether the claimant's legitimate interests have been infringed. In that situation, the claimant must make the specific legal duty do double duty: not only as showing that the defendant has acted unlawfully, but also that the claimant's right has been infringed. This is difficult to do, unless there is something in the way the provision is formulated to suggest that it was meant to confer a right on the claimant. Cases of equitable wrongs such as breach of confidence and breach of fiduciary duty fit neatly into this approach. In cases of that sort, it is easy to see both that the breach is a wrong and that it can be said to damage the rights of specific people (*Boulting v Association of Cinematograph, Television and Allied Technicians* [1963] 2 QB 606, 636, Upjohn LJ). But misbehaviour in the course of a court case, while obviously wrong, might be seen as harming the public interest rather than the rights of any one individual. So it has been held that there is no liability where the defendant punishes the claimant for giving evidence in a legal action, even though this is a contempt of court (*Chapman v Honig* [1963] 2 QB 502). But exceptionally, misconduct in litigation may be held to infringe individual rights.

> **Acrow (Automation) v Rex Chainbelt [1971] 3 All ER 1175:** Acrow obtained an injunction against SI Handling Systems, to force it to honour a licence agreement it had entered into with Acrow. Rex, a company associated with SI, attempted to subvert the injunction by refusing to supply Acrow with essential equipment. Held: Acrow could sue Rex for deliberate interference with its business.

6.30 Difficult problems arise where the claimant relies on the same statutory provision both to establish the 'unlawfulness' *and* the legitimacy of the interest interfered with. The cases where this is easiest to do is where the statute was meant to grant the claimant an interest in property, or something analogous. So in *Ex p Island Records* [1978] Ch 122 it was held that breach of the Dramatic and Musical

Performers' Protection Act 1958 (since repealed) gave an action to the performers and record companies affected. But Shaw LJ dissented in that case, arguing that the statute could not be read as conferring a right to sue for breach of its provisions. The House of Lords has since confirmed that Shaw LJ's is the right approach (*Lonrho v Shell Petroleum Co (No 2)* [1982] AC 173, 187, Lord Diplock).

It remains controversial whether the claimant has to show that the statute was one on which a civil action lies, or whether it is sufficient that the statute confers a right on the claimant with which the defendant has interfered. A good example of the sort of statute that will do is provided by *Associated British Ports v Transport and General Workers' Union* [1989] 3 All ER 796. The statute in the case established a dock labour scheme. Interference with this scheme was held capable of giving rights to the employers affected, *even though* there was no action for breach of statutory duty available. More controversially, it has been held that the making of an agreement which is 'unlawful', in the sense of contravening legislation on anti-competitive practices, is sufficient to give a competitor a right of action (*Daily Mirror Newspapers v Gardner* [1968] 2 QB 762).

'Eurotorts' and public law

6.31   Breach of EU law, a specialized form of breach of statutory duty, can give rise to an action, so long as the *Lonrho v Shell* test, that the duty was meant to give rise to rights, is satisfied (*Garden Cottage Foods v Milk Marketing Board* [1984] AC 130). But this is a highly complex area, which is still developing; and consideration must be given to the range of remedies available for breach. So in one context at least the Court of Appeal has ruled that action for damages is not normally available against the government, the alternative remedy of judicial review being adequate to achieve justice (*Bourgoin SA v Ministry of Agriculture, Fisheries and Food* [1986] QB 716). And EU directives will not be read as giving rights of action to private individuals where this is unnecessary to achieve their purposes (*Three Rivers District Council v Bank of England (No 3)* [2001] UKHL 16). But there are plainly some cases where an award of damages is justified, so long as a 'manifest and grave' breach is shown (*R v Secretary of State for Transport, ex p Factortame* [1999] 4 All ER 906). This can include judicial flouting of EU law, even by the highest court within a particular nation (*Köbler v Austria* [2004] All ER (EC) 23).

Analogous and somewhat related is the very uncertain tort of 'misfeasance in a public office', which seems to require deliberate misbehaviour by a public official either with the intention of injuring the claimant, or with reckless indifference (*Three Rivers District Council v Bank of England (No 3)* [2001] UKHL 16). It does not appear to be necessary to prove that the claimant was in any way targeted, or even that the claimant was known to the misbehaving official (*Akenzua v Secretary of State for the Home Department* [2002] EWCA Civ 1470). A live issue is of what counts as actionable injury for the purposes of this tort: so far it appears that loss of liberty will do so (*Karagozlu v Metropolitan Police Commissioner* [2006] EWCA Civ 1691), but infringement of privacy will not (*Watkins v Secretary of State for the Home Department* [2006] UKHL 17). In a case involving the forcible removal of the inhabitants of the Chagos Islands, an attempt to extend the tort by analogy to create a tort of 'unlawful exile' was unsuccessful (*Chagos Islanders v A-G* [2003] EWHC 2222 (QB)).

Assessment

'The economic torts are in a mess'

6.32   The confusion of the economic torts is manifest. The confusion is partly linguistic, partly over how creative we want our judges to be, and partly over the merits of various proposed patterns of liability. Nor is it obvious that squeezing all the economic torts into a single 'genus' tort of unlawful interference with trade or business will improve matters. What is 'unlawful'? Why 'trade or business' and why not other losses? How does 'interference with trade' differ from mere competition? 'The economic torts are in a mess. The acceptance, without definition, of the genus tort...only adds to that mess. Definition of this tort is vital' (Carty 'Intentional violation of economic interests: the limits of common law liability' (1988) 104 LQR 250, 278).

Liability for lawful behaviour

Should it exist at all?

6.33   Cases where the defendant neither commits nor induces any unlawful act at all, and yet is still held liable for an economic tort, are rare. Many of these cases consider them anomalous. In these cases—'conspiracy to injure' (**6.18**) and cases of interference with contract without inducing a breach (**6.22**)—there is a strong case for there being no liability at all. Yet to others it seems a pity not to have the option of finding liability for conduct which was intended to cause harm, and which serves no conceivable beneficial purpose.

Can we trust the judges?

6.34 An entirely different kind of objection to this type of liability is that, while it might often be a useful addition to the law, its development should be left to Parliament and not to the judges. The development of this head of the law over the past century or so is no glowing advertisement for the merits of the common law system. The issues it raises are broad and complex. So while it seems worrying that the common law gives no remedy in the *Mogul* type of case (**6.18**), it would be even more worrying if the courts attempted to fashion a remedy without due regard to the many policy issues involved. So while the ability of a busy legislature to keep every part of the common law under its eye must be doubted, nonetheless there is a strong case for the judges leaving well alone.

Liability for unlawful behaviour

6.35 It seems less problematical to impose liability where the defendant's conduct was in some sense unlawful, and judicial creativity here is correspondingly less worrying. Again, however, the over-enthusiasm and lack of rigour displayed in the deployment of the economic torts against trades unions throughout the last century have not enhanced the judiciary's reputation in this area. And what is left of the law seems much too specific. What can it matter whether the defendant's conduct is rightly described as 'intimidation' or not? Why should it matter whether the defendant had help or acted alone? This was precisely why the 'genus' approach seemed desirable—though it appears that the current House of Lords thinks otherwise. If the 'genus' approach is right, then perhaps we can abandon the other, more specific torts entirely—and good riddance. As it is, what good do these individual categories do?

Yet what job should the 'genus' tort be doing? Time and again, we find the 'unlawfulness' issue turning on matters which should surely be resolved under another head of the law. Few think it enough that the defendant was engaged in activity which was undoubtedly illegal. The question is not merely whether the defendant's behaviour is illegal, but also whether the claimant is entitled to complain of it. It is not enough that the defendant has done wrong, if the claimant has suffered no infringement of rights. This leads many to suspect that the emphasis is entirely wrong, and that the 'genus' tort is a mistake. If the question is whether the defendant's procurement of a breach of contract should enable the claimant to sue, then we should look for the answer to that question in the policies and purposes of contract law, not tort. If the defendant has infringed a statute, then the matter should turn on whether the statute is one breach of which gives a right to sue, or whether the imposition of liability can be said to further the policy of the statute (**1.47**). On this view, the establishment of the 'genus' tort would be an intellectual error of the highest order.

FURTHER READING

Bagshaw 'Can the economic torts be unified?' (*review article*) (1998) 18 OJLS 729.

Carty 'Intentional violation of economic interests: The limits of common law liability' (1988) 104 LQR 250.

Carty 'The economic torts in the 21st century' (2008) 124 LQR 641.

Craig 'Once more unto the breach: the Community, the State and damages liability' (1997) 113 LQR 67.

Howarth 'Against *Lumley v Gye*' (2005) 68 MLR 195.

Neyers 'Rights-based justifications for the tort of unlawful interference with economic relations' (2008) 28 LS 215.

Sales and Stilitz 'Intentional infliction of harm by unlawful means' (1999) 115 LQR 411.

Simester and Chan 'Inducing breach of contract: one tort or two?' (2004) 63 CLJ 132.

Tridimas 'Liability for breach of community law: Growing up and mellowing down?' (2001) 38 CMLR 301.

SELF-TEST QUESTIONS

1 What is the 'genus' tort, and is it currently part of the law (**6.27**)?

2 Is it possible to sue the defendant in deceit when all the defendant has done is express an opinion (**6.5**)?

3 Can the tort of conspiracy be used to protect the claimant's reputation (**6.19**)?

4 How much does the defendant need to know about a contract before he or she can be said to 'intentionally interfere' with it (**6.23**)?

5 Why is action over 'two-party intimidation' rare (**6.14**)?

7

Land use and the environment

SUMMARY

Various torts provide a patchwork of protection in respect of land use:

- Trespass to land

- Private nuisance

- Public nuisance

- Strict liabilities for dangerous activities

The torts here have only a small part to play in the law's protection of the environment, and have little overall coherence in themselves. Arguably, however, they remain a useful supplement to the law's general provision in this area.

7.1 The law of tort has some impact on the protection of the environment. However, the law is complex and uncertain, even by the charitable standards which must be applied to tort law; and the rules have traditionally been seen in a quite different light, protecting the rights of individual landowners rather than 'the environment' as such. The result is that several quite distinct torts, each of considerable age, provide a crazy quilt of protection for land use and environmental interests. No-one would argue that these miscellaneous torts make any overall sense as a response to the problems of protecting the environment; but it is another question whether they form a valuable, if small, part of the law's overall response to the problem. This matter is taken up when the individual torts have been considered (**7.51**).

Trespass to land

7.2 The defendant commits trespass by any unjustified intrusion onto the claimant's land. The claimant need not prove loss or damage, and the intrusion may be trivial—though the claimant may also use the tort to remedy damage deliberately done by the defendant while trespassing. The tort catches not only intrusion by the defendant in person, but also intrusions for which the defendant is responsible. So the defendant may commit trespass if the defendant's animals stray onto the claimant's land; and if the defendant leaves property on the claimant's land, there is a continuing trespass, with a fresh cause of action every day, until it is removed.

Below and above

7.3 In principle, the claimant may sue for an intrusion at any height or depth above or below the land; but some qualifications must be made. Different strata or levels may have different owners, and so might need to be treated as separate territories: for example, different floors of the same building may be in different ownership, and each owner can complain only of trespass to their own area. Cases of split levels aside, intrusion below the surface of the claimant's land is actionable unless permitted by statute; though who is entitled to any minerals may be a complicated question. Intrusion above the surface is actionable as well, at least in the case where the intruder is still attached to the ground. So where a crane used for building on the defendant's land swings its jib over the claimant's land, this is usually trespass: *Woollerton & Wilson v Richard Costain* [1970] 1 All ER 483. But where the intruder is not attached to the ground, this is not always the case.

> **Bernstein of Leigh v Skyviews and General [1978] QB 479:** Skyviews took aerial photographs of Bernstein's mansion, with a view to selling them to him. Instead, Bernstein sued in trespass. Griffiths J held that the action failed because *(i)* there was no evidence that the aircraft was ever directly above Bernstein's land, *(ii)* if it was, Bernstein had no reasonable use for the air space at that height and so no right to complain of a trespass, and *(iii)* Skyviews were protected by statute.

This statutory provision (now embodied in the Civil Aviation Act 1982, s 76) gives a complete defence to trespass for an aircraft flying at a height which is reasonable in all the circumstances, though there is strict liability for any actual physical damage caused.

Whose land?

7.4 The claimant is entitled to complain of intrusions onto any land of which the claimant is in possession—that is, land over which the claimant has physical control. Where the claimant is not now in possession, but has a legal right to go into possession, then if the claimant does so, the possession is, by legal fiction, backdated to the time when the claimant's right arose, and so the claimant acquires a right to sue those who trespassed since that time. (This is called 'trespass by relation'.) There is no defence that the claimant ought never to have been in possession of the land (no defence of *jus tertii*), unless the defendant personally has a better right to possession. If land is subject to a lease, it is the tenant, not the landlord, who is legally in possession and can sue for intrusions. Those with lesser rights, such as lodgers, do not displace the owner's possession, and have no remedy in trespass for intrusions—though conceivably the owner's failure to expel the intruders might be a breach of contract with the lodger.

Need the defendant be at fault?

7.5 Deliberate conduct by the defendant which is *in fact* an intrusion is actionable. It is no defence that the defendant did not appreciate that it was an intrusion, or realize that it was unlawful. It is no defence, therefore, that the defendant had lost his or her way, even after taking the greatest of care not to do so. However, the defendant has a defence if the intrusion was an involuntary act, as where the defendant is pulled onto the claimant's land despite protests and struggles. Where the intrusion is by the defendant's property (usually the defendant's animals), the courts ask whether the intrusion was the product of intention or carelessness on the defendant's part, or whether the defendant was blameless.

> *League Against Cruel Sports v Scott* **[1986] QB 240:** In the course of hunting, Scott's staghounds ran onto the League's deer sanctuary. Park J held that Scott would be liable if he meant the hounds to trespass or had been negligent in failing to prevent trespass. Persistent hunting in circumstances where trespass was impossible to prevent was evidence of intention to trespass. £180 damages and an injunction were awarded.

Defences

7.6 The main defences open to the defendant are:

- exercise of the defendant's own property rights, such as a private right of way;
- putting right some wrong which is the claimant's responsibility, such as by 'abatement of nuisance' (**7.29**);

- statutory authority to enter the claimant's land, such as under the Police and Criminal Evidence Act 1984;
- public right, such as the right to walk the highway;
- permission (**7.7**); and
- necessity (**7.8**).

These rights to enter land are very specific, and the defendant must stay within their limits. Simply because the defendant has the right to walk the highway going over the claimant's land does not entail a right to spy on the claimant—even if the defendant is careful to keep walking as he spies (*Hickman v Maisey* [1900] 1 QB 752). If the defendant's intrusion is initially justifiable but then the defendant does some positive and unlawful act, then the defendant is treated by fiction of law as having been a trespasser all along. (This is called 'trespass *ab initio*', 'trespass from the very beginning'.)

Permission

7.7 The claimant cannot sue the defendant in trespass if the defendant had the claimant's permission ('licence') to be on the land. Permission can be implied from circumstances: this is why the defendant does not usually commit trespass by walking onto the claimant's land and knocking on the front door, unless the claimant has already made it clear that the defendant is unwelcome. The defendant will become a trespasser if he or she acts in a manner not permitted by the terms of the licence. If the claimant revokes the licence, then the defendant becomes a trespasser if still present after a reasonable time for leaving has expired. However, the claimant may surrender this right by contract.

> **Hurst v Picture Theatres [1915] 1 KB 1:** During a cinema show, Hurst, sitting in the audience, was suddenly and unjustifiably told by one of the staff to leave. When Hurst refused, he was forcibly ejected. Held: Hurst could sue in assault.

Necessity

7.8 Necessity is usually said to be a defence to an action in trespass, but the courts are not always very consistent in their treatment of the defence. So it has been held that a need for shelter, however desperate, cannot justify the defendant's trespass, because to hold otherwise would be open to abuse (*Southwark London Borough Council v Williams* [1971] Ch 734). Yet it has also been held that the defence is available to a police force using inflammable CS gas against a psychopath on the claimant's property, even though their use of it was held negligent (*Rigby v Chief Constable for Northamptonshire* [1985] 2 All ER 985). It is safe to say that extreme circumstances are needed before the defendant will have a defence of necessity (**11.42**). There is no general right at common law for the defendant to enter the claimant's premises to effect repairs to the defendant's own property, though by statute (Access to Neighbouring Land Act 1992) a court may grant the defendant access for this purpose.

Remedies

7.9 The claimant may claim damages from the defendant for any trespass. The claimant may recover any financial loss proved to flow from the trespass, or (if none) a nominal sum. If the defendant took over property which had some value in the rental market, the claimant may also recover a reasonable rental for the period of the defendant's occupation (this remedy is called 'mesne profits'). Some cases apply this principle also where the defendant wrongly acted as if the defendant had a right of way, allowing the claimant to charge the market value of such a right ('wayleave'). There will not usually, however, be any question of an award of exemplary damages (**10.10**).

7.10 In appropriate cases, the claimant may seek a court order evicting the defendant from the land. Self-help to achieve the same result is tightly controlled by the Criminal Law Act 1977, s 6: it is an offence to use or threaten force to enter premises occupied by another, subject to a rather limited defence for displaced residential occupiers. In any event, the claimant must use no more force than the circumstances reasonably justify. Where the claimant never ceased to occupy, an injunction may sometimes be necessary to curb the defendant's trespassory activities (**10.2**), or again the claimant might use self-help, provided again that the claimant uses the minimum force reasonably necessary for the purpose. Where the defendant's property is trespassing on the claimant's land, the claimant has the right to impound it and retain it until paid compensation (the remedy is called 'distress *damage feasant*'), though the claimant has to keep good care of it in the meantime.

Private nuisance

7.11 A private nuisance consists of an unjustified interference by the defendant in the claimant's enjoyment of land. The remedy usually consists of an award of damages and/or an injunction to force the defendant to rectify the situation. The tort is 'private' in the sense that it is a right of one private individual (the claimant) against another (the defendant); a nuisance which affects a significant section of the public is 'public' and so may involve criminal proceedings against the defendant as well (**7.30**).

It is not always clear where nuisance (= interference) ends and trespass (= intrusion) begins. One old case holds that if the defendant lets a pile of rubbish fall onto the claimant's wall, this is trespass (*Gregory v Piper* (1829) 9 B & C 591), but the modern position is unclear. The test is usually said to be that of directness. So if the defendant deliberately throws a cricket ball into the claimant's garden, this is trespass; but if the defendant organizes a cricket match and balls are hit over the boundary, this is nuisance, if anything (*Miller v Jackson* [1977] QB 966).

7.12 Nuisance may take many forms. Perhaps the claimant's land has been physically damaged, say by the emission of poisonous fumes from the defendant's factory; or perhaps noise and smell from the defendant's farm have ruined the claimant's enjoyment without any discernible physical damage. Nuisance tends to involve continuing sources of annoyance, but one-off events may constitute nuisances if sufficiently severe. The older cases sharply distinguish between actual property damage, on the one hand, and mere aesthetic offences, on the other. Modern cases place less emphasis on this distinction, which is in any event hard to apply in many cases.

Balancing the rights of the parties: relevant factors

7.13 It is impossible to give a definitive account of which activities constitute nuisances, beyond saying that the defendant's behaviour must be unreasonable in view of the damage it does to the claimant's interests. In each case, the court balances the defendant's right to act against the claimant's right not to be injured, and decides whether the defendant has overstepped the line which the court (retroactively) draws. The court usually asks the general question whether the defendant acted 'reasonably' in view of the harm to the claimant. However, there is some constancy in the factors the courts regard as relevant to this balancing process, and in that limited sense it is possible to generalize about the way the courts resolve disputes of this kind.

How severely did the defendant hurt the claimant?

7.14 The seriousness of the injury—both its extent and its duration—is a major factor in the balance. If the defendant temporarily delays in removing piles of manure, rendering nearby conditions very unpleasant, this may not be a nuisance, even though there would undoubtedly be a nuisance if the defendant left them there permanently (*Swaine v Great Northern Rly* (1864) 4 De GJ & Sm 211). Some judges have insisted that there must be a 'continuing state of affairs' before action will lie in nuisance. Yet it is hard to see why this should be necessary, particularly as a 'state of affairs' can be discovered in retrospect. So in *Spicer v Smee* [1946] 1 All ER 489, where fire in the defendant's house spread to the claimant's and damaged it, the defective state of the defendant's electrical wiring, which caused the fire, was found to constitute the 'continuing state of affairs' for this purpose. In practice, despite occasional *dicta* to the contrary, there seems to be no difficulty in suing for one-off incidents, provided they are sufficiently severe. It is also sometimes said that private nuisance requires material damage to the claimant's property; but anything serious enough to constitute a nuisance is likely to have an effect on the value of the property, and that seems to be enough.

What was the type of injury?

7.15 Different types of injury are treated in different ways, partly because of current judgments as to which injuries are serious, and partly as a reflection of the judgments of previous generations of judges. It is no longer realistic (if indeed it ever was) to draw a very sharp line between physical injury to property and merely aesthetic offences. However, the law lord who drew that distinction was undoubtedly right that the claimant will have an easier time of it in private nuisance if physical damage can be proved (Lord Westbury LC in *St Helens Smelting Co v Tipping* (1865) 29 JP 579). Property rights are much better protected than the right to leisure activities.

> **Hunter v Canary Wharf [1997] 2 All ER 426:** Several hundred claimants complained that the Canary Wharf building development had created clouds of dust which deposited itself on their property, and that Canary Wharf Tower, the centrepiece of the development, interfered with their TV reception. Held: the dust was actionable if it could be shown to have damaged claimants' property (by impairing the utility or value of whatever it was deposited on), but the interference with TV reception was not actionable.

But even on those facts, the distinction between cases involving damage to property and other cases is no magic talisman. The House of Lords ruled against the TV claim principally because it seemed analogous to a claim that the defendant's building has ruined the claimant's view, which the courts have always rejected. It might be different, hinted Lord Hoffmann, if the defendant had interfered with the claimant's TV reception through electrical machinery.

How valuable is the defendant's activity?

7.16 The defendant has a better chance of winning the case if the defendant's activity has some obvious and significant utility to the public. However, it must not be forgotten that the claimant, too, is part of the public; the defendant cannot usually cast a significant loss on the claimant by a simple plea of 'public interest'. Moreover, there is often scope for disagreement about what constitutes a valuable activity.

> **Miller v Jackson [1977] QB 966:** The Millers complained that cricket balls from matches organized by Jackson often landed in their garden, and that a few had done

damage to their house. Held (by Geoffrey Lane LJ): an actionable nuisance had been committed and the Millers were entitled to damages and an injunction to prevent repetition; (by Cumming-Bruce LJ) that damages could be awarded for the nuisance, but it would be against the public interest for an injunction to issue; (by Lord Denning MR) that the social utility of cricket outweighed the inconvenience to the Millers, who accordingly had no remedy.

What sort of locality did the events happen in?

7.17 The less pleasant the area in which the alleged nuisance occurred, the worse must be the defendant's behaviour if it is to be held a nuisance. Accordingly, what is permissible behaviour in one place might be a nuisance in another.

> ***Murdoch v Glacier Metal Co* [1998] 7 LS Gaz R 31:** Murdoch claimed that the night-time noise from Glacier's factory was a nuisance. Held: the court had to take into account the character of the neighbourhood. Given that the factory was based on an industrial estate and was not the only major source of noise (Murdoch's house was close to a bypass), no actionable nuisance was established.

> ***Laws v Florinplace* [1981] 1 All ER 659:** Laws complained of the opening of a sex shop and cinema club by Florinplace, in premises close to his home; he relied particularly on the adverse effect on property values and the attraction of undesirables to the previously placid residential area. Vinelott J held that it was arguable that a nuisance had been committed, and restrained Florinplace from continuing its activities, pending full trial.

Several old cases suggest that the character of the locality is irrelevant if the claimant is complaining of actual physical damage, rather than less tangible matters. Views differ on whether this is still the law, if indeed the distinction can sensibly be drawn at all.

The general character of the area will, of course, be under the oversight of the local planning authority. It is not strictly relevant in nuisance whether the defendant had planning permission. Nonetheless, a grant of permission *which was intended to change the character of the neighbourhood* may form an important part of a case that the neighbourhood's character has in fact changed—with the result that what would earlier have been a nuisance is not now a nuisance (*Wheeler v Saunders* [1996] Ch 19).

How sensitive is the claimant?

7.18 A claim in nuisance may be rejected on the ground that the claimant's unusual sensitivity to the defendant's activity gives no right of action. This may sound at first like an obvious deduction from the first factor (**7.14**)—that the claimant cannot complain of trivial inconveniences—but it is in fact a quite different idea. Unusually sensitive claimants are not protected *even if the effect of the defendant's activities is catastrophic.*

> **Robinson v Kilvert (1889) 41 Ch D 88:** Kilvert heated his premises to assist him in his trade of making paper boxes. Robinson, who occupied the floor above, complained that the heat affected the brown paper he warehoused there, drying it and considerably reducing its value. Held: activities which would not injure any but the most sensitive of trades were not actionable as nuisances.

However, more recent authorities stress that there is no special rule here. If the claimant is the only person to suffer from the defendant's activities, and only suffers because of unusual sensitivity on the claimant's part, then this is a hefty indication that the defendant's activities are reasonable ones when viewed in the broad way that the law of nuisance requires. But this is simply an application of the ordinary balancing exercise, not a special rule about sensitive claimants (*Network Rail Infrastructure Ltd v CJ Morris* [2004] EWCA Civ 172).

It is quite different if the claimant successfully establishes nuisance, but it then becomes clear that the extent of the injury was much greater than would have been suffered by most claimants. The defendant's plea is then one of remoteness of loss, and will fail unless the claimant's loss is of a *different type* from that which was foreseeable; it is irrelevant whether the defendant could have foreseen the extent (**7.23, 10.32**).

Did the defendant set out to hurt the claimant?

7.19 Conduct which might be unexceptionable in normal circumstances might be a nuisance if intentionally used to provoke, annoy, or harm the claimant: see *Christie v Davey* [1893] 1 Ch 316 (loud domestic noises) and *Hollywood Silver Fox Farm v Emmett* [1936] 2 KB 468 (shooting rabbits near the claimant's farm and disturbing his stock). An apparent exception is provided by one old case (*Bradford Corpn v Pickles* [1895] AC 587), where the defendant deliberately diverted water running under his land away from the claimant's reservoir, in revenge for the claimant's refusal to pay the defendant for it. The House of Lords held that no action lay. The exception is only apparent, however. If in principle the claimant and the defendant both have a right to do what they have been doing, the presence of malice is helpful in striking a balance between them. But, as the Lords pointed out in *Pickles*, the claimant had no legal right to the water at all—and so there was nothing to balance.

Who can sue?

7.20 It is usually considered that the claimant can only complain of a private nuisance if the claimant has either possession of the land or has a property right in it. The typical claimant will therefore be the freehold owner of the property, but those with subsidiary property rights can also sue if their interest is affected: for example a tenant, or the holder of a private right of way. A landlord can sue for injury to the residual rights which are retained (the landlord's 'reversion'). Even a 'tolerated trespasser', liable to eviction whenever the freehold owner chooses, has sufficient title to sue in nuisance (*Pemberton v Southwark London Borough Council* [2000] 3 All ER 924). But others with no property right may not, on the traditional view, sue, however good their right to be on the premises: the tenant's spouse, for example (*Malone v Laskey* [1907] 2 KB 141). This traditional view has now been reaffirmed by the House of Lords in *Hunter v Canary Wharf* [1997] 2 All ER 426. However, it seems that the owner's right includes the right to sue for damage which occurred before he or she became owner (*Delaware Mansions v Westminster City Council* [2001] UKHL 55).

7.21 There have been various attempts to relax this requirement, to extend the protection of the tort to those who live on the land without in any sense 'owning' it. In *Khorasandjian v Bush* [1993] QB 727, the claimant complained that the defendant had threatened her with violence, followed her about, and persistently harassed her in person and over the phone. She sought an injunction to prevent a repetition. The defendant admitted that an injunction was available to prevent violence or threats of violence (**2.3**), but denied that it was available against non-violent harassment. This could not be nuisance, he argued, because the claimant did not own the property at which she was harassed: she lived at home with her parents. Controversially, and by a majority, the Court of Appeal held that the claimant may sue despite this objection. However, the House of Lords in *Hunter v Canary Wharf* [1997] 2 All ER 426 said that this is wrong. The law would today almost certainly catch the defendant on harassment (**2.10**), but as to the tort of nuisance the defendant's argument was perfectly correct.

A potentially more successful argument, though as yet of uncertain impact, is based on Art 8 of the European Convention on Human Rights, where a claimant asserts a 'right to respect for his private and family life [and] his home'. This protection overlaps with the tort of nuisance, but differs from it in subtle ways. It focuses on where the claimant's home is, not on who owns the property in question. It probably represents a more demanding standard than nuisance: it is a strong thing to say that the claimant's human rights are infringed, and evidence of trivial annoyances would presumably not do. And, as ever in these cases, the defendant will remind the court that defendants have rights too; it may be, for example, that whatever the claimant complains of is in itself something the defendant has a human right to do. These cases are therefore likely to involve the court in a balancing exercise, similar to that already required by the tort of nuisance (see **7.13**). At all events, the courts are only at the start of this enquiry. Article 8 was one factor leading to a ruling that noise from a military airport was a nuisance actionable by those living nearby (*Dennis v Ministry of Defence* [2003] EWHC 793 (QB)). And it has been held to be arguable that the Convention gives a right of action to children living on land even though they have no right of action in nuisance (*McKenna v British Aluminium* (2002) Times, 25 April). However, the Convention did not help a claimant whose house was flooded by the activities of the defendant water company: the House of Lords reviewed the relevant statutory scheme of liabilities and remedies, found it to be a fair one, and held that individual complaints of unfairness could not impugn the validity of the scheme overall (*Marcic v Thames Water Utilities* [2003] UKHL 66). And the European Court of Human Rights has refused to say that the rights of residents living around Heathrow Airport were infringed by arrangements for night flights (*Hatton v United Kingdom* (2003) 37 EHRR 28). However, *Hatton* is very far from the final word on that subject, especially given the powerful dissenting judgments in the case.

Must the claimant prove that the defendant was negligent?

7.22   It is sometimes said that liability in private nuisance is 'strict' and is therefore quite different from negligence liability, which requires proof of fault. However, two careful qualifications must be made, before we can see what the true issue is.

• First, it is absolutely true that the defendant may blunder into liability for private nuisance through ignorance of law, or through practical inability to meet the law's standard of fault. If the defendant lights a bonfire which is a nuisance to the claimant's neighbouring land, it is irrelevant whether the defendant knew enough law to appreciate the possibility of liability. So certainly nuisance is in that sense 'strict', but so too is negligence. For example, the learner driver is liable for not attaining the law's standard of the reasonably experienced and careful driver, whether or not the driver appreciates that, or is practically able to attain that standard (**4.14**).

• Second, where the claimant is claiming an injunction to prevent or suppress a nuisance from the defendant's land, it is irrelevant whether the nuisance is the defendant's fault. The injunction looks forward to demand that the defendant ameliorate the situation, not backward to whose fault it was (**10.2**).

A quite distinct question, however, is whether if the claimant sues for the loss caused by the defendant's nuisance, the defendant may plead *lack of fault* as a defence.

7.23   The claimant complains of a nuisance from the defendant's land and sues for the loss caused. The defendant admits that the situation amounts to a nuisance, but denies fault in the way in which it came about. Must the court investigate the defendant's plea, or can the claimant retort that liability is 'strict'? This is a controversial question; all that can be said with certainty is that when the courts have been asked this question in recent years, they have tended to treat the liability as a negligence liability:

> **Leakey v National Trust [1980] QB 485:** A mound of earth on the National Trust's land collapsed onto Leakey's land. Held: the Trust had anticipated the danger and, as they had unreasonably done nothing about it, they were liable.

> **Holbeck Hall Hotel v Scarborough Borough Council [2000] QB 836:** A landslip on land near a cliff led to the collapse of the claimant's hotel, which had to be demolished. The claimant argued that the local council, which owned the land between the hotel and sea, should have foreseen the problem and dealt with it, especially given that eight years earlier they had been warned of a possible problem by a firm of consulting engineers. Held: it was unreasonable to expect the council to engage in extensive geological investigations, and so it was not liable.

This assimilation of private nuisance with negligence has been adopted in several leading cases, including *Bolton v Stone* [1951] AC 850 (**1.40**) and *Cambridge Water Co v Eastern Counties Leather* [1994] 2 AC 264 (**7.36**). Of course, to say that the liability is 'negligence-based' rather than 'strict' is only the beginning of the enquiry. Negligence law is hardly static or settled, and many of the unanswered questions it poses resonate in nuisance cases—particularly the question of when the defendant may plead that removing the risk to the claimant would have been too expensive. Nonetheless, it seems likely that future issues will be fought about in that framework, and not on the assumption of 'strict' liability. In particular, it is settled that, just as in negligence, the defendant has a defence that the type of loss caused was unforeseeable and hence too remote (*The Wagon Mound (No 2)* [1967] 1 AC 617) (**10.30**). (For the contrary view, that liability in nuisance is still strict, see e.g. Cross, 'Does only the careless polluter pay? A fresh examination of the nature of private nuisance' (1995) 111 LQR 445.)

Defence: the defendant not in control at all

7.24 It follows that it will be a defence to an action in private nuisance that the defendant had not, and could not reasonably have had, control over the land from which the nuisance arose. So the claimant will have to prove either intention or lack of care on the defendant's part. The defendant may be liable if the defendant directly created the nuisance, whether it emanates from the defendant's own land or elsewhere (*Hubbard v Pitt* [1976] QB 142). The defendant may also be liable if a contract between the defendant and a landowner gives the defendant control of a hazard arising from the land (*LE Jones (Insurance Brokers) Ltd v Portsmouth City Council* [2002] EWCA Civ 1723). If a nuisance occurs on land which the defendant occupies, the defendant may be liable if the defendant knew or ought reasonably to have known of it in time to do something about it, but not otherwise (*Sedleigh-Denfield v O'Callaghan* [1940] AC 880). If the defendant instructs others to do building work, the defendant will be liable if the work would have resulted in a nuisance however it was done. And some authorities say that if the project obviously risks creating a nuisance, the defendant will be liable for any negligence on the part of those doing the work, *whether or not* the defendant can be said to be vicariously liable for the workers' actions (*Matania v National Provincial Bank* [1936] 2 All ER 633; for vicarious liability see **9.2**). Where the defendant allows others to occupy the land, the defendant may be found liable if those others act in a foreseeable way to harm the claimant.

> **Lippiatt v South Gloucestershire Council [2000] QB 51:** The council allowed travellers to occupy a strip of land. Lippiatt, a tenant farmer of adjoining land, complained of repeated acts of trespass and nuisance, especially the dumping of rubbish on her land. The council applied to have the action struck out, as they could not be held responsible for the acts of the travellers, at least where the acts complained of were on Lippiatt's land. Held: repeated acts of nuisance of which the council had knowledge, and which they did nothing to stop, were a ground of liability.

Landlord and tenant

7.25 Where the first defendant leases land to the second defendant, and a nuisance then emanates from that land, liability in nuisance follows the legal right of control.

The tenant is responsible if:

- the nuisance is the result of the tenant's own activities; or
- the nuisance results from the state of any part of the premises which the tenant knows about or could reasonably be expected to know about.

There are *dicta* (in *St Anne's Well Brewery Co v Roberts* (1928) 26 LGR 638) that the tenant may be liable even where the landlord has a duty to repair, though the tenant can then sue the landlord to pass the loss on.

The landlord is responsible if:

- he or she knew or ought reasonably to have known about the nuisance at the time of letting (*Brew Bros v Snax (Ross)* [1970] 1 QB 612); or
- he or she retains a right to repair, and the nuisance arises from failure to repair (Defective Premises Act 1972, s 4); or

- the nuisance arises from the tenant's activities, of which the landlord had knowledge before the letting (*Tetley v Chitty* [1986] 1 All ER 663).

However, the courts are markedly reluctant to make landlords responsible for voluntary misbehaviour by their tenants. The role of landlord should not be confused with that of the local authority, even (or perhaps especially) when the landlord *is* the local authority:

> **Hussain v Lancaster City Council [2000] QB 1:** Hussain's shop on a housing estate was subjected to a campaign of racial harassment and intimidation by many of those living on the estate. Hussain sued the local authority, as landlord of the estate. Held: the landlord had not authorized or encouraged these acts, and so was not liable in nuisance. (Action in negligence also failed.)

> **Southwark London Borough Council v Mills [1999] 4 All ER 449:** Mills, a local authority tenant, complained that the soundproofing was so poor that neighbouring tenants were clearly audible as they went about ordinary activities. Held: even if the noise from those ordinary activities constituted a nuisance (which it did not), landlords are not responsible for ordinary activities of their tenants.

Prescription

7.26 The defendant has a defence if the defendant has carried on the nuisance now complained for at least 20 years (Prescription Act 1832, s 2). However, it is not enough that the defendant has been carrying on the same activity for 20 years if it is only more recently that it became a nuisance; time runs only from the point at which the claimant was first unlawfully affected, not from when the defendant began the activity.

Statutory authority

7.27 Whether a statute relating to the defendant's activities provides a defence in nuisance depends on its construction. As a rule, the claimant may not sue for a nuisance if the defendant's activities were authorized by statute, either expressly or by necessary implication. So statutory authorization to build an oil refinery bars action both for building and for ordinary operation of the refinery (*Allen v Gulf Oil Refining* [1981] AC 1001). The claimant's claim will therefore fail if the nuisance is an inevitable consequence of the type of activities the statute authorizes. However, authority to carry on a certain type of activity is not to be equated with authority to carry it on carelessly. More generally, if the defendant had appreciable freedom of action under the statute, the claimant may demand that the defendant use it with due regard to the claimant's interests, and sue if the defendant's activities are unreasonable in relation to the claimant's interests (*Metropolitan Asylum District Managers v Hill* (1881) 6 App Cas 193).

Consent

7.28 The claimant's consent to the defendant's activities is a defence, and consent need only be tacit. Two major qualifications must be made, however. First, consent to the defendant's activity being carried on at all is not the same as consent to the defendant's running it carelessly. If the defendant was in fact careless, and the loss would probably not have occurred if the defendant had acted carefully, the defendant will have to prove consent *to carelessness*; which may be difficult. Second, it is traditionally said that consent cannot be inferred merely from the fact that the claimant has 'come to the nuisance' by acquiring property near it, even with full knowledge of the defendant's activities. If the defendant then has a defence at all, it is by reference to the 'character of the neighbourhood' (**7.17**). This is a controversial area. In *Miller v Jackson* [1977] QB 966, where the claimant bought a new house just next to a cricket ground where cricket had been played for over 60 years, Lord Denning MR held that there was consent. Geoffrey Lane and Cumming-Bruce LLJ, by contrast, held the defence inapplicable—though Cumming-Bruce sided with Denning in holding that the case was not appropriate for an injunction.

Remedies: damages, injunction, self-help

7.29 Once nuisance is established, the claimant may recover any proven financial loss, subject to a defence of remoteness (**7.23**). (For discussion of the measure, and its relation to damages under the Human Rights Act where both are available, see *Dobson v Thames Water Utilities Ltd* [2009] EWCA 28.) It will often be desirable to forestall a nuisance, or obtain an order to make the defendant stop it: an injunction to that effect is very often available (**10.2**). Traditionally it was also said that the claimant had the right, after giving the defendant notice, to 'abate' the nuisance, that is, to enter the defendant's land and use the minimum force reasonably necessary to stop it, or to curb its effects. However, a recent case suggests that this self-help remedy is rather narrow.

> **Burton v Winters [1993] 3 All ER 847:** The Winters' garage, built by the people from whom they had bought the land, protruded some 4½ feet onto Burton's land; Burton applied for, but was refused, an injunction to have it knocked down. Could Burton knock it down herself? Held: she could not.

The court seemed to think that the right to abate was available only in two cases: where the case was a simple one where legal proceedings would have been inappropriate, or where urgent action was plainly necessary. Where a legal action not only could have been, but actually was, brought before a court, there was no longer a right to private self-help.

Public nuisance

7.30 Where a nuisance affects a substantial number of people, it is said to be a 'public' nuisance. The nuisance need not interfere with the use of land as such, but may interfere with any aspect of the public's rights, and may accordingly take many forms. Cases include obstructing the highway (*Chaplin v Westminster Corpn* [1901] 2 Ch 329), making obscene telephone calls (*R v Norbury* [1978] Crim LR 435), and organizing raves (*R v Shorrock* [1994] QB 279). The uncertain and broad ambit of the tort allows the judges to spring occasional surprises. So, for example, in *Thomas v National Union of Mineworkers* [1986] Ch 20 Scott J ruled that picketing might amount to a public nuisance. This was on the ground that it was an unreasonable harassment of those at whom it was directed—even though it did not constitute an assault on them, and had no prospect of preventing them from going where they wished. In each case the court must, if necessary, go through the same process of balancing the defendant's rights against those of others as in private nuisance cases. To many minds this notion allows too much scope for judicial creativity, and it is only the rarity with which it is invoked that saves it from being a serious infringement of civil liberties. This is yet another area where the Human Rights Act 1998 (**1.22**) might be expected to have an impact, as either party might claim that their human rights have been infringed.

A crime, and sometimes a tort

7.31 If the defendant is responsible for the public nuisance, the defendant is liable to be prosecuted criminally. An injunction to prevent or curb a public nuisance can only be sought by the Attorney-General or by local authorities (under the Local Government Act 1972, s 222), though a private individual may proceed with the Attorney-General's permission (this is called a 'relator action'). Individual, civil right of action is more limited. First, the fact a nuisance may be public does not prevent the claimant from arguing that it infringes the claimant's private rights, protected by the tort of private nuisance. Second, if the claimant has suffered a particular injury, in some way going beyond the loss inflicted on all affected by the nuisance, there is a right of action for public nuisance.

Who can sue?

7.32 If the claimant is contemplating a civil action for public nuisance, the claimant must show some loss resulting from the nuisance which goes beyond the loss suffered by all affected. However, it seems that the *type* of loss is irrelevant, may consist of personal injury (*Re Corby Group Litigation* [2008] EWCA 463), and may even (it seems) include a purely economic loss. Liability relating to the highway illustrates the need to give separate consideration to public and private aspects of nuisance here. If the defendant blocks the claimant's access to the highway, this is an infringement of the claimant's private rights, and the claimant may sue in private nuisance; but if the defendant blocks the highway just outside the claimant's land, this is at most public nuisance, and the claimant will have to prove particular damage.

> **Tate & Lyle Industries v Greater London Council [1983] 2 AC 509:** The GLC were responsible for the construction of ferry terminals on the Thames, causing silting. Tate & Lyle paid over £500,000 to dredge the Thames, without which the silt would have prevented large vessels from reaching their jetty. Held: there was no private nuisance, as there was no injury to Tate & Lyle's jetty. However, as there was a hindrance to navigation generally, there was a public nuisance, from which Tate & Lyle had suffered an unusual degree of damage. Accordingly, they had a right of action.

Who is liable?

7.33 The test for liability is whether the defendant had control over the nuisance. The question whether liability in private nuisance is 'strict' was discussed above (**7.22–7.23**), and much of that discussion applies also to public nuisance. Ignorance of the law is no defence. But if the defendant argues that the defendant had no control over the events leading to the nuisance or could not reasonably have prevented it, the questions are, whether the defendant could reasonably have been expected to foresee the nuisance; and, if so, whether the defendant could reasonably have been expected to prevent it.

> **Wandsworth London Borough Council v Railtrack [2001] EWCA Civ 1236:** Pigeons roosting under one of Railtrack's bridges were held to constitute a public nuisance. Were Railtrack liable to compensate the council for the cost of constantly cleaning the pavements, necessary only because of the pigeons' presence? Held: they were. While the presence of the pigeons was not Railtrack's fault, nonetheless on becoming aware of the nuisance they were bound to take reasonable steps to remedy the matter. There was no relevant distinction between cases of physical damage to property and cases of mere smell and discomfort.

However, there may be an exception where the defendant erects an artificial projection overhanging the highway: the defendant is sometimes said to be strictly liable for loss caused by these projections (*Tarry v Ashton* (1876) 1 QBD 314, Lush and Quain JJ; Blackburn J to the contrary). If there is such a special rule, it does not apply to natural objects such as trees, where the defendant has a defence if all reasonable care was taken (*Wringe v Cohen* (1876) 1 QBD 314). In any event the general tendency of the modern law is to give strict liability as narrow an interpretation as possible, negligence liability being the norm.

> ***Rowe v Herman* [1997] 1 WLR 1390:** Herman, a house-owner, employed a contractor to build a garage on his land. In the course of the work, the contractor laid metal plates over a footpath to protect it, but forgot to remove them when the work was done. Rowe, a user of the footpath, tripped over the plates, fractured his ankle, and sued Herman. Held: as the laying of the plates was not a necessary part of the work, the strict liability for acts on the highway did not apply. Herman was not liable unless he could be shown to be at fault himself.

Strict liabilities relating to land

7.34 We have already seen that liability for nuisance has often been thought of as 'strict', though today it is increasingly being assimilated to negligence (**7.22–7.23**). At common law, there were two cases where liability was on any definition strict: liability for damage caused by animals, and liability for fire. In the famous case of *Rylands v Fletcher* (1868) LR 3 HL 330, the House of Lords generalized from these instances to create a general principle of liability for the escape of dangerous things from the defendant's land, a principle which was meant also to include the escape of dangerous products of new technologies. Since that case, however, the courts have tended to stress negligence rather than strict liabilities. Liability for animals is now statutory (**7.44**); whether liability for fire still has an independent existence is considered below (**7.42**). Various other special cases are dealt with by statute (**7.43**).

The principle in *Rylands v Fletcher*: escape of dangerous things

7.35 If the defendant accumulates some dangerous thing, as part of some non-natural use of land, then the defendant is strictly liable to the claimant if the thing escapes and does damage to the claimant. This rule was laid down in *Rylands v Fletcher* (1868) LR 3 HL 330, where the defendant constructed a dam on his land to provide water for his mill. As a result of negligence by the defendant's contractors (though not by the defendant himself), the water burst through into the claimant's mines and flooded them. The liability is strict, in the sense that the claimant need not prove negligence, but there are extensive defences, which are considered below (**7.40–7.41**).

This principle has a rather antique air to it, and the suggestion has often been made that its more distinctive features should be abolished, or at least that it should be absorbed into the tort of negligence. However, as the whole area of environmental liability has received a great deal of legislative attention, the judges have been reluctant to tinker; the current approach is that while they will smooth away the rougher features of the doctrine, complete abolition would be an inappropriate move (see especially *Transco plc v Stockport Metropolitan Borough Council* [2003] UKHL 61).

How 'dangerous'?

7.36 It is usually said that a thing is 'dangerous' for this purpose if it is likely to cause damage if it escapes, and there seems no advantage in expanding this definition further. The following have, at one time or another, been held to be 'dangerous': gas (*Batcheller v Tunbridge Wells Gas Co* (1901) 65 JP 680), a poisonous yew tree (*Ponting v Noakes* [1894] 2 QB 281), fumes from creosote (*West v Bristol Tramways* [1908] 2 KB 14), and a fun-fair 'chair-o-plane' ride (*Hale v Jennings Bros* [1938] 1 All ER 579). However, the House of Lords now appears to have held that a thing cannot be 'dangerous' if its escape was not foreseeable at all.

> **Cambridge Water Co v Eastern Counties Leather [1994] 2 AC 264:** Eastern Counties Leather used a powerful toxic solvent in their tanning process, much of which was spilled on the factory floor. Over several years of use, a large quantity of this solvent seeped under their property, several thousand metres along an aquifer, and into Cambridge Water's borehole. New EU regulations on water quality meant that the solvent rendered the water legally undrinkable. Held: no action lay, as the pollution was unforeseeable.

In *Crown River Cruises v Kimbolton Fireworks* [1996] 2 Lloyd's Rep 533, where the defendant's fireworks display caused a fire on the claimant's river vessel, Potter J was reluctant to base liability on *Rylands v Fletcher* principles. '[I]n the light of the current judicial and academic reserve which appears detectable towards extension of the principle' ([1996] 2 Lloyd's Rep 533, 547), he based liability on nuisance instead.

Is there a requirement of 'non-natural use'?

7.37 It is not clear what, if anything, the requirement of 'non-natural use' adds to the requirement of dangerousness. Not all of the classic formulations of the rule mention it. It may have been meant only to imply that the defendant must deliberately accumulate something, rather than fail to remove a pre-existing ('natural') accumulation. Most modern cases assume, however, that the test is one of how ordinary the defendant's activity is and (possibly) of how justifiable. So activities such as erecting or demolishing buildings (*Thomas and Evans v*

Mid-Rhondda Co-operative Society [1941] 1 KB 381) or mining in an ordinary way (*Rouse v Gravelworks* [1940] 1 KB 489) are not 'unnatural'. Indeed, it was even suggested that the manufacture and storage of high explosives might be 'natural', at least in wartime (*Read v J Lyons* [1947] AC 156). Yet in the *Cambridge Water* case it was said that the storage of chemicals was 'an almost classic case of non-natural use' ([1994] 1 All ER 53, 79, Lord Goff). On this view, the defendant would not escape liability merely because it was common in that industry, or because it provided employment, or was otherwise to be encouraged. This all suggests that the true test is now dangerousness, though the House of Lords did not say so expressly. This area of the law is badly in need of clarification.

'Escape'

7.38 The claimant cannot complain of events if their effects were felt only on the defend-ant's land, or which affected the claimant while on the defendant's land: such as an explosion in the defendant's factory where the claimant is an employee (*Read v J Lyons* [1947] AC 156), or a leak affecting the claimant's gas main running across the defendant's land (*Transco plc v Stockport Metropolitan Borough Council* [2003] UKHL 61). The requirement is often confusingly stated to require an 'escape' of *the thing accumulated*, but that is not strictly accurate. An accumulation of explo-sives, which detonate causing damage to neighbouring landowners, is actionable (*Miles v Forest Rock Granite Co* (1918) 62 SJ 634), even though it is at best a rather confusing metaphor to describe this as an 'escape' of the explosives. *Something* must escape as a result of the accumulation, but it need not be the accumulation itself.

Who may sue?

7.39 The usual claimant in these cases is a landowner who has suffered property dam-age. 'Landowners' for this purpose include anyone with an interest in land. Some authorities say there are no other possible claimants (e.g. *Weller & Co v Foot and Mouth Disease Research Institute* [1966] 1 QB 569). However, other cases hold that the claimant may sue for damage to personal property, whether or not it was on the claimant's land when damaged (e.g. *Halsey v Esso Petroleum Co* [1961] 2 All ER 145). Some cases also hold that the claimant may sue for personal injury (e.g. *Hale v Jennings Bros* [1938] 1 All ER 579), though other authorities doubt it, suggesting that the tort concerns only the rights of property owners (*Read v J Lyons* [1947] AC 156). The modern trend is to confine the action narrowly, and *Hale v Jennings* has to be regarded as very doubtful today (see e.g. *Transco plc v Stockport Metropolitan Borough Council* [2003] UKHL 61).

Who is liable, and how strict is the liability?

7.40 The liability arises whenever the defendant has control over land where there is a dangerous accumulation. The liability is usually described as strict. However, various defences together drag the tort in the direction of liability for fault.

- If the immediate cause of the incident was the act of a trespasser, there is no liability unless the defendant ought reasonably to have foreseen and prevented the trespasser's action (*Perry v Kendricks Transport* [1956] 1 All ER 154).

- If the immediate cause of the incident was some unforeseeable natural cause ('Act of God'), such as unforeseeably heavy rainfall, the defendant is not liable (*Nichols v Marsland* (1876) 2 Ex D 1). The result, though not the principle, of *Nichols* has been questioned in later cases, which point out that the possibility of heavy rain should surely have occurred to reasonable people considering the matter.

- The claimant cannot complain of an escape which was the claimant's own fault. On the question whether the claimant can complain of a loss which would not have happened but for the claimant's abnormal sensitivity, the authorities conflict.

- If damage of the type the claimant suffers was not foreseeable at all, the claimant cannot claim (*Cambridge Water* case, **7.36**).

These rules do not *quite* add up to a general defence of due care by the defendant, but their joint effect is somewhat similar in many cases. However, the defendant remains liable if the risk to the claimant was plain but the defendant decided (reasonably or not) that the cost of defending the claimant against the risk was more than the defendant was prepared to pay; arguably that would be the case if the facts of the *Cambridge Water* case recurred today.

Other defences

7.41 The defendant also has a defence on proof of any of the following:

- That the claimant *consented* to the dangerous accumulation. Consent may often be inferred from mere knowledge of the accumulation. However, if the claimant knows of the accumulation, but not that the defendant has acted negligently, then the defendant remains liable for negligence, to which the claimant has not consented (*Peters v Prince of Wales Theatre* [1943] KB 73).

- If the accumulation was carried on for the *common benefit* of the claimant and the defendant, it can usually be taken that the claimant has consented to it (*Prosser & Son v Levy* [1955] 3 All ER 577).

- That the defendant had a *statutory duty or authority* to make the accumulation, despite the danger. But the case law is confused, and each statute must be interpreted on its own merits. It appears that if the statute places the defendant under a *duty* to act (as where a water company is placed under an obligation to maintain pressure in its pipes), the defendant will probably not be liable for the unavoidable risk of escape unless negligence is proved (*Dunne v North Western Gas Board* [1964] 2 QB 806). But if the statute merely *authorizes* the defendant to act, then the authorities conflict on whether the defendant is liable in the absence of negligence, though they are unlikely so to hold if the risk was obviously incidental to activities of the sort the defendant was engaged in.

- That the accumulation was a created as a reasonable response to a danger facing both the defendant and the claimant (the 'common enemy' rule) (*Arscott v Coal Authority* [2004] EWCA Civ 892).

Special case: fire

7.42 Strict liability for fire predates *Rylands v Fletcher*, and only fits rather awkwardly within it. Nonetheless it is customary today to discuss it as an example of *Rylands* liability, which exists alongside negligence liability for fire. So where the defendant's carburettor caught fire in his garage and the fire spread to the claimant's premises, the court applied *Rylands*. The court did not seem unduly bothered by questions of what precisely was the 'accumulation', whether cars are 'natural', or whether what escaped was the same thing as what was accumulated (*Musgrove v Pandelis* [1919] 2 KB 43).

> **LMS International Ltd v Styrene Packaging and Insulation Ltd [2005] EWHC 2065 (TCC):** The defendants manufactured expanded polystyrene. A spark accidentally produced while cutting some of the polystyrene resulted in a fire, damaging neighbouring properties including the claimants'. Held: the storage of the finished polystyrene close to the manufacturing process created a very real risk of fire. This was itself enough to demonstrate a non-natural user of the land, leading to strict liability for any fires which occurred.

By ancient statute (Fires Prevention (Metropolis) Act 1774, s 86), there is no liability for fires which start 'accidentally'. But the courts have construed this narrowly, holding that no fire is 'accidental' if it starts or is made worse by the defendant's negligence (*Goldman v Hargrave* [1967] 1 AC 645), or falls within the *Rylands v Fletcher* principle (*Mason v Levy Auto Parts of England* [1967] 2 QB 530). The defendant is also liable for the negligence of all lawful visitors on the land. Who is a lawful visitor is sometimes a difficult question.

> **H & N Emanuel v Greater London Council [1971] 2 All ER 835:** The GLC hired contractors to remove two prefabricated bungalows, prohibiting them from burning any

rubbish involved, because of the risk that the fire would spread. The workers nonetheless burnt the rubbish, and the fire spread to Emanuel's property. By their act of setting fire to the rubbish, the workers technically became trespassers, and so the GLC disclaimed responsibility for the fire. Held: there was an obvious risk that the workers would disobey their instructions, and the GLC had done nothing to guard against that risk. Accordingly, they could not plead that the workers were trespassers.

Other special cases

7.43 Strict liability is imposed for particular hazards by statute: notably for underground storage of gas (Gas Act 1965, s 14, as amended), illegal disposal of waste (Environmental Protection Act 1990, s 73(6)), and incidents involving radioactive matter (Nuclear Installations Act 1965, s 12, on which see *Blue Circle Industries v Ministry of Defence* [1999] Ch 289). In each case there are certain defences, and so the liability is not strictly speaking 'strict'.

Liability for animals

7.44 By the Animals Act 1971, the 'keeper' of animals is under a strict liability for damage caused by those animals, in two situations described in the following paragraphs. 'Keeper' is defined in s 6(3), and the definition is broad. The defendant is 'keeper' of an animal if the defendant owns it, or possesses it (except where the defendant has temporarily taken possession of the animal to stop it from doing damage, or to return it to its owner). If the defendant is head of a household, the defendant is 'keeper' of all animals kept by members of the household who are under 16. Once the defendant is 'keeper' of a particular animal, the defendant remains its 'keeper' for the purposes of the Act until the animal has a new 'keeper'. It is therefore perfectly possible for a particular animal to have more than one keeper at any one time. Indeed, both the claimant and the defendant may be keepers. Assuming that the claimant can establish the requirements of the Animals Act, the mere fact of being keeper herself does not prevent her suing the defendant for any injuries sustained (*Flack v Hudson* [2001] QB 698).

Animals of a dangerous species

7.45 If the animal of which the defendant is the keeper is a member of a 'dangerous species', then the defendant is strictly liable for any harm it does. A species is 'dangerous' if:

- it is not commonly domesticated in the British Isles; and

- fully grown members of the species either are likely to do severe damage unless restrained, or are such that any damage they do is likely to be severe (s 6(2)).

'Species' is defined as including sub-species and varieties (s 11); so (for example) each different breed of dog is a different 'species' to a lawyer, even though a zoologist would have a different view.

Individually dangerous animals

7.46 The defendant is also strictly liable as keeper of an animal from a non-dangerous species, if three specific matters are proved by the claimant:

- the damage the animal caused was of the sort it was likely to cause unless restrained, or which was likely to be severe if that animal did it; and

- the animal's dangerous characteristics are not usually found in animals of that species, or are usually found only in particular circumstances; and

- the defendant knew of the danger, or (if the animal has been left in someone else's charge) the person in charge knew of the danger. If the defendant is keeper because he or she is head of household and the junior keeper is under 16, it is enough that the junior keeper knew of the danger.

These provisions are obscure, and have led to controversial decisions.

> ***Gloster v Chief Constable of Greater Manchester Police* [2000] PIQR P114:** Two constables, Gloster and Owen, were running after a car thief. Owen was leading Jack, a police Alsatian. Owen tripped, accidentally releasing Jack, who bit Gloster twice in the leg. Alsatians are not naturally aggressive, though they can easily be trained to attack on command; Jack had done nothing less than he had been trained to do. Held: Jack had no 'dangerous characteristics ... not usually found in animals of that species', as any Alsatian had sharp teeth and could be trained to act as Jack had. Accordingly, there was no strict liability under the Animals Act. (However, Hale LJ expressed surprise that the trial judge had not found Owen to have been negligent.)

And yet Jack had been specifically trained to bite, at least in limited situations! It is odd to say that police dogs do not have dangerous characteristics; they are employed by the police precisely because they do. The Animals Act strikes a statutory bargain, under which people are allowed to own dangerous animals so long as they pay for the damage those animals do. It is unclear why this bargain does not apply to the police.

> ***Mirvahedy v Henley* [2003] UKHL 16:** Henley's horses were suddenly panicked, escaped from a secure paddock, and eventually ran into a road, where one of them collided with Mirvahedy's car. Held: Henley had known of the possibility of the horses'

behaviour, and it was irrelevant that he was unaware of the precise incident that had panicked them.

It seems to follow that animal conduct 'usually found only in particular circumstances' will attract liability *even if it was entirely normal for such an animal in those particular circumstances*. This broadens the liability considerably. *Mirvahedy* has also been applied in a case where a horse suddenly reared, in circumstances where (as its keeper knew) such rearing was entirely possible, if not common (*Welsh v Stokes* [2007] EWCA Civ 796); however, it was not applied when a horse passing a car unexpectedly veered into it for no clear reason (*Clark v Bowlt* [2006] EWCA Civ 978). It was also distinguished in a case where a cow showed unexpected abilities:

> **McKenny v Foster [2008] EWCA Civ 173:** McKenny's car collided with a cow that had escaped onto the road, killing her passenger as well as the cow. It emerged that the cow had recently been weaned, and was attempting to rejoin its calf; this was not unexpected behaviour in cows, though the extent of motivation and jumping ability the cow had shown was exceptional. Held: the degree of agitation shown by the cow was far beyond the normal, and as it was not known to the farmers they were not liable.

Plainly there is still a great deal of confusion over the definition of the 'characteristics' to which the Act refers.

Defences

7.47 The liability of the keeper under the Animals Act 1971 is strict, and it is quite irrelevant whether the harm done by the animal has anything to do with its dangerous characteristics. So if the defendant's tiger escapes and ruins the claimant's paintings by leaving paw-prints on them, the defendant is strictly liable. Nonetheless, the Act recognizes certain defences:

- *The claimant's own fault.* Damage which is wholly the claimant's fault attracts no liability at all (s 5); damage which is partly the claimant's fault may lead to a reduction in damages (ss 10 and 11; **11.17**).

- *The claimant's consent.* As with most torts, the claimant cannot sue where the claimant earlier agreed to run the risk of harm (**11.2**). Note that consent may very often be inferred where the claimant runs a risk which is very obvious (**11.6**) (for an example see *Freeman v Higher Park Farm* [2008] EWCA Civ 1185).

- *The claimant is a trespasser.* The claimant cannot recover for an injury caused by the defendant's animal if the defendant shows that it occurred when the claimant was trespassing on the defendant's land. There is an exception if the defendant kept the animal deliberately to guard the land: in that case, the defendant has a defence only if the defendant also shows that it was reasonable to use the animal in that way (s 5(3)). Note that the Guard Dogs Act 1975 strictly regulates the use of guard dogs. Breach of that Act's provisions does not in itself entail civil liability, but will almost certainly stop the defendant from arguing that the use of the dog was reasonable—and so it indirectly gives an injured trespasser a right to sue under the Animals Act 1971.

Application of other torts

7.48 The Animals Act 1971 abolished the special common law rules on liability for animals. So we need no longer concern ourselves with the old rules, or their concern with distinguishing animals *ferae naturae* (= of a wild nature) from those *mansuetae naturae* (= of a peaceable nature). Nonetheless, the general law of tort still applies, and so the defendant's misbehaving animals may involve the defendant in liability in a number of situations.

- If it was foreseeable that the defendant's animals might become dangerous, the defendant may be liable in negligence (e.g. *Draper v Hodder* [1972] 2 QB 556, the facts of which arose before the Animals Act 1971 was in force). In particular, the defendant may be liable in negligence for leaving animals where they might stray onto the highway (s 8(1)), though there is a statutory exception where the defendant lawfully left animals on common land, or on a town or village green, or in an area where fencing is not customary (s 8(2)). (For examples of claims in negligence, both ultimately unsuccessful, see *Jones v Whippey* [2009] EWCA Civ 452 and *Glaister v Appelby-in-Westmorland Town Council* [2009] EWCA Civ 1325.)

- The defendant's animals may involve the defendant in liability for nuisance, as by creating noise, smells, obstruction, or other disturbances (**7.11**; and note especially the case of the messy pigeons, **7.33**).

- Trespass to land (**7.2**) or trespass to the person (**2.1**) may be committed through an animal, as where the defendant deliberately sets his dog on the claimant.

For that matter, if the defendant trains a mynah bird to repeat words which ridicule the claimant, this might involve the defendant in liability for defamation; though it might be a difficult question whether the defendant is liable in slander or in libel (see **8.20**). Potentially, then, the defendant's animals may make the defendant liable for just about any tort, though some are a great deal more likely than others.

Special cases

Dogs harming livestock

7.49 Where the defendant is keeper of a dog which harms the claimant's livestock, the defendant is strictly liable to the claimant (Animals Act 1971, s 3). 'Livestock' is precisely defined in the Act, as meaning 'cattle, horses, asses, mules, hinnies, sheep, pigs, goats and poultry, and also deer not in the wild state and, while in captivity, pheasants, partridges and grouse' (s 11). This special rule is somewhat anomalous, for it means that property is better protected than the person.

Straying livestock

7.50 Where the defendant's livestock strays onto another's land, there is strict liability for property damage done as a result (s 4). There is also a statutory right to detain the offending animals, to charge for their care while so detained, and ultimately to sell them if not reclaimed (s 7).

Assessment

Current trends in the law

7.51 The torts under consideration in this chapter develop slowly, receiving relatively little attention either from the legislature or from litigants. Various key points stand out. The torts are very diverse: they cover a wide range of situations, and because they must therefore be based on very broad principles, they are unpredictable. The torts, by and large, protect individual rights, not the public interest (**7.20, 7.31**). It is true that the courts pay some attention to the public interest (**7.16**), but the courts seek no evidence on this from anyone but the parties. The question before the court is essentially whether one private individual has infringed the rights of another, rather than what the public interest in the environment requires. The claimant is allowed only to protect the claimant's own interests and is not a representative of all who might have some objection to the defendant's activities. It is increasingly clear that the courts see the answer to such problems in the application of negligence principles, rather than in ideas of strict liability (**7.22–7.23**):

> ...I incline to the opinion that, as a general rule, it is more appropriate for strict liability in respect of operations of high risk to be imposed by Parliament, than by the courts... [G]iven that so much well-informed and carefully structured legislation is now being put in place for [dealing with environmental pollution], there is less need for the courts to

develop a common law principle to achieve the same end, and indeed it may well be undesirable that they should do so (*Cambridge Water Co v Eastern Counties Leather* [1994] 1 All ER 53, 76, Lord Goff).

It is possible that the Human Rights Act 1998 (above, **1.22**) will have a major impact in this area, particularly in the light of European Convention, Art 8(1), guaranteeing rights to the home and to private and family life.

Part of a wider system

7.52 This narrow incidence of the law of tort would be impossible to defend if it were all the law had to say on the protection of land use and the environment; but it is not. The common law runs alongside an extensive system of 'statutory nuisances' for which local authorities may take proceedings; further powers are vested in the Environment Agency. There is also the all-pervasive system of planning controls, which pre-empt many issues of land use before they get the chance to raise issues of nuisance (**7.17**). Parliament has not neglected questions of civil liability either: one reason why catastrophes such as tanker disasters tend not to give rise to litigation is that Parliament has already settled the ground rules of civil liability, without the need for the courts to do so. When we consider, therefore, what the proper scope of common law liability should be, we are asking what should be done in the marginal or unexpected cases which have not *already* been provided for by legislation. What, in the light of that, should be done?

Distinguish more between remedies?

7.53 For some, the law on nuisance is unnecessarily complicated because the courts tend to pose the blanket question 'whether there was a nuisance', when they should ask simply whether the claimant should have the remedy claimed. The question whether the claimant can close the defendant's factory down is quite different from whether the claimant is entitled to loss caused by its operations. Yet, as these both depend on whether these operations constitute a nuisance, arguably the courts are unfair to claimants. They hesitate to grant damages, because that could in other cases open the way to a claim to an injunction.

Strict liability or negligence liability?

7.54 Others suggest that it is too ungenerous to claimants to insist on proof of fault. The argument, which is at its strongest where the defendant's activities carry obvious dangers to others, may be put morally or economically: that justice, or economic efficiency, or both, require that the defendant must carry the costs as well as the benefits to be made from the dangerous activity. (How strongly the economist would put the argument would depend on several factors; if it is relatively easy for the defendant to bargain with claimants or potential claimants, the 'Coase theorem' suggests that bargains made by the parties will settle the matter regardless of the law's allocation of risk. The law's main role, on this view, is to facilitate bargains between the parties.)

More public, less public?

7.55 Finally, it is often suggested the current law is defective for placing too much emphasis on individual rights, with the result that the public interest is neglected. There might be many reasons an injured party might not sue. If one injured party does sue, there is no enquiry into the loss the defendant has caused generally— indeed, the court would not normally hear from other injured parties at all. Damages are awarded strictly for the claimant's own loss, and there is no question of punitive damages, or the award of a 'global' sum to compensate all those injured by the activities complained of. Moreover, many interests, and in particular individuals' interests in their own health and safety, are barely recognized at all by the tort of nuisance. The same is true of interests such as good air quality: the air does not belong to anyone, and so has no-one to guard its interests unless a particular claimant can establish and quantify a loss to him personally. Many argue, therefore, that the current structure of liability almost invariably underestimates the harm done by environmentally dangerous activities.

FURTHER READING

Buckley 'The march of negligence: Has nuisance a future?' (2007) 58 NILQ 395.

Chevalier-Watts 'Civil liability for animals' (2007) 11 Mountbatten JLS 56.

Davey 'Neighbours in law' (2001) 65 Conv 31.

Garwood-Gowers 'Improving protection against indirect interference with the use and enjoyment of home' (2002) 11 Notts Law Jour 1.

Kidner 'Nuisance and rights of property' [1998] Conv 267.

Lee 'What is private nuisance?' (2003) 119 LQR 298.

McManus 'Noise law in the United Kingdom—A very British solution?' (2000) 20 LS 264.

Morgan 'Nuisance and the unruly tenant' (2001) 60 CLJ 382.

Murphy 'The merits of *Rylands v Fletcher*' (2004) 24 OJLS 643.

Nolan 'The distinctiveness of *Rylands v Fletcher*' (2005) 121 LQR 421.

O'Sullivan 'Nuisance, local authorities and neighbours from hell' (2000) 59 CLJ 11.

Wightman 'Nuisance—The environmental tort?' (1998) 61 MLR 870.

SELF-TEST QUESTIONS

1 Angie's factory, which has been operating for 30 years, last year added a new unit. The machinery makes a loud humming noise. As a result Bernard, who last month bought a house nearby, cannot get to sleep at night. Assuming that there is a nuisance, does Angie have a defence *(a)* of prescription (**7.26**); *(b)* of consent (**7.28**); or *(c)* that she obtained planning permission before adding the new unit (**7.17**)?

2 Is it a defence to an action in nuisance that the defendant's conduct was, on the whole, for the public benefit (**7.16**)?

3 May the same conduct by the defendant amount to both a public nuisance *and* a private nuisance (**7.31**)?

4 In what sense or senses is the liability for the tort in *Rylands v Fletcher* 'strict' (**7.40–7.41**)?

5 Charles, while exploring tunnels under his land, discovers a large and impressive cave, which he regularly visits on later occasions. It turns out that the cave is in fact directly under Donna's land. Has Charles committed trespass (**7.3**)? Does it matter whether Charles reasonably thought it was under his own land (**7.5**)? What damages, if any, may Donna recover (**7.9**)?

8

Protection of reputation

SUMMARY

A statement which lowers the claimant's reputation may constitute defamation. Key points are:

- Was the defendant responsible for the statement?
- What defences are available?
- What is the appropriate remedy?

Other torts may occasionally be used to protect reputation. Reform of the law is highly controversial, particularly in relation to the size of awards and the legal costs involved.

8.1 Reputation is protected principally by the tort of defamation, though a few other torts are relevant (**8.42**). Defamation is the most antique part of tort law you are ever likely to meet. The law is byzantine, the procedure archaic, and the remedies draconian. Reforms have smoothed away the rougher edges of the law, but the result keeps few happy. The expense of the remedy pushes all but the very rich away. Legal aid has never been available, the framers of the scheme never believing the law was in a fit state to justify it. This unavailability will certainly have to be reconsidered, as it has been held to put the UK in breach of Art 6 of the European Convention on Human Rights in cases where there is serious 'inequality of arms' between the claimant and the defendant (*Steel and Morris v United Kingdom* (European Court of Human Rights, 1 February 2005)).

Defamation is sometimes divided into slander (spoken defamation) and libel (written or broadcast defamation). But the law is very similar for both and it will only be necessary to distinguish the two when we consider damages (**8.21**).

The role of the jury

8.2 Defamation is almost unique among the torts: it is very often heard before a judge and jury, rather than a judge alone. The role of the jury is to determine matters of fact and to determine the level of damages. The role of the judge is to decide issues of law and procedure, including (if necessary) the decision to withdraw from the jury any questions to which there can only be one reasonable answer. This division of responsibility is a major factor in the complexity of defamation proceedings. Yet it also means that at least some of the major decisions are in the hands of a body representative of the public. However, it also adds to the length and cost of trials; and for this and other reasons the current tendency is to resolve the matter without a jury where possible.

Current procedures are curiously ambivalent about the use of juries. On the one hand, the courts have insisted on the prominent place of jury trial in defamation cases. The use of a jury is not merely one possible mode of trial, it is a right which either party may claim, which may only be refused for clear reasons (*Alexander v Arts Council of Wales* [2001] EWCA Civ 514). On the other, the courts have been so insistent on the limited role of juries as to remove almost all force from this right. Under current procedures, a jury may be refused altogether on the ground that the case would be too complex for them. Particular questions may be withdrawn from them, on the ground that the answer to them is either a matter of pure law, or is so plain that there is only one way they could reasonably resolve it. And the courts have been absolutely ruthless in correcting juries they consider to have reached the wrong answer, particularly on the assessment of damages (e.g. *John v MGN* [1997] QB 586, **8.22**). How genuine can the 'right' to jury trial be, when the judges have no hesitation in imposing their own verdict where it differs from that of the jury?

Liability

The meaning of statements

8.3 Much of the law of defamation assumes that we can give a definite meaning to what the defendant said or wrote. The meaning will often be clear: the defendant might say outright that the claimant is a thief. But defamation may take any form, if a derogatory impression is given.

> **Monson v Tussauds [1894] 1 QB 671:** Monson was tried for murder by shooting; the (Scots) criminal court returned a verdict of 'Not Proven'. Tussauds exhibited a waxwork of Monson, with a gun, near the entrance of its Chamber of Horrors. This was held, for defamation purposes, to amount to a statement that Monson was a murderer.

Where the meaning of the defendant's statement is disputed, it is the claimant's job to specify what the meaning is, and the jury's to say whether the claimant is correct. The judge may refuse to put the question to the jury if the suggested meaning is an unreasonable one. The form of the statement does not matter. The test is: *what meaning would reasonable people give to the statement?*

> **English and Scottish Co-operative Society v Odhams Press [1940] 1 KB 440:** A newspaper story about incorrect tax returns was headlined 'False Profit Return Charge Against Society'. The Society said that this amounted to an accusation that it had *deliberately* made false returns. Held: the headline could reasonably be read in that way, and the jury was entitled, having regard to the whole story, to treat it as an accusation of fraud.

The process of spelling out the supposed meaning often results in something barely recognizable to its original author, or at the very least involves a plodding elucidation of fleeting references in the original article. In *Cruise and Kidman v Express Newspapers* [1999] QB 931 the passage complained of read (in part) as follows:

> Since [Kidman] married himbo hunk Tom Cruise and the couple inaugurated themselves as Hollywood royalty—not difficult when the competition is led by Bruce 'n' Demi—there has been a persistent trickle of speculation. Their failure to produce offspring (like everyone else in uptown LA, they adopted some poor children) set Hollywood tongues wagging. He was gay, they said; he was impotent; *she* was gay. The whole marriage thing was no more than a business arrangement, they sniggered, and, most sinister of all, the wedding had been ordered by the Church of Scientology, which was keen to establish the couple as a beacon of clean living and an example to the young. Scientology has become the religion of choice in A-list Hollywood, and the Cruises are very keen on it. The only one of the world's major faiths whose founder is called Ron, its adherents include such models of continence and rectitude as Lisa Marie Presley and Kirstie Alley.

This contains a number of distinct assertions about the claimants. Here is their version of its meaning. Do you agree that it is the true meaning?

> 4.2 that, far from being the 'golden couple' that they seek to portray, the 'Hollywood royalty' in which they have cast themselves, and the 'great love match' suggested by the second plaintiff..., the likely truth is that their marriage is a hypocritical sham, there being good reasons to believe that it is a cover for the homosexuality of one or both of them and/or a cynical business arrangement and/or a marriage ordered by the Church of Scientology so that the Scientologists might dishonestly hold up the plaintiffs as an example to the young;

> 4.3 that there are good reasons to believe that the first plaintiff's failure to father children is attributable to impotence and/or sterility and his vehement public denial of sterility probably a lie;

4.4 that the 'plaintiffs adopted some poor children' because it is the fashion in 'uptown LA'; ...

(The article contained a number of allegations about the claimants, in addition to those mentioned here. The case went to the Court of Appeal to settle various pleading points, including what facts would have to be proved to establish defences of justification or fair comment. Two months after the ruling of the Court of Appeal, a settlement was agreed, under which Express Newspapers made a public admission that their article was completely wrong, and paid damages (believed to be in the order of £100,000 to each claimant) and costs (believed to be about £150,000).)

Slang

8.4 The claimant may rely on slang meanings, but must explain them to the court.

> **Allsop v Church of England Newspaper [1972] 2 QB 161:** A newspaper published a hostile review of Allsop's performance on television ('We need religious television we can understand'), and complained of a 'pre-occupation with the bent'. Held: while this phrase was plainly derogatory, it was ambiguous. Allsop was ordered to spell out in more detail what he took it to mean, if his libel action was to continue.

Inferences

8.5 Perhaps the defendant's statement does not directly say anything against the claimant, but reasonable listeners would nonetheless *infer* something against the claimant. The defendant is responsible not only for the statement, but also for reasonable inferences from it.

> **Tolley v JS Fry & Sons [1931] AC 333:** Tolley, a famous amateur golfer, was depicted in an advertisement for Fry's chocolate, with a limerick praising both Tolley and the chocolate. Held: reasonable readers might infer that Tolley had received money for allowing his name to appear in this way, and accordingly might believe that he had compromised his amateur status.

> **Gillick v British Broadcasting Corpn [1996] EMLR 267:** A participant in a live TV programme commented that 'there were at least two reported cases of suicide by girls who were pregnant'. Gillick, a prominent campaigner against contraceptive advice for young girls, claimed that these words accused her of being morally responsible for those deaths. Held: in the context in which they were spoken, the words were capable of bearing that meaning.

But this is potentially a highly oppressive rule and the courts have refused to apply it to its fullest extent.

> **Lewis v Daily Telegraph [1964] AC 234:** The *Daily Telegraph* reported, accurately, that the Fraud Squad of the City of London Police were investigating a particular firm. Lewis, its managing director, sued, arguing that readers might believe that 'there was no smoke without fire', and therefore would infer that he must be guilty of something. Held: many people might draw that inference, but nonetheless it was not a reasonable inference. Lewis would not be allowed to treat the story as an allegation of fraud against him.

Inferences based on special facts

8.6 Sometimes the inference on which the claimant relies could only have been drawn by someone with special knowledge, the statement appearing quite innocuous to someone without this knowledge. The claimant must carefully plead this special meaning (known as an 'innuendo'), as well as the special knowledge on which it relies. Further, even if the claimant succeeds in this argument, the claimant has only been defamed in the eyes of those with this special knowledge—a point which may reduce the damages payable. However, there is no rule that the defendant must have known of the special facts, and accordingly the principle may have unexpected results from the defendant's point of view.

> **Cassidy v Daily Mirror Newspapers [1929] 2 KB 331:** The *Daily Mirror* published a photograph of Mr Cassidy with a woman, implying that they were engaged. Mrs Cassidy sued, saying that this gave her acquaintances the impression that she was not married to Mr Cassidy, and so it amounted to a charge that she was 'living in sin' with him. The *Mirror* argued that, as they had not mentioned Mrs Cassidy, they could not be said to have defamed her. Held: to those who knew Mrs Cassidy, the photograph would have conveyed the meaning she argued for, and so she was defamed in the eyes of those people.

> **E Hulton & Co v Jones [1910] AC 20:** The *Sunday Chronicle* published an account of a motor show in Dieppe, suggesting that one Artemus Jones, a married clergyman, was seen behaving immorally. A barrister called Artemus Jones sued, producing friends who swore they thought the story referred to him. The *Chronicle* pleaded that the account was light-hearted, and 'Artemus Jones' manifestly an invention. Held: the test was whether reasonable people would infer that the claimant was meant; in view of the unusual name, the jury was entitled to infer that the claimant had been defamed.

This rule is potentially a very harsh one. If either case were to recur, the defendant might plead the statutory defence of unintentional defamation (**8.25**). (Though on the facts of the *Jones* case itself this would have been unlikely to succeed: Mitchell 'Artemus Jones and the Press Club' (1999) 20 JLH 64).)

The term 'innuendo' is sometimes also used to refer to slang, topical references, or other meanings which might need to be explained to the judge, but which are nonetheless the ordinary meanings of the words used (**8.4**). These are technically known as 'false innuendoes', as distinct from 'true innuendoes' which rely on proof of extrinsic facts.

Is the defendant responsible for publishing the statement?

8.7 Distinguish carefully between the person with whom the statement originates (the 'primary publisher') and those who repeat it ('secondary publishers').

Primary publishers are strictly liable

8.8 Good motive is no defence, nor is a reasonable belief that the statement is true. Communication to a single person other than the claimant is enough. If the claimant shows that the defendant put the statement into general circulation, it is for the defendant to prove that no-one read it or understood it. Indeed, some old cases say that if the defendant sends the claimant an insulting postcard, defamation is established, unless the defendant can prove that it was not read by postal workers en route, or that the insults would not have been understood by those readers. The defendant is not necessarily safe even in the case of a sealed envelope.

> **Theaker v Richardson [1962] 1 All ER 229:** Richardson sent an abusive letter to Theaker, correctly addressed. Her husband opened it. Held: Richardson was liable for the publication to Theaker's husband. While refusing to lay down a presumption that husbands read their wives' letters, the Court of Appeal did not fault the jury's verdict that this was a natural and probable consequence of Richardson's behaviour.

The primary publisher may sometimes also be held liable for the greater harm done when the statement is repeated. Traditionally this is said to be so in three cases: *(i)* where the defendant requests or authorizes the repetition; *(ii)* where the defendant means it to be repeated; and *(iii)* where the repeaters do so because they feel morally bound to do it. But in practice the defendant seems to be held liable whenever repetition is foreseeable as a consequence of the defendant's behaviour, and some authorities say that this is indeed the law (e.g. *Baturina v Times Newspapers Ltd* [2010] EWHC 696 (QB)).

> **McManus v Beckham [2002] EWCA Civ 939:** While in McManus's shop, Beckham saw various signed photographs of her husband. She observed in a loud voice that the signatures were forged, and advised customers not to buy them. The incident was widely reported in the press, under such headlines as 'Posh goes stropping—Beck's "Forgery

Fury" ' (*Daily Mirror*). A preliminary issue was whether Beckham could be held liable for the wide publicity given to her accusation, or was liable only for its publication to the three customers who actually heard her. Held: as a celebrity, Beckham was aware that her accusation was likely to be reported widely, and was liable accordingly.

(A settlement was reached in March 2003, under which Beckham's counsel made an apology in open court, and she provided for McManus a set of official merchandise signed by her husband, as well as a payment of £55,000 and costs.)

Secondary publishers are liable for negligence

8.9 At common law, those who merely repeat defamatory statements may have a defence if they neither knew nor could reasonably have known that they were repeating defamatory matter; but they are otherwise liable (*Goldsmith v Sperrings* [1977] 2 All ER 566). The common law rule on the matter has now been replaced by statute (Defamation Act 1996, s 1); the new rule is somewhat more precise, but to the same general effect. 'Authors', 'editors', and 'publishers' of statements are strictly liable; others have a defence if they can show they took all reasonable care in relation to the statement, and did not know, and had no reason to believe, that they were contributing to the publication of a defamatory statement. The definitions used in the section are complex; how the courts will react to them can only be a matter for speculation at this early stage.

One important ruling in relation to the internet holds that messages posted to bulletin boards expose those who operate the boards to an action as secondary publishers (*Godfrey v Demon Internet* [2001] QB 201). They have a defence if they could not have known of the defamation—an easy plea to make given the bulk of messages—but if the person defamed complains of it, then the defence is very hard to sustain. In practice, therefore, an offending message has to be removed as soon as their attention is brought to it, or they face liability in defamation if no defence can be established. The result in *Godfrey v Demon* is controversial, and not at all obvious. It seems rather like saying that a shop which hires TVs 'publishes' whatever images then appear on the screen, or (for that) matter that a telephone company 'publishes' whatever words are spoken down the phone line. It is to be hoped that the higher courts will reconsider this ruling. Nonetheless it is well established for now, and has led to a much-reported action against friendsreunited.co.uk for enabling a former pupil to libel his former teacher. Those who run bulletin boards may also be the subject of orders to make them identify the senders of defamatory messages (*Totalise Ltd v Motley Fool Ltd* [2001] EWCA Civ 1897). Attempts have been made to extend this liability still further, to cover an Internet Service Provider who carried messages to and from the message board. But this has failed, either on the ground that such a merely 'passive' role does not amount to publication, or falls within a statutory defence for 'mere conduits' of information over the Internet (*Bunt v Tilley* [2006] EWHC 407 (QB); Electronic Commerce (EC Directive) Regulations 2002, reg 17). Further, it will not be presumed that a defamatory message on a board or other site has been read by anyone: it is for the claimant to prove that it has been accessed and downloaded by someone within the jurisdiction of the court (*Al Amoudi v Brisard* [2006] EWHC 1062 (QB)).

> **Metropolitan International Schools Ltd v Designtechnica Corp [2009] EWHC 1765 (QB):** In an action for defamation on an internet discussion forum, the question arose whether the owners of Google could be added as defendants, when a search for the article threw up a defamatory snippet of text as part of the search results. Held: No. ' ... [Google] has no role to play in formulating the search terms. Accordingly, it could not prevent the snippet appearing in response to the user's request unless it has taken some positive step in advance. There being no input from [Google], therefore, on the scenario I have so far posited, it cannot be characterised as a publisher at common law' (Eady J).

The liability of secondary publishers is one of the heavily criticized aspects of the modern law of defamation. It is not practical for printers and distributors to read everything they publish, let alone to check whether individual statements are true. The standard of care required from them has never been spelled out with any precision. Threats of action against distributors may be enough to suppress the offending publication entirely; yet the courts refuse 'prior restraint' when asked for it directly (**8.23**), and so should not allow it in through the back door. In fact, legal action is only rarely taken against distributors, but the threat is always there, and it is a potent one. Here, as at many points throughout the modern law of defamation, there is the potential impact of European Convention, Art 10, guaranteeing freedom of expression (see **1.22**).

The law's neat distinction between 'primary' and 'secondary' publishers sits rather uncomfortably with modern publishing practice. If a newspaper story criticizes the claimant, is there a 'publication' when the journalist types a first draft, another if a colleague sees it, another when seen by a sub-editor, another when seen by the libel reader? Technically speaking there is a fresh 'publication' each time the statement comes to someone's attention. However, most of the internal workings of the newspaper are covered by qualified privilege (see **8.36**), and in practice the claimant usually treats the printing of the newspaper as the 'primary publication'.

Does the statement defame the claimant?

8.10 It is not sufficient that the statement annoys or embarrasses the claimant. The statement must lower the claimant's reputation. In the traditional formula, it must stir up 'hatred, ridicule or contempt' against the claimant. Yet this formula is misleading, for the claimant is not bound to produce witnesses who say they are now inclined to loath, mock, or despise the claimant. On the contrary, the claimant often produces witnesses who say they never for a moment believed what the defendant said. It is not any particular, real person who must feel these emotions of hatred, ridicule, and contempt. Rather, the test is whether the defendant's statement arouses them in the breast of The Reasonable Person.

The Reasonable Person

8.11 The courts have often acknowledged that The Reasonable Person differs somewhat from the citizenry at large. The Reasonable Person represents what people *should* be, in the court's eyes, even if they *are* rather different. If the defendant accuses the claimant of a particularly ingenious fraud, this defames the claimant, because The Reasonable Person hates and despises those who commit fraud. It is irrelevant that many people might feel awe at the skill supposedly displayed (*Tournier v National Provincial Bank* [1924] 1 KB 461, 487, Atkin LJ).

To satisfy the 'hatred, ridicule or contempt' formula when the claimant's *property* is disparaged, we must ask whether the state of affairs described reflects on the claimant personally. So it is not necessarily defamatory to say of a shopkeeper that some of the goods he sells are defective, but it probably would be defamatory to say that they *all* are. This can lead to awkward borderline cases, and it is an open question whether the English courts will follow this Australian case:

> **John Fairfax Publications v Gacic [2007] HCA 28:** Gacic published a review of a new Sydney restaurant, 'Coco Roco', criticizing the food as overpriced and sub-standard. Held: this was plainly capable of defaming the restaurant's owners. 'It is unimaginable...that the estimation of the [owners] in the mind of any adult person, let alone a reasonable reader, would not be lowered by a statement that they sold unpalatable food and provided bad service at their restaurant, and did so for considerable sums of money' ([2007] HCA 28, para 190, Callinan and Heydon JJ).

Beyond 'hatred, ridicule or contempt'

8.12 The traditional formula is at best a loose indication. It is impossible to be precise here, for a number of reasons. First, changing values mean that older cases are not a reliable guide. Second, whether a particular statement is defamatory is ultimately a jury question, and juries cannot give their reasons; the cases tell us only which cases are so clear that the judge can *withdraw* them from the jury. Third, the cases are often inconsistent. For example, some cases say that it is not defamatory to call the claimant a bankrupt, because this could be for many reasons, not all of which reflect on the claimant's character; whereas others say that this allegation obviously damages the claimant's reputation, especially if the claimant is involved in professional or commercial work.

As another example, is it defamatory to say that the claimant is a homosexual? This is clearly stated in the older cases to be defamatory. Yet with modern changes in values, it is hard to imagine a court relying on them: '[t]here is no common view that sexual conduct of any kind between consenting adults is grossly immoral' (*Stephens v Avery* [1988] 2 All ER 477, 480, Browne-Wilkinson V-C). It does not follow, however, that the defendant may allege homosexuality with impunity.

> **Donovan v 'The Face'** (April 1992, unreported): A magazine, *The Face*, purported to 'out' the actor Jason Donovan. Donovan sued, saying that he had been accused, not merely of being homosexual, but also of concealing his supposed sexuality to preserve his stage image as a heterosexual. A jury found the statement defamatory, awarding £200,000.

(For another example, where a charge of homosexuality was also regarded as defamatory *because it implied that the claimants had tried to fool the world that they were heterosexual*, see *Cruise and Kidman v Express Newspapers* [1999] QB 931, **8.3**.)

Again, it has traditionally been assumed that it is defamatory to say that the claimant suffers from a serious disease. There is no sign of a retreat from this position merely because hatred, ridicule, and contempt are not today seen as appropriate responses to disease.

And for a sufficiently shocking allegation, some judges will abandon the traditional formula entirely.

> **Youssoupoff v Metro-Goldwyn-Meyer Pictures** (1934) 78 SJ 617: MGM produced a film which, while it used fictitious names, nonetheless plainly portrayed the claimant, and suggested that she had been raped by Rasputin the Mad Monk. Held: this was a defamatory allegation because (per Scrutton LJ) the story was plainly to her discredit, or (per Atkin LJ) the law of defamation also protects claimants from statements which would cause others to shun or avoid them.

Neither reason seems satisfactory. Scrutton's approach, which assumes that the claimant herself was at fault, is strange. Atkin's formulation is more satisfactory, and also explains why it is defamatory to say that the claimant has a serious communicable disease; but how was his criterion satisfied on the facts? This reformulation seems to broaden the scope of liability very wide indeed, to include claimants much less deserving than Princess Youssoupoff.

> ***Berkoff v Burchill* [1996] 4 All ER 1008:** Burchill's review of a horror film *The Creature* compared the eponymous creature to the actor Steven Berkoff, though noting that the creature itself was 'marginally better looking'. Berkoff sued in libel. Held: on the assumption that the review meant that Berkoff was hideously ugly, it was capable of being defamatory.

There is much force in the dissenting judgment of Millett LJ, who concluded that 'Miss Burchill made a cheap joke at Mr Berkoff's expense; she may thereby have demeaned herself, but I do not believe that she defamed Mr Berkoff. If I have appeared to treat Mr Berkoff's claim with unjudicial levity it is because I find it impossible to take it seriously' ([1996] 4 All ER 1008, 1020). A similar attitude was displayed in a later case.

> ***Norman v Future Publishing* [1999] EMLR 325:** In an article otherwise extremely complimentary to the claimant, an internationally famous opera singer, there appeared the following sentence. 'This is the woman who got trapped in swing doors on her way to a concert, and when advised to release herself by turning sideways replied: "Honey, I ain't got no sideways".' This was said to amount to a charge that '(*1*) [she] had used a mode of speech which was (*a*) vulgar and undignified and/or (*b*) conformed to a degrading racist stereotype of a person of African–American heritage; alternatively (*2*) [she] had been guilty of patronising mockery of the modes of speech stereo-typically attributed to certain groups or classes of black Americans, and was therefore guilty also of hypocrisy'. Held: the sentence, read in the context of the whole article, was not reasonably capable of being read in any of those suggested senses.

'Vulgar abuse'

8.13　There is no liability for mere insults which no reasonable person would treat as factual allegations. It is sometimes said that there is no liability for 'vulgar abuse'. But that is misleading. Rather, the rule is that ridicule is not actionable if, rationally considered, it suggests nothing to the claimant's discredit.

> ***Charleston v News Group Newspapers* [1995] 2 AC 65:** The *News of the World* portrayed the claimants, who played a married couple in the soap opera *Neighbours*, apparently committing an indecent act. The headline was 'Strewth! What's Harold up to with our Madge?' The text made it clear that the claimants' faces had been superimposed on pictures of pornographic actors. Held: the article must be read as a whole, and when so read was not defamatory.

> ***John v Guardian News and Media Ltd* [2008] EWHC 3066 (QB):** In a spoof diary entry describing a charity fundraising event, it was suggested that nearly all of the funds

raised were consumed in the event itself rather than going to charity. Held: while the article was clearly critical of the event and its funding, nonetheless it was written in a humorous spirit, and would not have been understood in the literal sense the claimant relied on. 'The words complained of ... could not be understood by a reasonable reader of *The Guardian Weekend* section as containing the serious allegation pleaded ... If that was the allegation being made, a reasonable reader would expect so serious an allegation to be made without humour, and explicitly, in a part of the newspaper devoted to news' (Tugendhat J).

'It is rumoured . . .'

8.14 To repeat the defamatory utterances of others is usually regarded as attracting liability for defamation in itself. To preface a defamatory remark with the tag 'There is no truth in the vile rumour that ...' is likely to be regarded as a ploy, and no better than simple repetition without comment.

A more tricky case (which never came to trial) was as follows. Rumours circulate in journalistic circles that the Prime Minister is having an affair. *New Statesman and Society* magazine suspects that these rumours have been manufactured to discredit the Prime Minister, and publishes a leading article saying so, necessarily repeating the rumours as it does so. Does this defame the Prime Minister? The matter is unclear. The *Statesman* had a strong case, though they had certainly not done themselves a favour by their front-page reference to 'Major's "Mistress" '. The settlement gave Major only £1,001, though costs and compensation to their distributors drove the *Statesman's* total bill up to around £250,000.

Meanwhile, the courts have been sending out mixed messages as to whether someone who repeats a rumour may defend themselves on the ground that there was in fact such a rumour.

> **Stern v Piper [1997] QB 123:** A columnist in the *Mail on Sunday* quoted allegations made against Stern, made in the pleadings of a legal action against Stern. Stern sued the newspaper. Held: the newspaper could not establish a defence of truth merely by proving that the allegations had in fact been made in judicial proceedings.

> **Shah v Standard Chartered Bank [1999] QB 241:** SCB made various allegations of fraud against Shah to Bank of England officials. Shah sued, saying that he had been accused of fraud, and that SCB could only justify these accusations by proving them true. SCB said that they meant no more than that Shah had acted suspiciously and seemed to be guilty, both of which they thought they could prove. Held: it was a jury question which of the two meanings was the right one, as either view could reasonably be held. However, if the statements meant only that Shah was apparently guilty, this could be justified only by evidence of actual conduct by Shah, not by repeating hearsay.

An attempt to challenge the law laid down in *Shah* as infringing the European Convention on Human Rights was rejected by the Court of Appeal (*Chase v Newsgroup Newspaper Ltd* [2002] EWCA Civ 1772).

Values of particular class

8.15 The claimant may argue that while the defendant's statement does not defame the claimant in the eyes of the general public, it nonetheless does so in the eyes of some smaller class. Stated baldly, this argument must be rejected. The claimant must appeal to the values of the whole community—even if the claimant and the defendant both belong to some narrower grouping. Yet as explained above (**8.6**), the claimant is perfectly entitled to rely on matters of *fact* known only to a narrow class, and the line is often hard to draw.

> ***Byrne v Deane* [1937] 1 KB 818:** A private club had been running an illegal gaming machine, which the police confiscated. A satirical poem was then prominently posted at the club, suggesting that Byrne had tipped the police off ('But he who gave the game away / May he byrnn in hell and rue the day'). Byrne sued Deane, who ran the club. Held (by a majority): no reasonable person would regard it as wrong to inform the police of illegal conduct, and so the poem was not defamatory.

Yet Greer LJ was able, on those facts, to find liability. Byrne had in effect been accused of disloyalty to other members of the club, which is a sin in the eyes of the whole community. 'Whether that was justified or not is quite another matter' ([1937] 1 KB 818, 830). Some care is needed, therefore, in applying this rule.

> ***Shah v Akram* [1981] LS Gaz R 814:** Akram published a pamphlet attacking Shah's standing as a Muslim, saying that he had insulted Islam. Both were devout Muslims. Held: a reasonable person, of any religion or none, would think poorly of someone who insulted the faith of others. Accordingly, Akram's statement was defamatory by the standards of the community in general.

> ***Singh v Eastern Media Group* [2010] EWHC 1294 (QB):** Singh, a Sikh holy man, was accused of being a 'cult leader' and an 'impostor'. Held: this was not actionable, as judicial consideration of it could not in practice be divorced from questions of Sikh doctrine and practice. 'Of course, I recognise that if an all   egation were made of someone, who happened to be a religious leader, that he had his hand in the till, or assaulted a follower, this could be determined separately and without reference to religious doctrine or status, but that is far from this case. The issue whether this Claimant is or is not fairly described as an "impostor" cannot be isolated and resolved without reference to Sikh doctrines and traditions' (Eady J).

Group defamation

8.16 There is no rule that the claimant must be mentioned by name. The same statement may defame tens or even hundreds of people, if reasonable hearers would take it to reflect on each one of them. Yet the courts are reluctant to treat insults against a class as defaming each member of it. If the defendant broadcasts racial abuse against black people, the claimant may not sue merely because he or she is black. But the same remarks might be defamatory if, in context, they single out the claimant in some way.

Defaming corporate bodies

8.17 A statement that a corporate body is poorly or dishonestly run may reflect on its officers and be actionable by them.

> *Orme v Associated Newspapers Group* **(1981) Times, 4 February:** A newspaper alleged misconduct against the Unification Church (the Moonies). Orme, the Church's leader in England, was not mentioned in the piece, but said that it could be taken to mean that he knew about, and condoned, the conduct complained of. Held: the statement was capable of being read that way by reasonable readers.

Can the corporation itself sue? A corporation is a person in law (unlike unincorporated bodies such as trade unions), and it does not require excessive mental gymnastics to think of a corporation having a reputation of its own. So companies may sue in defamation. But it has been held that local authorities cannot, whatever the injury to their 'governing reputation', as this would have a chilling effect on political debate (*Derbyshire County Council v Times Newspapers* [1993] AC 534). For the same reason, a political party cannot sue in defamation either (*Goldsmith v Bhoyrul* [1998] QB 459). After the hugely unsatisfactory 'McLibel' case (*McDonald's Corpn v Steel and Morris* (1997, unreported)), there is certainly a school of thought that business corporations do not need the right to sue in defamation at all, and that this right is too open to abuse. However, the courts have proved unresponsive to this, rejecting even the argument that they should have to prove special damage before an action will lie (*Jameel v Wall Street Journal Europe SPRL* [2006] UKHL 44).

'No substantial tort'

8.18 A new defence appears to be emerging, that the alleged defamation does not amount to a substantial tort. In principle it has always been the law that trivial claims are not maintainable (*de minimis curat lex*, 'the law does not concern itself with trifles'), but a new willingness to hold that particular claims are indeed trivial is manifesting itself.

> ***Kaschke v Gray* [2010] EWHC 1907 (QB):** A posting in a blog suggested that Kaschke had once been investigated by the German police for possible involvement with a terrorist group, though it also accepted her denial of any such involvement. Held: while there were minor differences between what the blog post alleged and what Kaschke accepted as the truth, these differences would not result in a significant award of damages, and the cost of a trial would be out of all proportion to the loss suffered. The action should not proceed further.

Remedies

Financial loss: 'special damages'

8.19 A successful claimant in defamation is entitled to all financial loss that can be shown to flow from the defendant's statement ('special damages'), subject to defences of remoteness (**10.28**) and mitigation (**10.36**).

Injury to feelings and other unquantifiable losses: 'general damages'

8.20 Defamation is sometimes 'actionable per se'—that is, actionable in itself, without proof of special damage. The claimant is then entitled to a sum for injured feelings, lost dignity, and unprovable but likely financial loss ('general damages'). It is important for this purpose to distinguish between libel, which is always actionable per se, and slander, which is only actionable per se in certain situations.

Libel or slander?

8.21 Defamation by word of mouth is slander; written defamation is libel. The test is sometimes said to be that slander is temporary, libel permanent; but this is misleading. Defamatory newspaper stories are libel, even if every reader throws the newspaper away immediately on finishing it; speech is slander, even if it is remembered for many years after.

The following have been settled by case law to be libel, not slander: pictures, sculptures, films (with or without sound track), and reading out defamatory letters. Statute establishes that stage plays, TV, and radio broadcasts for general reception are libel (Theatres Act 1968, s 4; Broadcasting Act 1990, s 166). The status of email is unclear, but it too is probably libel; several cases involving email have already been decided, but seemingly without broaching the libel/slander issue. Sound recordings (records, tapes, CDs) are of uncertain status, as are radio broadcasts intended to be private.

The following slanders are actionable per se: *(i)* that the claimant committed an offence punishable with imprisonment; *(ii)* that the claimant has a serious communicable disease; *(iii)* that the claimant, being female, is guilty of 'unchastity or adultery' (Slander of Women Act 1891); *(iv)* that the claimant does his or her job, or the duties of some official post, ineptly or dishonestly. As to the last exception, if the defendant's statement plainly reflects on the claimant's work, it does not matter whether the defendant mentioned the job or post; so a charge of dishonesty is almost bound to fall within it. There is some dispute over the types of post covered by the exception; it seems that if the post is a purely honorary one, then a charge of dishonesty is actionable per se, but a charge of ineptitude is not.

General damages: relevant factors

8.22 Where general damages are available, the following are relevant: the number and identity of those who heard the statement; the reactions of particular hearers; evidence relevant to financial loss, such as a falling-off of custom after the statement; and whether, when, and how the defendant offered an apology. Where the defendant's statement plainly contributed to a knock against the claimant's reputation, it is irrelevant that others besides the defendant made the statement, unless the claimant obtains compensation from them as well; though it is open to the defendant to join those others as co-defendants (**9.26**).

Large awards by juries have given rise to criticism, and may be reduced on appeal. The courts have made it clear that their supervision will be strict, both as to compensatory damages and exemplary damages (*Rantzen v Mirror Group Newspapers* [1994] QB 670; *John v MGN* [1997] QB 586); in one case, where the House of Lords suspected that the jury had ignored a clear direction on damages, they reduced a £85,000 award to a nominal £1, and then ordered the claimant to pay roughly two-thirds of the costs, believed to be over £1m - (*Grobbelaar v News Group Newspapers Ltd* [2002] UKHL 40). The largest award ever in a defamation case, £1.5m, was challenged before the European Court of Human Rights, which ruled that the jury's award violated the defendant's right to free expression under Art 10 of the European Convention on Human Rights (*Tolstoy Miloslavsky v United Kingdom* (1995) 20 EHRR 442); and five-figure sums have also been held inconsistent with the Convention, in a case where the defendants' means were very modest (*Steel and Morris v United Kingdom* (European Court of Human Rights, 1 February 2005)). However, while the issue was not before the court, there are hints in its judgment that the control of juries outlined in the *Rantzen* case ensures that the modern law is not subject to the same criticism.

Evidence as to the claimant's *general reputation* at the time the statement was made is highly relevant, and may be introduced by the defendant or the claimant. There are three qualifications to this:

- The evidence must have some connection with the subject matter of the statement; evidence that the claimant is reputed to be stingy is irrelevant if the charge was dishonesty.

- The question is as to the claimant's *reputation*, and so evidence as to the claimant's actual (but hitherto secret) conduct, or as to the claimant's real character, is out of order. Specific instances of good or bad behaviour by the claimant are admissible only as evidence of reputation.

- The defendant will not be allowed to confuse the question of reputation with the separate question of whether the statement was true. So rumours and suspicions that the claimant did indeed do what the defendant said are only admissible, if at all, as part of a case that the statement was true.

The circumstances leading up to the statement are relevant, and the defendant may produce evidence of provocation by the claimant. The defendant's behaviour and motivation are also relevant. In this respect defamation differs for other torts: if I smash your stereo, I pay the same amount whether I did it deliberately or merely clumsily. In defamation, compensation is for injured feelings, and so a defendant who is openly hostile inflicts a greater injury than a defendant who plainly made a slip of the tongue (**10.16**). The defendant's manner, and any additional insults thrown in, may inflate the damages. Nonetheless, the goal is to *compensate* the claimant. The defendant's hostility is said to 'aggravate' the defamation, but the object of these 'aggravated damages' is still to compensate.

Occasionally, the claimant can go beyond compensation, and demand a sum explicitly meant to punish the defendant. The rules governing these 'exemplary' or 'punitive' damages, which apply to all torts, are described below (**10.10**).

Are awards in defamation truly compensatory, or truly punitive? The line is always blurred—ordering the defendant to compensate the claimant necessarily deters others who might end up in the defendant's position. In practice there are usually elements of both.

Injunctions

8.23 It is sometimes possible for the claimant to obtain an injunction (a court order backed up with the threat of imprisonment) against repetition of the defamation (**10.2**). Pre-trial injunctions ('interim injunctions') are very rare indeed, and are almost never granted where the defendant intends to prove the statement true, unless this is clearly a hopeless endeavour (**10.4**). Post-trial injunctions ('final injunctions') are less tightly restricted in theory, but are nonetheless uncommon.

Absolute defences

8.24 Some defences to an action for defamation are 'absolute', that is, they may be asserted whatever the defendant's state of mind. Others are only 'qualified', that is, they are unavailable if the defendant had an improper motive for making the statement. There are a number of specific defences, though they are rather narrow.

Unintentional defamation: offer of amends

8.25 The Defamation Act 1996, ss 2–4, introduces what amounts to a defence that the defendant did not mean to defame the claimant. The defendant can, however, only take advantage of this defence if the defendant is prepared to apologize and to offer a sum in compensation. The defendant must make an 'offer of amends' to the claimant, which must include a reasonable offer to make a correction and apology, to publish it, and to pay compensation and the claimant's legal expenses.

- If the claimant accepts the offer of amends, the claimant cannot sue in defamation, but the terms of the offer of amends are enforceable by legal process (s 2). In appropriate cases, the claimant may make a statement in open court (*Winslet v Associated Newspapers Ltd* [2009] EWHC 2735 (QB)).

- If the claimant wishes to accept an offer but does not think the terms offered are reasonable, s 3 establishes procedures for resolving this dispute. This may involve a full enquiry into damages. The defendant may rely on any relevant fact or matter in mitigation of damages, though the defendant may not allege directly or indirectly that the defamatory statement was true (*Abu v MGN Ltd* [2002] EWHC 2345 (QB)). The use of this procedure may itself go a long way towards mitigating any loss suffered by the claimant, and if so this will be reflected in a reduction of damages (*Nail v News Group Newspapers Ltd* [2004] EWCA Civ 1708).

- If the claimant refuses the offer and sues, then the claimant can only succeed by proving that the defendant knew or had reason to know that the statement referred to the claimant, *and* that it was false, *and* that it defamed the claimant. It is not enough to show that the defendant ought to have had the relevant knowledge (*Milne v Express Newspapers Ltd* [2004] EWCA Civ 664). However, if the defendant relies on the offer of amends as a defence, the defendant cannot also rely on other defences, such as that the statement was true or privileged (s 4).

There is also provision for 'qualified offers', where the defendant's offer of amends relates only to certain specified possible meanings of the defamatory utterance, but not others.

This provision apart, there is no defence of 'due diligence'. Of course, if the defendant acted reasonably, and could not reasonably have doubted the statement, that is relevant to other defences—not least because if due care is taken, there is a good chance that the statement is in fact true. However, there is no explicit defence of due care, and this may have implications under the European Convention on Human Rights, as the Norwegians discovered:

> **Bladet Tromsø v Norway (1999) 29 EHRR 125:** A government inspector made allegations of animal cruelty against some hunters. The newspaper *Bladet Tromsø* gave a fair and accurate account of that report. The hunters sued *Bladet Tromsø*, and it became clear that the report was inaccurate; *Bladet Tromsø* were found liable in defamation. Held: it was reasonable for the newspaper to rely on the government report, and so Norwegian libel law contravened their right to freedom of expression.

Consent

8.26 If the claimant assented to the publication, no action lies. So if the defendant privately insults the claimant and the claimant challenges the defendant to repeat this before witnesses, no action lies if the defendant does so. Consent is also established if the claimant passes up an easy opportunity to prevent publication:

> **Carrie v Tolkien [2009] EWHC 29 (QB):** Tolkien posted various comments on Carrie's website, which (if untrue) were clearly defamatory of Carrie. Held: as Carrie had control over the website, he could have removed the comments as soon as he became aware of them. The period before he became so aware was short, and accordingly no substantial tort was proved.

Truth ('justification')

8.27 As a rule, the defendant has a complete defence on proving that the statement was true. The jargon is that the defendant 'justifies' the statement, and this defence is often referred to as 'justification'. The onus of proof is on the defendant, who must carefully set out what it is intended to prove. What the defendant must justify is not the literal statement, but the defamatory allegation, which may be very different (above, **8.3**).

This has counter-intuitive results, illustrating the startling effects of the rule that the defendant is judged as reasonable listeners understand the statement, and not as the defendant reasonably meant it. If the defendant says (correctly) that the claimant was sacked for dishonesty, reasonable hearers might perhaps take this as meaning that the claimant actually *was* dishonest—and if they would, the defendant must prove *actual* dishonesty. (The same logic applies if the defendant reports that the claimant has been convicted of a criminal offence, though by Civil Evidence Act 1968, s 13, the conviction is conclusive evidence for this purpose that the claimant is indeed guilty.)

Particular problems are caused when the very meaning of the statement is disputed. Where the claimant and the defendant are not agreed on the meaning of the statement, the defendant must put in a so-called *Lucas-Box* pleading (after *Lucas-Box v News Group Newspapers* [1986] 1 All ER 177), specifying which meaning it is that the defendant will justify. It is important to clarify the issues in this way, because the whole direction taken at trial may depend on precisely what the allegation is taken to mean.

> **McPhilemy v Times Newspapers [1999] 3 All ER 775:** McPhilemy, a journalist, produced a documentary alleging the existence of a widespread conspiracy in Northern Ireland to murder prominent republicans. A newspaper claimed that the documentary was a hoax, which no reputable broadcaster would have produced. McPhilemy sued. The question was whether the newspaper was to justify their claim by proving that McPhilemy was a hoaxer, or whether they could broaden the issue by disproving the conspiracy. Held: keeping defamation actions within manageable and economic bounds was an important consideration. However, here the newspaper had made it clear from the start that they disputed the existence of the alleged conspiracy, and so should be allowed to lead evidence on that point.

A similar point might have arisen in *Irving v Penguin Books* [2000] All ER (D) 523, where the claimant was accused of being a holocaust-denier who distorted historical evidence to favour his relatively benign portrayal of Nazi activity. However, there was a potential problem, as Gray J refused to make factual findings on historical questions: 'it is not for me to form, still less to express, a judgement about what happened' ([2000] All ER (D) 523, para 1.3). The issue was in fact treated by the parties as being whether or not the claimant had shown sufficient objectivity in his historical work. Therefore the judge was able to conclude that a defence of justification was made out, without broaching wider historical issues.

Where the defendant's statement was very specific, the court is concerned not so much with its literal truth as with the accuracy of its 'sting'—the reason why it is defamatory. So if the defendant says that the claimant raped a specified woman on a particular occasion, the defendant may justify by proving that the claimant raped *another* woman on that occasion, or possibly even on another occasion, so long as the court thinks that the 'sting' amounts to the same thing.

> **Alexander v North Eastern Rly Co (1865) 29 JP 692:** The defendant said that the claimant had been convicted of a criminal offence, and had served three weeks in prison in consequence. In fact, the claimant had served two weeks. Held: the jury was entitled to regard the statement as justified, if they thought this appropriate.

At common law, if the defendant made several specific charges, each one has to be justified if the defence is to succeed. But by the Defamation Act 1952, s 5, the defendant may prove some only, and then invite the court to say that the 'sting' of the statement is true. So if the defendant accuses the claimant of five distinct thefts and then proves three, the defendant may argue that the claimant's reputation has not been unfairly or materially damaged by the other two charges, even if they are completely untrue. That case aside, however, a partial justification is no defence, though the evidence to support it may sometimes reduce the damages.

Where the allegation is vaguer, such as that the claimant is generally dishonest, the range of admissible evidence is wider. Accordingly, in a case where the defendant alleges a specific act of misconduct, but can only prove another and different type of misconduct, the claimant will usually try to treat the issue as narrowly as possible, and the defendant will seek to broaden it.

> **Bookbinder v Tebbit [1989] 1 All ER 1169:** Tebbit accused a local council of spending £50,000 on over-stamping its notepaper with 'Support Nuclear Free Zones', which he considered a 'damn fool idea'. Bookbinder, leader of the council, sued over that single allegation, even though this was only one of several charges on the same theme. Could Tebbit justify by proving that the council had wasted money in *other* ways, or did he have to prove over-stamping? Held: Tebbit could not broaden the issue, but had to justify what he actually said.

These cases are difficult, however, and a number of factors are relevant; for example, in *Bookbinder* Ralph Gibson LJ suggested the result would have been different if instances of actual dishonesty had been alleged.

> **Dee v Telegraph Media Group Ltd [2010] EWHC 924 (QB):** The *Daily Telegraph* published an account of a tennis victory by Dee under the headline 'World's worst tennis

pro wins at last'. It was agreed that Dee had earlier lost 54 consecutive matches in world-ranking tournaments, which was the longest string of such defeats in the world. Dee argued that the headline was nonetheless defamatory, especially as the article made no reference to his successes in domestic Spanish tournaments, and it so painted an unfair picture of his talents. Held: a defence of justification was bound to succeed, and the action was struck out accordingly.

When is truth not a defence?

8.28 In a sense, truth is fundamental. If true statements damage the claimant's reputation, then it was plainly an inflated one, which the law should not protect. Nonetheless, two qualifications must be made, where the law pursues different policies from those usually at work in defamation cases.

First, criminal convictions committed very far in the past may become 'spent' under the Rehabilitation of Offenders Act 1974. This has a number of consequences, designed to discourage subsequent revelation of the offence. One consequence is that if the defendant's statement reminds others of the claimant's conviction, and the claimant sues in defamation, the defendant's plea of justification will be defeated if the claimant proves that the defendant was motivated by spite or other improper considerations (s 8). How quickly convictions become 'spent' depends on a variety of factors; no offence can ever become 'spent' if the penalty was prison for 2½ years or more.

Second, revelation of the truth very often allows the claimant to sue in breach of confidence. Indeed, it is possible to combine this action with action for defamation. Lurid retellings of the life of pop stars have led to claims for breach of confidence in so far as the stories are true and for defamation in so far as they are false (e.g. *Woodward v Hutchins* [1977] 2 All ER 751). For claimants who wish no further intrusion into their private lives, however, the law's solution here may be worse than the problem they hoped to solve by invoking it.

Absolute privilege

8.29 Certain governmental duties attract absolute immunity from suit for participants. This privilege applies even if malice is proved. The potential for abuse is obvious; the traditional view, which is not without its critics, is that absolute freedom from suit is a necessary shield for those involved.

First, *proceedings in Parliament* are privileged (Bill of Rights 1688, Art 9), as are the reports of the various parliamentary commissioners (ombudsmen) (e.g. Parliamentary Commissioner Act 1967, s 10(5)). MPs accused of accepting bribes in return for asking parliamentary questions found that they could not sue their accusers, as the courts could not investigate the charges without infringing this privilege. They persuaded their colleagues to enact the Defamation Act 1996, s 13, which enables individual MPs to waive the privilege in so far as it concerns them. The 'sudden and humiliating' collapse of the resulting libel action may possibly discourage other MPs from invoking the section in future (see Williams '"Only flattery is safe": Political speech and the Defamation Act 1996' (1997) 60 MLR 388). Section 13 has been given a wide interpretation, so as to allow the canvassing of allegations which could otherwise not have been fairly tried without infringing parliamentary privilege (see *Hamilton v Al Fayed* [2001] 1 AC 395). It has long been suggested that this immunity would not survive challenge under the European Convention on Human Rights. However, arguments that the immunity infringed Art 6 (right to a fair and public hearing) and Art 8 (respect for private life) were rejected by the European Court of Human Rights in *A v United Kingdom* [2002] ECHR 811.

Second, *courts* attract immunity for those involved in their activities. Statements in court are privileged, as are statements at any stage of the legal process, and even conversations between solicitor and client when the client seeks advice. There is no clear definition of a 'court' for this purpose, and the same body may be a court or not, depending on the activity it is engaged in. Magistrates' courts are (for this purpose) courts when trying a criminal charge, but not when deciding whether to renew a liquor licence; the European Commission is not usually a 'court', but may be sufficiently like one when engaged in enforcing competition law (*Hasselblad (GB) v Orbinson* [1985] QB 475). The privilege does not apply to an outburst which is irrelevant to the court's proceedings—even an outburst by a judge. The privilege also extends to documents which only see the light of day because of legal proceedings (*Taylor v Serious Fraud Office* [1999] 2 AC 177).

The privilege applies to a statement in the context of an investigation of crime:

> **Westcott v Westcott [2008] EWCA Civ 818:** Westcott complained to the police that her father-in-law had assaulted her and her six-month-old baby. The complaint did not however result in a prosecution. Held: all participants in a criminal investigation were entitled to an absolute privilege in respect of statements made.

However, the privilege does not apply simply because legal proceedings *might conceivably* be in the offing:

> **Waple v Surrey County Council [1998] 1 All ER 624:** The council removed the claimant's son from her, and placed him with foster parents. It then served a notice demanding a contribution to the son's maintenance. In the ensuing correspondence, the council

made an allegation as to the claimant's conduct in relation to her son. Held: the immunity could cover witness statements made with a view to legal proceedings. But mere service of a contribution notice did not inevitably mean that judicial proceedings would ever start. No sufficient link to judicial proceedings was shown here, and the immunity did not apply.

Third, communications between *high-ranking officials* are privileged: it seems that a defamatory statement by a Secretary of State to a Parliamentary Under-secretary is not actionable (*Chatterton v Secretary of State for India* [1895] 2 QB 189). It is unclear whether or when, if at all, this principle protects officers at lower grades. Certainly the courts do not seem willing to extend this absolute privilege, and certainly not in cases where a qualified privilege is already available (see below, **8.36**):

> **S v Newham London Borough Council (1998) 96 LGR 651:** The council sent a letter to the Department of Health containing various allegations about S, one of its own social workers, and suggesting that his name should be placed on the register of those unsuitable for work involving children. Held: the allegations in this letter attracted only a qualified privilege, not an absolute one.

Qualified defences

'Malice'

8.30 Rather more extensive defences are available if the claimant cannot establish 'malice'. The precise meaning of 'malice' in this context is much disputed. The core idea is that the defendant's statement was motivated by improper considerations— usually, but not necessarily, hatred of the claimant.

Strictly speaking, the definition of 'malice' varies with each defence to which it is relevant: each privilege is granted for a particular reason of public policy, and 'malice' means attempting to use the defence for some other reason. But little clarity would be achieved by separating the defences in this way.

The burden of proof as to malice is usually on the claimant, and it is heavy. Evidence to establish malice may include: lack of candour or reasonableness; violent or exaggerated language; previous or subsequent words or behaviour showing hostility against the claimant; or lack of reasonable grounds for believing the statement. None of these is conclusive. The claimant only establishes malice if it is more likely than not that the defendant had an improper motive.

Fair comment

8.31 There is a defence if the defamatory remark was *(i)* a comment on facts, *(ii)* within the bounds of fairness, and *(iii)* on a matter of public interest. The claimant may defeat this plea by showing malice, which usually means showing either that the defendant did not believe the statement, or was hopelessly and unreasonably prejudiced against the claimant. A purely factual statement is not comment; it is either true or false.

This last point requires emphasis, because it goes completely against the common, non-legal, use of the phrase 'fair comment'. If the defendant recites certain suspicious facts about the claimant and then tentatively suggests that the claimant might therefore be guilty of some crime, a non-lawyer might describe this as 'fair comment'. However, to a defamation lawyer, 'fair comment' has nothing to do with it. Either the claimant is guilty or the claimant is not; if the defendant has a defence it is justification, not fair comment. 'Fair comment', to a defamation lawyer, is always comment on some facts; the defendant cannot invent facts and then say he was commenting on his invention.

8.32 The defendant must explain to the court the facts on which the comment was based, and (if they are disputed) prove them. For example, if the defendant says that the claimant is cruel to his children, this cannot be fair comment if the claimant has no children, no matter what other evidence of cruelty the defendant can produce. The defendant often resorts to the so-called 'rolled-up plea', that in so far as the statement was factual it was true, and in so far as it was comment it was fair. It is sufficient if the 'sting' of the facts is true—details may be wrong, so long as the substance is accurate (Defamation Act 1952, s 6). It seems that the defendant may comment on statements protected by privilege; so the defendant may comment on a report published by Parliament without proving that what it says is true—so long as the defendant does not personally assert that it is true.

Given this requirement of a factual basis, it follows that the defendant cannot comment on the claimant's character under the guise of commenting on more limited issues. For example, the defendant cannot use a review of the claimant's book to comment on the claimant's sexual habits, unless they are relevant to the book; and the reviewer must distinguish carefully between saying that a *book* is absurd or immoral and saying that *its author* is absurd or immoral. It is often a very difficult question whether (say) the reviewer of a play, who says that one of the participants is a bad actress, is making a comment on the performance or a statement about the actress (e.g. *Cornwell v Myskow* [1987] 2 All ER 504).

> **British Chiropractic Association v Singh** [2010] EWCA Civ 350: Singh wrote
> a newspaper article critical of chiropractic, denouncing it as based on 'not a jot of

evidence', and claiming that the British Chiropractic Association 'happily promotes bogus treatments'. The issue was whether this last remark was fact or comment. Held: it was comment. The 'sting' of the article was that Singh did not consider the evidence for chiropractic reliable (a legitimate matter for comment), rather than a factual allegation about the Association's honesty or lack of it.

It does not matter whether the relevant facts are common knowledge or not, so long as the defendant can prove them at trial, and so long as the facts existed at the time when the comment was made (*Lowe v Associated Newspapers* [2006] EWHC 320 (QB)). The defendant need not have set out in the statement the facts on which the comment was based, if they would have been clear to those who read it.

> **Kemsley v Foot [1952] AC 345:** Foot wrote a newspaper article violently critical of another newspaper, heading it 'Lower than Kemsley'. He did not otherwise mention the Kemsley Press, or the newspapers it controlled. Lord Kemsley sued. Foot argued that the headline was fair comment on Kemsley's management of his newspapers. Held: Foot was entitled to put this defence to a jury. The headline sufficiently indicated the facts on which the comment was based.

Surprisingly, in a later case the House of Lords ruled that, where the statement was a comment on an earlier statement, the court had to determine whether the statement was fact or comment *without* looking at the earlier statement (*Telnikoff v Matusevitch* [1991] 4 All ER 817). The reason given was that not everyone who read the statement would have read the earlier statement too. But this seems to demand a great deal from critics; as Lord Ackner, dissenting, put it, it should be enough for the defendant 'to have identified the publication on which he is commenting, without having [to] set out such extracts therefrom as would enable his readers to judge for themselves ...' ([1991] 4 All ER 817, 830).

Comment must be fair

8.33 This is simply one aspect of absence of malice: comment is indefensible when it goes beyond the limits of fairness, even if the defendant personally believes it fair. Nonetheless, these limits are broad, and even sustained ridicule or prejudiced, obstinate and eccentric remarks may be 'fair' for this purpose. Indeed, one law lord has suggested that the word 'fair' is misleading, as the test really relates to the defendant's good faith, not the defendant's fairness (*Reynolds v Times Newspapers* [1999] 4 All ER 609, 615, per Lord Nicholls). While it is not absolutely clear what the test is, it is plainly misleading to say *simply* that the comment must be 'fair'.

In *Reynolds*, where the claimant, a former Irish Prime Minister, had resigned in controversial circumstances, the defendant had put a discreditable interpretation on those events. The House of Lords was not prepared to allow a defence of fair comment, principally because the defendant had failed to mention the claimant's own explanation for the events in question, and because of sloppy journalism on their part. Lord Nicholls suggested ten relevant factors, though he also said that his list was not exhaustive:

(1) The seriousness of the allegation. The more serious the charge, the more the public is misinformed and the individual harmed, if the allegation is not true. (2) The nature of the information, and the extent to which the subject matter is a matter of public concern. (3) The source of the information. Some informants have no direct knowledge of the events. Some have their own axes to grind, or are being paid for their stories. (4) The steps taken to verify the information. (5) The status of the information. The allegation may have already been the subject of an investigation which commands respect. (6) The urgency of the matter. News is often a perishable commodity. (7) Whether comment was sought from the plaintiff. He may have information others do not possess or have not disclosed. An approach to the plaintiff will not always be necessary. (8) Whether the article contained the gist of the plaintiff's side of the story. (9) The tone of the article. A newspaper can raise queries or call for an investigation. It need not adopt allegations as statements of fact. (10) The circumstances of the publication, including the timing ([1999] 4 All ER 609, 625).

The modern operation of the defence therefore brings standards of responsible journalism into what is traditionally a tort of strict liability, though it has recently been stressed that the test cannot be stated as simply a negligence standard (*Branson v Bower* [2002] QB 737); the core question was whether the journalists have behaved responsibly (*Jameel v Wall Street Journal Europe SPRL* [2006] UKHL 44). The precise detail of the defence is still a matter of controversy (for detailed examples see *Loutchansky v Times Newspapers (No 2)* [2001] EWCA Civ 1805; *Charman v Orion Publishing Group* [2007] EWCA Civ 972).

Galloway v Telegraph Group Ltd [2006] EWCA Civ 17: A *Daily Telegraph* reporter found documents in Baghdad which appeared to show that Galloway had accepted significant sums of money from Saddam Hussein. Based on these documents, the *Telegraph* publicly accused Galloway of having taken the money. At trial, the *Telegraph* accepted that the allegations were untrue, but pleaded privilege. Held: the defence of privilege undoubtedly allowed some scope for reportage or repetition of allegations made by others. Here, however, the *Telegraph*'s adoption of the allegations as true, and their embellishment of the allegations going beyond anything in the documents, was fatal to the defence.

Flood v Times Newspapers [2010] EWCA Civ 804: The *Times* reported on allegations that Flood, a Detective Sergeant, had taken bribes. A subsequent investigation found that there was no evidence to justify the allegations. Held: the initial reporting of the allegation was protected by *Reynolds* privilege, but when it became clear that there was no evidence to back up the allegations, the privilege collapsed, and any republication of the original article would be defamatory. Leaving the article available on the *Times* website constituted such a republication.

This new version of the defence is much criticized. If the defendant's falsehoods concerning the claimant have received wide circulation, it is not obvious that the defendant should be left with no liability merely because the defendant is considered to have acted responsibly.

The defence of fair comment only applies to matters of public interest or importance

8.34 Any aspect of national or local government, or of the legal system, satisfies this requirement. Whether the running of a private concern is 'of public interest' depends largely on its size and significance.

> ***South Hetton Coal Co v North-Eastern News Association*** **[1894] 1 QB 133:** A newspaper criticized the sanitary conditions of cottages rented by a colliery, which was landlord to most of the village's 2,000 inhabitants, as well as the major local employer. Held: the conduct of such a firm could be a matter of public interest.

A claimant who has deliberately attracted the public's attention is a fit subject for public comment. So any published work, any newspaper article, any literary or artistic performance open to the public, and any advertisement, is open to public criticism—as indeed is the criticism itself.

Qualified privilege at common law

8.35 There is a defence if the defendant was under a duty to make the statement, or had a legitimate interest in so doing, *and* the person to whom he made it had a duty to listen, or a legitimate interest in so doing. For example, if the defendant honestly reports to the police that her property has been stolen and that she thinks the claimant is responsible, the privilege is made out; the defendant has a legitimate interest in reporting the theft of her goods, and the police have a duty to listen. There is a defence, therefore, even if the claimant is not the thief. However, the defendant must confine herself to her legitimate interest, and must not be motivated by malice. So she has no defence if she did not believe the claimant to be the thief, or she lied in any respect, or had some improper motive; and the privilege does not protect her in relation to irrelevant remarks, such as that the claimant is a pervert.

8.36 Duty and interest are matters for the court. They must arise in fact: a mistaken belief by the defendant, however reasonable, that there is a duty will not do. However, the duty or interest need not be a legal one. Relatives may be candid with each other about matters affecting one another's welfare, such as whether the claimant is a suitable husband for one of them; and employer and employee may be candid with one another when doing their jobs.

> *Bryanston Finance v de Vries* **[1975] QB 703:** Defamatory letters were dictated, typed up and sent. When was the tort committed? Held: each communication to a distinct individual amounted to a publication, but all the work before the letters were sent was covered by qualified privilege.

Defence of assets or reputation against the claimant's attacks is a good ground of privilege, though criteria of appropriateness and relevance must be borne in mind. So if the claimant attacks the defendant's character and the defendant tries to rebut the charges, this may attract privilege; the defendant may even call the claimant a liar, provided the claimant's veracity is relevant. It is also now clear that this privilege protects the defendant's solicitor, at least so long as what the solicitor says is 'reasonable self-defence' and not 'a counter-charge or diversionary attack' unconnected with the claimant's criticism (*Regan v Taylor* [2000] NLJR 392). But the privilege cannot excuse a general attack on the claimant's character; it is no defence to slander that it avenges earlier slander.

It is often legitimate to invoke the help of others in pursuing one's legitimate interests, even if this inevitably leads to the spread of defamatory material.

> *Beach v Freeson* **[1972] 1 QB 14:** Freeson, an MP, wrote letters to the Law Society and the Lord Chancellor, repeating defamatory complaints made by a constituent. Held: Freeson had acted properly and was protected by qualified privilege.

> *Kearns v General Council of the Bar* **[2003] EWCA Civ 331:** The General Council, the governing body of the Bar, received unverified information that Kearns was not a qualified solicitor and was not entitled to instruct counsel. The General Council circulated the entire Bar to that effect. Held: even though no steps had been taken to check the information (which was wrong), nonetheless it was clearly relevant to the General Council's legitimate functions and so was privileged.

8.37 It is not enough that the defendant has a legitimate interest in the subject matter of the statement, if the communication does not serve it.

> *Watt v Longsdon* **[1930] 1 KB 130:** A company director received a letter accusing the managing director of alcoholism, dishonesty, and adultery. He passed on copies to the chairman and to the managing director's wife. Held: the communication to the chairman was privileged, but the communication to the wife was not; she had a legitimate interest in receiving the letter, but the director had none in sending it.

8.38 The defendant must take care not to broadcast the statement too broadly; the recipients must each have a duty or a legitimate interest in the communication.

> ***Chapman v Lord Ellesmere* [1932] 2 KB 431:** The Jockey Club 'warned off' Chapman from Kempton Park racecourse, in such a way as to suggest he was responsible for the doping of a racehorse. Held: publishing this by notices in the *Racing Calendar* was legitimate, as the racing public had an interest in the matter; but the general public had none, and so the publication in *The Times*, and to news agencies, was not privileged.

Where there is an official channel for complaints of the type the defendant is making against the claimant, use of that channel is usually privileged, and broader communication is usually not. It appears that the preparation of a petition to Parliament attracts a qualified privilege, if indeed it is not within the absolute parliamentary privilege. But the courts have, to date, set their face against any general defence of 'fair information on a matter of public interest'. The public is not regarded, for this purpose, as having a 'right to know' (*Blackshaw v Lord* [1984] QB 1).

It might be different, the court added, if the case was one involving immediate public danger, such as cases of suspected terrorism, or contaminated food. A similarly narrow line has been taken by statute: reversing earlier case law, the Defamation Act 1952, s 10, disallows the defence of privilege in election campaigns where it relies purely on the voters' right to know about issues relevant to the election. More recently, the House of Lords have refused to allow a general defence of 'comment on an issue of public interest', though they emphasized the value of free expression (*Reynolds v Times Newspapers*, above, **8.33**).

Privilege by statute

Court reporting

8.39 Reports of legal proceedings attract privilege, which is now stated in the Defamation Act 1996, s 14. The privilege is there said to be 'absolute', though it applies only if the report is 'fair and accurate', and contemporaneous with the proceedings themselves. The privilege is lost if the reporter repeats allegations made against the claimant but fails to mention evidence or argument on the other side. It is legitimate for a newspaper to report on a long case day by day, despite the inevitably partial picture given; but an account given after the trial is over is not allowed this leeway. It is unclear whether a paper which relates allegations against the claimant on day one of a trial loses privilege retroactively if it fails to publish the claimant's rebuttal on a later day.

Parliament

8.40 Qualified privilege applies to fair and accurate extracts and abstracts of papers published by parliamentary authority (Parliamentary Papers Act 1840, s 3). Unusually, it is for the defendant to establish absence of malice, not the converse.

Other official bodies and meetings

8.41 The Defamation Act 1996, Sch 1, Pt I extends privilege to reports of public proceedings of foreign legislatures, international organizations, and courts, as well as copies or extracts from official registers and notices published by courts. In cases covered by Pt II, there is a right to publish fair and accurate reports, but it is lost if the defendant, being the original publisher of the statement, refuses to publish a reasonable letter from the claimant by way of explanation or contradiction of what the defendant published. Part II protects the proceedings of associations to promote science, religion, or learning; trade associations; associations to promote particular sports; general meetings of public companies; local authorities; magistrates; committees of persons holding enquiries authorized by statute; public meetings on matters of public concern. The last category has been held to include press conferences, and to apply not only to what was said openly there, but also to the contents of press releases issued at the conference (*McCartan Turkington Breen v Times Newspapers* [2001] 2 AC 277). Where a publisher includes additional facts or comments in the report, it can be a difficult question of degree whether the report is still 'fair and accurate' (see, for example, *Curistan v Times Newspapers* [2008] EWCA Civ 432).

Other torts protecting reputation

8.42 Various torts in addition to the tort of defamation may be used to protect the claimant's reputation. No detailed treatment will be given here.

  • The tort of *malicious falsehood* is largely aimed at protecting business interests and requires proof of express malice. However, there is no reason why it cannot be used to protect personal reputation (*Joyce v Sengupta* [1993] 1 All ER 897), though the courts have so far been reluctant to 'borrow' rules from libel law (*Ajinomoto Sweeteners Europe SAS v Asda Stores* [2010] EWCA 609). It appears that the claimant cannot succeed without proving financial loss of some kind (*Allason v Campbell* (1996) Times, 8 May). However, damage of that sort may be presumed if the words injure the claimant in a professional or business capacity, or are in writing and likely to cause financial harm (Defamation Act 1952, s 3). Moreover, once the claimant has established a right of action, damages for injury to feelings are available (*Khodaparast v Shad* [2000] 1 All ER 545).

• The tort of *negligence* may be invoked, even when an action for defamation on the same facts would be barred by privilege (*Spring v Guardian Insurance* [1995] 2 AC 296 (**5.45**)). However, the fact that the claimant was a foreseeable victim of a misstatement by the defendant is not in itself enough to guarantee that the defendant owed the claimant a duty. So where the claimant was refused a job because of a discouraging report on her by the employer's in-house doctor, the Court of Appeal held that the doctor's duty was owed only to the employer, and not to her (*Kapfunde v Abbey National* [1999] ICR 1).

• False accusations of crime leading to an attempt to prosecute the claimant may be remedied through the tort of *malicious prosecution*. The tort has strict requirements; in particular, it must be shown that the defendant had an improper motive, and the criminal proceedings must ultimately have ended in the claimant's favour. (An argument that human rights considerations demand a more claimant-friendly rule was rejected in *Moulton v Chief Constable of the West Midlands* [2010] EWCA Civ 524.) It used to be thought that the tort could only be used where the defendant was actually the prosecutor. It now appears that it can also be invoked against those who make false complaints with a view to instigating a prosecution, at least where 'in substance' they are themselves prosecutors (*Martin v Watson* [1996] AC 74).

Reform of the law

Reforms: small or large?

8.43 The present state of the law pleases no-one. But there is no agreement on whether the problems are relatively minor, or whether they go to the roots of the present system. As to minor reforms, several have recently been made, such as widening the defence of unintentional defamation (**8.25**), and narrowing the liability of secondary publishers (**8.9**). Other reforms, such as allowing the Court of Appeal to reduce excessive awards by juries, have been enacted in recent years (**8.22**). Recent procedural reforms have done a great deal to speed up the process, and to resolve the dispute by means short of a full trial. And the Court of Appeal in *Rantzen v Mirror Group Newspapers* [1994] QB 670 and elsewhere has proclaimed that in doubtful cases the courts will lean in favour of freedom of speech. But is this fine-tuning sufficient? To clarify the issue, compare the tort of defamation with the other torts you have already learned about. What are the main differences? Several stand out:

• large awards for injury to feelings;
• juries;

- a complex and bewildering mix of strict and fault liability;
- high legal costs.

These are all bound together. Juries are thought necessary because of the highly subjective level of the damages. Complex rules are necessary to control juries. And the high costs of administering these rules is only sustainable because the possibility of massive damages prompts parties to pay their lawyers well; no-one would contemplate incurring a legal bill in five or six figures unless the sum at stake was large as well. The introduction of contingent fees into this area may change the pattern somewhat, but there are difficulties here. (In particular, it has proved difficult for claimants to secure insurance against the possibility of having to pay costs to the defendant, which means that the arrangement is very risky from the claimant's point of view.)

Compensation or deterrence?

8.44 Let me briefly play devil's advocate, to show what the present system is good at. Compare a typical personal injury action with a typical defamation action. The personal injury claimant will recover a sum largely designed to reflect actual financial loss, though of course it may include a sum for pain and suffering as well. The defamation claimant will typically have suffered no financial loss at all, yet will receive an award despite this—possibly quite a large one. Plainly, then, the principal object of defamation is not to give compensation, at least not in any ordinary sense. If the current law is justifiable, it can only be on the ground that it deters potential defamers.

Seen this way, many of the more common criticisms of the law miss the point. Relatively few defamation cases reach court; if the sole deterrent against defamation is to be the court's reaction in those cases, that reaction must be correspondingly gruesome. It is unsurprising that awards in defamation cases are so much more generous than awards in personal injury cases. There is a battery of legal regulation on health and safety, with the result that the law on personal injury *damages* need not deter, but may simply ask how much each injured claimant deserves to get. The higher levels of damages in defamation therefore reflect the law's very different purposes. From this point of view, the unpredictability of jury decisions is an advantage rather than a disadvantage: few cases result in a really huge award, and the deterrent effect would be entirely lost if potential defendants *knew in advance* which of them were running a serious risk.

Options for change

8.45 None of this is to support the current law, but only to focus the issue. In most defamation cases, there is no injury to compensate for, other than an injury to feelings; this requires some legal response, but it does not have to take the form of a large money award, or indeed any money award at all. The main issue is therefore over deterrence, and what form it should take. There appear to be three main possibilities: *(1)* no fundamental change; *(2)* a considerable reduction in awards for general damages; *(3)* complete abolition of general damages and introduction of other forms of deterrence.

Option 1: no fundamental change

8.46 The case for no fundamental change is not completely unarguable. Many blemishes in the law have been removed, especially by giving the Court of Appeal the power to correct excessive jury awards. And it is unfair to judge the current system by what happens in individual cases alone; it is the deterrent effect that has most impact on people in general. Yet by placing all the weight on deterrence before the event, the current law sadly neglects the position of those who have been defamed despite it. None but the very rich can afford to sue. Effectively, the more powerful an individual is, the more congenial he finds the law of defamation, which is arguably the wrong way round for a democratic legal system to be.

Option 2: substantial reduction in general damages

8.47 A defendant who stands to lose a very large sum is slow to settle, and inclined to spend correspondingly large sums on a defence. A sharp reduction in the range of possible awards could be a major part of a package to speed up procedure, widen the range of those who can afford to sue, and encourage rapid settlement. A range of measures to implement this change would probably involve the following and more: abolition of juries; explicit limits on awards for non-pecuniary loss; encouragement of arbitration; and simplification of the law, such as on the test for a defamatory utterance. Modern controls on jury awards, and the procedural changes in the Defamation Act 1996, go a long way down this road, accelerating the procedure and providing avenues to terminate more cases before they reach full trial. The overall effect should be to speed up and cheapen litigation, and to shift more of the disputes from the full trial to the preliminary (interim) stages.

Changes of this sort would amount to a reorientation of defamation law towards a relatively poorer clientele. The emphasis on deterrence would remain the same, as would the mechanism of deterrence: namely the impact of damages awards on the editorial budget of potential defamers. The law would be more predictable, less exacting, but also broader in its grasp. If the reform were done well, it would widen access to potential claimants considerably. Many who can now do no more than write impotent letters of protest to their defamers would be able to start county court proceedings. Newspapers would still have to employ libel readers, and many would have to take on litigation managers as well. No-one can predict whether the impact on editorial budgets will ultimately be greater or smaller; it will simply be different, a drip-drip-drip of relatively small claims, rather than occasional thunderbolts threatening the defendant's very existence. Which is preferable?

Option 3: abolition of awards of general damages

8.48 Other means of deterring defamation exist, and are arguably preferable to a money award. Common suggestions are a right of reply; a right to an apology in some cases; a specific criminal offence of 'character assassination'; or a statutory Press Council to implement any or all of these changes and to enforce journalistic standards generally. All of these would rely ultimately on the criminal law for their efficacy, though the reforms would have failed in their purpose if recourse to the criminal law became an everyday event. (There is already an offence of 'criminal libel', though it is rarely prosecuted for.) This would bring the element of deterrence out into the open, and precisely for that reason would attract a great deal of hostility. The civil liberties implications of an extension of the criminal law would need careful thought, though they might on balance be thought preferable to the threat of bankruptcy implicitly wielded by the current law.

Conclusion

8.49 Reform of the law of defamation is much discussed, but little ever comes out of the discussion; when it does, it is usually fairly timid. Public discussion of the issues is dominated by the press itself, which often seems reluctant to accept even that the grossest cases of defamation should attract any legal response, and which regards any suggestion that it should apologize for misstatements as a breach of its human rights. Only an unusually powerful and self-assured government could push through any reform unacceptable to a large part of the press. As a result, the law is labyrinthine in its complexity, entirely unaffordable to most potential claimants, and thoroughly capricious in its treatment of those who can afford it.

FURTHER READING

Barendt 'What is the point of libel law?' (1999) 52 CLP 110.

Cooke 'Twilight of the libel jury?' (2006) 14 Tort Law Rev 64.

Gibbons 'Defamation reconsidered' (1996) 16 OJLS 587.

Loveland 'The ongoing evolution of *Reynolds* privilege in domestic libel law' (2003) Entertainment Law Rev 178.

Mullender 'Defamation, qualified privilege and the European Convention on Human Rights' (1999) CLJ 15.

Treiger-Bar-Am 'Defamation law in a changing society: The case of *Youssoupoff v Metro-Goldwyn-Mayer*' (2000) 20 LS 291.

Weaver 'Defamation law in turmoil: The challenges presented by the Internet' (2000) 3 JILT (<http://www2.warwick.ac.uk/fac/soc/law/elj/jilt/2000_3/weaver>).

Williams 'Defaming politicians: The not so common law' (2000) 63 MLR 748.

Young 'Fact, opinion and the Human Rights Act 1998' (2000) 20 OJLS 89.

SELF-TEST QUESTIONS

1   Arnold insults Bernard before a large audience, but speaking in Swahili. Does this defame Bernard (**8.6**)? If yes, what factors are relevant in assessing damages (**8.22**)?

2   Connie writes an editorial in the *Tiddlywinks Times*, claiming that only those brought up in the UK are likely to show sufficient commitment when part of the national team. Dot, a member of the UK Tiddlywinks Team, who spent most of her early years abroad, sues in libel. Will she succeed (**8.5**)? Does it matter whether her recent performance has been good or bad (**8.32**)?

3   Edna states publicly that Frank is a thief who has often stolen money from his mother. When Frank sues, Edna cannot prove theft from Frank's mother, but has evidence of theft from Frank's former girlfriend. Can Edna use this evidence to support a plea of justification (**8.27**)? If not, can Edna introduce it to reduce Frank's damages (**8.22**)?

4   Gordon chairs an official enquiry into whether Harry, Imogen, and Jeremy broke the law by authorizing arms exports to warring states. In what circumstances will Gordon's report be privileged (**8.41**)?

9

Parties, and liability for others

SUMMARY

The defendant may be liable for torts committed by others, in a number of situations. These situations include:

- where the defendant's employee commits a tort;
- where the defendant was under a duty to prevent others committing torts; and
- where the defendant's duty was non-delegable.

Where a number of different people are responsible for the same damage, then as between themselves the law may make a rough apportionment of blame. But each one of them is liable to the claimant for the whole of the loss. The principles in this chapter vastly expand the range of tort liability, by making many, beyond the obvious perpetrator of the tort, liable to compensate the claimant.

9.1 Tort texts are often written as if the person who must pay damages for a tort is the person primarily responsible for it. This is not usually so, however. Most tort liability in practice is liability for the actions of others. There are a number of legal doctrines under which the tort of the first defendant may render the second defendant liable to compensate the victim. The discussion here commences with the most frequently encountered one, the doctrine of *vicarious liability*.

While much of the detail here may seem obscure, it is nonetheless one of the most practically important chapters in the book. It explains how to connect a tort committed by the first defendant to other defendants, who may in an ordinary sense be blameless, but on whom the law nonetheless fastens liability. Very often the main perpetrator of a tort is penniless or untraceable: establishing liability in tort might seem academic. Nonetheless the claimant may be able to obtain an effective remedy against a solvent defendant.

Vicarious liability

9.2 Where the first defendant is engaged in carrying out his or her obligations under a contract of employment, and while doing so commits a tort against the claimant, then the claimant may sue not only the first defendant but also his or her employer. It is irrelevant whether the employer was at fault. However, the doctrine applies only where the first defendant is *employed* by the second defendant; the mere existence of a contract between the first and second defendants is not sufficient, if it is not a contract of employment. It is also not enough merely that the first defendant committed the tort in work time: it must be committed 'in the course of the employment', a more demanding requirement.

It is usually assumed that this doctrine applies to all torts. A defendant recently questioned whether it applied to the statutory tort of harassment (considered above, **2.10**), in a case where the claimant could demonstrate a campaign of bullying against him by his departmental manager. The House of Lords laid down a presumption that vicarious liability applies to any statutory tort; that presumption could be rebutted by any indication that Parliament intended otherwise, but there was no such indication in the case of the harassment legislation, even though it had originally been aimed at a very different type of problem, namely stalking (*Majrowski v Guy's and St Thomas's NHS Trust* [2006] UKHL 34).

Who is an employee?

9.3 The law in this area has its origins several centuries back. Employer and employee (or, more probably, 'master and servant') may well have lived in the same house, and the employer's right to give orders to employees was seen as analogous to a husband's right to give orders to his wife and to his children. In that context, the distinction between an employee and an 'independent contractor' was simple enough. The employee's time belonged to the employer, who could therefore give precise orders as to how it was to be used, whereas an independent contractor was hired to achieve particular results without detailed direction. Therefore, if there was some doubt whether a particular contractor was an employee or not, it was usually sufficient simply to ask whether he was subject to the 'control' of an employer, or whether he was an 'independent' contractor. Did the employer control how the work was done, or only what results were to be achieved?

Ideas of social deference and hierarchy have changed somewhat in the intervening period. Moreover, in all but the simplest jobs, the scope for detailed control of employees is rather limited. In *Mersey Docks and Harbour Board v Coggins and Griffith (Liverpool)* [1947] AC 1 a crane driver had been temporarily seconded by his employers to a firm of stevedores. The issue was whether the stevedores had become his employers. Attempting to apply the 'control' test, counsel asked him which firm's orders he accepted. He replied 'I take no orders from anybody' ([1947] AC 1, 4). Many employees would, no doubt, give this answer today; and the very idea that skilled employees such as surgeons or airline pilots might need detailed control would be a worrying one.

Technically there may still be a right of control, but this is theory, not fact. Who is an employee, and who an independent contractor, remains an important question today, for many reasons: different taxation, health and safety, and employment protection regimes apply, quite apart from the issue of vicarious liability with which this chapter is concerned. But 'control' cannot be the sole or main criterion today.

The modern law

9.4 The courts have many times had to consider who is an employee and who is not. This has not always been for the purposes of the law relating to vicarious liability. Employment status is relevant for a wide variety of purposes, and the orthodox view is that the question of status has a unique answer in each case. X cannot be an 'employee' for one purpose but an 'independent contractor' for others; either X is an employee or X is not. Relevant factors are said to be the following:

- *How have the parties themselves described the legal relationship between them?* The way in which the parties have themselves described the relationship is obviously a factor. Some care is needed, however. The question is not which category the parties would like their relationship to fall into, but rather, which category best describes the rights and duties they have created. So if the relationship is clearly an employment relationship, the court will not be put off by the parties' own description of it as a 'labour-only sub-contract' (*Ferguson v John Dawson & Partners (Contractors)* [1976] 3 All ER 817). The courts are also aware of the risk that the parties may deliberately have misdescribed their relationship, to secure tax advantages to which they are not entitled.

- *Is the work done an integral part of the business, or incidental to it?* This test was enunciated by Denning LJ in *Stevenson Jordan & Harrison v Macdonald and Evans* [1952] 1 TLR 101, 111. It is also called the 'organization' test: is the worker employed as part of a wider organization, or a self-employed independent contractor?

- *Who has the risk of loss and the chance of profit?* This is the 'entrepreneur' test: is the worker simply selling a set proportion of his time at a fixed rate, or can the worker be said to be in business on his or her own account? So an architect who retains control over his own number of hours is likely to be an independent contractor, even when other factors point to his being an employee (*WHPT Housing Association v Secretary of State for Social Services* [1981] ICR 737). The test is sometimes called the 'economic reality' test, though this label begs rather a lot of questions. Moreover, the distinction can be a fine one.

> **Ready Mixed Concrete (South East) v Minister for Pensions and National Insurance [1968] 2 QB 497:** A driver was hired by a concrete company on terms that he would always have his lorry ready to carry concrete. He was obliged to maintain the vehicle at his own expense, to have it painted in the company's colours, and he had to wear the company's uniform. He was, however, permitted to hire a substitute driver. Held: the driver was not an employee.

- *Is it sensible to speak of 'control' and, if so, who has control?* It has been clear since *Cassidy v Ministry of Health* [1951] 2 KB 343 that control is not conclusive: there can be employment relationships where the employee is so skilled that control is obviously impossible. Control was still emphasized as a factor as late as the decision in *Market Investigations v Minister for Social Security* [1969] 2 QB 173, though that is probably the last major case to give it a prominent role. Nonetheless, it can still be a significant factor. When a part-time drama teacher claimed he was an employee of the school which hired him, the lack of control the school exercised was an important consideration. The school did not prescribe a syllabus, and left him free to teach as he wished. He was held to be an independent contractor (*Argent v Minister for Social Security* [1968] 3 All ER 208).

- *'Borrowed' employees.* Control may also be relevant where there is no doubt that the worker is an employee, but it is unclear *whose* employee (e.g. *Mersey Docks and Harbour Board v Coggins and Griffith (Liverpool)* [1947] AC 1, above, **9.3**). But it is only one factor. *Thompson v T Lohan (Plant Hire)* [1987] 2 All ER 631 appears to hold that clauses transferring control from the main employer to a temporary 'borrower' may sometimes be invalid under the Unfair Contract Terms Act 1977, s 2. Probably, however, the point of the case was that the main employer retained control and so the clause was a sham. There is a strong presumption that the 'lending' company is still the employer (e.g. *Biffa Waste Services v Maschinenfabrik Ernst Hese GmbH* [2008] EWCA Civ 1257), though there are occasional examples of the presumption being rebutted (e.g. *Gibb v United Steel Companies* [1957] 2 All ER 110). Controversially, it has recently been held in the Court of Appeal that there will sometimes be joint control of the employee and hence joint vicarious liability in both employers (*Viasystems*

(Tyneside) Ltd v Thermal Transfer (Northern) Ltd [2005] EWCA Civ 1151); though a differently constituted Court of Appeal was quick to point out that such cases will be rare (*Hawley v Luminar Leisure Ltd* [2006] EWCA Civ 18).

No one test is conclusive. On one side, there is the stereotypical employee, who sells a certain number of hours of time, in which the employee does precisely what he or she is told. On the other side, there are the stereotypical independent contractors, who perform a set task, by their own methods and using their own equipment. Which stereotype is closest to the actual facts is largely a matter of impression. Modern judges still make some use of the tests outlined above, but they emphasize their limitations, and that the role of a higher court is only to correct manifest errors of law, rather than to substitute its own verdict on such an open-ended enquiry (e.g. *Hall (Inspector of Taxes) v Lorimer* [1994] 1 All ER 250).

'The course of employment'

9.5 The employer is liable for the employee's tort only if the employee was genuinely trying to do the job at the time. Or, as it is usually put, the tort must be committed 'in the course of the employment'. There is therefore no vicarious liability if the tort occurred while the employee was (in the antique but well-established phrase) 'on a frolic of his own'. Of course, no employer would want its employees to act so badly as to land the employer in court as defendant in a tort action. Nonetheless, the courts insist that there is a difference between doing a job badly and ceasing to do it all, and that is the distinction they apply. The basic idea is clear enough, despite numerous borderline cases, which are probably impossible to reconcile with one another.

Honest attempt to do the job

9.6 So long as the employee was trying to do the job at the time when he or she committed the tort, the courts are likely to hold that the employee was still 'in the course of the employment'. Occasionally, the employee's actions are so outrageously dangerous that the court rebels and holds that the employee was outside the course of the employment. But such cases are rare.

> ***Keppel Bus Co v Sa'ad bin Ahmad* [1974] 2 All ER 700:** A ticket collector on a bus attacked Ahmad, a passenger, smashing his glasses. The ticket collector was under the mistaken impression that this was necessary to prevent a fight breaking out on the bus. Held: the bus company was not vicariously liable.
>
> ***Allen v London and South Western Rly Co* (1870) LR 6 QB 65:** A railway booking clerk accidentally gave Allen a foreign coin in his change. An argument followed; Allen

then tried to take a replacement from the till, whereupon the clerk had him arrested. Held: prosecuting defaulting customers was not the clerk's job, and therefore his employers were not vicariously liable for assault and false imprisonment.

The decision in *Allen* is, however, probably too nit-picking for modern tastes.

Fennelly v Connex South Eastern [2001] IRLR 390: Fennelly bought a railway ticket but was subsequently challenged by Sparrow, a ticket inspector working for Connex. An altercation followed, in the course of which each was offensive to the other. It ended when Sparrow put Fennelly in a headlock and evicted him from the station. Held: Sparrow was in the course of his employment throughout. It was not the right approach to look at each of Sparrow's actions in isolation, and to ask whether each was in the course of his employment. The entire matter was in effect a single incident, which was part of Sparrow's attempt to perform his duties.

Incidental activity while doing the job

9.7 In general, activities which the employee carries out while engaged in work are treated as part and parcel of the work itself. The courts do not usually have any truck with the idea that the employee might be working with the right hand but 'on a frolic of his own' with the left.

Century Insurance Co v Northern Ireland Road Transport Board [1942] AC 509: Davison, a petrol lorry driver, was engaged in pumping petrol from his lorry into the tank of a filling station, while smoking a cigarette. Held: his employers were vicariously liable for his causing the ensuing explosion.

Photo Production v Securicor Transport [1978] 3 All ER 146: Musgrave, a security guard, was patrolling premises late at night, guarding them against fire. It was bitterly cold, and he lit himself a small fire to warm his hands. The fire unexpectedly grew and engulfed the entire premises. Held: the employers were vicariously liable for Musgrave's misconduct.

The last is a very strong case, for the guard's carelessness was sufficiently gross to sustain a prosecution against him for arson! Perhaps the case would have been different if he had been a *deliberate* arsonist, though the distinction between deliberate arson and reckless arson is rather a fine one. There can certainly be cases where the employee's tortious activities can sensibly be separated from work activities being carried on at the same time. For example, there was no vicarious liability for an office cleaner who used her time in the office as an opportunity to make long-distance calls from the office phones (*Heasmans v Clarity Cleaning Co* [1987] ICR 949). Nor was the Post Office liable for an employee who scrawled racial abuse on a letter bound for his neighbours (*Irving and Irving v Post Office* [1987]

ICR 949). While in general an employee who does the job slowly is still doing the job, nonetheless there are exceptions; deliberately doing an urgent job slowly is often indistinguishable from refusing to do it at all.

> **General Engineering Services v Kingston and St Andrew Corporation [1989] 1 WLR 69:** Firefighters were in dispute with their employers, and operated a go-slow policy. When summoned to a fire, they took about 17 minutes to reach it, rather than the three minutes it would ordinarily have taken them. Held: their employers were not vicariously liable for the failure to put out the fire.

Forbidden method of doing the job

9.8 Employees do not step outside the scope of their employment merely because they employ methods which their employers have forbidden. Difficult questions of degree arise when employer and employee have different conceptions of what the job entails.

> **Limpus v London General Omnibus Co (1862) 27 JP 147:** Omnibus drivers were specifically forbidden to race one another, even with the object of beating a rival omnibus to a group of potential customers. Held: a driver who caused an accident while racing under such conditions was still in the course of his employment.

One special case is where an employed driver is forbidden to carry extra passengers, but nonetheless does so. If the driver later injures the forbidden passenger through negligence, is the employer vicariously liable? Plainly on any ordinary interpretation the driver will usually have been driving in the course of the employment, as would quickly be made plain if the driver injured some other road user. But when the passenger is the claimant, the courts have tended to ask the slightly different question whether *the offer of a lift* was made in the course of the employment.

> **Twine v Bean's Express [1946] 1 All ER 202:** A driver picked up a hitch-hiker, despite express instructions not to do so. The driver's poor driving injured the hitch-hiker. Held: the hitch-hiker was a trespasser in the employer's vehicle, and so could not sue the employer.

> **Rose v Plenty [1976] 1 All ER 97:** Contrary to his employer's orders, Plenty, a milk delivery driver, paid Rose, a 13-year-old boy, to help him with his deliveries. Rose was injured by Plenty's poor driving. Held: the employers were vicariously liable, despite their direct orders.

It is sometimes suggested that the case would be different if the passenger *knew* of the prohibition, but this suggestion has yet to be confirmed in an actual decision.

Honest attempt to do someone else's job

9.9 The employee is likely to be held to have stepped outside the course of the employment if he or she attempts to perform some task which is *someone else's* job. This is especially so if the task is one requiring special skills which the defaulting employee does not have. So the employer will not be liable where a bus conductor attempts to move a bus (*Iqbal v London Transport Executive* (1973) 16 KIR 329). But where the employee was hired to move obstacles in a warehouse, and so ought to have pushed a lorry out of the way, the employee remained in the course of the employment when he attempted to drive it out of the way instead (*Kay v ITW* [1968] 1 QB 140). It would be hopeless to attempt to reconcile all of the many and varied cases on this issue, though it is safe to say that an honest attempt to serve the employer's interests is likely to attract vicarious liability.

> **Poland v John Parr & Sons [1927] 1 KB 236:** An employee thought he saw a boy stealing sugar from his employer's cart; he attacked the boy, who fell and injured his leg. The employee was off-duty, and in any event was not employed to guard the sugar. Held: the employer was nonetheless vicariously liable for the employee's act.

The driver who frolics

9.10 Where employed drivers, for their own private purposes, deviate from the route they ought to be following, it is a matter of degree whether they can be held to be 'on a frolic of their own'.

> **Harvey v RG O'Dell [1958] 2 QB 78:** A builder took a five-mile detour to buy tools and to get lunch. Held: he was still in the course of his employment.

> **Hilton v Thomas Burton (Rhodes) [1961] 1 All ER 74:** A lorry driver who had had lunch took a detour to get tea. Held: he was no longer in the course of his employment.

After some initial controversy, it now seems to be settled that driving to or from work is not usually travel 'in the course of the employment', unless the terms of the employment make it so.

> **Smith v Stages [1989] AC 928:** Employees were sent out to do emergency work about 200 miles away from their usual place of work. They used their own cars and were paid for their time while driving. Held: they were still in the course of their employment while driving.

The criminal employee

9.11 Crimes committed as part of a bona fide attempt to do the job, or otherwise to serve the employer's interests, are within the scope of the employment. Crimes committed for the employee's own personal benefit or amusement are not. So deceit by an employee will be in the course of employment if intended to benefit the employers, even though the employers did not know about it and would have forbidden it had they known (*Barwick v English Joint Stock Bank* (1867) LR 2 Exch 259). But a teacher who uses school trips as an opportunity to commit sexual assaults on his students is arguably not acting in the course of his employment; this cannot be construed merely as an unauthorized mode of doing his job (*Trotman v North Yorkshire County Council* [1999] LGR 584). There are a few cases which extend liability beyond this, but it will be argued below that these cases are better explained on other grounds (see **9.18**, **9.19**).

However, the result in *Trotman* has now been called into question. In *Lister v Hesley Hall* [2001] UKHL 22 the claimants were systematically and regularly subjected to sexual abuse by the warden of their school. After the warden's conviction for various sexual offences, the claimants sued his employer. The Court of Appeal refused to find liability, but the House of Lords, overruling *Trotman*, proposed a slightly broader test. Liability could be established if the defendants had undertaken to care for the claimants through the services of their employee, and there was a 'very close connection' between his employment and the torts he committed. On the facts, there was held to be a sufficiently close connection.

This is a significant departure from the older case law, as the employee's behaviour could not possibly be described as merely a mode of doing his job. However, the new test is extremely vague, and their Lordships only gave rather superficial consideration to the wider effect of adopting their new test. In its immediate context, therefore, the decision is immensely significant, but it is far from clear that it has much effect outside it. It has been decisive in two recent claims, both of which would have been doubtful (though not completely unarguable) under the pre-*Hesley* law.

> *Mattis v Pollock* **[2003] EWCA Civ 887:** Cranston was employed as a nightclub doorman. At an incident where Mattis was present, a fight broke out, as a result of which Cranston was chased away and escaped. Returning soon after with a knife, he stabbed Mattis in the back, which resulted in paraplegia. Held: Cranston had a history of violence, and had been encouraged by his employer to act aggressively. He was returning to the club to seek revenge for the earlier incident, and so there was a direct connection with his duties. It was entirely fair to conclude that he was still within the scope of his employment when he stabbed Mattis.
>
> *Weir v Bettison* **[2003] EWCA Civ 111:** Dudley, an off-duty police constable, unlawfully 'borrowed' a police van to help his girlfriend move house. In the course of the work, Dudley wrongly formed the view that Weir was rifling his girlfriend's belongings, whereupon he

manhandled Weir into the restraining cage in the van, inflicting considerable injuries. Held: Dudley was apparently acting as a constable, 'albeit one who was behaving very badly', and so his actions attracted vicarious liability.

Hesley Hall was also relied on in *Gravil v Carroll* [2008] EWCA Civ 689, where a rugby club was held liable for a punch thrown by one of their players/employees during a match. But this is a result that might easily have been reached pre-*Hesley Hall*, given that the court regarded such fights as 'an ordinary (though undesirable) incident of a rugby match', and was not much impressed by the lengths clubs went to discourage such behaviour. A more striking result was reached in another sexual abuse case:

> **Maga v Trustees of the Birmingham Archdiocese of the Roman Catholic Church [2010] EWCA Civ 256:** The claimant was repeatedly sexually assaulted by a Catholic priest over a number of months. The priest's employers resisted an argument for vicarious liability, pointing out that the claimant was not a Catholic and had only minimal contact with the church. Held: a sufficiently strong connection was established on the facts, amongst which were that the priest had developed his relationship with the claimant under guise of performing his pastoral duties, and that a number of the incidents occurred on church premises.

The employer's indemnity

9.12 The employer is liable to an action by the victim of the employee's tort. However, the employee is still liable for the tort; and the employer can, in theory at least, recoup any money paid out to the claimant from the employee personally.

> **Lister v Romford Ice and Cold Storage Co [1957] AC 555:** The Listers, father and son, were employees of Romford Ice. The son negligently injured his father, who sued Romford Ice. Romford Ice paid the father, then sought to recoup the damages from the son. Held: the son's negligence was a breach of his employment contract, for which his employer could recover damages.

This claim can only be made if the employers were themselves blameless, their liability being vicarious only. In practice, such a liability would be very heavy for the individual employee to bear. Most employers find that the financial benefits of trying to pass on such liabilities to the employees concerned are far outweighed by the price they would have to pay in poor industrial relations. Their liability insurers might not always take the same attitude, but after the *Lister v Romford* decision the major liability insurers entered into a 'gentlemen's' agreement' not to take advantage of it. Poorly unionized employees are not always in a position to resist such claims if made.

Joint and several liability

9.13 There is a variety of legal doctrines under which one person may be liable for the tort of another. The doctrine of vicarious liability is the most important, but others are encountered on a regular basis. It was at one time necessary to distinguish carefully between 'joint liability', where there is a single legal wrong for which both the first and the second defendants are responsible (as where they jointly planned and executed some dangerous building operation which injures the claimant) and 'several liability', where the wrongs were entirely independent but led to the same damage (as where the first and second defendants both drive negligently and injure the claimant when they crash into one another). The distinction is very hard to apply in practice, and in modern conditions it can usually be forgotten. It may, however, occasionally be relevant on the finer points of law.

Joint tortfeasors: vicarious liability and analogous cases

9.14 This is the most common form of joint liability: employer and employee are jointly liable for the same tort. Vicarious liability (**9.2**) is the most common example. By statute, in certain cases, there is a liability analogous to vicarious liability, even though there is no employment relationship:

- Trade unions are liable for the acts of their officials, unless they repudiate them under a specific statutory procedure (Trade Union and Labour Relations (Consolidation) Act 1992, ss 20–21).
- Chief Police officers are liable for the actions of constables under their direction and control (Police Act 1996, s 88, as amended). The liability attaches to 'any unlawful conduct of constables under his direction and control in the performance or purported performance of their functions', and that the liability arises 'in like manner as a master is liable in respect of any unlawful conduct of his servants in the course of their employment'.

Other examples of joint liability

Joint enterprises

9.15 Where the first and second defendants together carry out some risky enterprise, it appears that they may both be liable for torts committed by one of them.

> **Brooke v Bool [1928] 2 KB 578:** His tenant being away, the landlord looked round the rented premises to try to locate the source of a gas leak. His lodger, who had come to

help, lit a match to help them see where they were going. Held: the landlord was jointly liable with the lodger for the resulting explosion.

The principle is clear enough, though its application to the facts of *Brooke* is not. The full facts of the case are not entirely clear. Joint enterprise is mentioned as one ground of liability; but so is agency; also the point that the landlord had legal and factual control of the situation—though it was unclear whether he realized what the lodger was up to in time to forbid him to do it. Nonetheless, the basic rule is clear. It is a broad liability, making one party liable even though they have themselves done nothing wrong, and the courts have not allowed the liability to be extended still further by adding in the doctrine of vicarious liability:

> ***Crédit Lyonnais v Export Credits Guarantee Department* [2000] 1 AC 486:** An employee of ECGD assisted a non-employee in a scheme to defraud CL. The employee's acts were not in themselves tortious, but nonetheless were part of the plan under which CL was defrauded. CL argued that the employee was liable as joint tortfeasor, and ECGD were vicariously liable for his acts. Held: even though the employee's acts were in the course of his employment, nonetheless this did not render ECGD liable unless those acts were tortious in themselves.

Extra-hazardous acts

9.16 Where the first defendant carries out an especially dangerous task on the second defendant's instructions, it appears that the second defendant may be liable for the first defendant's negligence, even though the first defendant is an independent contractor rather than an employee.

> ***Honeywill and Stein v Larkin Bros* [1934] 1 KB 191:** Contractors, hired to install sound equipment in a theatre, themselves hired photographers to take pictures of their work. At that date, flash photography was a risky operation, generating momentary quantities of very intense heat. The photographers negligently set fire to some curtains and there was extensive fire damage as a result. Held: the contractors were liable to the theatre-owners for the photographers' negligence.

This doctrine is rarely invoked, and it is not entirely clear which activities are sufficiently 'extra-hazardous' for this purpose. However, it has been held to apply where the owner of a house hired a contractor to re-roof it, resulting in penetration of damp in his neighbour's property (*Alcock v Wraith* [1991] NPC 135); though the court in that case relied also on the notion of a 'non-delegable duty' (**9.22**). *Honeywill* has recently been said to be good law and binding on at least courts of first instance (*Bottomley v Todmorden Cricket Club* [2003] EWCA Civ 1575). However, a differently constituted Court of Appeal has recently declared that the doctrine is 'so unsatisfactory that its application should be kept as narrow as possible', and it 'should be applied only to activities that are exceptionally dangerous whatever precautions are taken' (*Biffa Waste Services v Maschinenfabrik Ernst Hese GmbH* [2008] EWCA Civ 1257). Its overall status is therefore in some doubt.

Delegated duties

9.17 Analogously with vicarious liability, where the first defendant commits a tort in the course of carrying out a task delegated to the first defendant by the second defendant, then the second defendant may be liable for the first defendant's tort. Nearly all of the modern cases involve the first defendant's temporary use of the second defendant's car. The rule is that if the first defendant drives it negligently while doing a job for the second defendant, then the second defendant will be liable.

> **Ormrod v Crosville Motor Services [1953] 1 All ER 711:** Murphie lent his car to the Ormrods, so that they could visit friends in Normandy and then drive on to meet him in Monte Carlo, where they would have a holiday together. Held: Murphie was liable for the Ormrods' poor driving en route.

However, attempts to extend the doctrine further were prevented by the House of Lords in 1972.

> **Morgans v Launchbury [1973] AC 127:** A husband borrowed his wife's car to go to work and then to go on to the pub. He had promised her that if unfit to drive, he would not attempt to do so, but would get a friend to drive for him. Held: the wife was not liable for the friend's poor driving.

In particular, the Lords refused to hold that the wife's desire for her husband's safe return made the friend's driving a task 'delegated' to him; nor would they give any legal status to the notion of a 'family car'. The line the Lords drew in *Morgans* has forced later courts to make some rather fine distinctions, such as deciding precisely when a wife who has gone shopping has done so as a delegated task and when she has gone on her own account (*Norwood v Navan* [1981] RTR 457). As Ormrod LJ commented in the case, it is absurd that liability might turn on whether the driver's shopping basket contained a preponderance of goods for herself or for her family, if indeed the distinction can sensibly be drawn at all ([1981] RTR 457, 461). It is not clear that this doctrine serves any useful purpose at all, given the existence of the MIB scheme for the protection of those injured by uninsured drivers (**4.13**).

Agency

9.18 The legal concept of agency is primarily relevant to contracts. If A authorizes B to make particular contracts on A's behalf, then if B negotiates contracts as A's agent, the contracts which result will bind A. No doubt it is possible for A to authorize B to commit torts, and no doubt A is liable in that case also, but these cases seem to be rare. However, the concept of agency may sometimes extend to cover acts which were never authorized. So if A grants B a general authority to make contracts, A may sometimes be liable even if B makes contracts which A would certainly never have permitted had A known the facts. It is in this connection that a confusion with tort is likely.

> **Lloyd v Grace, Smith & Co [1912] AC 716:** Lloyd entered the offices of Grace Smith, solicitors, to ask for investment advice on property she owned. Sandles, the managing clerk, advised her to sell, and she signed documents which she supposed were necessary to effect a sale. In fact, they were conveyances of the properties into Sandles' own name, and he quickly disappeared with the proceeds. Held: the solicitors were liable for Sandles' fraud.

The result makes sense in terms of agency. The solicitors had left Sandles in charge of the office, and Lloyd's assumption that he was an authorized member of the firm was not an unreasonable one. So in terms of agency law, it seems plausible to say that Sandles was clothed with authority by the firm, and so contracts he made bound the firm. But as a decision on vicarious liability, the result seems a little odd, as Sandles was plainly acting for his own benefit, rather than 'in the course of his employment'. Moreover, if the liability is based on vicarious liability, then presumably it would have been quite different if Sandles had been an independent contractor rather than an employee—a surprising result from Lloyd's point of view. Nonetheless, even though the opinions in the case squarely base the liability on agency, it is often said to be an example of vicarious liability. The orthodox view at present is that it can properly be regarded as an example of vicarious liability, but that in this particular context the test for the existence of liability is not 'the course of employment' test. Rather, the test is whether the fraud was within the scope of the agent's authorization (*Armagas v Mundogas SA, The Ocean Frost* [1986] AC 717, 783, Lord Keith).

> **Hornsby v Clark Kenneth Leventhal [1998] PNLR 635:** Young was an employee of CKL. For several years he conducted a successful fraud, under which he persuaded over 100 people to deposit funds with him. CKL permitted Young to carry out his own personal business from CKL's property, though they knew nothing of any fraud; Young's clients never supposed they were dealing with CKL, but only with Young in a personal capacity. Held: giving an employee permission to run his own business on the firm's property was not to be equated with adopting that business as their own. If CKL had no notice of possible fraud, they had no duty to investigate.

In fact, I have already quietly relied on agency principles at various points in this book. It is usually quite uncontroversial. Suppose the first defendant, an official of the second defendant (a company), gives advice to the claimant in circumstances where a *Hedley Byrne*-type duty applies (see above, **5.14**). The advice is wrong, and the claimant sues the second defendant. It is hard to say that the claimant 'relied on' the second defendant without implicitly adopting agency notions—we can say that the first defendant spoke with the second defendant's authority, or that the second defendant adopted the first defendant's behaviour, or whatever. A company has no vocal cords of its own; it can only 'speak' through agents. In most cases, this can quietly be skated over. Occasionally it cannot, and difficult questions arise.

> ***Williams v Natural Life Health Foods* [1998] 2 All ER 577:** Mistlin was managing director of NLHF. NLHF entered into a franchise agreement with Williams, under which Williams was to run a health food shop in Rugby. Williams had been encouraged to enter the agreement by an enthusiastic prediction of profits prepared largely by Mistlin, and NLHF's general reputation was largely based on his expertise. Both the franchised shop and NLHF subsequently failed; Williams sought to hold Mistlin personally liable for negligent misstatement. Held: there had been no sufficient assumption of personal responsibility by Mistlin to find him personally liable.

> ***Merrett v Babb* [2001] EWCA Civ 214:** Merrett applied to a building society for a loan to finance a house purchase. Babb prepared a careless valuation report on the house for his employers, valuers acting for the building society. This report was eventually passed on to Merrett, though with details of its authorship removed. The valuers subsequently became insolvent. When defects in the house appeared, which Babb should have noticed but had not, Merrett sued Babb personally for negligent misstatement. Held: even though Merrett did not know the author of the report, nonetheless she had relied on it, as having being produced by a person competent to do so. Liability was established.

Several liability

Bailment and custody of goods

9.19 Where one person agrees to look after goods for another, various obligations arise under the law of bailment. In particular, there may be a duty to guard the property against theft or damage by third parties. Accordingly, where the first defendant steals or damages the claimant's goods which are bailed to the second defendant, then the second defendant may be liable for the loss. Where the first defendant happens to be the second defendant's employee, this looks confusingly like vicarious liability.

> ***Morris v CW Martin & Son* [1966] 1 QB 716:** Morris left a fur stole with Beder for cleaning. Beder sub-contracted the work, with Morris's consent, to Martin. The job was given to Morrissey, an employee of Martin; but Morrissey committed theft. Held: Martin was responsible for its employee's theft.

Whether this is regarded as a special rule relating to bailment, or as an example of vicarious liability, may be a mere matter of taste. However, there are certainly some situations in which it would matter, and there are various questions which need to be asked:

• *Was the thief in the course of his employment?* Even after making full allowance for the rule that an unauthorized mode of performing the employment contract may still be 'in the course of the employment' (**9.8**), it seems strange to regard stealing an article as merely an unauthorized mode of looking after it. Equally, where the claimant's car has been left with a garage for repairs, the garage is liable to its owner when one of their employees drives it around for his own purposes (*Aitchison v Page Motors* [1935] All ER Rep 594). If this is vicarious liability, then, it is of a special type, subject to its own special rules.

• *Does the nature of the bailment matter?* If this is truly vicarious liability for the tort of the employee, it is hard to see how the nature of the bailment matters. However, *dicta* in *Morris* suggest that it does. In particular, where the second defendant is looking after goods gratuitously, there would be no liability for theft by the first defendant even if the first defendant is employed by the second defendant (see [1966] 1 QB 716, 725, Lord Denning MR, 737, Diplock LJ; though compare *Port Swettenham Authority v TW Wu & Co (M) Sdn Bhd* [1979] AC 580).

• *Does it matter whether the thief is an employee or not?* If the basis of the liability is vicarious liability, then obviously it is vital; if the liability is in bailment, it is not obvious why it should. The point appears to be open.

So there appears to be a special rule that where the claimant entrusts property to the second defendant under contract and the second defendant entrusts it to its employee the first defendant, then the second defendant is liable to the claimant for the first defendant's misbehaviour with it. This appears to be so even on facts where the first defendant was obviously on a 'frolic of his own'. There are conflicting *dicta* on whether the second defendant would be liable if the thief was an employee, but *not* the particular employee to whom the goods had been entrusted.

The economic torts

9.20 Under the economic torts, the claimant may sue the defendant for loss deliberately inflicted on the claimant by 'unlawful' means (**6.27**). The precise meaning of 'unlawful' varies from context to context. Where the means adopted are 'unlawful' in the sense that they constitute a tort for which the claimant could have sued someone else, then in effect the 'economic torts' become a means for imposing several liability for the tort.

Second defendant negligently allows first defendant to commit a tort

9.21 At various points, we have already encountered situations where the second defendant is liable to the claimant for failing to prevent the first defendant injuring the claimant (see **3.4**). There are always arguments against holding one person responsible for what another person did; when the second defendant is held responsible, it is usually on the ground that the second defendant was personally responsible for the circumstances in which the first defendant acted. The fact that the first defendant's behaviour is tortious is usually completely incidental in such cases, though of course the possibility of suing the first defendant as well or instead of the second defendant is likely to have been very important to the claimant when considering legal strategy.

- The first defendant may be incapable of looking after himself or herself, and it is precisely for that reason that the second defendant owes a duty to others, perhaps because the first defendant is a child (e.g. *Carmarthenshire County Council v Lewis* [1955] AC 549 (**1.30**)).

- The second defendant may be under a particular duty to prevent the first defendant harming others. Perhaps the first defendant is a prisoner (e.g. *Home Office v Dorset Yacht Co* [1970] AC 1004 (**1.33**)), or a potentially dangerous child (*Wilson v Governors of Sacred Heart Roman Catholic School* [1998] 1 FLR 663—though on the facts the second defendant was found to have acted reasonably), or an irresponsible employee of the second defendant (e.g. *Hudson v Ridge Manufacturing Co* [1957] 2 QB 348—where the first defendant's behaviour would almost certainly have been held to be outside the scope of his employment).

- It may be the second defendant's fault that the first defendant is so dangerous in the first place. Perhaps the second defendant carelessly hired the first defendant and put him in a position of trust, when a little care would quickly have established that the first defendant was a professional burglar (*Nahhas v Pier House (Cheyne Walk) Management* [1984] 1 EGLR 160).

- The second defendant has ordered the first defendant to carry out activities which would be dangerous no matter how carefully they were done. Perhaps the second defendant hires the first defendant for building operations inherently likely to create a nuisance (*Matania v National Provincial Bank* [1936] 2 All ER 633 (**7.24**)).

Non-delegable duties

9.22 Sometimes the second defendant is held liable because, while the second defendant reasonably delegated performance of a legal duty to the first defendant, nonetheless the first defendant failed to perform it. The reason for this is sometimes said to be that certain duties are 'non-delegable'. But this way of putting it leads to confusion. *All* duties are non-delegable, at least in the sense that they must be performed, and if they have not, it is no answer to say that someone else was (ineffectively) asked to do so. The practical answer to any question of 'delegation' is usually to ask precisely what the duty on the second defendant is.

An example may help. Take the (fictitious) Nutrition of Children (Civil Liability) Act 2008, which provides that if any parents have not given their children their tea by 5pm on a given day, the parents have committed a tort against them. Plainly, there is a sense in which this statute imposes a duty on parents. Is this duty 'delegable'? There are really two questions:

• If the parents arrange for a neighbour to provide tea on a particular day, and the neighbour does so, are the parents in breach? The answer is that they are not, unless there is something in the legislation to say that the parents must provide tea *in person*. So if the statute allows others to perform the duty on the parents' behalf, it is in one sense a 'delegable' duty.

• If the parents arrange for a neighbour to provide tea, but the neighbour *fails* to do so, what is the position? Almost certainly, the next question is whether the Act imposes an absolute duty to provide tea, or only provides that the parents must act reasonably. In the first case the parents will certainly be in breach; in the second they are only in breach if their attempt at delegation was unreasonable. Only if the parents satisfy their duty by doing their best is the duty 'delegable', in this sense.

In general, tort lawyers are more interested in results than in who achieves them. And so it is the later distinction that is usually most important. Where tort law imposes an absolute duty to produce a certain result, then the defendant is in breach unless it is in fact achieved; 'delegation' only avoids liability if it was successful. Where the duty is only to act reasonably, then the defendant may usually escape liability by showing that the task was delegated to someone else, so long as that delegation was reasonable. However, there is a limited class of exceptional cases, where even a reasonable delegation will be held not to be a satisfaction of the defendant's duty.

Absolute liabilities

9.23 Where the second defendant is under an absolute duty not to harm the claimant in a particular way, then it is no defence that the second defendant took a (reasonable but ultimately misguided) decision to tell the first defendant to deal with the problem. This rule applies to the strict liability for breach of statutory duty and to the strict common law liabilities such as nuisance liability for activities adjacent to the highway, *Rylands v Fletcher* (1868) LR 3 HL 330 liability, interference with a private right of support (*Alcock v Wraith* [1991] NPC 135), and liability for fire. In these cases, then, the duty is 'non-delegable'. Two very minor qualifications need to be made to this proposition:

• Where an employer is in breach of statutory duty, and an employee is injured as a result, it appears to be a defence that the task of complying with the statute was reasonably delegated *to the very employee who was injured*. However, this defence will only be successful where the entire responsibility both for the breach and for the injuries themselves can be put on the employee's shoulders.

> ***Ross v Associated Portland Cement Manufacturers* [1964] 2 All ER 452:** Ross was killed when he fell off a ladder while repairing wire netting in Associated's factory. His widow sued for breach of statutory duty, saying that Associated had failed to 'provide a safe means of access to the place of work'. Associated replied that the decision to work at the top of a ladder was Ross's own. Held: the work had been beyond Ross's experience, and so responsibility for the breach of statute could not be attributed to him alone, though his widow's damages should be reduced by one-third for contributory negligence.

• Where the second defendant has a strict common law duty to render a harmful situation safe, and hires the first defendant to put it right, it appears that the second defendant will only be liable for a failure by the first defendant to do the task properly. The second defendant is not liable for 'collateral' acts by the first defendant, not intimately connected with the removal of the danger. The reason seems to be that the second defendant is not vicariously liable for the acts of the first defendant, but is responsible only for the source of danger. So the second defendant should not be held responsible for misbehaviour by the first defendant which is unrelated to the task. There is no particular logic to this—the point that the danger cannot be removed except by workers who may misbehave is surely part of the reason why it is dangerous—but the exception seems well established.

> ***Padbury v Holliday and Greenwood* (1912) 28 TLR 494:** Contractors were hired to put metal window frames into a building. One worker left a tool on a window-sill, not in the ordinary course of doing the work. The wind blew the tool off and it hit the claimant. Held: the tool had not been left as part of doing the work, and therefore the owner of the building was not responsible for the worker's collateral negligence.

Negligence duties

9.24 In general, where the defendant's only obligation is to act reasonably, the defendant may sometimes satisfy the duty simply by instructing someone else to deal with the problem. This will of course only be so if this was a reasonable thing to do, and there is nothing else that the reasonable person would do in that situation. If the defendant's decision to delegate is reasonable, then it cannot retrospectively become unreasonable simply because the delegate turns out to be incapable of handling the situation. So, for example, if it is reasonable for the occupier of premises to turn over some repair job to an independent contractor, the occupier need not do it personally. He or she need only act reasonably in selecting the contractor and in checking the work after it was done (Occupiers' Liability Act 1957, s 2(4)(b), **4.24**).

There are a limited number of exceptions to this basic rule. It has been held that if the defendant advertises that he runs a fleet of mini-cabs, then he owes customers a non-delegable duty to ensure that the cabs he refers them to are reasonably safe. If customers are injured, he cannot plead (contrary to the impression he deliberately fostered) that the cab drivers are all independent contractors over whom he had no control (*Rogers v Night Riders* [1983] RTR 324). A broader exception relates to employment. Employers owe their employees a duty to make their work environment reasonably safe (**4.32**). This duty has been held to be non-delegable, in the sense that the employees are entitled to this safe environment wherever they have been sent, even if it is to some site over which the employer has no control. So if an employer temporarily 'lends' an employee to another firm, then the employer remains liable for any deficiencies in the employee's work environment (*McDermid v Nash Dredging and Reclamation Co* [1987] AC 906 (**4.35**)). Further, by statute, if an employee is injured by defective equipment, the employer is liable if the defect was due to negligence, whether the employer's or anyone else's (Employers' Liability (Defective Equipment) Act 1969) (**4.38**).

Conclusion

9.25 It is important to remember that there is no magic in 'delegation'. If the defendant is supposed to secure a certain result, and the defendant gets someone else to do it, then the duty is discharged. But that is because the defendant has *performed* the duty, not because the defendant has 'delegated' it to someone else. In other cases, the duty may demand more. So the duty a hospital owes its patients is not merely its vicarious liability for the sum total of the duties the members of its staff owe. There is in addition a primary duty to care for the patient (*Cassidy v Ministry of Health* [1951] 2 KB 343, 363, Denning LJ). Again, if harm comes to a child at school, the school is vicariously liable for any misbehaviour by the teachers and other staff, but it also owes a primary duty to care for the children. To show that there was no one teacher whose job it was to guard against the particular harm that befell the claimant may make the school's legal position worse, as that could be precisely what the claimant is complaining of (*Carmarthenshire County Council v Lewis* [1955] AC 549).

Contribution

9.26 If the first defendant is liable to the claimant in respect of a certain loss, the claimant is entitled to sue the first defendant for the whole of it. It is no defence that others too are liable. Nor is this a ground for reducing damages. The claimant need not justify the decision to sue the first defendant rather than anyone else. However, it is open to the first defendant to seek a 'contribution order' against any other person whom the claimant could have sued in respect of the same damage. If the first defendant can show that the second defendant was also liable to the claimant, the court will divide ('apportion') the liability between the first and second defendants.

It is vital to appreciate that contribution does not usually affect the claimant's position: the claimant may sue the first defendant or any possible defendant, and it is no concern of the claimant's whether that defendant manages to recoup a share of the damages from someone else. Indeed, the claimant may sue *more* than one defendant, though the claimant will not be able to recover legal costs in the second or subsequent actions unless the court agrees it was reasonable to bring them (Civil Liability (Contribution) Act 1978, s 4). In any event, the claimant cannot recover more than 100 per cent of the loss suffered.

It is sometimes suggested that where the first defendant alone is sued but others are liable too, the first defendant should be entitled to a defence of 'proportionate fault', reducing the damages—*even if* the claimant has no prospect of recovering damages from anyone else. But this is not currently part of the law (**11.25**).

9.27 The first defendant has the right to claim compensation 'from any other person liable in respect of the same damage' (Civil Liability (Contribution) Act 1978, s 1(1)). It is irrelevant whether the second defendant was liable as joint tortfeasor, several tortfeasor, or indeed was liable for breach of contract or breach of trust. The main situation the Act envisages is where the first and second defendants could each be sued by the claimant, but it also allows for other cases:

- The first defendant does not lose the right to seek contribution merely because the second defendant has settled with the claimant (s 1(2)). Indeed, where the second defendant has settled with the claimant, the first defendant is entitled to claim contribution without having to prove that the claimant could have sued the second defendant—even if the second defendant never admitted liability to the claimant (s 1(4)).
- If the second defendant was at one point liable to the claimant, then the second defendant remains liable to contribute even if the claimant can no longer sue the

second defendant (s 1(3)). There is an exception to this in a very limited class of case—'expiry of a period of limitation or prescription which extinguished the right on which the claim against' the second defendant 'was based'. This applies, however, only to the tort of conversion, the usual effect of limitation being merely to bar the claim, not the right on which it was based.

However, if the claimant has already sued the second defendant and failed on the merits of the claim, it appears that the first defendant cannot claim contribution (s 1(5)). Moreover, if the second defendant settles with the claimant in such a way as to make it clear that the sum is a full and final settlement of the claimant's claim, then the claim is gone, and the claimant has no basis for proceeding against the first defendant at all (*Jameson v Central Electricity Generating Board* [2000] 1 AC 455). The practical effect of this is that if the claimant means to proceed against the first defendant after settling with the second defendant, the terms of the settlement with the second defendant should make this clear.

Apportionment

9.28 The court may make any apportionment of liability 'such as may be found by the court to be just and reasonable having regard to the extent of that person's responsibility for the damage in question' (s 2(1)). This may be as high as 100 per cent or as low as 0 per cent in appropriate cases (s 2(2)). However, the maximum the court may order the second defendant to pay is the amount which the claimant could have recovered from the second defendant, even if the first defendant's own liability is greater (s 2(3)). Express agreement between the first and second defendants apportionment, whether before or after the claimant's injury, in effect excludes the court's discretion (s 7(3)).

Relation to contributory negligence

9.29 What is the correct approach when the claimant also bears some of the responsibility for the accident? In *Fitzgerald v Lane* [1989] AC 328 the claimant attempted to cross a pelican crossing without waiting for the lights to change in his favour. The first defendant's car ran into him and he was thrown onto the other side of the road, where the second defendant's car ran into him. The trial judge found that the first defendant and the second defendant had both been driving too fast; he considered that all three of the parties involved had acted equally badly. Accordingly, he argued that each should bear one-third of the loss. In the result, therefore, the claimant could recover one-third of the loss from each of the first defendant and the second defendant, bearing one-third himself.

The House of Lords held that this was the wrong approach, as it telescoped two quite different questions. The first question was as to the proper size of the claimant's claim. If the claimant sues either defendant, then a court should say that the claimant and the defendant were equally to blame, and therefore the claimant is entitled to recover 50 per cent of the loss he suffered. The result is the same whichever defendant the claimant sues, and in neither case is the existence of another possible defendant relevant. Second, how is this claim to be apportioned between defendants? Since they are equally to blame, each must pay half. Accordingly, the claimant must bear 50 per cent of the loss himself, and the first and second defendants must each pay 25 per cent.

Assessment

9.30   Much of the material in this chapter may have seemed rather esoteric, or antiquarian, or simply marginal. Yet it is one of the more important chapters in the book. For it is only through the principles outlined here, and through the mechanism of insurance, that most tort claimants are able to link the liability to a financially substantial defendant, and hence actually recover damages. Indeed, the whole edifice of tort liability, with its strong emphasis on concepts of personal fault, rests on distinctly collectivist foundations. Defendants are able to meet these awards because policy decisions were taken to force liability on those with deep pockets, rather than the more 'obvious' defendants.

Why is employment special?

9.31   The doctrine of vicarious liability makes much turn on whether or not the person whose fault the accident was is an employee of the defendant. Why should this be? The old idea that employees are 'under the control' of the employer, whereas independent contractors are not, is long discredited; in any event there is no suggestion that the liability should be any less where the employer was not in a position to prevent the accident. It is often suggested today that, whatever may be the orthodoxy, the courts do in fact ask themselves *why* it is necessary to determine, in any one case, whether a particular worker is an 'employee' or not, and adapt their answer to the policies relevant to that issue. Whether someone is an 'employee' or not does in reality, and arguably should, depend on why the question is being asked. But this approach, while probably correct, points an even sharper finger at the lack of principled reasoning behind vicarious liability. It is all very well to say that we should hold workers to be 'employees' when the proper policy basis to vicarious liability points in that direction. But when is that, precisely?

Tort as a just response to wrongdoing?

9.32 If we regard tort as society's response to wrongdoing, as a system for the ascription of responsibility, then it emerges as a (crude but workable) answer to the problem of how we make business enterprises liable. It says, in effect, that business enterprises are guilty of wrongdoing where one of their employees, attempting to do his job, is guilty of wrongdoing. This is obviously not perfect, but it is not easy to improve on, either. How else can we hold companies responsible, given that a company has 'no body to be kicked, and no soul to be damned'?

Tort as a system of deterrence?

9.33 Alternatively, we might regard vicarious liability as part of a system for deterring companies from wrongful behaviour. The threat that companies will be held responsible for the torts of their employees is supposed to terrify them into controlling the employees. It is possible that it has this effect to some extent; but it has to be said that there is very little evidence for it. A firm worried by this prospect is likely to insure against it, and while it is possible for an insurer to know enough about its client's business to recommend appropriate improvements to procedures and safeguards, and hence to stop the problem at source, this seems to be relatively rare.

Tort as loss-distribution?

9.34 If we regard tort as a mechanism for spreading losses across society, we would see vicarious liability as merely one step in the chain linking the unfortunate victims of accidents to those who bankroll them, namely the general public. If particular industries or professions cause great harm to the population, then their extensive legal liability will ultimately be reflected in the prices they charge. By their individual decisions whether to buy the goods or services in question or to spend their money elsewhere, the individuals who constitute the market effectively decide whether society can afford it. This is not an implausible way of describing the modern system; but it suggests that the law is not only unduly complicated but also unduly narrow. Why should it matter whether employees do the harm or not? And why should it matter whether the harm was done 'in the course of employment'? Surely it should be enough if the employee's access to work facilities made it easier for him or her to do damage?

Conclusion

9.35 The various legal institutions described in this chapter extend liability considerably. Yet their basis and justification are rather obscure. Simultaneously, they cast into doubt the justification for many other areas as well, for they provide the mechanisms whereby doctrines seemingly aimed at imposing personal responsibility in fact impose it on those who bear no responsibility at all for the events in question.

FURTHER READING

Armour 'Corporate personality and assumption of responsibility' [1999] LMCLQ 246.

Barron 'The impact of post-Lister vicarious liability on the licensed trade in the United Kingdom' (2007) 4(3) ESLJ (<http://www2.warwick.ac.uk/fac/soc/law/elj/eslj/issues/volume4/number3/barrona>).

Brennan 'Third party liability for child abuse: Unanswered questions' (2003) 25 Jour Social Welfare & Family Law 23.

Brodie 'Enterprise liability: Justifying vicarious liability' (2007) 27 OJLS 493.

Giliker 'Rough justice in an unjust world' (2002) 65 MLR 269.

Kidner 'Vicarious liability: For whom should the "employer" be liable?' (1995) 15 LS 47.

McIvor 'The use and abuse of the doctrine of vicarious liability' (2006) 35 CLWR 268.

Murdoch 'Negligent advice: Whose duty is it?' (2001) 17 Prof Neg 123.

Stevens 'A servant of two masters' (2006) 122 LQR 201.

Townshend-Smith 'Vicarious liability for sexual (and other) assaults' (2000) 8 Tort Law Rev 108.

Yap 'Enlisting close connections: A matter of course for vicarious liability?' (2008) 28 LS 197.

SELF-TEST QUESTIONS

1 Can an employee acting directly contrary to the employer's orders still be 'in the course of the employment' (**9.8**)? What about an employee who is acting solely for his own benefit (**9.11, 9.18, 9.19**)?

2 What is the modern relevance of the 'control' test for vicarious liability (**9.4**)?

3 Given that police officers are not employees, how do you account for the vicarious liability of their chief officers (**9.14**)?

4 When can the defendant defeat the claimant's claim by pointing out that others are more at fault than the claimant (**9.26**)?

5 If the claimant, the first and the second defendants are all equally at fault for the accident in which the claimant was injured, how are damages apportioned between them (**9.29**)?

Remedies

SUMMARY

This chapter summarizes the various remedies available to the claimant. The main remedy is damages. Generally speaking these damages are calculated so as to provide a quite precise assessment of the claimant's loss. After dealing with general principles of assessment, the chapter goes on to consider in detail methods of calculation of personal injury damages.

10.1　There could in principle be many responses from the law to a tort committed by the defendant against the claimant. In practice, by far the most common is an award of compensatory damages. I come to this possibility last (**10.18**). In a few cases, the claimant may be able to exercise self-help (see **7.29**). The claimant may sometimes be able to claim an injunction forbidding the defendant to continue with tortious behaviour (**10.2**). Alternatively, the claimant may seek an award of money not calculated on compensatory principles (**10.8**).

Injunctions

10.2　An *injunction* is a court order instructing the defendant to behave in a particular way. Disobedience is a contempt of the court which issued the injunction: it is a criminal offence, and can be punished by imprisonment or a fine. Most injunctions are *prohibitory* injunctions, telling the defendant to abstain from doing something or other, though some injunctions are *mandatory* injunctions telling the defendant positively to do something or other.

The injunction is a discretionary remedy, but the principles on which the courts will decide its availability in any one case are relatively settled. The principles on which injunctions are granted vary considerably with the point in time at which the claimant claims the injunction. If no tort has yet been committed, but the claimant has good reason to believe that it will be, the claimant may claim a *quia timet* injunction to nip the tort in the bud. Where a tort has already been committed, the claimant may start an action for damages and seek an *interim* injunction, before trial. Alternatively, the claimant may wait until trial and seek a *final* injunction.

Quia timet injunctions

10.3 Sometimes the claimant seeks an injunction '*quia timet*' (= because he or she fears) that a tort will be committed. Where no tort has yet been committed, the courts are reluctant to act without clear evidence that a tort is likely. It is not entirely clear how imminent a tort must be. Evidence that the defendant's tree roots are likely to grow so as to infringe the claimant's rights within three years has been held insufficient to justify an immediate court order to cut them back (*Lemos v Kennedy Leigh Development Co Ltd* (1961) 105 SJ 178). It has been said that the only rule is that no court will issue an injunction 'prematurely' (*Hooper v Rogers* [1975] Ch 43). Certainly the court will consider possible alternative remedies, such as making a declaration of the claimant's rights with liberty to apply for an injunction if circumstances later warrant it.

Interim injunctions

10.4 Particular problems arise when the claimant alleges that a tort has already been committed, and seeks an injunction before the trial of the main action. Basic issues in dispute may not yet have been resolved. If an injunction is issued, it may turn out that the claimant in fact did not have the right claimed and that the defendant was perfectly entitled to act in the way the court forbade. So the claimant will certainly not be awarded an injunction without making an undertaking to compensate the defendant, should the claimant's claim turn out to be misconceived. Further, while the claimant is no longer put to proof that there was a prima facie case against the defendant, nonetheless the claimant must show that there is 'a serious issue' to be dealt with at trial. In deciding whether to grant an interim injunction, the courts take into account various factors:

- If the claim is right, will damages be enough to compensate the claimant?
- If the claimant's case is wrong, will the claimant's undertaking adequately compensate the defendant?
- Is the preservation of the status quo a worthwhile objective?

These criteria were laid down in *American Cyanamid Co v Ethicon Ltd* [1975] AC 396 as being of general application. However, it is clear that different approaches will be required in different kinds of case. In defamation cases, considerations of freedom of speech predominate. If the defendant intends to prove at trial that the statement was true or was fair comment, a court will almost never restrain the defendant before he or she has had a chance to do that (*Bestobell Paints Ltd v Bigg* [1975] FSR 421).

> **Holley v Smyth [1998] QB 726:** Smyth claimed that Holley had extracted £200,000 from him by false pretences, and sent Holley draft press releases detailing the alleged fraud, saying that he would publish them unless he recovered his money. Holley sought an injunction, arguing that Smyth's conduct amounted to blackmail. Held: in sufficiently extreme circumstances the courts will restrain a libel, but will never do so merely because of the defendant's motives, or the threatened mode of publication, or the potential damage to the claimant. Injunction accordingly refused.

It has been held that this result is still good today, despite the Human Rights Act 1998, s 12(3), which seems to say that a defendant may be restrained if the claimant is 'likely to establish' liability at trial. The reasoning is that s 12 was intended to buttress press freedom, and therefore should not be read in such a way as to diminish it (*Greene v Associated Newspapers Ltd* [2004] EWCA Civ 1462). The 'likely to establish' test is more relevant in attempts to restrain breaches of confidence, though even there considerations of freedom of expression are likely to predominate (*Cream Holdings v Banerjee* [2004] UKHL 44).

In labour law cases, by contrast, almost certainly the dispute will have been resolved long before the matter comes to a trial, and what the court says at the interim stage will effectively decide the matter. Accordingly, a court will be strongly influenced by which side's case on the ultimate issues looks stronger at that stage (*NWL v Woods* [1979] 3 All ER 614).

Final injunctions

The inadequacy of damages

10.5 The ordinary remedy for a tort is damages. The claimant cannot claim an injunction unless the claimant can show that damages alone would not be an adequate remedy. Where the defendant is plainly doing serious and continuing damage to the defendant's property, it is almost axiomatic that an injunction to stop the damage is a superior remedy to damages, and so an injunction is readily available (e.g. *Pride of Derby and Derbyshire Angling Association v British Celanese* [1953] Ch 149). Differing views are expressed in cases concerning relatively slight property damage, often in the course of the same judgment. On the one hand, if the damage is truly trivial, it would be wrong to allow the heavy machinery of an injunction to be invoked. On the other, there is unease that a deliberate taking of the claimant's property can in effect be condoned by the legal system, merely because the claimant's loss is small in monetary terms. So if the defendant deliberately extends his house in such a way as to diminish the claimant's light, and then dares the claimant to take legal action over it, some may doubt 'whether it is complete justice to allow the big man, with his big building and his enhanced rateable value and his improvement of the neighbourhood, to have his way, and to solace the little man for his darkened and stuffy little house by giving him a cheque that he does not ask for' (*Leeds Industrial Co-operative Society v Slack* [1924] AC 851, 872, Lord Sumner). Much depends on whether the court truly regards the claim as trivial. The monetary value of the loss is only one factor, and the fact that only a small sum would be awarded in an action for damages might be precisely why the court decides that an injunction is the most appropriate remedy.

The court's discretion

10.6 It is sometimes said that the courts will only grant final mandatory injunctions if certain strict conditions are satisfied: that there is a strong probability of future harm to the claimant, that the defendant has acted 'wantonly or unreasonably', and that it is possible to state precisely what the defendant is being required to do (*Redland Bricks v Morris* [1970] AC 652). Other factors may be taken into account in deciding whether to grant an injunction, including some factors which would be irrelevant if the action were for damages:

- *The degree of difficulty to which the injunction would subject the defendant.*

- *The claimant's behaviour.* Misconduct by the claimant, such as by leading the defendant on or misleading the defendant, may lead to the refusal of an injunction.

- *Public interest?* Some cases assert that the public interest can be a factor in deciding whether to grant an injunction, particularly where the activity the claimant seeks to restrain benefits many besides the defendant (e.g. *Miller v Jackson* [1977] QB 966 (**7.16**); *Dennis v Ministry of Defence* [2003] EWHC 793 (QB) (**7.21**)). Other judges have criticized this, however, as giving insufficient weight to the claimant's rights in the matter (e.g. *Kennaway v Thompson* [1981] QB 88).

Watson v Croft Promosport Ltd **[2009] EWCA Civ 15:** Croft started to use their land as a motor circuit. Watson, a neighbouring landowner, sought an injunction to limit the number of days that Croft could carry on this noisy activity. At first instance, Simon J gave damages only, stressing both that the activity was an extremely popular one, and that Watson himself had indicated a willingness to accept damages if Croft's activities were limited somewhat. Held: damages in lieu of an injunction should only be awarded in very exceptional circumstances, such as where an injunction would be oppressive to the defendant. There was a substantial injury to the claimant, and the benefit to the public did not outweigh it.

Substitution of a damages award

10.7 The courts have power to substitute an award of damages for an injunction (Supreme Court Act 1981, s 50). This is a curious provision, the origins of which go back to the days before 1875, when injunctions and damages had to be claimed in different courts. Judges sometimes assume that it applies in any case where a court could in theory have granted an injunction, whether or not it would have been wise to do so (e.g. *Hooper v Rogers* [1975] Ch 43, 48, Russell LJ). In cases of deliberate invasion of property rights, the orthodox position seems to be that if the claimant has established a right to an injunction, the court will not substitute an order under s 50 unless damages would adequately compensate the claimant, and it would be oppressive to the defendant to issue an injunction (*Shelfer v City of London Electric Lighting Co* [1895] 1 Ch 287).

Types of damages

10.8 Damages are usually compensatory. That is, they represent the value of something to which the claimant was entitled, and of which the defendant deprived the claimant. While an award of damages always punishes the defendant at some level, however it may be calculated, nonetheless the point of asserting that damages are compensatory is that they are measured by what the claimant has lost, rather than as a measure of how wicked the defendant has been. Where the claimant's rights have been violated, but the court is unable to award any sum as compensation, the court may give *nominal* damages (currently £10); and where the claimant brought the action simply to establish that the right exists, this remedy may be quite adequate for the claimant's purposes. In defamation cases, it is open to the court to award *contemptuous* damages of 1p, to indicate that the claimant was indeed defamed but that the claimant should nonetheless never have brought the action. In such a case, the claimant will probably find that the court is reluctant to award any legal costs against the defendant.

General damages and special damages

10.9 A contrast is often made between *general damages* and *special damages*. These expressions are used in various different senses, though the underlying contrast is always the same: 'special damages' represent specific items of which the claimant can give details, whereas 'general damages' represent some loss for which the claimant is entitled to compensation without giving details. So, for example, some torts are said to be actionable 'without proof of special damage': action lies in assault (**2.1**) or libel (**8.1**) without establishing any damage as such. Negligence, by contrast, is not actionable even in theory unless loss to the claimant is proved. However, when discussing damages in negligence, it is common to distinguish between 'special' damages that can be itemized before trial (e.g. clothing torn in the accident) and 'general' damages which cannot (e.g. future wages, or damages for the claimant's pain and suffering). It is not necessary for the claimant to prove 'special damage' in *this* sense as a precondition of bringing the action.

The different uses of the 'general'/'special' distinction are slightly baffling at first. The root meaning is always the same, and the distinction is about the duties of the lawyers involved in fighting the case. 'Special' damage is damage which the claimant's lawyer must itemize and prove, 'general' damage is damage which the claimant's lawyer is entitled to assert without proving, or at least without proving it in detail. But the precise nuances vary with the context.

Exemplary damages

10.10   In a very limited number of cases, the claimant is entitled to an award of damages which exceeds the sum necessary for compensation, and which is explicitly meant to punish the defendant for misbehaviour. Exemplary damages are highly controversial, many arguing that the law of tort should only concern compensation. Put like that, the argument is rather circular: it does not give any reason why exemplary damages should not be available, or suggest any limit that should be placed on them, but merely asserts that they should not be regarded as part of the law of tort. A more sophisticated argument is that punishment of wrongdoing is more appropriately carried out through the criminal law. This is for several reasons, notably that better procedural safeguards are open to defendants in the criminal law, and that if a criminal court orders the defendant to forfeit money, it will go to the state rather than to the claimant. How strong this objection is must depend on the context.

Exemplary damages are only available in a limited class of cases.

- First, where the conduct complained of was done on behalf of an organ of government, and committed the tort in an arbitrary, unconstitutional, or oppressive way.

- Second, where the defendant committed the tort after calculating that the benefit the defendant would gain from the tort exceeded any likely claim for damages in respect of it.

These narrow limits to the doctrine were established in *Rookes v Barnard* [1964] AC 1129. That decision was much criticized, but the Lords reaffirmed it in *Cassell & Co v Broome* [1972] AC 1027. There are a few statutes which seem to authorize the award of exemplary, or at least non-compensatory, damages: Reserve and Auxiliary Forces (Protection of Civil Interests) Act 1951, s 13(2); Copyright, Designs and Patents Act 1988, s 97.

Arbitrary, oppressive, or unconstitutional conduct

10.11 This category is traditionally stated to apply to 'servants of government', but it appears to apply to all governmental activity, whether or not the individuals who do it are technically 'servants' (employees). It is not always clear who is 'governmental' and who is not. It has been held that a (privatized but heavily regulated) public utility is not 'governmental' for this purpose (*AB v South West Water Services* [1993] QB 507). It appears to be enough if the conduct complained of is unconstitutional *or* oppressive *or* arbitrary (*Holden v Chief Constable of Lancashire* [1987] QB 380).

It may be asked why oppressive and arbitrary behaviour by government entitles the claimant to more generous remedies, when equally unpleasant behaviour from private bodies would not. A possible answer is that it is often very difficult to use the criminal law against governmental bodies, and especially against the police, whose conduct is often impugned in these cases. The law of tort is here being used as a substitute for the criminal law, and accordingly takes on rather crime-like characteristics.

The defendant sets out to make a profit

10.12 This category has been broadly stated to apply 'whenever it is necessary to teach a wrongdoer that tort does not pay' (*Rookes v Barnard* [1964] AC 1129, 1227, Lord Devlin). Provided that the wrong was clearly deliberate, it usually seems to be enough to show that the defendant's motive was straightforwardly economic. Typical cases are where a landlord seeks to evict a tenant in order to seek another tenant at a higher rent (*Design Progression Ltd v Thurloe Properties Ltd* [2004] EWHC 324 (Ch)), or where a publisher includes libels in a publication to increase its circulation (*McCarey v Associated Newspapers (No 2)* [1965] 2 QB 86). 'What is necessary is that the tortious act must be done with guilty knowledge for the motive that the chances of economic advantage outweigh the chances of economic, or perhaps physical, penalty' (*Cassell & Co v Broome* [1972] AC 1027, 1079, Lord Hailsham LC). (See also *AT v Dulghieru* [2009] EWHC 225 (QB), where the facts involved trafficking, coerced prostitution and false imprisonment.) Complex questions can arise when a defendant is liable both for exemplary damages and for a criminal confiscation order arising out of the same facts (*Borders (UK) Ltd v Commissioner of Police of the Metropolis* [2005] EWCA Civ 197).

The law set in concrete?

10.13 There are many examples of exemplary damages in the law reports; but not all the torts are represented. The decision in *Rookes v Barnard* [1964] AC 1129 certainly discouraged any further expansion. It is sometimes suggested that the existing cases should be regarded as definitive, so that exemplary damages will not be awarded for any tort unless there is a pre-*Rookes* authority allowing it for the same tort. This is a proposition it is hard to justify from *Rookes* itself, and is inconsistent with a number of cases since *Rookes* (e.g. *Bradford City Metropolitan Council v Arora* [1991] 2 QB 507). Nonetheless until recently it was the current view (see e.g. *AB v South West Water Services* [1993] QB 507).

Relevant considerations

10.14 Where exemplary damages are available, the courts have tended to emphasize the need for restraint, once the remedy has been cut loose from the notion of compensation. Various factors are mentioned as relevant:

• The claimant's own position must be considered. So it is a factor tending to reduce exemplary damages that the claimant provoked the defendant's conduct (*Lane v Holloway* [1968] 1 QB 379). Where there are a number of claimants, the appropriate course is first to calculate how much the defendant should fairly pay, and then determine how it should be shared between the various claimants (*Riches v News Group Newspapers* [1986] QB 256).

• Obviously the defendant's own behaviour is a vital consideration. It is also appropriate to consider the defendant's means in determining how much would be an appropriate punishment. If there is more than one defendant, then the award of damages should be that which is appropriate for the *least* blameworthy of the defendants (*Cassell & Co v Broome* [1972] AC 1027).

• The court should first calculate a compensatory award, and then consider whether the defendant merits further punishment beyond that. There is, however, a conflict of authority over the relevance of other punishments to which the defendant was subjected. One case holds that if the defendant has been criminally punished for his behaviour, there is no scope for further punishment through an award of exemplary damages (*Archer v Brown* [1985] QB 401).

There is currently considerable controversy over the level of damages in these cases, especially in cases brought against the police, where cases are typically decided by juries. Should jury awards be under the same rigid control by the courts as are now applied in cases of defamation (see *John v MGN* [1997] QB 586 (**8.22**))? The two classes of case are not entirely analogous; most of the police activity in issue is straightforwardly criminal, and tort is being used to redress the deficiencies in the criminal justice system that fail to deal with them as such. It seems very strange to lump the treatment of serious crimes by police officers in with the frivolities of defamation cases. Nonetheless, the Court of Appeal has ruled that similarly tight controls are appropriate in these cases too. And so exemplary awards against the police of £50,000 and £200,000 respectively were reduced, the court ruling that £25,000 and £15,000 were the right figures (*Thompson v Metropolitan Police Comr* [1998] QB 498).

Reform

10.15 The Law Commission has proposed that exemplary damages (or, as it prefers, 'punitive' damages) should be available more broadly, at least in cases where the defendant has deliberately flouted the claimant's rights (*Aggravated, Exemplary and Restitutionary Damages*, Law Com Report No 247, December 1997).

Injury to feelings, and aggravated damages

10.16 In a limited number of cases, the claimant is treated as having suffered an injury for which substantial compensation should be given, even though there is no quantifiable pecuniary loss in any ordinary sense. So victims of defamation (**8.1**), malicious falsehood (**8.42**), trespass to the person (**2.1**), and trespass to land (**7.2**) may be entitled to substantial sums even though their wallets are none the worse as a result of the defendant's behaviour. In those circumstances, if the defendant has infringed the claimant's rights in a particularly nasty way, the compensation may be correspondingly larger than normal. The damages are said to be *aggravated*.

> **Jolliffe v Willmett & Co [1971] 1 All ER 478:** A private detective entered Jolliffe's house; in the ensuing struggle, the detective gave Jolliffe a glancing blow. Held: Jolliffe was entitled to £250 compensation for the 'insolent and high-handed' trespass, and £150 for assault.

As well as the torts already mentioned, it appears that aggravated damages are available in deceit (*Archer v Brown* [1985] QB 401). An attempt to claim them in negligence for 'horrific' pain failed, the court considering that they would serve no purpose not already covered by an award for pain and suffering (*Kralj v McGrath* [1986] 1 All ER 54; on pain and suffering generally see **10.58**). But they were awarded where a mother sued her former solicitors for negligently losing her custody of her children (*Hamilton Jones v David and Snape (a firm)* [2003] EWHC 3147 (Ch)). It seems that the courts have no rooted objection to such awards in negligence cases, so long as they do not duplicate other heads of damage.

Aggravated damages are technically compensation for a wrong, not punishment. An argument for aggravated damages is thus quite distinct from an argument for exemplary damages. Indeed, the claimant is free to argue in an appropriate case first, that the damages are aggravated and, second, that even when so enhanced they do not adequately punish the defendant for the wrongdoing in the case.

> **Rowlands v Chief Constable of Merseyside Police [2006] EWCA Civ 1773:** After an altercation at her home with a police constable, Rowlands was arrested, handcuffed in front of her own children, and taken to the police station. A jury subsequently found the police conduct unjustifiable, and she claimed damages. A jury awarded her £2,500 for malicious prosecution, £2,000 for psychological injury, and £850 for false imprisonment. Held: in addition to those sums, she was entitled to *(i)* £6,000 aggravated damages—while there was an obvious danger of double compensation, nonetheless the injury to her feelings was distinct from the psychological harm she had suffered, and so demanded additional compensation; *(ii)* £7,500 exemplary damages for arbitrary police conduct.

In practice, however, exemplary and aggravated damages are available in much the same sets of circumstances, and it is often hard to say which is the more appropriate label for a particular award; cases before *Rookes v Barnard* [1964] AC 1129 often did not distinguish the two at all. The Law Commission proposed that statute should rigorously divide up the two, by stating that aggravated damages can only compensate for mental distress, and cannot be used to punish the defendant (*Aggravated, Exemplary and Restitutionary Damages*, Law Com Report No 247, December 1997).

Restitutionary damages

10.17 Where the defendant tortiously takes some valuable asset from the claimant, then the court may sometimes award the claimant the amount the claimant might reasonably have charged the defendant for the use of the asset.

> **Swordheath Properties v Tabet [1979] 1 All ER 240:** Tenants became trespassers, when they stayed on in leased premises after their leases expired. Held: the landlords could recover the reasonable market rental for the period of occupation, as damages for trespass.

Such an award might be justified as compensatory damages if it is shown that the claimant would have made this profit but for the claimant's tort. However, this doctrine is not confined to cases of that sort, and may be available even if it is clear that the claimant could not have used the asset profitably elsewhere. There has been considerable academic controversy over whether these cases should be regarded as compensatory damages, or as illustrating a principle of 'unjust enrichment' (compare Sharpe and Waddams 'Damages for lost opportunity to bargain' (1982) 2 OJLS 290, and Birks *An Introduction to the Law of Restitution* (1985) 330).

While the cases could be fitted into either mould, they fit neither very well. The Law Commission have recently proposed considerable extensions to the availability of restitutionary damages, though their proposals would leave a great deal of discretion to the courts as to both the availability and the method of calculation (Report No 247 'Aggravated, Exemplary and Restitutionary Damages' December 1997).

Compensatory damages: general principles

10.18 I now turn to strictly compensatory awards, which form the bulk of claims in tort. It is first necessary to establish what the claimant will receive compensation *for*. The basic principle is that the claimant is entitled to be compensated to the extent that the defendant's tort made the claimant worse off. In other words, the courts will compare the claimant's position as it is and the claimant's position as it would have been had the defendant's tort not occurred, and will compensate the claimant for the difference between the two states. So if the defendant destroys the claimant's property, in principle the claimant is entitled to the value of that property; if the claimant suffers personal injury, the claimant is entitled to the amount by which this injury makes the claimant worse off. Personal injury damages are treated in detail below (**10.51**).

Destruction of the claimant's property

10.19 The claimant is entitled to the value of property which is destroyed by the defendant's tort. But how is that value to be ascertained? An obvious measure, if it can be applied, is the market cost of a replacement. Indeed, the courts have applied this measure even where the claimant was in a position to manufacture a replacement at a cheaper cost (*Smith Kline & French Laboratories v Long* [1989] 1 WLR 1). When the claimant buys a superior replacement, the courts have occasionally awarded the claimant the entire cost of so doing, where the claimant had no sensible alternative (*Harbutt's 'Plasticine' v Wayne Tank and Pump Co* [1970] 1 QB 447). Where there is an appreciable delay before replacement, which the claimant cannot reasonably avoid, the damages may include a figure for loss caused by the delay (*Moore v DER* [1971] 3 All ER 517), or for the reasonable cost of hiring a temporary substitute (*Martindale v Duncan* [1973] 2 All ER 355). In principle, the claimant is entitled to all financial costs occasioned by the destruction of the property.

> **Owners of Dredger Liesbosch v Owners of SS Edison [1933] AC 449:** The *Edison*
> negligently sank the *Liesbosch*, which was engaged in profitable contract work. Held: the

owners of the *Liesbosch* were entitled to the cost of a replacement dredger, plus the costs of adapting it and transporting it, and for losses under the contract caused by the delay.

Damage to the claimant's property

10.20 Where the defendant has merely damaged the claimant's property, without destroying it outright, the court will usually have to chose between two measures: the diminution in value of the property and the cost of putting the damage right. The diminution-in-value measure is most obviously appropriate if the claimant does not intend to do any repairs, or intends to sell the property before any repairs are done, though even there *dicta* occasionally favour the cost-of-repair measure (e.g. *The York* [1929] P 178, 184–5, Scrutton LJ). Where the claimant in fact repairs, the cost of so doing is the obvious measure of damages, though it can be displaced if the defendant convinces the court that the amount spent on repairs was unreasonable. The claimant may also recover for other losses which result from any delay while repairs are taking place, such as the need to hire a replacement. Such claims occasionally fade into claims for restitutionary damages (**10.17**).

> *Owners of Steamship 'Mediana' v Owners, Master and Crew of Lightship 'Comet'* **[1900] AC 113:** The defendant collided with the claimant's light-ship, damaging it and putting it temporarily out of action. While it was being repaired, the claimant used a substitute ship, which it kept available for precisely this sort of emergency. The substitute ship would, but for the emergency, not have been used for any purpose at all. Held: the claimant's damages could include a sum for the use of the substitute lightship.

Probably the result on the facts is justifiable on ordinary principles, as the sum was mostly for additional expenses which the claimant would not have incurred had it not had to push the substitute vessel into service. Nonetheless, it appears that the House of Lords meant to go further: 'Supposing a person took away a chair out of my room and kept it for 12 months, could anybody say you had a right to diminish the damages by showing that I did not usually sit in that chair, or that there were plenty of other chairs in the room? The proposition so nakedly stated appears to me to be absurd...' ([1900] AC 113, 117, Earl of Halsbury LC). The precise rationale is unclear. Perhaps this means merely that where the defendant has effectively deprived the claimant of the use of an asset for a certain period, the courts will be inclined to award the value of that asset for the relevant period. The alternative is to engage in refined calculations which may, in the end, do no better justice than simply awarding the rough figure. After all, no-one contends that the assessment of damages is a very precise process, and the more refined the procedure, the more it costs the parties to apply.

Causation

10.21 If there is no causal connection between the claimant's loss and the defendant's conduct, then the defendant is not responsible for the claimant's loss.

> *Performance Cars v Abraham* **[1962] 1 QB 33:** The defendant damaged the claimant's car, necessitating a respray. However, the car already needed a respray because of earlier damage, for which the defendant was not responsible. Held: the defendant was not responsible for the claimant's loss.

Problems in relation to causation are particularly acute for torts which require proof of special damage—a list headed, in terms of practical importance, by the tort of negligence. An entirely different approach is taken for torts which do not. So, for example, it is taken for granted that a defamatory statement 'causes' injury to the claimant's reputation (**8.20**). It is in effect possible to deny causation between the claimant's utterance and the defendant's poor reputation, but it must be done indirectly, such as by arguing that the defendant had no reputation to lose (**8.22**), or that the statement was spread about by persons for whom the claimant had no responsibility (**8.8**). These problems are pursued in the chapter on defamation itself, as they raise problems peculiar to that tort.

The 'but for' test

10.22 The starting point in causation is usually assumed to be the 'but for' test: the defendant is liable to the claimant only if the claimant would not have suffered the injury but for the defendant's tort. Many cases can be resolved on this criterion. Certainly, if the criterion is satisfied, the defendant is unlikely to be able to deny causation; and few claimants who fail it can hope to establish liability.

> *Barnett v Chelsea and Kensington Hospital Management Committee* **[1969] 1 QB 428:** Barnett was admitted to hospital with stomach pains and vomiting. The duty officer negligently failed to diagnose his condition, telling him merely to consult his own GP if the symptoms persisted. Barnett soon died from acute arsenic poisoning. Held: as Barnett's death would have been a certainty even if the hospital had accurately diagnosed his condition, the hospital was not liable for the death.

In cases of that sort, the argument is really that the defendant's conduct, however reprehensible, had nothing to do with the claimant's injury. It is not so much a factual argument as a denial of responsibility. Accordingly, it may sometimes be convincingly employed even in cases where it is entirely unclear what would have happened had the defendant acted properly.

> *The Empire Jamaica* **[1957] AC 386:** The owner of *The Empire Jamaica* was in breach of statutory duty in not obtaining a certificate of competence for the mate on his ship. However, the mate was in fact perfectly competent. When the mate was in charge of the

ship, it was involved in a collision due to his negligence. Held: the owner's breach of statutory duty was not a cause of the collision.

Cases where there is no duty

10.23 Confusion enters in some cases where the defendant fails to prevent the claimant
coming to some kind of harm. Sometimes the court denies causation, but seems
really to mean that there is no duty. So in *East Suffolk Rivers Catchment Board v
Kent* [1941] AC 74, where the claimant suffered a long period of flooding which
the defendant could easily have prevented, liability was refused. This was put both
on the ground that the defendant had no duty to prevent the flooding, *and* that
the defendant's behaviour was not the cause of the flooding. It seems preferable to
describe such results in terms of duty. Certainly the claimant's loss was caused by
weather conditions, but it was also caused by the defendant's failure to act with due
care; whichever way the question is asked, we come sooner or later to the question
whether the defendant had a duty to act, and 'causation' seems a red herring.

The same sort of confusion was apparent in *Reeves v Metropolitan Police Commissioner*
[2000] 1 AC 360, where police paid insufficient attention to the danger that one of
their prisoners might commit suicide. The police conceded that they were in breach of
duty, but nonetheless argued that the actual suicide was a voluntary act, breaking the
causal chain. So, they said, the death was caused not by the police but by the suicide
himself. But the House of Lords rightly held that this was misconceived. Once it was
established that the police were at fault for failing to guard against suicide, they could
not then claim that suicide was a breach of the causal chain. (However, damages were
reduced by 50 per cent for contributory negligence; see below, **11.21**.)

Cases of multiple tortfeasors

10.24 Many commentators have pointed out that the 'but for' test breaks down where the
first and the second defendant both engage in dangerous behaviour and simultaneously injure the claimant. Say both are reckless members of a hunting party, who
carelessly discharge their firearms in the claimant's direction at the same time.
Can each of them say that his bullet did not cause the claimant's death, because
the other bullet would have killed the claimant anyway? Common sense suggests
that neither defendant should be allowed to escape on that ground. But such cases
are rare. Simultaneity of that kind usually suggests that the two of them are acting
in concert, and if they are then they will both be liable as joint tortfeasors (**9.15**).
Indeed, sometimes the courts seem prepared to stretch a point in the claimant's
favour even though the two have not acted together.

> **Lambton v Mellish [1894] 3 Ch 163:** Mellish and Cox were rival merry-go-round opera-
> tors, each of whom played pipe organs. Lambton, who lived nearby, argued that, while
> neither organ was loud enough to constitute a nuisance in itself, nonetheless their joint

sound constituted a nuisance. Held: as Mellish had been aware of Cox's music but had continued, he was liable in nuisance.

In cases where both defendants shoot the claimant, in practice the first defendant's bullet will not be precisely simultaneous with the second's. So it appears that the earlier defendant will be liable, the later fortuitously being able to plead that the damage was done before he acted (*Performance Cars v Abraham* [1962] 1 QB 33 (**10.21**) is of that type). A more credible hypothetical case, though it is hard to find a case where it has occurred, is where the first defendant negligently disables the brakes on the second defendant's car, and then the second defendant collides with the claimant after negligently failing to apply them at all. It would be strange if the claimant's case against either defendant were to fail on causation grounds, even though both can say that the 'but for' test was not satisfied.

Factual uncertainty

10.25 A further difficulty with the 'but for' test is that it is often very unclear what would have happened if the defendant had not committed the tort. The court knows what *did* happen, but what would have happened if the defendant had behaved carefully is often a matter of speculation. Generally speaking, the claimant has to prove his or her case on the balance of probabilities. The claimant will therefore lose unless it is more likely than not that proper conduct by the defendant would have avoided the injury the claimant suffered.

> *Hotson v East Berkshire Area Health Authority* **[1987] AC 750:** Hotson fell from a tree and entered hospital in such a poor way that he had only one chance in four of ever being able to walk again. However, the hospital entirely failed to treat him, and his chances of avoiding being a cripple reduced to zero. Held: Hotson would probably have ended up that way even if the hospital had acted with reasonable speed, and accordingly the hospital was not liable.

This principle has been applied many times. An obvious criticism is that it is unreasonably generous to the defendant. Where the defendant is guilty of serious wrongdoing, which deprived the claimant of a significant chance of avoiding injury, it seems wrong to give the defendant the benefit of doubts over what precisely would have happened. But this is often what the courts have done.

• In *McWilliams v Sir William Arrol & Co* [1962] 1 All ER 623, Arrol failed to provide safety harnesses for its employee scaffolders, including McWilliams. McWilliams later fell to his death. The House of Lords held that Arrol was without responsibility for the death, relying on evidence that McWilliams would not have worn a harness had one been provided. The decision has been much criticized. It seems a classic case of both the claimant and the defendant being to blame, and it is hard to see how ruminations about 'causation' take it out of that category (**4.40**). It may be true that scaffolders in general very rarely wore harnesses, leading to an 'irresistible' inference that McWilliams would not have done ([1962] 1 WLR 295, 300, Lord Kilmuir LC). But those very facts seem to point to significant and widespread neglect of employers' obligations.

• In *Bolitho v City and Hackney Health Authority* [1998] AC 232, a registrar was summoned to Bolitho's hospital bedside to advise on his acute respiratory difficulties. She failed to attend; Bolitho died. The registrar's evidence was that her presence would not have helped: in the event, the only thing that might have made a difference would have been if she had intubated, but (fully in accord with medical practice) that is not what she would have done. The court held that there was no causation: if she had complied with her duty of care, Bolitho would still have died.

Factual uncertainty and 'material contribution to risk'

10.26 Some of the leading cases depart from the usual approach.

> **McGhee v National Coal Board [1972] 3 All ER 1008:** McGhee worked in a brick kiln. He contracted dermatitis due to the high concentrations of brick dust. There was evidence that the risk of the workers getting dermatitis would be significantly reduced if the employer had installed showers for them to use at the end of their shifts. It was, however, impossible to say that if the showers had been available, then McGhee would never have suffered dermatitis. Held: there was sufficient evidence that the employer's breach of duty had made a contribution to the dermatitis, and the employers were liable.

Plainly, these facts are very similar to those in *Hotson* (**10.25**), and if there is a real difference it is hard to see what it is. In both cases, the defendant deprived the claimant of a chance; yet in both, the claimant would probably have suffered the same fate whatever the defendant did. The reasoning is a little obscure: it was assumed to be enough that the employers had made a 'material contribution' to the risk of dermatitis, and how this was to be reconciled with the 'but for' criterion was not spelled out. The case is similar to, but goes further than, *Bonnington Castings v Wardlaw* [1956] AC 613, where the claimant was injured by the escape of silica dust from two of his employer's machines. Neither machine was well ventilated, but the employer was only in breach as to one of them, as there was no practical means for ventilating the other. There too, it was thought sufficient to establish causation that there had been a 'material contribution' to the claimant's injury by the machine in breach.

There have been attempts to squeeze *McGhee* and *Bonnington* into the ordinary 'but for' approach. For example, the cases were approved, though some of their reasoning was criticized, in *Wilsher v Essex Area Health Authority* [1988] AC 1074. There, five independent causes appear to have contributed to the risk of the damage which the claimant suffered while in the defendant's hospital, but the House of Lords refused to hold the hospital liable simply because one of those causes was the result of negligence, and they remitted the case for retrial. Few commentators were convinced that *McGhee* and *Bonnington* could be seen as examples of the 'but for' approach, and in *Fairchild v Glenhaven Funeral Services* [2002] UKHL 22 the House of Lords at last accepted that the cases have to be seen as an exception to it.

Fairchild involved a number of claims brought against employers by their former employees. In each case, the employees had contracted mesothelioma as a result of asbestos dust at work. However, while it was clear that the employers were in breach of their duty in this respect, each of the employees had been exposed to such dust in more than one employment, so that it was impossible on a 'but for' standard to trace the disease to any one employer. The Lords held that in circumstances of that kind, justice demanded the application of a 'material contribution' test. *Fairchild* was applied in *Barker v Saint Gobain Pipelines plc* [2004] EWCA Civ 545, where the claimant had been exposed to asbestos dust for just under 30 years, for 8½ of which he had been the defendants' employee. He had been self-employed for almost all of the remainder of the period. The defendants were held liable, though with a 20 per cent reduction for the claimant's own contributory negligence. A similar approach was taken in *Chester v Afshar* [2004] UKHL 41 (below, **11.5**), where again the House of Lords considered that justice required the recognition of the defendant's contribution to the injury even though it did not satisfy a 'but for' criterion. While it is clear that cases of this sort are the exception and not the rule (*Paul Davidson Taylor v White* [2004] EWCA Civ 1511), nonetheless in their own area they appear to be well established. More unsettlingly, it has recently been stated (in a medical negligence case) that 'one cannot draw a distinction between medical negligence cases and others', suggesting an even broader application (*Bailey v Ministry of Defence* [2008] EWCA Civ 883).

However, a significant limit on this type of liability has been introduced by *Barker v Corus UK* [2006] UKHL 20. In that case (which involved further mesothelioma claims, by employees who had both worked for a number of employers and acted as self-employed for a period), the House of Lords ruled that the various claims were several, not joint; that is to say, that an employer who was responsible for x per cent of the risk is liable only for x per cent of the damages. It follows that the effect of one defendant's becoming bankrupt is that their share of the damages is never paid, rather than falling on other defendants as the Lords seemed to have envisaged in *Fairchild*. The rationale of this ruling is unclear, and (controversially) it was immediately reversed by statute, but in relation to mesothelioma claims only (Compensation Act 2006, s 3). This new provision bites where it is shown that the defendant's conduct made a material contribution to the risk of mesothelioma, regardless of whether a balance-of-probabilities criterion is met (*Sienkiewicz v Greif (UK) Ltd* [2009] EWCA Civ 1159).

Factual uncertainty and damages for a lost chance?

10.27   Another approach to factual uncertainties would be to award the claimant damages for a lost chance. So a court faced with the facts of *Hotson* might argue that the claimant had been deprived of a 25 per cent chance of recovery, and accordingly award 25 per cent of the amount the claimant claimed as representing the whole loss. (Note that while support for loss-of-chance damages is usually regarded as a pro-claimant position, nonetheless it might reduce damages in cases where the claimant lost a chance of more than 50 per cent but significantly less than 100 per cent.) Damages for lost chances are well established in some areas of damages assessment (see e.g. **10.59**), but the controversial question is whether they can be awarded in a case where the claim will otherwise fail completely on the ground it fails the 'but for' test.

The *Hotson* case itself provides no support for damages for loss of chance, but neither does it rule them out. Such cases are well established in the law of contract. In tort, there are a few recent examples, where it is stressed that the loss of the chance has to be proved on the balance of probabilities; but if it can be so proved, then it can be sued for.

> **Allied Maples Group v Simmons and Simmons [1995] 4 All ER 907:** Allied Maples took over Kingsbury, the subsidiary of a rival group, with a view to selling off unwanted properties and keeping the rest. However, they found that Kingsbury had certain onerous legal liabilities of which they had been unaware. They sued Simmons & Simmons, who had been advising them on the takeover, arguing that if they had been warned of these liabilities, they might have been able to secure indemnities against them. Held: as there would have been a substantial chance that they would have been able to secure an indemnity, they were entitled to damages to reflect that chance.

Allied Maples was a tort case rather than a contract case, but nothing seems to turn on the point.

> **First Interstate Bank of California v Cohen Arnold & Co [1996] 5 Bank LR 150:** First Interstate Bank became concerned about the financial stability of one of its clients, to whom it had lent some £5m. It consulted Cohen Arnold, who negligently assured it that there was nothing to worry about. Accordingly, the bank waited rather

longer than it would otherwise have done before realizing property it held as security for the loan. Held: there was a two-thirds chance that it would have received more money but for Arnold Cohen's poor advice, and accordingly it could recover two-thirds of the likely extra amount.

Acton v Graham Pearce & Co [1997] 3 All ER 909: Acton, a solicitor, was convicted of legal aid fraud. His solicitors had negligently failed to order an inspection of certain key documents, which might have shown that the most damning evidence against him was in fact perjured. If his solicitors had done their work more carefully, there would have been a 50 per cent chance that he would never have been convicted. Held: he could recover 50 per cent of the loss caused by his conviction.

As the discussion in later cases such as *Charles v Hugh James Jones & Jenkins* [2000] 1 All ER 289 shows, assessing a loss of chance of winning litigation can be a very complicated business. Further, the courts are not prepared to be strictly logical where this seems to lead to absurdity. The claimant suffered serious injuries in a road accident; the defendant, her solicitor, secured an admission of liability but then lost the action by missing a time limit. How were damages for the defendant's negligence to be assessed? In principle, the test was the value of the claimant's lost action, which involved asking how strong her case would have looked at the date at which trial would have taken place had the defendant conducted the action properly. But in fact the claimant's condition worsened after that date, and the court felt that it would be unfair not to take this into account. So in fact the claimant received a greater sum than could be justified on strict loss-of-chance reasoning.

Given that the courts are prepared to give damages for lost chances in cases of purely economic losses, including lost chances to secure compensation for personal injury, it would be surprising if the courts were not equally prepared to give damages for lost chances in personal injury cases. This has, however, only rarely happened (e.g. *Doyle v Wallace* [1998] 30 LS Gaz R 25), and the House of Lords in *Gregg v Scott* [2005] UKHL 2 has now ruled it out for the future. In a case where the defendant's negligence reduced the claimant's chances of recovering from cancer from 42 to 25 per cent, a majority of the court held that this loss of a chance was not a compensatable head of claim.

Remoteness

10.28 Where the defendant's tort has caused loss to the claimant, the defendant may sometimes argue that the loss was too remote a consequence of the defendant's conduct. Too many other causes may have intervened, or the injury may be very unexpected, or it may simply be out of all proportion to the fault the defendant was guilty of. The argument is often confused and undeserving, and many commentators have cynically concluded that 'remoteness' arguments are simply a device for controlling claims which seem too large.

To which torts is it a defence?

10.29 In general, torts involving deliberate wrongdoing by the defendant do not allow remoteness as a defence. This applies to assault and battery, deceit, and the economic torts. It is therefore enough in these cases if the claimant establishes a causal link between the defendant's conduct and the claimant's loss.

> *Doyle v Olby (Ironmongers)* **[1969] 2 QB 158:** Olby sold Doyle an ironmongery business, making various false statements about its accounts. Doyle put considerable money into the business, but ended up making a loss. Held: Doyle could recover all sums he had expended on the business.

It is less clear whether torts of strict liability are subject to a remoteness defence. The tort in *Rylands v Fletcher* (1868) LR 3 HL 330 certainly is, as is liability for fire. It is unclear whether liability for animals is. Probably the tort of breach of statutory duty is not: it is no defence that a breach of duty was unforeseeable or unpreventable, and so it would be surprising if the consequences of a breach could be avoided by a plea of remoteness. But there is no clear authority on the point. In practice, the rule that the claimant's loss must be of the same type as that which the statute was intended to prevent (**1.49**) fulfils a similar function. Most of the case law on remoteness concerns the tort of negligence; it appears that nuisance applies similar rules (**7.23**).

Competing approaches

10.30 The actual test for remoteness is a matter of some controversy. In a leading case early in the 20th century, the courts tended to stress causation issues: so long as the defendant had committed a breach of duty against the claimant, the defendant was liable for all direct physical consequences of the claimant's behaviour.

> *Re Polemis and Furness, Withy & Co* **[1921] 3 KB 560:** Furness Withy's employees, in the course of unloading Polemis's ship, carelessly dropped a plank into the hold. This caused a spark, which lead to an explosion, which seriously damaged the ship. Held: Furness Withy was responsible for the entire loss.

It was stressed in the case that this doctrine applied only where 'the damage is in fact directly traceable to the negligent act, and not due to the operation of independent causes having no connection with the negligent act' ([1921] 3 KB 560, 577, Scrutton LJ). Yet the case was subsequently heavily criticized, by a court possibly under misconceptions as to the breadth of the decision, and a test based on foresight was substituted.

> **Overseas Tankship (UK) v Morts Dock and Engineering Co, The Wagon Mound [1961] AC 388:** OT's employee deliberately discharged furnace oil into Sydney Harbour. The oil spread over the harbour. MDE's employees, seeing the oil on the water, consulted their manager on whether it was safe to continue welding; he said that it was. Held: the fire which resulted was too remote a consequence for MDE to recover from OT.

However, there is a certain amount of ambiguity in the application of this test. In subsequent litigation over the same incident, another claimant, whose ship was some way away from where the fire started, and so who was presumably even less 'foreseeable' and more 'remote', nonetheless established to the court's satisfaction that the fire *was* foreseeable. The reasonable person in the defendant's position would have realized that there was a (small but non-negligible) risk of fire (*Overseas Tankship (UK) v Miller Steamship Co Pty, The Wagon Mound (No 2)* [1967] 1 AC 617). Plainly, then, there is a certain amount of flexibility in the test. What may have been going on is that the claimant in *The Wagon Mound* was not anxious to obtain a ruling that the defendant should have foreseen the fire, as the defendant would then have retorted that the claimant should have foreseen it too. The defendant would then have raised a defence of contributory negligence, whereas the claimant in the second action laboured under no such handicap. But whatever may be the explanation of the discrepancy between the cases, it is clear that *The Wagon Mound* is not such a terrifying decision for claimants as it was at first thought to be. Certainly it does not mean that the *precise* facts which happened have to be foreseeable before the event.

> **Hughes v Lord Advocate [1963] AC 837:** Hughes, an eight-year-old boy, was playing in a temporary shelter left by council workers digging up the road. He accidentally knocked over a paraffin lamp, which fell down an open access hole: the paraffin effervesced, and there was a fuel-air explosion which injured Hughes. Held: the harm to Hughes was of a foreseeable type, and it was unnecessary for the extent of a foreseeable type of harm to be foreseeable.

Accordingly, the modern rule is sometimes stated to be that while the *type* of loss must be foreseeable, its *extent* need not be, nor need the precise manner of its infliction. Nonetheless, this is a rather flexible criterion.

> **Jolley v Sutton London Borough Council [2000] 3 All ER 409:** A boat was abandoned on council land. Jolley (14 years old) and a friend decided to repair it; they jacked it

> up and began work. It fell on Jolley, causing severe spinal injuries. Held: the boat was an allurement to children, and therefore the council were in breach of duty to leave it there. While the conduct of Jolley was hard to guess beforehand, nonetheless all loss flowing from the failure to remove the boat was recoverable.

The narrower view of the Court of Appeal, that an attempt to repair the boat was unforeseeable, was rejected. The range of uses to which the claimant could put it without allowing the council to escape liability extended to 'whatever use the rich fantasy life of children might suggest' (Lord Hoffmann).

Different doctrinal labels

10.31 Very often, essentially the same argument about liability can be put in various different ways, using different terminology. Where the defendant injures the claimant in circumstances where it is pretty amazing that the claimant was affected by the defendant's activities, it is common to discuss the issue as being 'whether the claimant was too remote a victim'. But equally the issue might be discussed under the rubric of whether the defendant was in breach of duty to the claimant at all. For example, the 'rescuer' cases have this ambiguous quality (**3.31**). It is usually completely unimportant which classification is adopted. I treat denials that the claimant was in any way a foreseeable victim of the defendant's activities as a denial of duty, rather than an assertion of remoteness. But this is purely a point about the arrangement of the book: if they were treated as 'remoteness' cases, as they are by many writers, the result would not be that the law was stated differently, but merely that it was stated in a different order. Again, where the defendant's argument is that the chain of events leading from the defendant's conduct to the claimant's loss is too long and convoluted, in many situations it makes little difference whether we say that the claimant's loss is 'too remote' or whether we say it is 'not caused' by the defendant's tort. In this treatment, 'remoteness' and 'causation' are initially treated as separate notions, but the major part of the text treats them together.

A common talking point here is the famous New York case of *Palsgraf v Long Island Railroad Co* 59 ALR 1253 (1928), where guards employed by the defendant railroad were careless in helping a passenger on to a train, just as it was pulling out of the station. A package was dropped. Unfortunately it contained fireworks, and the resulting explosion injured the claimant (who was some distance away) by knocking over a set of scales standing next to her. No doubt liability would be refused in England, just as it was refused by Cardozo J in the New York Court of Appeals; but on what ground? No duty? No breach of duty? Remoteness? Insufficient causation? Lack of 'proximity'? Each solution has its supporters.

Direct physical consequences of the defendant's conduct

10.32 As a generalization, if the defendant is in breach of duty to the claimant, the defendant is liable for direct consequences of the defendant's behaviour, except where the type of loss which occurred was of an unforeseeable type.

> **Doughty v Turner Manufacturing Co [1964] 1 QB 518:** A foundry worker accidentally knocked the asbestos lid of a cauldron into the molten metal in the cauldron itself. After a few minutes, an unforeseeable and violent chemical reaction between the metal and the asbestos took place, showering Doughty, who was working underneath, with molten metal. Held: the foundry owners were not liable for this unforeseen event.

Nonetheless, a broad view is taken of the 'type' of loss and, if the type is the same, the extent does not matter.

> **Vacwell Engineering Co v BDH Chemicals [1971] 1 QB 88:** BDH delivered chemicals to Vacwell, without a warning that they would explode on contact with water. One of Vacwell's employees put them in a sink, and there was an explosion of immense proportions. Held: BDH was liable for the whole loss.

> **H Parsons (Livestock) v Uttley Ingham & Co [1978] QB 791:** Through its breach of contract when supplying farm equipment, Uttley Ingham poisoned Parsons' pigs. It was foreseeable that the pigs would be ill as a result, but the death of most of the herd was unforeseeable. Held (on the assumption that remoteness rules were the same in contract and in tort): the entire loss was recoverable.

Remoteness and 'mere matters of assessment'

10.33 What is sometimes treated as a variant on the 'type and extent' rule, but is perhaps better treated as a distinct notion, is that matters of mere assessment are not subject to a remoteness test. So if the defendant negligently smashes the claimant's vase, the defendant is liable to pay for a replacement, even if (unforeseeably) it turns out to be an exceptionally valuable antique. Or if the defendant negligently runs over the claimant, who looks like a tramp, the claimant may recover for the consequences of the personal injury, without having to meet any argument that it was 'unforeseeable' that he was in fact remuneratively employed (*The Arpad* [1934] P 189, 202–3, Scrutton LJ). Most such cases can be explained by arguments about the 'range of foreseeable consequences' of the defendant's action, or considerations of the type of injury the defendant could reasonably foresee. But it seems that the claimant can recover whether or not those arguments could be made.

The 'thin skull' rule

10.34 Where the defendant is responsible for the infliction of personal injury on the claimant, and then because of some pre-existing condition, the damage is more extensive than could have been foreseen, the defendant is nonetheless liable for it all. The defendant must 'take his victim as he finds him', and cannot protest that it was unreasonable for the claimant to have such a 'thin skull' or such a delicate constitution.

> ***Bradford v Robinson Rentals* [1967] 1 All ER 267:** Robinson Rentals sent out Bradford, an employee, in freezing conditions, in a van without a heater. Bradford sustained severe frostbite. Held: Robinson Rentals was liable for the full extent of his injury.

> ***Smith v Leech Brain & Co* [1962] 2 QB 405:** Smith, a factory worker, was burnt on the lip by a piece of molten metal, in an accident for which his employer was responsible. It turned out that Smith had a pre-malignant condition, which the burn turned into a full-blown and fatal cancer. Held: Smith's widow could sue for her husband's death.

There is an obvious incompatibility between the 'thin skull' approach and the general approach in *The Wagon Mound* [1961] AC 388, at least in cases where the claimant's injuries were of a type which could not have been foreseen before the event. One case has held that where the approaches conflict, there can be no recovery.

> ***Tremain v Pike* [1969] 3 All ER 1303:** Rats infested Pike's farm. They bit Tremain, one of Pike's employees. He then contracted Weil's disease, a rare condition transmitted through rats' urine. Held: Pike was not liable for this unforeseeable harm.

However, that case was decided relatively soon after *The Wagon Mound* [1961] AC 388 itself. Later decisions tend to fudge the issue, wavering between a 'thin skull' approach on the one hand, or liability for loss of a foreseeable 'type', broadly defined. Either approach is more generous to the claimant than was the court in *Tremain*, and it is very hard to see how the case can be regarded as rightly decided.

What happens after the accident

10.35 In many cases, the measure of the claimant's loss is immediately obvious. If the defendant destroys the claimant's car, the obvious measure is the value of the car, and often it will not matter what happens later on—the damages will be the same. However, sometimes the court looks further, particularly where the claimant says that further loss occurred at a later stage. Many concepts are used in this enquiry. We might ask whether any additional loss is 'too remote' or was 'unforeseeable', or question whether it was really caused by the defendant. In the following paragraphs I follow a thematic approach, rather than trying to isolate particular legal doctrines.

It is sometimes said that the results in these cases owe relatively little to legal doctrine and rather a lot to policy choices by the judges. However, even if that is a meaningful distinction to make, it is misleading, not least because it ascribes to the judges rather more clarity of thought than really seems to be the case.

The claimant's subsequent conduct

10.36 The defendant is liable for all foreseeable consequences of the tort. So the defendant does not cease to be liable for the consequences of the tort merely because the claimant has reacted in some way, even in a way which increases the loss suffered. However, the defendant may disclaim liability where the claimant 'breaks the chain of causation', or commits a *novus actus interveniens* (a 'new and intervening act'), or behaves in a manner which is unreasonable.

It is sometimes said that the claimant is under a *duty to mitigate the loss*, that is, a duty to take reasonable steps to reduce the loss, or at least prevent it from getting any larger. However, this is a very confusing way of putting it. The claimant is not under a *duty* in any normal sense: the claimant commits no legal wrong by being extravagant. However, the claimant is not entitled to be extravagant *at the defendant's expense*. The defendant can therefore refuse to pay any expenses which the claimant could readily have avoided.

Reasonable response to the accident

10.37 Where the claimant's increased loss is the result of the claimant's own decisions in the wake of the accident, the defendant's liability for the increased loss turns on the reasonableness of the claimant's behaviour. The need to contain the loss is one factor which ought reasonably to influence the claimant. But it is not the only one. The courts will not allow the defendant to be charged for items of expense which the claimant incurred unreasonably. Equally they do not expect the claimant to sacrifice *all* other considerations to the reduction of the bill which the defendant must pay.

> **McKew v Holland & Hannen & Cubitts (Scotland) [1969] 3 All ER 1621:** As a result of negligence for which Holland was responsible, McKew suffered an injury to his leg which occasionally made it give way. McKew suffered further injury when he collapsed while descending some stairs, which he had tried to do without assistance. Held: Holland was not responsible for the further injury.

> **Wieland v Cyril Lord Carpets [1969] 3 All ER 1006:** As a result of negligence for which Cyril Lord was responsible, Weiland had to wear a surgical collar, which made it hard for her to move her head, and hence to see around her. Held: Cyril Lord was liable for her further injuries when she fell over obstacles she could not see.

Doubt has been cast on *McKew*, in a case where the claimant lost a leg by the defendant's negligence, and subsequently tripped while attempting to fill his car's petrol tank without using either his prosthetic leg or sticks. Liability was found for the second injury, subject to a deduction of one-third for contributory negligence (*Spencer v Wincanton Holdings Ltd* [2009] EWCA Civ 1404).

Again, the courts almost never hold that rescuers are responsible for the injuries they suffer while rescuing (**3.31**). Indeed, anyone placed by the defendant's behaviour in a life-or-death situation where he must act quickly can plead that his behaviour was not, 'in the agony of the moment', unreasonable—no matter how foolish it can be made to appear in retrospect.

Mental disorder

10.38   Where the defendant's tort interfered with the claimant's mental stability or mental health, subsequent activity by the claimant will not necessarily be judged by ordinary standards of reasonableness, but is judged by more generous standards of 'foreseeability'.

> *Pigney v Pointer's Transport Services* **[1957] 2 All ER 807:** After a head injury for which Pointer's was liable, Pigney became a depressive, and ultimately committed suicide. Held: his widow could sue Pointer's in respect of his death.

Pigney has been doubted, as dating from a time before the requirement of foreseeability was firmly established, but on similar facts the House of Lords has now reached the same conclusion (*Corr v IBC Vehicles* [2008] UKHL 13).

> *Brice v Brown* **[1984] 1 All ER 997:** Brice had a hysterical personality disorder, though it was fairly moderate and well controlled. After suffering nervous shock for which Brown was responsible, her condition worsened considerably, including various examples of bizarre behaviour, a suicide attempt, and three admissions to mental hospital. Held: everything that had happened was within the range of the foreseeable, and Brown was liable for her condition.

A controversial decision holds the defendant liable even for the consequences of very serious criminality by the claimant.

> *Meah v McCreamer* **[1985] 1 All ER 367:** Meah suffered brain damage as a result of an accident resulting from McCreamer's drunken driving. This led to a personality disorder, and Meah ended up as a category 'A' prisoner for life following a succession of sexual assaults. Held: Meah's damages could include an element to compensate him for his imprisonment.

This is a highly controversial result. The verdict left Meah considerably richer than most convicted rapists. This prompted his victims to sue him for assault, and they obtained damages (*W v Meah, D v Meah* [1986] 1 All ER 935). Meah then sued McCreamer again, claiming that these additional sums were also recoverable. However, Woolf J held them too remote (*Meah v McCreamer (No 2)* [1986] 1 All ER 943), a result which it is hard to reconcile with the first ruling. (The correctness of *Meah (No 1)* is now in doubt, though on grounds not relevant here: see **11.31**.) There is similar judicial ambivalence in cases where the claimant divorces, and alleges that his divorce is traceable to personality changes he suffered as a result of the defendant's negligence. In *Jones v Jones* [1985] QB 704, this argument was accepted, but in *Pritchard v JH Cobden* [1988] Fam 22, *Jones* was overruled. There are serious conceptual difficulties in these cases, not least because of the conflict between tort's usual assumption that people are responsible for their own actions, and the very clear psychiatric evidence that these particular claimants were not.

Financial decisions

10.39 The claimant must act reasonably when taking decisions which affect the amount the claimant will subsequently be claiming.

> ***Patel v Hooper & Jackson* [1999] 1 All ER 992:** Patel bought a house on the strength of a valuation report provided by H&J. However, he realized almost immediately that the house was uninhabitable. Held: damages for the negligent report could include the cost of making the house habitable, and the claimant's reasonable costs in extricating himself from the transaction, which would include the reasonable cost of accommodation elsewhere until the house could be sold. But the damages could not include expenses which the claimant would have incurred anyway, such as mortgage payments on the house he bought next.

> ***Darbishire v Warran* [1963] 3 All ER 310:** Warran damaged Darbishire's car, valued at £85. Darbishire had it repaired at a cost of £180; he thought it impossible to get a replacement for £85, though it seems that there would have been other similar vehicles available at that price. Held: he could recover no more than £85.

The limits of the latter ruling are unclear. It appears that the claimant had simply not looked for a replacement at all, and accordingly the court was unimpressed with his argument that none was available. It also seems that the court was unsympathetic to any argument that he attached sentimental value to the particular vehicle; though the court suggested that it might be different if the vehicle in question were unique (as in *O'Grady v Westminster Scaffolding* [1962] 2 Lloyd's Rep 238). It is unclear when, if ever, the claimant is reasonably allowed to be motivated by non-financial considerations.

> ***Admiralty Commissioners v SS Amerika* [1917] AC 38:** A submarine was sunk, with the loss of all crew, by the negligence of the *SS Amerika*. One item of loss claimed was the

pensions paid by the Navy to the crew's widows. Held: these payments were voluntary payments, which could not be added to the damages.

A rather different sort of case is *Calvert v William Hill Credit Ltd* [2008] EWCA Civ 1427, where the claimant, a compulsive gambler, asked the defendants to exclude him from telephone gambling for a period. In accordance with their code of practice on the matter, the defendants said they would do so, but failed to enforce their own policy. The claimant gambled repeatedly with the defendants and lost. Could he sue them to recoup amounts gambled? The Court of Appeal held not. They were prepared to find that the defendants owed a duty and were in breach of it. However, if the defendants had complied with their duty, the consequence would simply have been that the claimant would have lost his money with another bookmaker. Accordingly, no causal connection was shown and the claim failed.

The impecunious claimant

10.40 Perhaps the claimant chooses a relatively expensive solution to the problem caused by the defendant's negligence, because the claimant cannot afford the immediate costs associated with a cheaper solution. For example, if the claimant is forced into borrowing large amounts of money in a hurry, the total amount the claimant will ultimately have to pay is likely to be more than if the claimant could have paid the immediate expenses out of the claimant's own capital. The view was traditionally taken that the claimant cannot pass these higher expenses on to the defendant (*Owners of Dredger Liesbosch v Owners of SS Edison* [1933] AC 449).

But the *Liesbosch* rule was always rather hard to justify, as it seemed an unprincipled exception to the general attitude that tortfeasors must take their victims as they find them. The rule was whittled away in a succession of decisions (e.g. *Dodd Properties (Kent) v Canterbury City Council* [1980] 1 All ER 928; *Mattocks v Mann* [1993] RTR 13) and has now been repudiated by the House of Lords:

> **Lagden v O'Connor [2003] UKHL 64:** Lagden's car was damaged in an accident which was wholly the fault of O'Connor. While Lagden's car was being repaired, he obtained the free use of another vehicle by a contract with a credit hire company, under which they would recover their costs by suing O'Connor. In a long-term perspective this was a relatively expensive way for Lagden to acquire a replacement car, but his parlous financial position left him with no alternative. Held: Lagden's full loss was recoverable unless O'Connor could show that there had been a cheaper alternative open to him, which she could not do.

Subsequent conduct of third parties

10.41 Where the defendant causes injury to the claimant, and subsequent activity by others (not under the defendant's control) makes matters worse, the claimant may sometimes argue that the defendant is nonetheless responsible for the whole. Perhaps it is only because of the defendant's activity that the other parties had the chance to injure the claimant's interests at all. As noted above, the courts are generally reluctant to find the defendant liable for wrongdoing committed by others (see e.g. **1.31**). So it is not unusual for the courts to hold that the third party intervention is a *novus actus interveniens*, or is for some other reason not something for which the defendant can be held responsible.

Criminal acts

10.42 No formal line is drawn between lawful and unlawful third party conduct, but nonetheless the courts are highly likely to hold that third party criminality breaks the chain of causation.

> **Lamb v Camden London Borough Council [1981] QB 625:** Negligence by the local council in relaying a water main led to subsidence in Lamb's house. Her tenants deserted it and squatters soon moved in. Held: the council was not liable for damage done by squatters.

Each of the judges in the case gave a different reason, and the case is a puzzling one, especially since it is hard to deny foreseeability. The court's reluctance to hold anyone liable for the uncontrolled acts of squatters was palpable. But such claims do not inevitably fail.

> **Ward v Cannock Chase District Council [1985] 3 All ER 537:** The council allowed its property to fall into disrepair. It collapsed, damaging Ward's house, which had to be abandoned. The council accepted responsibility, but did not proceed with repairs at any great speed. Ward's house, left abandoned, was vandalized. Held: the council was liable.

Scott J distinguished *Lamb* on the ground that the vandalization of the claimant's property was 'virtually certain' unless the council acted with great speed ([1985] 3 All ER 537, 553).

Criminal acts as supervening cause?

10.43 A slightly unusual argument was deployed in *Baker v Willoughby* [1970] AC 467. The defendant injured the claimant's leg by poor driving. The claimant permanently lost about 30 per cent of the use of the leg, and in normal circumstances would have been entitled to damages to reflect this loss for the rest of his life. However, three years after the accident, the claimant was attacked by armed robbers, who further injured the leg, so that it had to be amputated. The defendant admitted liability for restricted use of the leg for three years, but suggested that after that time there was no further liability. The claimant no longer had a leg at all, and to award him money for having *restricted* use of the leg was to compensate him for a loss which he had not, in the event, suffered. In other words, the argument was that the criminal attack on the claimant was a 'supervening' cause, of such proportions that it made the earlier history of injury by the defendant merely past history.

The argument failed, and the claimant kept the damages for 30 per cent loss of use for the duration of his life. In other words, the claimant recovered damages for having only restricted use of his leg, when in fact (through no fault of the defendant's) he had no leg at all. The case is unusual, and the reasons for sympathy to the claimant are obvious enough. Perhaps the simplest explanation of the case is that as the claimant's misfortunes were entirely the result of two torts, all his loss should be recoverable from the tortfeasors together; yet the robbers could not be sued for the loss of a good leg, for they had only deprived the claimant of a 70 per cent-useful leg. (The question of the robbers' liability was not academic, since it could then have been recovered from the CICB: see **2.6**.) Nonetheless, the reasoning in the case is rather obscure, and the result has been criticized.

Responses to the crisis precipitated by the defendant

10.44   By contrast, where the third party conduct was an attempt to deal with the problem caused by the defendant's own negligence, the courts will not be quick to call it unreasonable or unforeseeable.

> **The Oropesa [1943] P 32:** Bad navigation by the master of the *Oropesa* caused it to collide with the *Manchester Regiment*. The master of the *Manchester Regiment*, which was badly damaged, set out in a lifeboat to talk to the master of the *Oropesa* about saving it. The lifeboat capsized, drowning the occupants; the widow of one of them sued the owners of the *Oropesa*. Held: the decision to set out in a lifeboat had been a reasonable response to the situation, and did not break the chain of causation.

The courts have been reluctant to hold the defendant liable for the consequences of bad medical treatment in response to an injury caused by the defendant, perhaps because it is always open to the claimant to sue the doctor. Nonetheless, where it must have been obvious that the claimant would need medical treatment as a result of the defendant's tort, the defendant may sometimes be held liable.

> **Robinson v Post Office [1974] 2 All ER 737:** Robinson suffered a cut for which his employer was responsible. A doctor gave him an anti-tetanus injection, to which Robinson suffered a violent allergic reaction. Held: Robinson's employers were liable for all injuries.

Market movements

10.45 Where the defendant gives the claimant bad advice in a financial matter, yet much of the claimant's loss is due to subsequent market movements, it appears that that element of the claimant's loss will not be recoverable.

> **South Australia Asset Management Corpn v York Montague [1997] AC 191:** SAAM lent considerable sums of money to borrowers offering property as security. It would not have made the loans but for the over-valuation of the property by YM. The lenders defaulted on the loans, and SAAM could not recoup all its money because of the inadequate value of the property. Its loss was further compounded by a steep fall in the property market. Held: SAAM could not recover from YM any element of loss fairly attributable to the fall in the property market. In any event, SAAM could recover no more than the difference between the sum lent and the true value of the property at the time the loan took place.

Expressing this in algebraic terms, let:

A = actual loss, i.e. (amounts paid out by SAAM)−(amounts eventually recovered);

V = the valuation initially placed on the property by YM; and

V* = the actual value of the property at the time YM valued it.

Then the amount recoverable is the lesser of (A) and (V–V*). The actual loss is (A), but there is an artificial cap on the damages to prevent defendants being held liable for the effect of market conditions, for which they have no more responsibility than does anyone else.

This leads on to a further question: What if, under the doctrine of contributory negligence (**11.17** below), the court regards the claimant as partly responsible for the loss? Suppose that the court assesses the defendant's responsibility as r (with $r = 1$ meaning that it was all the defendant's fault, $r = \frac{1}{2}$ meaning that the claimant and the defendant were equally to blame, etc.). A naïve approach would be to say that we simply calculate the figure the court would have granted had the defendant been wholly to blame, and apply a factor for contributory negligence, so that the claimant recovers:

$r \times$ (lesser of (A) and (V–V*))

But this ignores the point that (A) is the true loss, and (V–V*) merely an artificial cap. The true measure, the Lords have now told us (*Platform Home Loans v Oyston Shipways* [2000] 2 AC 190), is:

lesser of $((r \times A)$ and (V–V*))

This is, unfortunately, a complex area of law, even for specialists.

Benefits subsequently received by the claimant

10.46 The claimant suffers injury; one consequence of the injury is that the claimant receives money or other benefits as compensation. Should these sums go to reduce the defendant's liability to the claimant? In principle, the answer is 'Yes'; the defendant need only compensate the claimant for loss actually suffered. To the extent that the loss has been put right by others, it is no longer something for which the claimant deserves compensation from the defendant. However, there are two exceptions, both of uncertain extent.

Insurance and analogous benefits

10.47 Where a benefit the claimant receives is an entitlement for which the claimant previously paid, then the sum does not reduce damages. So if the claimant pays for private insurance against accidents, sums received from the insurer do not reduce the claimant's damages. This rule is clear enough where the claimant deliberately purchased and paid for the insurance, but it is unclear how far outside that it stretches.

> **Parry v Cleaver [1970] AC 1:** Cleaver's bad driving injured Parry, a policeman. This resulted in Parry's premature retirement from the force. Cleaver suggested that Parry's damages should be reduced to reflect the invalidity pension payable to Parry in respect of the years before Parry would have retired in normal circumstances. Held: this sum should not be taken into account to reduce damages.

The decision is a controversial one, reached only by a majority. In justifying the decision, the majority emphasized that the entitlement was closely analogous to private insurance. It was therefore unfair, it was said, to penalize the claimant because the claimant merely takes the insurance as part of his or her remuneration package, rather than taking a higher salary and paying for insurance out of that. However, this approach has not struck all the judges as realistic, especially if there is no reason to suppose that the claimant had the option of taking the money in higher salary rather than insurance benefits. Certainly the courts will not allow the claimant to invoke the rule in respect of sick pay (*Hussain v New Taplow Paper Mills* [1988] AC 514), and why that situation should be any different from *Parry* is not altogether clear. And again, the claimant cannot apply the rule to insurance paid for entirely by the employer (*Gaca v Pirelli General plc* [2004] EWCA Civ 373). The current situation is awkward, and seems to reflect an illogical compromise between incompatible principles.

> **Longden v British Coal Corpn [1998] AC 653:** Longden, 36, suffered injuries at work which forced him to retire. Under the company's pension scheme, he was then entitled to a lump sum of £10,000 and an annual pension of £5,000. Had he continued in his job

until age 60 he would have received a lump sum of £33,000 and an annual pension of £11,000. Was he entitled to claim these latter sums as damages, or was he entitled only to the *difference* between those sums and the amounts he actually received? Held: in respect of the period before Longden reached 60, he need not give credit for benefits received. For the period after, however, he would be overcompensated if he received more than the *net* loss of pension, and so the court would reduce his damages to avoid overlap.

Where the claimant is insured against the very sort of loss which the defendant causes, typically the insurers will seek to be *subrogated* to the claimant's claim—that is, they will stand in the claimant's shoes for legal purposes, and claim the damages which the claimant could have claimed. In cases of that sort, the claimant has in fact been compensated, and the real quarrel is between the claimant's insurer and the defendant. Can the defendant argue that in those circumstances the claimant has in reality suffered no loss, and so there is no claim for the insurers to be subrogated to? Usually the answer will be 'No', but the real question is as to the purpose of the insurance.

> **Europe Mortgage Co v Halifax Estate Agencies [1996] EGCS 84:** EM lent money on security, but subsequently claimed they would never have done so but for the negligent valuation of the security by HEA. HEA pointed out that EM had already been fully compensated for this under their mortgage indemnity guarantee insurance. Held: this insurance was taken for EM's benefit, not HEA's, and should therefore be ignored.

An analogous situation occurs where the claimant happens to make a gain as a result of a legislative rule.

> **Dimond v Lovell [2002] 1 AC 384:** Lovell negligently damaged Dimond's car. While it was being repaired, Dimond hired a replacement, under a legal agreement by which the hirers were to be paid, if at all, out of the damages Lovell was found liable to pay. However, the hire agreement failed to comply with statutory regulations, with the result that Dimond was not liable to pay anything for the hired car. Lovell argued that, as Dimond had in fact obtained the use of the hire car for nothing, she had not suffered any loss in that regard. Held: to allow full recovery would in effect be to allow the hirers to recover hire, and thus to subvert the statutory rule that such agreements were invalid. Accordingly, nothing was recoverable under this head.

Friends and family

10.48 Where the claimant receives money freely given by others after the accident, and which was meant to benefit the claimant rather than to reduce the defendant's liability, then it will usually be treated as having that effect. It will accordingly be ignored in calculating the damages the defendant must pay. The doctrine is simple enough where the claimant receives cash or other gifts from family or relatives; these sums are simply ignored in calculating the claimant's damages. More complicated considerations enter when the gift consists of services.

> **Donnelly v Joyce [1974] QB 454:** Donnelly, aged six, was injured by Joyce in such a way as to require regular re-bandaging of the wound. This was done by Donnelly's mother, who gave up her nursing job in order to find time to do it. Held: her loss of wages was recoverable as an additional item of damages by Donnelly.

It is obvious that torts involving personal injury will have some impact on the claimant's family as well as the claimant personally. Nonetheless it is not usual to regard them as victims of the tort, in the eye of the law. However, the reasoning in *Donnelly* was considered too artificial in later cases. The loss had in reality been incurred by his mother, and the law should recognize that: it should 'enable the voluntary carer to receive proper recompense for his or her services' (*Hunt v Severs* [1994] 2 All ER 385, 394, Lord Bridge). One consequence of this is that where such damages are awarded, they are held on trust for the carer, rather than belonging to the claimant beneficially. However, another consequence is to undermine the whole concept, for if these are 'really' damages to give compensation to the carer, how can this be justified, given that no tort against the carer is established? This thought seems to have been a factor in a controversial case.

> **Hardwick v Hudson [1999] 3 All ER 426:** Hardwick was a partner in a garage business; his wife worked there for one day a week. When he was injured through Hudson's negligence, his wife temporarily took over his management functions for no additional pay; the business continued to do well. Hardwick claimed the reasonable value of his wife's services as damages from Hudson. Held: the cases on personal injury care should not be extended to a case such as this. Unlike those cases, the services provided by the wife were such that they would normally be provided under contract, and there was no public policy in encouraging their provision free of charge.

So the claimant does not recover on those facts, though it seems that he would have done had he entered into a formal employment contract with his wife, under which a salary for additional work was fixed. This seems artificial, to say the least.

An even more controversial case is where the defendant is a member of the claimant's family, and provides part of the care the claimant needs after the accident. In *Hunt v Severs* [1994] 2 All ER 385 the claimant fell off the defendant's motorcycle, on which she had been riding pillion; the defendant was held responsible for her injuries. The claimant and the defendant later lived together, and eventually married. The defendant in fact provided much of the nursing care the claimant needed.

Should the claimant be able to include an item in her damages claim for nursing care, or could the defendant's insurers retort that the claimant had in effect already received compensation for that through the defendant's care for her? The House of Lords ultimately held that she had no claim. The claimant could not force the defendant (or in reality, the defendant's insurer) to pay for nursing care which had in fact been provided by the defendant in person.

Subsequent natural events

10.49 Where the defendant has caused loss to the claimant, the courts are in principle prepared to hold the defendant responsible also for subsequent physical consequences. Nonetheless, there comes a point at which they decide that the claimant's problem is no longer one for which the defendant can fairly be asked to take responsibility. The defendant's tort becomes a mere part of the history, not a ground for further liability. The argument is usually made in the form that later supervening events 'submerge' the loss originally caused by the claimant, making it irrelevant to what follows.

> *Carslogie Steamship Co v Royal Norwegian Government* **[1952] AC 292:** The *Heimgar* was damaged when it collided with the *Carslogie*, in an accident which was the fault of the *Carslogie*. The *Heimgar* headed into port for repairs, but was further damaged in stormy weather, necessitating further repairs. The *Heimgar* would have taken ten days to repair, but because of the storm, repairs took 30 days. The collision damage and the storm damage were repaired concurrently. The owners of The *Heimgar* claimed for loss of profit over ten days. Held: no damages for loss of profit were recoverable at all.

The Lords stressed that the storm had turned the ship from a seaworthy, albeit damaged, ship into a ship that would not be seaworthy until 30 days' worth of repairs were completed, and accordingly they regarded the storm as wiping out the earlier cause of loss. The defendant's tort had become a mere part of the history, rather than a cause operating in the present. The same point has also come up in relation to personal injury.

> *Jobling v Associated Dairies* **[1982] AC 794:** As a result of an injury for which his employers were responsible, Jobling suffered partial disablement, being fit only for sedentary work. Three years after his accident, he was struck down by a spinal condition that made him unfit for any work at all. Held: his employers were not responsible for his injuries after the date when the spinal condition supervened.

There is much insistence in the case that the claimant is expected to bear the ups and downs of life without attempting to pass them on to others. The problem in the case is caused by the factual uncertainties involved. If it had been clear that the claimant's spinal condition predated the original accident and was all along inevitable, the employer would certainly not have been liable (**10.21**). If, by contrast, it could have been shown that it was an indirect and unexpected consequence of the work injury, then the employer would probably have been liable under the 'thin skull' rule (**10.34**). As it was, it was very hard to know what was going on. The result is easier to understand if we say, as some of the law lords did, that the total disability was 'inevitable' regardless of the work accident. But it is hard to see how the evidence justified that.

Jobling is obviously similar to *Baker v Willoughby* [1970] AC 467 (**10.43**) where, however, the supervening cause was the activities of armed robbers who attacked the claimant. The Lords there had refused to treat the legal amputation after the robbers' attack as 'supervening'. *Baker* was criticized in *Jobling*, but most of the criticism seems to miss the mark. It is not true, for example, that *Baker* created a risk of double compensation if the claimant had claimed against both sets of tortfeasors. The robbers did not deprive the claimant of a healthy leg and would not have been made to pay damages as if they had. If the result of *Baker* is wrong, then the claimant would fail to recover the total loss suffered by suing all the tortfeasors, even though the tortfeasors' activities were the sole cause of the loss. Are the two cases consistent? They appear both to be still law, with the (rather unsatisfactory) distinction between them being that in *Baker* the allegedly supervening cause was tortious, whereas in *Jobling* it was not.

Subsequent events: taxation

10.50 If the claimant loses earnings as a result of the tort, almost certainly the claimant is also relieved of a tax liability. In other words, if the claimant loses £10,000 in earnings, then the claimant does not have to pay the tax on £10,000. And so to give the claimant £10,000 in damages may amount to overcompensation. The inevitability of taxation is proverbial, and so it would be surprising if the effect of the tax system on the claimant's loss was regarded as unforeseeable. However, there are substantial practical difficulties in asking what the claimant's tax liability would have been in hypothetical circumstances, or which part of the claimant's existing bill is attributable to the defendant's tort. The case law is accordingly somewhat confused. However, there is one clear and common case where the courts will act. When the claimant is deprived of some gain on which the claimant would certainly have been taxed, but the damages the defendant pays will certainly not be taxed at all, then the claimant's damages must be reduced to reflect this. So if the claimant claims for lost earnings, then the claimant will receive the amount the claimant would have received *after* tax (*British Transport Commission v Gourley* [1956] AC 185).

Personal injury damages

10.51 The assessment of personal injury damages might seem one of the most uncontroversial areas of the law of tort. Once liability for the claimant's personal injuries has been established, all that is left is the mechanical collation of information on the claimant's resulting disability and its consequences.

Yet the stated goal of providing full compensation for the claimant is taken for granted, rather than rationally demonstrated. Why should the defendant have to pay for all the consequences of the wrong? Much press criticism of tort is ultimately aimed at this feature of the law, reflecting a sentiment that damages should reflect other features, such as the defendant's relative blameworthiness. And when we compare tort with other methods for securing just compensation— insurance, social security—tort's goal of full compensation begins to stand out as rather unusual. Worse, the goal is impossible. The court cannot restore to the claimant what the claimant has lost, but only give money. Where what is lost is non-pecuniary—freedom from pain, enjoyment of life, freedom of movement—it is obvious that no one sum of money will ever be quite right. Even where the loss is pecuniary, there are numerous problems of assessment. Moreover, it is never possible to know quite what would have happened but for the tort, or indeed what has happened with it except by waiting for events. Yet the whole point of the award is lost if it cannot be made within a reasonable amount of time following the accident. Many guesses, some of them quite arbitrary, must be made in the course of estimating the likely consequences of an accident. As one law lord has commented:

> The award is final; it is not susceptible to review as the future unfolds, substituting fact for estimate. Knowledge of the future being denied to mankind, so much of the award as is to be attributed to future loss and suffering—in many cases the major part of the award— will almost surely be wrong. There is really only one certainty: the future will prove the award to be either too high or too low (*Lim Poh Choo v Camden and Islington Area Health Authority* [1980] AC 174, 183, Lord Scarman).

Indeed, this understates the difficulty, because while the claimant will eventually know what the future holds, the claimant may never know what it would have held but for the accident.

The process of assessment

10.52 Damages are today calculated by a judge sitting alone, applying relatively fixed principles, and subject to appeal. This is a recent state of affairs. Before the 1930s, it was still common for juries to set damages awards, and they were not completely excluded from such cases until the 1960s (*Ward v James* [1966] 1 QB 273). It is still theoretically possible for a jury to be summoned in such cases, but it is almost unheard of (see *H v Ministry of Defence* [1991] 2 QB 103). And it was not until *Jefford v Gee* [1970] 2 QB 130 that judges were required to itemize the awards they made. It then became the orthodoxy that 'plaintiff and defendant alike are entitled to know what is the sum assessed for each relevant head of damage and thus to be able on appeal to challenge any error in the assessments' (*George v Pinnock* [1973] 1 WLR 118, 126, Sachs LJ).

Today, the principles on which judges should act are stated with a fair degree of precision, though a degree of elasticity is well recognized. The appeal courts are unwilling to alter awards on appeal simply because it is rather more or less than the members of the court would themselves have awarded. Consistency in practice results from past cases, especially as collected in the sizeable reference work *Kemp and Kemp on Damages*. The Judicial Studies Board has attempted to increase consistency in the award of damages.

Consistency, of course, is not the same thing as justifiability. Not all commentators agree that the principles of damages 'have few parallels outside the world of witchcraft and sorcery' (Conaghan and Mansell *The Wrongs of Tort* (1993) 56), but it is fair to say that few are entirely happy with them either.

Assessment in practice

10.53 Very few cases come to court, and the tort system would be unworkable if they did. In practice, therefore, most awards are settlements reached between the claimant's solicitor and the defendant's legal department or insurers. Most of the claims are for a relatively small amount. Large claims, while not irrelevant to practice, do not constitute a very large proportion of it.

There is considerable delay involved in the system. A survey conducted in 2007 found that claims take, on average, two years to settle. Unsurprisingly, therefore, the tort system cannot provide help at an early stage. For that, the injured have to rely on sick pay and the social security system. The superior bargaining strength of defendants puts them in a strong position vis-à-vis claimants, and therefore in a position to drive damages levels down. This is not in itself a ground for criticizing the system, as strong centralized defendants are in a better position to meet damages awards than would be a more disparate grouping. But it is a point to be borne in mind when individual judicial decisions are criticized as too generous to claimants.

The lump sum

10.54 Damages are nearly always in the form of a lump sum, representing all of the claimant's loss. This sum will be received some time after the injury itself, and may represent items of loss sustained before and after the award. Where the money is being received later than the injury for which it compensates, interest may be payable, though the rates are rather low:

- Provable ('special') pecuniary losses attract interest from the date of the injury, at half the special interest rate for money paid into court.

- Non-pecuniary losses usually attract 2–3 per cent interest from the date the claim form was served.

Where money is paid early, as is common for compensation for injuries with long-term consequences, the damages will be lower to reflect this, though the calculations are rather crude. Where loss is recurrent, such as a loss of wages over a long period, the courts calculate a sum representing losses for a typical year (the 'multiplicand') and then select an appropriate 'multiplier' for the number of years over which the injury is suffered. This multiplier will usually be much less than the number of years involved. The claimant is expected to invest the money to secure a reasonable return over the future years, and the multiplier will also be reduced to reflect various contingencies.

Whether this rather crude technique is adequate is a matter of some debate. It has been suggested that the courts should fix the multiplier by reference to official statistics of mortality rather than guesswork, and this is now the norm, using the 'Ogden Tables'. There was controversy in the 1970s over whether inflation should expressly be taken into account in the calculations. The courts ultimately ruled that it should not, on the argument that if the claimant invests the damages wisely the effect of inflation should be offset (*Lim Poh Choo v Camden and Islington Area Health Authority* [1980] AC 174).

Avoiding the inconveniences of a lump sum

10.55 Various devices have been proposed for avoiding the disadvantages of a single lump sum. The Pearson Commission recommended in 1978 that the courts should be empowered to order periodical payments, adjustable in the light of changing circumstances. But this has only slowly been acted on. Various measures are in place:

- The court may order a *split trial*, to determine whether the defendant is liable, but then postponing any question of the amount of liability. This is most obviously appropriate where the claimant's prognosis is very unclear.

- The court may order an *interim payment* to the claimant where liability has been established or the court thinks it likely that it will be, so long as the defendant is an insurer, a public authority, or otherwise capable of making the payment. The court may order payment of a 'reasonable percentage' of the claimant's likely eventual claim.

- Where there is a chance that the claimant's condition will deteriorate seriously in the future, the claimant may claim *provisional damages*, assessed on the assumption that the chance will not materialize. The claimant has liberty to apply to the court again if it does (Supreme Court Act 1981, s 32A, inserted by Administration of Justice Act 1982, s 6). However, the courts have ruled that this provision can only be used in the case of 'clear and severable' risks, rather than in the more normal case where the claimant's existing condition seems likely to degenerate. So where the claimant has arthritis caused by the defendant's tort, the risk that the claimant will eventually have to stop work entirely is a matter for ordinary techniques rather than provisional damages (*Willson v Ministry of Defence* [1991] 1 All ER 638). If the claimant later dies, there may be a further claim (Damages Act 1996, s 3).

- If both claimant and defendant consent, any award of damages can include an order for *periodical payments*; in relation to future pecuniary loss, the court may make such an order without consent, and indeed is under a duty to consider whether it should do so (Damages Act 1996, s 2, as amended by Courts Act 2003, s 100). The legislation provides for the amount of the order to rise as prices rise, in accordance with the Retail Price Index (RPI), though in appropriate cases the court can substitute a different rule, such as that an award shall be tied to an index of wages rather than of prices (*Flora v Wakom (Heathrow)* [2006] EWCA Civ 1103; and general guidance on how such cases were to be approached can be found in *Thompstone v Tameside and Glossop Acute Services NHS Trust* [2008] EWCA Civ 5). If there is shown to be a chance that the claimant's condition may change significantly in the future, the court may now (under the Damages (Variation of Periodical Payments) Order 2005) provide for the order to be a variable one, which may be modified at a later stage to reflect such a change if it occurs.

For various reasons, however, none of these powers are much used. The lump sum is the norm.

Investments and structured settlements

10.56 A basic dilemma here is that the defendant will eventually pay a lump sum, but the claimant is being compensated not for the loss of a lump sum but for the loss of an income stream. The court assumes that the claimant will invest the lump sum, and that the stream of dividends from that investment will roughly compensate for the loss of income. It is assumed that the claimant's investments will be relatively safe, and inflation-free. But what rate of return will the court assume that this gives the claimant? The amount of the lump sum depends on what that rate is assumed to be. The courts presumed that a rate of about 4½ per cent would be available. The House of Lords then ruled that this was unrealistic, and that a rate of 3 per cent should normally be assumed (*Wells v Wells* [1999] 1 AC 345). Pro-claimant groups argued that even this was unrealistic, and that a figure of 2 per cent would be nearer the mark. The Lord Chancellor now has power to set a rate (Damages Act 1996, s 1), and in 2001 set it at 2½ per cent (see SI 2001/2301). There is much dissatisfaction over this rate, but the Court of Appeal has recently ruled that only on exceptional facts is it open to claimants to argue that the Lord Chancellor's rate is inappropriate (*Warriner v Warriner* [2002] EWCA Civ 81; *Cooke v United Bristol Healthcare NHS Trust* [2003] EWCA Civ 1370).

In general, tax is not payable on damages, or on sums received in settlement of personal injury claims. However, if the claimant uses the award to purchase a regular income, the claimant would usually expect to pay tax on that income. The tax liability can, however, often be avoided by a so-called 'structured settlement', under which the defendant pays a lump sum to purchase an annuity on the claimant's life, and passes on the periodic payments to the claimant. This arrangement has advantages to both sides. The claimant has a regular income without the administrative difficulties involved in buying an annuity personally, and the amounts received are not subject to tax as (by revenue concession) they are treated as payments of compensation. The defendant has the advantage of being able to treat the case as closed, its obligation being only to pass on the annuity payments as received. However, the system is far from perfect. The administrative burden on the defendant is still substantial. Moreover, it does not solve the problem of future uncertainties. It is possible to index-link annuities to avoid the risk of inflation, but it is not usually possible to buy annuities which vary with future contingencies such as the progress of the claimant's disease or the extent of the nursing care the claimant needs. Structured settlements have received a great deal of official encouragement, but the courts do not have any power to force structured settlements on parties who do not wish to agree to them. A proposal that they should be given this power has received official support, but has not yet been implemented.

Assessment: the live victim

10.57 Personal injury damages are calculated under different heads, in a standard way. Special damages compensate for specific items of pre-trial loss. General damages are roughly divisible into sums for injury to the claimant's feelings, sums for lost income, and future expenses. Certain benefits received or likely to be received in the future must be deducted from the total. In what follows, we will first assume that the claimant is still alive, or at least *was* alive in the period under consideration; the effect of the claimant's death is considered below (**10.66**).

Injury to feelings

10.58 This is commonly subdivided yet further, though it would be wrong to suppose that the division is very rigid, or very rigorously applied. Some commentators have fundamental difficulties with this head: it does not represent a loss of money, so how can money replace what is lost? However, the court has nothing else to give but money, and as such does its inadequate best to translate the claimant's injury into a precise sum.

- '*Pain and suffering*'. The pain the claimant has suffered is likely to account for the major part of the sum awarded. It is assumed that claimants who are unconscious are not in pain, and accordingly nothing is payable for any period of unconsciousness, however prolonged. The courts also generally refuse to give damages for pain and suffering to a claimant who died quickly, even in extreme pain (*Hicks v Chief Constable of the South Yorkshire Police* [1992] 2 All ER 65).

- '*Loss of the amenities of life*' or '*loss of faculty*'. This refers to loss of enjoyment of life, or of the possibility of enjoyment of life, as a result of the injury. Typically, awards emphasize deprivation of the chance to pursue a favourite hobby or pastime. Controversially, the courts have insisted that the compensation is for the loss of amenity, not for *knowledge* that the amenity has been lost. Accordingly even a claimant who has remained unconscious since the date of the accident can recover the full amount under this head (*H West & Son v Shephard* [1964] AC 326). There are arguments both ways over whether this should be so. It is hard to justify such damages if compensation is the sole aim. But if other goals are relevant, it might be argued that damages should not be reduced because the defendant has suffered a *more* severe injury—and indeed that the sum is as much to comfort the claimant's relatives as it is to comfort the claimant.

- '*Loss of expectation of life*'. Formerly, this was compensatable as a distinct item. However, this head of damages has been abolished by statute, which directs that the claimant's knowledge that his or her life has been cut short is to be counted as part of the pain and suffering arising from the injury (Administration of Justice Act 1982, s 1).

A single sum is usually awarded for all of these items, to reflect losses both pre- and post-trial. It will often not be necessary, and indeed it may be pointless, to insist on the precise subdivision of damages mentioned. So, for example, where the claimant is given damages for reduced likelihood of marriage following the accident, it is unnecessary to consider whether this is technically 'pain and suffering' or 'loss of amenity' (*Hughes v McKeown* [1985] 3 All ER 284). It appears to be irrelevant whether the money could be used effectively to alleviate the pain.

Here are some fairly typical examples:

• Male, aged eight at the date of the accident and 11 when the court approved the settlement. Two deep lacerations to right cheek, each about 7 mm long. Damage to facial nerve, leaving him with a deformed smile, fully healed after five months. The scars healed well, leaving only a slight blemish. Psychological reaction (dreams, flashbacks) and anxiety-related symptoms, including a twitch, lasting until trial, and expected to disappear on a timescale of years. General damages agreed at £6,750 (*S v Bloomfield* [2000] CLY 1551).

• Female, aged 60 at the date of the accident and 63 at trial. Bruising and injury to spine, with discomfort in the pelvis, lower spine, and legs. This pain ruined a holiday she took soon after the accident. Subsequently gradual improvement of symptoms, which caused her inconvenience, and prevented her from enjoying her hobbies of badminton, cycling, and ballroom dancing. General damages £3,000, plus the cost of the holiday (£440) (*Burgess v Electricity Sports and Social Club* [2000] CLY 1683).

• Female, aged 43 at the date of the accident and 46 at trial. Whiplash neck injury, immediately producing pain, headache, and shock. Pain severe at first, reducing to a persistent ache after six months. Still some aching and stiffness by the date of trial; these symptoms were likely to be permanent. She abandoned her hobby of swimming, because it provoked her symptoms. General damages £4,750 (*Twycross v Hilton* [2000] CLY 1689).

• Male, 41 at the date of the accident and 44 at trial. Soft tissue neck injury. Pain and stiffness in his neck, which for six months meant he had to reduce the length of his shifts as a minicab driver. The pain interfered, for a few months, with his sex life, and with his hobby of darts. By the date of trial, there was still occasional discomfort. General damages £3,750 (*Tower v Ali* [2000] CLY 1693).

The sums are fairly arbitrary. They 'could be multiplied or divided by two overnight and they would be just as defensible or indefensible as they are today' (Cane *Atiyah's*

Accidents, Compensation and the Law (5th edn, 1993) 139). Such evidence as there is (though it is not overwhelming) suggests that, left to his own devices, the average member of the public would be more generous than the courts are. This concern was reflected in Law Commission Report No 257 (*Damages for Personal Injury: Non-pecuniary Loss*, 20 April 1999), which recommended a general increase in non-pecuniary damages. The matter was reconsidered by the Court of Appeal in *Heil v Rankin* [2001] QB 272, where (fending off arguments that it was engaging in retrospective legislation contrary to Art 6 of the European Convention on Human Rights) it was decided that the larger awards, at least, were insufficiently generous. Awards at the very highest level should be increased by one-third; awards in the region of £10,000 or more but below the highest level should be increased by a lesser amount. This is considerably less than the Law Commission recommended, but significantly more than was awarded before. This ruling cannot be the last word on the subject, but when and in what forum the matter will be settled has yet to emerge.

Loss of earnings

10.59 Wages lost before trial are special damages, which must be itemized and proved. Future loss of earning is usually calculated on a multiplier–multiplicand basis. The multiplicand is usually the claimant's net annual loss: salary lost, less tax which the claimant no longer has to pay and expenses the claimant no longer has to incur. All lost income can in principle be taken into account, including perks and benefits in kind; equally, any income the claimant seems likely to secure in fact must be deducted. No allowance is made for likely general increases in earnings generally; and most factors affecting the claimant's own pay are taken into account via the multiplier, not the multiplicand.

Selection of the multiplier is a complicated affair, though the Ogden Tables (based on mortality statistics) take some of the arbitrariness out of the process. The figure is meant to reflect the number of years over which the claimant suffers the loss, but there is no simple relation between the number of years and the number selected as the multiplier. If a multiplier of 40 was selected and the claimant was able to invest the money at 2½ per cent interest per annum, then the claimant would receive as yearly income the sum represented by the multiplicand, in perpetuity.

The multiplier may be increased to reflect the claimant's lost prospects of promotion. It may be reduced to reflect the risk of injury other than by the defendant, the possibility of redundancy, and other 'vicissitudes of life'. There is some confusion over whether women claimants should have their multipliers reduced to allow for the possibility that they might have given up work to have children. Some judges have done so, though where appropriate they have also added a sum for diminution of marriage prospects (e.g. *Moriarty v McCarthy* [1978] 1 WLR 155). But others have simply assumed in a rough-and-ready way that these two alterations to the figures will cancel one another out, and so both may be ignored (*Hughes v McKeown* [1985] 3 All ER 284).

The courts have maintained that the multiplier will not, exceptional circumstances aside, be increased to take account of future inflation. This was partly on the (incontrovertible) ground that the court does not know what the future level will be, sometimes on the (debatable) ground that, properly invested, the real value of the claimant's money should be unaffected, and sometimes on the (despairing) ground that the claimant's fellow citizens have to put up with inflation and the claimant deserves no special protection. It is also not permissible to increase the multiplier to offset the higher rate tax the claimant will pay on investing the sum the court awards (*Hodgson v Trapp* [1989] AC 807).

The 'lost years'

10.60 Where one effect of the injury is to reduce the claimant's lifespan, so that the claimant is expected to die before the claimant would (but for the injury) have retired from work, there is a problem in assessing the claimant's loss of earnings in the period where the claimant would have been earning but cannot because the claimant is dead. This problem of 'wages in heaven' is solved by calculating the claimant's net income over the relevant period on normal principles, but including in the deductions from income a sum representing the claimant's ordinary living expenses. Where the claimant was part of a family, this will involve calculating an appropriate proportion of the family bill for food, housing, heating, and lighting (*Harris v Empress Motors* [1984] 1 WLR 212). Whatever is left is recoverable as damages, including sums which would certainly have been spent on the claimant's dependants had the claimant lived (*Pickett v British Rail Engineering* [1980] AC 136). The rule is plainly intended to safeguard the position of the claimant's dependants, though it applies even if the claimant has none. Where the claimant is very young, the courts are in principle prepared to entertain claims of this sort. But they are likely to award nothing under it if there is no good evidence of what the claimant's earnings are likely to have been (*Connolly v Camden and Islington Area Health Authority* [1981] 3 All ER 250).

'Loss of earning capacity'

10.61 In rare cases, the courts award damages for 'loss of earning capacity'. This is not distinct from lost earnings, but rather a different way of calculating it. If there were too many uncertainties to calculate a sensible multiplier or multiplicand, the court may nonetheless award a lump sum to reflect the diminution in the claimant's work prospects. This is usually because the loss involved will be suffered, if at all, far into the future. Perhaps the claimant is very young, or the effects of the injury rather speculative, or the claimant's employer has kept the claimant on at the old wage but the claimant plausibly argues that his or her future prospects have nonetheless been damaged. It is often arbitrary which approach is adopted. In one case where a 21-month-old claimant was injured (he was 7½ by the time of the trial), a majority of the Court of Appeal assessed damages on the basis of a multiplicand representing the national average wage and a multiplier of 5 (*Croke v Wiseman* [1982] 1 WLR 71); but an award for loss of earning capacity on those facts would not have been surprising. Almost by definition, awards are exceedingly imprecise; the courts tend to err on the side of caution.

Expenses

10.62   As with earnings, so with expenses. Actual expenses before trial must be proved as special damage. Future recurrent expenses will probably be calculated on a multiplier–multiplicand basis, with the multiplier being chosen to reflect the number of years for which the expense will continue. On general principles, the claimant can of course only recover for expenses *reasonably* incurred, but that can be extensive, including (for example) the conversion of the claimant's house to take account of her injury (*Moriarty v McCarthy* [1978] 1 WLR 155, 163, O'Connor J). A decision to obtain medical help privately is not be to be treated as unreasonable merely because the same help was available under the NHS (Law Reform (Personal Injuries) Act 1948, s 2(4)); and the test is one of reasonableness, not of what the court might think is in the claimant's best interests (*Sowden v Lodge* [2004] EWCA Civ 1370). The same principle applies to care and accommodation costs which the defendant's tort makes necessary, and there is no obligation to accept assistance from the public authorities rather than suing the defendant for the cost of private care (*Peters v East Midlands Strategic Health Authority* [2009] EWCA Civ 145). Sometimes there is a danger of overlap between the claimant's claim for expenses and the claimant's claim for lost earnings. If the claimant is hospitalized for a lengthy period and stays in a private hospital, the claimant will not be allowed to recover *both* the cost of the hospital care *and* the lost wages in full, for while staying in hospital the claimant presumably avoids a significant part of his or her ordinary living expenses (*Lim Poh Choo v Camden and Islington Area Health Authority* [1980] AC 174).

Deduction of benefits

10.63 The general principle has been explained above (**10.46**). In general, benefits received by the claimant as a result of the tort must be deducted, but there are two exceptions: one for benefits funded by the claimant at some time in the past, the other for acts of generosity to the claimant after the accident. The latter exception has caused a great deal of confusion down the years. In *Roach v Yates* [1938] 1 KB 256, where the claimant's wife and sister-in-law gave up their jobs to nurse him, a sum was added to the claimant's damages because 'he would naturally feel that he ought to compensate them for what they have lost' ([1938] 1 KB 256, 263, Greer LJ). But this precedent was rather neglected in the following few decades. The practice grew up whereby relatives who intended to care for the victims of torts would often be advised to sign formal contracts to care for them for specific sums of money, which could then be added to the claimant's claim. In *Donnelly v Joyce* [1974] QB 454 it was held that such contracts were unnecessary: where the defendant's tort had created the claimant's need for care, the claimant could recover the value of that care. The amount it had cost the claimant's relatives to provide it, whether by wages foregone or otherwise, was admissible as evidence of the proper amount of the claimant's claim. However, this approach remained unsatisfactory, not least because it perpetuated the fiction that the loss involved was really suffered by the claimant, whereas the reality was that the claimant's need for care had been catered for, but the court considered that the carer deserved to be able to claim. The reality of the matter was acknowledged first in *Housecroft v Burnett* [1986] 1 All ER 332, and then by the House of Lords in *Hunt v Severs* [1994] 2 All ER 385. The principle is not confined to relatives, but can be applied in favour of any voluntary care-giver, such as a private charity hospice (*Drake v Starkey* [2010] EWHC 2004 (QB)).

There are numerous problems with this analysis, which have yet to be resolved satisfactorily.

> **Lowe v Guise [2002] EWCA Civ 197:** Lowe, 31, lived with his mother and disabled brother, to whom he provided about 77 hours per week free care. He was then injured by the negligence of Guise, and as a result could only provide such services for 35 hours per week, the balance being made up by his mother. Held: Lowe's damages should include the value of the services he could not longer provide for his brother; it was irrelevant that, when he provided them, he had done so for no financial reward. The court suggested (though the point was not in issue) that he would hold these sums on trust for his mother.

A particular problem is where the claimant is a young child and the care is to be provided by a parent. There are obviously huge difficulties in estimating how much *extra* care will result from the claimant's injuries, and some have therefore argued that such claims should be looked upon with suspicion. However, the Court of Appeal have rejected this, stating that such damages are always available where they can be proved, and not just in very serious cases (*Giambrone v JMC Holidays Ltd* [2004] EWCA Civ 158).

Social security benefits

10.64 Where the claimant had received social security benefits as a result of the injuries inflicted by the defendant, the claimant would be receiving double compensation if these benefits were not deducted from damages. But equally, if the defendant were able simply to deduct benefits paid, then the state would be paying for a liability caused by the defendant. The solution adopted is to insist that any tortfeasor settling a tort claim should account to the state for the amount of benefits received by the victim. Those benefits are ignored for all purposes in the course of assessing the claimant's personal injury damages (*Wisely v John Fulton (Plumbers)* [2000] 2 All ER 545). But no payment of compensation can be made until the defendant receives a 'certificate of total benefits' from the appropriate governmental department; the definition covers most social security benefits. Certain benefits are excluded from the scheme. The law was restated and amended in the Social Security (Recovery of Benefits) Act 1997.

NHS costs

10.65 Another scheme, distinct from the social security benefits scheme, is that for recovery of NHS costs. Originally introduced in 1999 and then confined to motor accident cases, this has now been extended to cover all cases where a compensation payment is made in respect of an injury for which NHS care was given. On making the compensation payment, the payer is also obliged to pay the appropriate NHS charges (Health and Social Care (Community Health and Standards) Act 2003, s 150).

Assessment: the dead victim

Survival of actions in tort

10.66 At common law, the claimant's death brought the action to an end. However, this rule has been reversed by statute (Law Reform (Miscellaneous Provisions)

Act 1934, s 1). But a claim brought by the claimant's estate after the claimant's death cannot include any element for:

- exemplary damages (Law Reform (Miscellaneous Provisions) Act 1934, s 1(2)(a)); or
- loss of earnings in respect of the period after death (Administration of Justice Act 1982, s 4(2)).

In practice, therefore, any claim brought by the claimant's estate after the death will be restricted to claims in respect of the period before the claimant's death. As to the period after, the claimant no longer experiences pain or suffering, and is taken not to merit a claim for lost amenities; claims for lost earnings are excluded by statute; and the claimant no longer has any expenses. General damages are therefore zero. A claim for special damages may succeed.

In strict logic, the claimant's funeral expenses would not be recoverable in full. The claimant would have died some time anyway, tort or no tort, and so there is merely acceleration of an inevitable expense, rather than a straightforward loss. However, the Act specifically provides that where the claimant's death was the result of the tort, a sum is recoverable for funeral expenses. Strict logic is therefore held at bay. That special case aside, any gain or loss to the estate consequential on the death itself is ignored.

Fatal Accidents Act 1976

10.67 Where the claimant's death is the result of the defendant's tort, then in addition to any claim by the claimant's estate, there is a statutory claim available to the claimant's dependants. This reflects the degree of the 'dependency', that is, the benefits which they would have received from the deceased had he or she not died. The claim is quite distinct from the claim by the estate (see, for example, *Reader v Molesworths Bright Clegg* [2007] EWCA Civ 169). It is a claim for pure economic loss consequential on the death of a provider. However, the claim lies only if a claim could have been brought in respect of the tort at the date of the death. So if the deceased person had already successfully sued the defendant, no additional claim arises on death, and conversely any defences which the defendant could have raised against a claim by the deceased can also be raised against the Fatal Accident Act claim.

Who can claim?

10.68 The claim is only for the amount of the dependency, and accordingly can only be brought by someone who was in fact a dependant of the deceased. Further, the

Act demands that claimants must come from specific categories of dependant. The claimant must, by s 1 as amended, be one or more of the following:

- husband or wife of the deceased at the date of death, or former husband or wife (including cases where the marriage was annulled or declared void);

- the civil partner or former civil partner of the deceased (under the Civil Partnership Act 2004);

- any person 'living with the deceased in the same household' and so living 'as their husband or wife' at the time of the death and for the preceding two years (for an example see *Kotke v Saffarini* [2005] EWCA Civ 221);

- any parent of the deceased, or anyone treated by the deceased as his or her parent;

- any child of the deceased, or anyone treated by the deceased as a child of the deceased's family in relation to any marriage to which the deceased was party;

- any other ascendant or descendent relative; or

- any brother, sister, uncle or aunt, or the issue of any such person.

The section also provides that relationships by marriage ('affinity') count the same as relationships by blood ('consanguinity'), and makes provision for cases of relationships by half-blood. It adds (confusingly, given the earlier references to marriage) that an illegitimate child is to be 'treated as the legitimate child of [the] mother and reputed father'. The list is long, confused and confusing. It has been added to down the years, now being considerably longer than when the claim was first introduced in 1846. The Law Commission have provisionally recommended that the statutory list of dependants be abolished, the test in future being simply whether there is a dependency in fact (*Claims for Wrongful Death*, Law Com Consultation Paper No 148, September 1997).

In principle, each dependant has a distinct claim, but the Act insists that procedurally there must be a single claim (s 2), and it is usual for the court to assess a single figure for the dependency and then divide it between claimants. The requirement of a 'single claim' may sometimes work injustice, but the Court of Appeal has recently ruled that this phrase should not be given an interpretation which would deprive some of the dependants of the possibility of a claim (*Cachia v Faluyi* [2001] EWCA Civ 998). This is an example of a statute's being interpreted in a human-rights-friendly manner, as is required by Human Rights Act 1998, s 3(1). The court has complete discretion as to the division of any sum received between multiple claimants (s 3(2)).

Calculation of the claim

10.69 The claimant is entitled to a sum representing the value of benefits which he or she would have received from the deceased but for the death. Where (as is usually the case) the benefits were expected to be received over a period, the courts will usually employ a multiplier–multiplicand basis for the calculation. Where the deceased had not provided any benefits in the past but seemed likely to do so in the future, it is a purely evidential question whether the facts justify a claim.

> **Taff Vale Rly Co v Jenkins [1913] AC 1:** A 16-year-old girl, living with her parents, was about to finish her apprenticeship as a dressmaker at the time when she was killed. It was expected that her wages would have risen sharply after qualification. Held: as there was a reasonable possibility that she would have supported her parents, an award to reflect this dependency could be made.

In cases where the deceased was a breadwinner, in theory the claim is for the amount the deceased brought into the house, less expenses attributable to his or her *own* upkeep, as opposed to the upkeep of others in the family. In practice, there are difficulties in calculating this, and the courts have to resort to rough-and-ready presumptions. It would be unrealistic to expect that if one member of a two-person household dies, then future bills for rent, food, and heating will decline by 50 per cent. The courts usually start from the assumption that where there is a single dependant, the dependency will be two-thirds of the amount of money the deceased brought in, and that if there are children as well it will be three-quarters. The figure will then be adjusted up or down in the light of the evidence (*Harris v Empress Motors* [1984] 1 WLR 212). In cases where the deceased provided home-making services, the courts sometimes say that the dependency is to be estimated by the cost of buying replacement services commercially (*Hay v Hughes* [1975] QB 790). But if the services are in fact provided after the death by a partner or by relatives, a more obvious measure is any wages lost by that relative (*Mehmet v Perry* [1977] 2 All ER 529). Where the deceased had been an invalid, cared for by a spouse or other relative, then allowances paid in respect of that care can be regarded as the source of a dependency; in effect, the carer was being paid a wage for caring for the invalid, and financial loss resulting from the death is actionable under the Act (*Cox v Hockenhull* [1999] 3 All ER 582).

Losses which result from the death are not always part of the dependency. In particular, when one member of a family works for another, being paid the going rate for the job, neither side 'benefits' from the arrangement, and its loss is to that extent not a ground for a claim under the Act.

> **Malyon v Plummer [1964] 1 QB 330:** A wife regularly performed some rather nominal services for her husband's one-man company, for which the company paid her £600 per annum; it was found that her services were worth about £200 per annum. On her

husband's death, this arrangement ceased. Held: she could recover only £400 per annum as dependency.

Burgess v Florence Nightingale Hospital for Gentlewomen [1955] 1 QB 349: Husband and wife worked as professional dancing partners; the wife died through a surgeon's negligence and her husband claimed under the Act. Held: nothing was recoverable as compensation for the interruption of their professional relationship.

The award may also include a sum to cover burial expenses actually incurred by the dependants (s 3(5)).

Loss of chance of dependency

10.70 The claimant does not have to show that the dependency would certainly have existed but for the death, or even that this is more likely than not; but any chances involved are part of the calculus of benefits. So where a husband and wife were separated at the time of the husband's death, the House of Lords held that it was wrong to deny the widow any dependency claim merely because a reconciliation seemed less likely than not—though, not insignificantly, they refused an award on the facts, as being too speculative a possibility (*Davies v Taylor* [1974] AC 207). The Act specifically directs the court to take account (in the case of a claim by a cohabitant living with the deceased as husband or wife) of the lack of any enforceable claim to support during life (s 3(4)).

Disregard of benefits

10.71 Benefits received by dependants as a result of the death are to be disregarded in calculating the dependency (s 4). The Act also provides that the possibility, or indeed actuality, of remarriage by a widow of the deceased is to be disregarded in calculating her dependency (s 3(3)). However, the Act makes no mention of claims brought by any children of hers, and so the widow's remarriage to a man who turns out to be a better provider than her first husband may reduce the children's claim substantially. As drafted, the subsection does not cover remarriage by widowers, but in fact the same result has been reached in their case by broad interpretation of s 4 (*Stanley v Saddique* [1992] QB 1). The precise ambit of s 4 is unclear, and not all the decisions in that area seem consistent. So where her husband's death meant that a claimant would not receive the benefit of her husband's retirement pension, but she received a similar result from a death-in-service pension, it was said that overall she had suffered no loss and so had no claim (*Auty v National Coal Board* [1985] 1 All ER 930). Yet when the widow of a retired man died and accordingly lost the benefit of his occupational pension, her damages were not reduced by her receipt of a widow's allowance under the same scheme (*Pidduck v Eastern Scottish Omnibuses* [1990] 2 All ER 69). Since the abolition of the 'wages in heaven' claim by the estate, there is no longer any provision for deduction of benefits received in consequence of a claim by the estate under the 1934 Act (**10.60**, **10.66**).

Damages for bereavement

10.72 In addition to the claim for a dependency, there is now a claim for non-pecuniary loss, called 'damages for bereavement'. The claim is for a fixed amount, which is the same in each case and set by the Lord Chancellor. At the time of writing it is £11,800 (see SI 2007/3489). The claim can only be made by a narrow class of relatives:

- The spouse or civil partner at the date of the death.
- Where the deceased never married or partnered and never reached 18, the claim may be made by his or her mother and (if the deceased was legitimate) father.

Defences

10.73 Any defence which would have defeated a claim by the victim of the tort also operates to defeat a claim under the Fatal Accidents Act 1976. If a claim by the deceased would have been met by a plea of contributory negligence, leading to a reduction in the damages payable, then the claim under the Act will be similarly reduced (s 5). There are also additional defences that can be raised.

> **Burns v Edman [1970] 2 QB 541:** A widow claimed for loss of dependency when her husband was killed in a road accident. It appeared that most, if not all, of his past earnings had come from criminal activities, and that there had been no prospect of his earning a living in any other way. Held: no claim was maintainable.

An unusual situation arose in *Dodds v Dodds* [1978] QB 543, where a wife's bad driving led to her husband's death. In a claim brought by her husband's estate, it was suggested that negligence by one of the dependants would weaken the claim. However, the court held that the negligence of one dependant could not affect the claims of the others, and the children all recovered for their dependency without any reduction. In that case, the wife was solely responsible for the accident, and it was conceded that she had no claim herself; it seems that where a dependant is partly responsible for it, that dependency claim may be correspondingly reduced (*Mulholland v McCrea* [1961] NI 135).

FURTHER READING

Andoh 'Exemplary damages and the police: Some reflections' (2001) 5 Mountbatten Jour Leg Stud 90.

Beever 'The structure of aggravated and exemplary damages' (2003) 23 OJLS 87.

Evans 'The scope of the duty revisited' (2001) 17 Prof Neg 146.

Lewis 'Deducting collateral benefits from damages: Principle and policy' (1998) 18 LS 15.

Lewis 'Increasing the price of pain: Damages, the Law Commission and *Heil v Rankin*' (2001) 64 MLR 100.

Murphy 'Rethinking injunctions in tort law' (2007) 27 OJLS 509.

Porat and Stein 'Indeterminate causation and apportionment of damages: An essay on *Holtby, Allen*, and *Fairchild*' (2003) 23 OJLS 667.

Reid '*Gregg v Scott* and lost chances' (2005) 21 Prof Neg 78.

Stapleton 'Lords a'leaping evidentiary gaps' (2002) 20 Torts LJ 276.

Stapleton 'Loss of the chance of cure from cancer' (2005) 68 MLR 996.

Stauch 'Risk and remoteness of damage in negligence' (2001) 64 MLR 191.

Thomson '*Barker v Corus*: *Fairchild* chickens come home to roost' (2006) 10 Edin LR 421.

SELF-TEST QUESTIONS

1 It is much easier to obtain a final injunction against libel than an interim injunction against it. Why is this (**10.4**)?

2 Why might the claimant prefer to be the beneficiary of a 'structured settlement' rather than any other sort of settlement (**10.56**)?

3 Is remoteness a defence to a claim for *all* torts (**10.29**)?

4 In what circumstances will benefits received by the claimant in consequence of the tort be ignored in assessing damages against the defendant (**10.46**)?

5 Are 'aggravated damages' intended to compensate the claimant or to punish the defendant (**10.16**)?

11

Defences and other factors limiting damages

SUMMARY

A number of defences call for special attention. They are:

- consent and exclusion of liability;
- contributory negligence;
- illegality;
- limitation; and
- necessity.

They provide a number of safety valves for courts concerned to limit the scope of liability.

11.1　This chapter covers defences to tort actions. This is a diverse area. A list of everything that has ever been counted as defence to a tort action would be very long indeed. For that matter, there is little agreement on where rules relating to liability end and rules relating to defences begin. For example, it was at one time thought that there was a defence of 'inevitable accident' to actions in negligence, and some of the more traditional texts still refer to it. But the more modern tendency is to say that this is a denial of negligence ('the accident was inevitable') or a denial of causation ('it would have happened anyway'). Little turns in practice on which approach is adopted. Again, it is not entirely clear that all defences apply to all torts. This chapter will consider five defences of fairly general application: consent, contributory negligence, illegality, limitation, and necessity.

Consent and exclusion of liability

11.2 It is a defence to an action in tort that the claimant consented in advance to the behaviour of which the claimant now complains. The Latin maxim is *volenti non fit injuria*: 'No injury is suffered by one who consents'. A related idea (though not precisely the same idea) is that the claimant cannot sue if the claimant has entered into a contract to give up any right of action.

In essence the defence is very simple, but a number of factors make it very rash to generalize about it:

   • While the doctrine of consent supplies the explanation when the defendant erects a warning notice which is held to absolve the defendant from liability, *notices are of different types, and accordingly have different effects in law*. At one extreme, there are notices which give the claimant precise warning of the physical danger the claimant is running, in such a way as to enable the claimant to avoid it. At the other are legalistic notices informing the claimant that the defendant does not intend to assume any legal liability, but giving no clue as to the danger the claimant might be running. If either type of notice has any effect, it will be on the ground that the claimant 'consented' to the terms of the notice. But the questions to ask in each case are different, and for a number of reasons the first type of notice is viewed with a great deal more sympathy than the second.

   • *The defence of consent raises different issues in different contexts.* For example, a plea of consent in relation to a surgical operation where the claimant was given a false idea of the nature of the operation (as where the surgeon removed the wrong leg) is very different from a consent plea where the claimant's complaint is that the surgeon did not warn the claimant in advance of certain risks of the surgery. These differences are partly, but not wholly, explained by the point that in the first case the claimant would be suing in battery and in the second in negligence. In what follows, I will be assuming that there is a common core of principle in the area, applying to most cases, but have already discussed elsewhere individual situations and individual torts which need consideration (e.g. **7.7**).

The burden of proof on matters of consent is on the defendant (*Freeman v Home Office (No 2)* [1984] QB 524).

The claimant's ability to consent

11.3 The claimant can sometimes pre-empt any argument for consent by showing that at the time at which the claimant supposedly consented, he or she did not possess an adequate level of understanding to give a valid consent. So children may often be held not to have consented in circumstances where adults certainly would be. The leading case is *Gillick v West Norfolk and Wisbech Area Health Authority* [1986] AC 112, and the question whether the claimant has adequate understanding for this purpose is often called the question of '*Gillick* competence'. It is a matter of whether the claimant has 'sufficient understanding and intelligence' to comprehend what is being proposed and to decide whether to agree to it. On or after their sixteenth birthday, it is taken that children are so competent in the case of medical procedures (Family Law Reform Act 1969, s 8). Controversially, however, a 16-year-old anorexic has not been regarded as competent to refuse treatment to prevent her starving herself (*Re C (Detention: Medical Treatment)* [1997] 3 FCR 49). For those over 16, the law has recently been restated in statute (Mental Capacity Act 2005, ss 1–5, in force 1 October 2007), which lists various detailed criteria in aid of the central question whether a person is 'unable to make a decision for himself in relation to the matter because of an impairment of, or a disturbance in the functioning of, the mind or brain'.

Reality of consent

11.4 An apparent consent by the claimant may not always count as consent for legal purposes. In principle the claimant will not be held to have consented if her 'consent' was obtained by threats or bullying, though the leading case on the matter does not give much encouragement.

> **Latter v Braddell** (1881) 45 JP 520: Employers accused their maidservant of being pregnant, insisted on a medical examination to confirm their suspicions, and threatened to sack her if she did not consent to it. She underwent examination, protesting but believing she was legally bound to, and was found not to be pregnant. They sacked her anyway. Held: her consent, though reluctant, was genuine and she could not sue in battery.

It is often said that the claimant's consent will be vitiated if it was obtained by misleading the claimant on some fundamental matter. But examples are hard to come by. If the defendant obtains the claimant's consent to a surgical operation by telling the claimant that the defendant intends to perform *some other* medical operation, then the defendant has no defence to battery; but that is usually explained by saying that what the defendant did was not what the claimant consented to. It is not that the claimant's consent was vitiated, but rather that what the defendant did was not what the claimant consented to. The judges have resisted any broader notion of 'informed consent': it is enough that the claimant knows in general terms what the defendant proposes to do (e.g. *Freeman v Home Office (No 2)* [1984] QB 524). Again, judges in an earlier century held that the claimant's consent to sex was effective even though she would certainly have refused had she known that the defendant suffered from a venereal disease (e.g. *Hegarty v Shine* (1878) 14 Cox CC 145). There are good reasons for not treating that case, and others like it, as conclusive authority. They are antique. In any event, most of the authorities are from the criminal law: criminal lawyers are asking about 'consent' for different reasons and with different policy objectives. A judge who was reluctant to label the defendant a rapist might nonetheless be willing to order the defendant to pay compensation for the same behaviour. Nonetheless, action by the claimant in fraud or negligence probably has a better chance of success than action in battery.

Medical cases

11.5 If a doctor misleads the claimant about the treatment the doctor is about to administer to the claimant, then the operation may amount to a battery, on the ground that what the defendant does is not what the claimant consented to. The requirement is that the claimant understands 'the general nature' of what the defendant is up to (*Chatterton v Gerson* [1981] QB 432). In appropriate cases, the claimant must be informed not simply about the risks of what is proposed, but also as to the alternatives and the risks associated with them (*Birch v University College Hospitals NHS Trust* [2008] EWHC 2237 (QB)). Consent is not vitiated simply because the defendant is not as open as the defendant could have been about the operation, or did not explain all the risks associated with it. This seems to be so even if the claimant specifically asked to know the risks (*Sidaway v Board of Governors of the Bethlem Royal Hospital* [1985] AC 871).

Strong opinions are held on both sides of the question whether patients' consent should be 'informed'. Not everyone would agree with the view of the House of Lords in *Sidaway*, that confidence between doctor and patient can only be upheld by permitting systematic concealment of the risks inherent in whatever course of action the doctor proposes. It is sometimes said that fraud vitiates consent, but it is not clear whether this applies to all frauds, or simply to fraud as to the type of operation. Other torts may possibly be invoked: a doctor who lies about what is planned may be liable for deceit (**6.2**); a doctor who does not reveal facts which a reasonable medical practitioner would have revealed may be liable for negligence (**5.14**). However, in both cases, the claimant would not be able to recover damages unless it can be proved that he or she would not have agreed to the operation but for the doctor's misbehaviour. A possible way forward has been indicated by the High Court of Australia:

> **Chappel v Hart (1998) 72 ALJR 1344:** Hart sought treatment from Chappel, an ear, nose and throat specialist. He advised surgery, and failed to warn her of the inherent risk

of damage to her vocal cords. As a result of the surgery she suffered such an injury, which led her to retire from a senior music teaching position. She argued that had she known of the risk, she would have delayed the operation, and arranged for it to be carried out by a more experienced surgeon. No negligence in the conduct of the operation was proved. Held (by a majority): as it was Chappel's duty to give a warning, it was for him to prove that giving one would have made no difference. Liability was established.

It will be seen that the major difference between this and the standard English approach is not so much in recognizing that the surgeon has a duty, as in the treatment of causation issues (see above, **10.25**). The majority in *Chappel* expressly declined to treat this as a 'loss of chance' case, saying that Hart had not 'lost a chance', but rather had suffered physical injury. The point has proved similarly controversial in England, but a majority of the House of Lords has now decided to follow *Chappel* (*Chester v Afshar* [2004] UKHL 41). Where the risk was one which the claimant was entitled to be warned against, the result of the risk was to be regarded as connected to the failure to warn; to the extent that this is a departure from a more traditional approach to causation, it is one which is required by the justice of the case.

Doctors who act in circumstances where the claimant is unconscious, or for some other reason cannot be asked or give consent, are sometimes said to act on an 'implied consent'. But this legal fiction is misleading: cases of this sort are dealt with here under the heading of 'necessity' (**11.42**). There is some scope for 'implied consent' so long as it is genuine: the claimant's consent need not take any particular form, and consent to an operation will include consent to all procedures necessarily incidental to it.

Consent inferred from the existence of an obvious danger

11.6   In the mid-Victorian period, when personal injury actions by employees against their employers were a (not altogether welcome) novelty, it was common for actions to be defeated on the ground of consent. The consent was often inferred from the mere fact that the employee knew of the risk. Perhaps as a reaction against this, later cases stressed that mere knowledge of a risk was quite different from agreement not to sue anyone who created it (e.g. *Smith v Charles Baker & Son* [1891] AC 325). However, this can at best be described as a half-truth. Some potential claimants have better reasons than others for taking risks, and this seems to play a heavy part in the court's decision whether to infer consent from knowledge of the risk. So while knowledge of the risk seems to be a prerequisite for a finding that the claimant has agreed to run it, it is not always clear what else is necessary.

Car cases

11.7 The courts are reluctant to infer consent to bad driving, even where the claimant is well aware of an increased risk of danger.

> ***Dann v Hamilton* [1939] 1 KB 509:** Dann accepted a lift from Hamilton, whom she knew to be drunk, though he appeared to be still capable of exercising care. 'Hamilton seems to have been somewhere in the limbo which divides complete sobriety from mild intoxication.' Held: she did not consent to the injuries she suffered from his bad driving.

> ***Nettleship v Weston* [1971] 2 QB 691:** Nettleship, a driving instructor, was injured by the driving of his pupil Weston on her third lesson, when she crashed into a lamppost. Held: he could sue her for his injuries.

No doubt the existence of compulsory liability insurance is a factor here. In *Nettleship*, there was evidence that the claimant had checked in advance that the defendant was covered by insurance; however, it does not appear that the court's decision would have been any different if no check had been made. In any event, it seems that consent may today be irrelevant in car cases (**11.15**).

Sporting cases

11.8 The courts take it for granted that sports are risky and that the claimant has no business complaining of injury, unless it was of a quite different type from that which the claimant could reasonably have expected to encounter.

> ***Simms v Leigh Rugby Football Club* [1969] 2 All ER 923:** Simms played rugby at an 'away' game in a field, with a concrete wall seven feet three inches from the touchline. He sued the occupiers of the field in respect of injuries sustained through his head colliding with it. Held: by playing he consented to this risk.

> ***White v Blackmore* [1972] 2 QB 651:** White was catapulted into the air after an accident with safety ropes at a jalopy race. He had been standing on the wrong side of the ropes, but he would have been caught in the same way if he had been standing on the right side. Held: this risk was so unusual that he could not be taken to have agreed to run it. (Note, however, that White lost the case on another point (**11.13**).)

A similar approach has been taken to less comprehensively regulated games.

> ***Blake v Galloway* [2004] EWCA Civ 814:** Blake, Galloway, and several other children, all aged around 15, engaged in good-natured horseplay involving throwing twigs and pieces of bark at one another. Blake threw a particular piece of bark at Galloway; Galloway threw it back. Accidentally, it hit Blake in the eye, causing serious injury. Held: Galloway's conduct was not reckless, or intended to cause harm; neither did it depart from the tacit understandings of the participants as to the limits of the game they were

playing. Accordingly, it was within the range of conduct to which all had consented, and there was no liability.

The claimant cannot sue when the sport in question was an obviously foolish enterprise in the first place.

> **Morris v Murray [1991] 2 QB 6:** After an afternoon's drinking, Morris and Murray set out on a trip in a light aircraft, in conditions of poor weather and visibility which had grounded other air traffic. Held: neither could sue the other for injuries sustained.

> **Ratcliff v McConnell [1999] 1 WLR 670:** Ratcliff and friends, all students at the defendant college, decided after a night of drinking to dive into the college's (locked) swimming pool. Ratcliff dived into the shallow end, hit the bottom, and suffered injuries leading to tetraplegia. Held: the danger should have been apparent to any adult, even if drunk. There was no breach of duty, and even if there had been, Ratcliff had consented to run the risk involved.

Employment cases

11.9 Risks which are inherent in the job the claimant is employed to do will not come within the defence. The claimant will probably know of the risks all too well, but in reality has no choice but to run them, and so cannot be said to consent to them. However, where the risk in question is not only obvious but is also easy to avoid, then the courts may be able to infer consent to run it.

> **Gledhill v Liverpool Abattoir Utility Co [1957] 3 All ER 117:** Gledhill was employed as a pig-slaughterer. He was injured when a pig he had just killed fell on top of him, falling out of the slip-ring attached to its leg. The rings were well constructed, and Gledhill knew of the risk. Held: Gledhill had impliedly agreed to run the risk, and could not sue.

However, in most such cases, the defendant's real argument will be that the risk is inherent in the job and so not really avoidable by anything the defendant did. So it is really a denial that the employer's duty has been broken, rather than a defence of consent as such. Where the defendant is in a position to do something to lessen the risk, the courts will usually insist that it is done. Note also that the House of Lords has rejected the so-called 'fireman's rule', that workers in dangerous trades such as firefighting cannot sue those who made their services necessary. So if the defendant negligently starts a fire and the claimant is injured in putting it out, the claimant can sue (*Ogwo v Taylor* [1988] AC 431) (**4.21**).

A special case is where the claimant's action is based on breach of a statutory duty by the claimant's employer. It would offend against the policy of the employment safety legislation to allow a defence of consent to run the risks of the job. Accordingly, the defence is not usually available. In extreme circumstances, however, where the breach of statutory duty was itself the claimant's responsibility, the courts consider that it would be unjust not to allow it. But strict requirements must be observed. Suppose the complaint is that the claimant was injured through working on an unsafe roof without using a crawling board, contrary to statute, and the defendant's answer is that the claimant could easily have used a board if he had chosen to. This is generally a matter for the defence of contributory negligence, which may reduce the claimant's damages somewhat (**11.17**). The defendant may, however, be able to defeat the claimant's claim *entirely*, so long as the claimant's failure to use the boards is itself a breach of statutory duty *by the claimant*, and the defendant, while technically in breach of the law, was in no way at fault (*Ginty v Belmont Building Supplies* [1959] 1 All ER 414).

> **Imperial Chemical Industries v Shatwell [1965] AC 656:** A team of shot firers were testing their circuits before commencing blasting operations. Contrary to orders, they did not get under cover while making the tests; unexpectedly, their test caused an explosion which injured them. Their failure to get under cover put them and their employer in breach of statutory regulations. Held: the team were all experienced, and there was no argument for placing any of the blame on the employer. Therefore no action lay.

The defence of consent is therefore available to the defendant where the claimant is 'the sole author of his own misfortune'. It will be defeated if at least part of the blame lies with the defendant, as where the defendant failed to supply necessary equipment or training, or gave orders which contributed to the accident (see *Boyle v Kodak* [1969] 2 All ER 439).

Rescuer cases

11.10　In this area as in others (**3.31**), the courts are reluctant to condemn the behaviour of rescuers and would-be rescuers. The fact that the claimant proceeded despite the obvious dangers might, indeed, be grounds for the award of a medal. Generally speaking, then, a plea of consent will fail where the claimant is attempting to save others from a peril of the defendant's own making. A fairly typical case is *Haynes v Harwood* [1935] 1 KB 146. A rare case where such a claimant fails is *Cutler v United Dairies (London)* [1933] 2 KB 297. Here the claimant was injured during his rather inept attempt to catch the defendant's runaway horse. Possibly the decision is to be explained by the point that no-one was in immediate danger from the animal.

The mentally unbalanced claimant

11.11　In cases where the claimant was mentally unstable and the defendant knew it, the courts have been prepared to make the defendant liable for the consequences of the claimant's own voluntary act. So in *Reeves v Metropolitan Police Commissioner* [2000] 1 AC 360 (see also **1.32**), where the police should have taken precautions against suicide by one of their prisoners, they could not say that the prisoner consented to his own death, even though it was a voluntary act. Obviously it would be futile to rule in the claimant's favour on liability in such circumstances if the courts were then to apply the defence of consent, and of course they have refused to do that. The doctrinal basis for this is unclear, although presumably it is along the lines that the defendant, at least, cannot treat the claimant as a voluntary agent, whether or not the claimant would for other purposes be so treated. Certainly there are degrees of mental unfitness here; the tendency is to dismiss the defence of consent in all cases, but to subject the fitter claimants to a defence of contributory negligence (see below, **11.21**).

A redundant principle?

11.12 It is not obvious that a principle of 'consent' is necessary to explain these cases. The claimant does not very obviously 'consent', in any normal sense, in any of them. Where the courts refuse liability, this is usually better explained by the suggestion that the defendant did not break the duty, perhaps because all that the duty required was to warn the claimant of the danger. This is particularly obvious in the case of occupiers' liability, where the question whether the claimant was warned is clearly part of the duty the occupier owes (**4.25**), but is a point of general validity. Given the existence of a defence of contributory negligence, many have suggested that the ability to infer consent from the existence of danger is quite unnecessary.

Consent inferred from the posting of a legal notice

11.13 A rather different situation is where the defendant posts a notice which warns the claimant, in general terms, that the defendant accepts no legal liability to the claimant or to others in the claimant's position. The notice may or may not give any indication of what sources of danger the defendant might be concerned about. This problem is of most relevance to occupiers' liability. A typical notice would be positioned at the entrance to the defendant's land and grant general permission for entry on conditions, one of which would be that the occupier would be under no liability. By contrast with the cases discussed above, the case law discloses relatively little sympathy for the claimant. If the defendant is entitled to keep others out of his or her land, it follows that the defendant is entitled to let them in only subject to conditions, some of which may restrict the claimant's rights to sue. But these cases are old, and a very different attitude is taken today, at least if the defendant is a business or governmental body. This change of heart has been achieved through legislation, which is described below (**11.14**). First, the cases.

- The test is said to be whether the defendant has done enough to warn people generally that no liability is accepted. It follows that there is usually no very careful examination of the claimant's own situation, to determine whether in fact the claimant saw the warning. It seems clear that the claimant cannot escape the effect of the notice if the reasonable person in the claimant's position would have read it (*Ashdown v Samuel Williams & Sons* [1957] 1 QB 409). It is unclear to what extent the claimant can plead factors such as illiteracy or lack of age which made it impossible to read. In *Geier v Kujawa, Weston and Warne Bros (Transport)* [1970] 1 Lloyd's Rep 364 an 18-year-old German woman who spoke little English was held able to escape the effect of an exempting notice, in circumstances where it bound people generally.

- As the notice is a legal instrument removing the claimant's rights, it is read against the person relying on it (*contra proferentem*). It is read as narrowly as possible, any ambiguity being resolved in favour of the claimant rather than the defendant. Nonetheless, prominently displayed notices exempting the defendant from liability for accidents 'howsoever caused' have been held to mean just that, and to exclude all liability (e.g. *White v Blackmore* [1972] 2 QB 651).

- It is open to the claimant to argue that, while aware of the conditions the defendant meant to impose, nonetheless the claimant had no real choice but to enter, and accordingly cannot be said to have freely accepted the terms. So when the claimant entered the defendant's dock in the course of his job as a lighterman, and was injured by a defective rope, the defendant was held unable to rely on exempting conditions displayed at the entrance to the dock (*Burnett v British Waterways Board* [1973] 2 All ER 631).

It is not entirely clear on what legal basis the doctrine defeats the claimant's rights, when it does. The cases usually suggest that it is a doctrine of 'conditional licence': the claimant is only allowed onto the land on condition that no cause of action arises. If so, it would be distinct from the doctrine of consent generally. This point matters, for if the true basis is conditional licence, it is hard to see how it can apply to trespassers, as they enter without a licence and in defiance of the need for one. But there is no very obvious reason why trespassers cannot be subject to the doctrine of consent. The point is open (**4.29**).

Unfair Contract Terms Act 1977

11.14 A major limit is placed on the doctrine of consent by the Unfair Contract Terms Act 1977, s 2. This section absolutely bars exclusion or restriction of personal injury liability in negligence by 'any contract term or notice' (s 2(1)), and subjects liability in respect of property damage or pure economic loss to a test of reasonableness (s 2(2)).

'Notice' is defined as including 'an announcement, whether or not in writing, and any other communication or pretended communication' (s 14). This provision is aimed primarily at formal notices of the *Ashdown v Williams* type, but it may have broader effects:

- The Act applies only to 'business liability' (s 1(3)), though 'business' is defined to include 'a profession and the activities of any government department or local or public authority' (s 14). The defendant's business liability comprises 'things done or to be done by a person in the course of a business (whether his own business or another's)', as well as occupiers' liability in respect of business premises. But liability to those admitted only for 'recreational or educational' purposes can be excluded, so long as the admission cannot be treated as part of the business purpose of the occupier (amendments to s 1(3) effected by the Occupiers' Liability Act 1984, s 2).

- Where the test of reasonableness applies, various factors are relevant. In *Smith v Eric S Bush* [1990] 1 AC 831, Lord Griffiths mentioned particularly whether the claimant and the defendant were of equal bargaining strength, whether it would have been practical for the claimant to go elsewhere, how difficult it was for the defendant to take good care and do the act properly, and whether it was open to the defendant to insure ([1990] 1 AC 858–9) (**5.24**).

- It is not entirely clear where the Act leaves liability generally. The Act was meant to safeguard the claimant's right to have due care taken of his or her interests, and so presumably it will not be read as going further. In an occupiers' liability case, presumably it is still open to the defendant to argue a notice was all that was required to warn the claimant of the danger. In a negligent misstatement case, the defendant can argue that, in the light of the notice and its prominence, it was unreasonable for the claimant to rely on the defendant's statement. But the *Eric S Bush* case gives little encouragement to this argument, emphasizing that exemption clauses are caught by the Act *whatever* form they take (s 13) (**5.24**). Section 2(3) may have been meant to preserve the defence of consent in cases of obvious risk. However, it is very obscurely worded and there is no consensus on its meaning: 'Where a contract term or notice purports to exclude or restrict liability for negligence a person's agreement to or awareness of it is not of itself to be taken as indicating his voluntary acceptance of any risk'.

Other statutory controls

11.15 The Unfair Contract Terms Act 1977 put other statutory controls somewhat in the shade, but did not abolish them. Of particular interest to tort lawyers is the Road Traffic Act 1988, s 149, which applies to liabilities caught by compulsory third party insurance. The section provides that agreements by passengers not to invoke this liability are void, and '[t]he fact that a person so carried has willingly accepted as his the risk of negligence on the part of the user shall not be treated as negating any such liability of the user' (s 149(3)). This broad wording seems to catch not merely contractual exclusions, but any variety of the consent defence (*Pitts v Hunt* [1991] 1 QB 24). In general, liabilities stricter than the negligence duty may be excluded; though see Consumer Protection Act 1987, s 7 (absolute duty in respect of defective products is not excludable).

The limits of consent

11.16 There are certain situations where the criminal law does not permit a defence of consent; most famously in recent years in *R v Brown* [1994] 1 AC 212, where a group of sado-masochists were convicted of assaults upon one another. However, the criminal law and civil law pursue rather different objects, and it by no means follows that consent would be no defence in a civil action on the same facts. The practical answer is probably that any likely action would fail for illegality (**11.26**) and so the consent point would not arise.

Contributory negligence

11.17 Under the defence of contributory negligence, the defendant argues that the claimant was also to some extent to blame for the loss the claimant suffered. At common law, this was a complete defence to the claimant's action. The old doctrine generated a complex jurisprudence around it, and in particular around the idea that whichever of the claimant and the defendant had the 'last opportunity' to avoid the harm should bear the loss himself. The 'all or nothing' quality of the defence ensured that there were plenty of cases, but came to be seen as its principal disadvantage.

Under the modern law, statute provides for a *reduction* in damages if the defence is established, the judge having a discretion in the matter (Law Reform (Contributory Negligence) Act 1945, s 1). While the sophistications of the old law were never expressly abolished, they have quietly withered and can now be forgotten. In some ways, the existence of the defence is a curiosity, for it enables the courts to do something which they staunchly decline to do in other areas: namely, to reduce the liability of an admittedly guilty defendant on the ground that someone else is also responsible (see **9.26**). As the House of Lords has emphasized, the Act's philosophy is pro-claimant: it is not there to defeat claims on the ground of the claimant's fault, but to save claims which would otherwise fail for that reason (*Standard Chartered*

Bank v Pakistan National Shipping Corpn [2002] UKHL 43). Yet it is not entirely clear whether, on balance, the legislation has made matters better for claimants or not. Certainly it means that a finding of contributory negligence has less drastic consequences than it would have done before. It is also probably true that the change has made it harder to dismiss the claimant's claim outright on the ground of neglect of obvious risk and therefore contributed to the decline of the defence of consent. On the other hand, the existence of the defence is a good general weapon in the defendant's hand for the reduction of damages which before the Act the defendant would have had to pay in full.

11.18 Most of the case law concerns the defendant's liability in negligence, where it is well settled that the defence applies. It is not absolutely clear which other torts are caught:

- There is a conflict of authority on whether the defence can apply to assault or battery (*Lane v Holloway* [1968] 1 QB 379 says that it does not; *Murphy v Culhane* [1977] QB 94 says that that it does).

- It has been held that the defence is not available in cases of fraud (*Standard Chartered Bank v Pakistan National Shipping Corpn* [2002] UKHL 43) or conspiracy to bribe the claimant's employees (*Corporacion Nacional del Cobre de Chile v Sogemin Metals* [1997] 2 All ER 917). This is obviously fair in cases where the claimant is suing a fraudster. It seems unreasonable to allow a defendant who has exploited the claimant's gullibility to reduce the damages on the ground that the claimant should not have been so gullible. But the result is not so obvious where, as in *Standard Chartered* itself, the defendant's liability is vicarious only.

- In the tort of negligent misstatement, it is a prerequisite of liability that the claimant's reliance on the defendant's statement be reasonable. Accordingly, pleas of contributory negligence can be expected to be rare, possibly being confined to cases where the claimant's reliance was initially reasonable but ought reasonably to have stopped before it did. It has occasionally been assumed that the defence applies, without any consideration of the point (e.g. *Edwards v Lee* [1991] NLJR 1517).

- It is clear that the defence applies to breach of statutory duty (*Caswell v Powell Duffryn Associated Collieries* [1940] AC 152). This was not obvious, as much liability in breach of statutory duty exists precisely to save workers from the consequences of their own neglect of their safety. It is the careless workers, not the careful, who need the protection of the legislation. This problem is resolved by findings that the worker's share of the responsibility is typically relatively low.

- The defence applies to nuisance (*Trevett v Lee* [1955] 1 WLR 113, 121, Evershed MR), and to liability for animals (Animals Act 1971, ss 5(1) and 10).

11.19 In cases where the 1945 Act applies, '[w]here any person suffers damage as the result partly of his own fault and partly of the fault of any other person or persons, a claim in respect of that damage shall not be defeated by reason of the fault of the person suffering the damage, but the damages recoverable in respect thereof shall be reduced to such extent as the court thinks just and equitable having regard to the claimant's share in the responsibility for the damage' (s 1(1)). It seems clear that the Act applies in any tort action where the defence of contributory negligence is available. It is much disputed whether or when the Act may be invoked where the defendant has been found liable only in breach of contract. The Act implies that the defendant must be guilty of 'negligence, breach of statutory duty or other act or omission which gives rise to liability in tort ...' (s 4). In *Forsikringsaktieselskapet Vesta v Butcher* [1988] 2 All ER 43, 53, O'Connor LJ was prepared to agree that the Act applied in a contract action where the contractual duty was the same as the tort duty that would exist independently of the contract. But the point is controversial and it seems strange if the claimant, having established that the defendant is liable in contract, is required to discuss whether or not a claim could also have been brought in tort.

Contributory 'negligence' and causation

11.20 It is not absolutely correct to describe carelessness by the claimant as contributory 'negligence', for 'negligence' strictly implies breach of a duty of care (**1.26**). It is simply a well-established phrase meaning that the claimant is insufficiently careful in respect of his or her own safety. It is irrelevant that the claimant was careless at the incident at which the claimant's injuries resulted, if there is no causal link between the carelessness and the damage. The defence is not meant as a punishment for carelessness, but as a finding that the claimant as well as the defendant was responsible for the loss the claimant suffered. The claimant will escape a reduction of damages if there was no causal link. So if the defendant runs down a drunken pedestrian, the pedestrian will recover in full if it is clear that the incident would not have gone differently had the pedestrian been sober. Nonetheless, partly as a reaction to the tangled pre-1945 law, the courts are reluctant to involve themselves in any very precise analysis of causation here.

> *Jones v Livox Quarries* **[1952] 2 QB 608:** In defiance of work safety instructions, Jones accepted a lift on the back of a company quarrying machine as it drove along. He was crushed when another vehicle went into the back of it. Jones argued that the purpose of the safety instructions was to guard against workers being thrown off the machine as it drove, and his breach was therefore irrelevant to the accident which happened. Held: Jones was contributorily negligent and his damages should be reduced by 20 per cent.

It appears that the burden of proof on causation is on the defendant.

> ***Owens v Brimmell* [1977] QB 859:** The claimant was injured in a car accident. He had not been wearing a seat belt. It was unclear whether the claimant had been injured through being thrown forward, or through part of the car being forced back on him. Held: there would be no reduction for contributory negligence on this ground, though there would be reduction of 20 per cent for driving with a drunk driver.

The claimant's characteristics

11.21 The claimant's 'negligence' or lack of it will be judged by the standard of the reasonable person of the claimant's characteristics in the claimant's situation. Where the claimant is under 18, he or she is entitled to be judged by the standard of a reasonable person of that age (*Gough v Thorne* [1966] 3 All ER 398, which concerned a 13½-year-old). There are *dicta* that there are ages below which young children can never be found guilty of contributory negligence at all—though there are *dicta* to the contrary as well. A 12-year-old, who ran out into the road without looking, was held 75 per cent responsible for his injuries in *Morales v Eccleston* [1991] RTR 151. One Scots case, *McKinnell v White* 1971 SLT 61, considered a five-year-old contributorily negligent for running out into the road; it is doubtful whether this would be followed south of the border. As a rule of thumb, we can say that the law usually makes allowance for the claimant's physical infirmities, though not the claimant's mental ones. Where the reason why the defendant is under a duty is because of the claimant's unusual characteristics, it is reasonable for those characteristics to be taken into account in assessing contributory negligence. So where the police pay insufficient care to the risk of suicide by one of their prisoners, who then kills himself, the courts have regard to the extent to which the deceased was responsible for his own actions. A profoundly depressed suicide might not be found to be contributorily negligent at all (e.g. *Kirkham v Chief Constable of Greater Manchester* [1990] 3 All ER 246, **1.32**), whereas someone in better mental health might be regarded as 50 per cent to blame (e.g. *Reeves v Metropolitan Police Commissioner* [2000] 1 AC 360).

> ***St George v Home Office* [2008] EWCA Civ 1068:** St George, who had become addicted to alcohol and drugs at age 16, was at age 29 sentenced to four months in prison. In his cell, he was assigned the top bunk, despite the foreseeable risk that he might suffer an epileptic seizure and fall, which was precisely what happened on his sixth day in the cell. The Home Office argued that, as he had been responsible for his own addiction, the accident was partly his own fault, and damages should be reduced accordingly. Held: technically 'fault could be established', but the addiction was so far

into the past that it was no longer right to regard this as a matter contributing to the accident; and/or the appropriate reduction was zero per cent.

Examples

Motoring and road use

11.22 The duties required of drivers and other road users are very diverse. It sometimes happens that the court considers that the reasonable driver would not have set out on the journey which the claimant did, so that the entire drive is one long example of contributory negligence.

> ***Gregory v Kelly* [1978] RTR 426:** A passenger accepted a lift in a car. Both the passenger and the driver knew that the foot brake was not working. Neither wore a seat belt. When an accident resulted, the passenger sued the driver. Held: the passenger could recover damages, but with a reduction of 40 per cent.

The courts have not only been reluctant to lay down many general rules here, but have positively stated that it will usually be wrong to do so. To see why, consider the suggestion made in *Bailey v Geddes* [1938] 1 KB 156 that if a car collides with a pedestrian, then this cannot be contributory negligence if the collision took place on a pedestrian crossing. As rules go, this is not a bad one, but almost immediately exceptions began to be made. So *Bailey* was distinguished in cases where the pedestrian stepped in front of the car unexpectedly (*Knight v Sampson* [1938] 3 All ER 309). Case law began to tackle such questions as precisely when the claimant was required to be 'on the crossing' for this purpose, and what counted as the 'crossing'. For example, was a traffic island in the middle of the road part of the 'crossing'? (Held: No (*Wilkinson v Chetham-Strode* [1940] 2 KB 310).) Later cases found it necessary to emphasize that the reasonable driver must be prepared for ill-advised acts by pedestrians, while not blaming them for anything truly unforeseeable (e.g. *Hurt v Murphy* [1971] RTR 186). Clearly, any hope for a clear rule dividing responsibility between the claimant and the defendant was almost hopeless before the 1945 Act, and entirely hopeless after it. The point is not that the behaviour of the courts is random and unpredictable, but merely that it cannot be reduced to a clear set of rules. Indeed, any judge who tries to extract *rules* from past authorities, as distinct from using them as examples for comparison to the instant case, is likely to be making a mistake.

Having said that, some straightforward situations recur with regularity. So without denying that each case is to be judged on the basis of its own peculiar facts, nonetheless it is possible to generalize about what the court will say. One such area is that of accidents caused by the defendant where the claimant was (if a car driver) not wearing a seat belt or (if a motorcycle rider) not wearing a crash helmet. *Froom v Butcher* [1976] QB 286 established that contributory negligence in such cases will be somewhere in a band running from 0 to 25 per cent, the precise point on the band being established by reference to a number of factors:

- *Causation is the major factor.* If the claimant's injuries would have been wholly avoided if the claimant had been wearing a belt, a 25 per cent deduction will be appropriate. If wearing a belt would have made no difference, or if it would have meant that the claimant would have suffered different but equally serious injuries, then no deduction should be made. Fifteen per cent would be a typical reduction, where the claimant's injuries would have been considerably less severe if the claimant had been wearing a seat belt.

- *Unreasonableness of wearing a belt.* Certain claimants will be able to escape a reduction if they have particular reasons why it would have been pointless, unsafe, or otherwise for them to wear a belt. Possible examples are if the claimant is heavily pregnant, or is unusually fat, or has a phobia about constraint (*Condon v Condon* [1978] RTR 483).

- *Other factors.* If there are other heads of contributory negligence by the claimant, this may push the total reduction up beyond 50 per cent, as where the claimant fails to wear a belt in the knowledge that the ride is likely to be a little rough.

It seems to make relatively little difference whether the case against the defendant is an unusually strong one, or whether it is just an ordinary example of negligence. Since the time of *Froom v Butcher* [1976] QB 286, legislation has provided that it is a criminal offence, in most situations, not to wear a belt (Road Traffic Act 1988, s 14, consolidating a provision in force since 1983). However, this does not seem to have altered the seriousness with which the courts view failure to wear a belt. This is no great surprise, as *Froom v Butcher* was happy to amalgamate the law on failure to wear a belt (not then illegal) with the law on failure to wear a motorcycle helmet (already at that time illegal).

It remains to be seen whether the courts will in time rule that cyclists injured in road accidents will have their damages reduced for failure to wear a cycle helmet. As with seat belts, there are arguments both ways. How much safer do the helmets make cyclists? Is the gain in safety really so significant that a decision not to wear one is comparable to life-threatening negligence on the road? Do the helmets in fact make cyclists *less* safe, by bestowing a feeling of security and therefore encouraging more risk-taking?

Employment

11.23 The duties of employers are extremely diverse, whether under the tort of negligence or through the many statutory duties applicable to the employment relationship. It appears that in such cases the courts pay some attention to the seriousness of the defendant's breach, and so will attribute a lesser share of the responsibility to the employee in cases where the defendant's breach was a relatively serious one (*Quintas v National Smelting Co* [1961] 1 All ER 630). While the exercise is in essence one of comparing the claimant's fault and the defendant's fault, however, there is no pretence that the claimant and the defendant are to be judged by the same standards:

- *Burden of proof.* It is for the defendant, not the claimant, to establish the defence, and accordingly there will not be a finding of contributory negligence merely because this is one possibility and the claimant has not established precisely how the accident occurred (*Smithwick v National Coal Board* [1950] 2 KB 335).

- *Allowances made for the claimant's situation.* Not too much will be expected of the claimant. Attention must be paid 'to the long hours and the fatigue, to the slackening of attention which naturally comes from constant repetition of the same operation, to the noise and confusion ... to his pre-occupation in what he is actually doing at the cost perhaps of some inattention to his own safety' (*Caswell v Powell Duffryn Associated Collieries* [1940] AC 152, 178–9, Lord Wright). Much of the point of industrial safety legislation is lost if a momentary lapse of concentration deprives the claimant of a claim—no matter how foolish this lapse can be made to appear in the calm of a later court hearing. Indeed, in one case it was said that industrial safety legislation is not merely for the protection of the careful, 'but, human nature being what it is, also the careless, the indolent, the inadvertent, the weary, and even perhaps in some cases, the disobedient' (*Carr v Mercantile Produce Co* [1949] 2 KB 601, 608, Stable J).

- *Care by employer.* The claimant is entitled to assume that the employer has been careful and has complied with all relevant statutory duties. The courts will be unsympathetic to an argument that the claimant ought to have realized that this was unrealistic (*Westwood v Post Office* [1974] AC 1).

- *The claimant's 'fault' does not occur in a vacuum.* The employer's duties may include a duty to warn the claimant of poor work practices, and accordingly any argument that an accident is 'wholly' the claimant's fault will receive close and suspicious scrutiny (e.g. *General Cleaning Contractors v Christmas* [1953] AC 180).

One example of the lack of symmetry between the claimant's fault and the defendant's fault is where the 'fault' attributed to the defendant consists wholly of some default by the claimant. In *Stapley v Gypsum Mines* [1953] AC 663 the claimants were instructed by their foreman to bring down the roof of a certain section of mine before they began work there. This proved more difficult than they had anticipated. In defiance of their orders, they began work there anyway. The roof collapsed on its own. Their widows sued the company: for the men to be working with the roof in that condition put the employers in breach of their statutory responsibilities. Even though the Lords considered that there was no failure of supervision—the employees were responsible and had considerable experience—they nonetheless held that their widows could recover, subject to a deduction of 80 per cent for contributory negligence. There are occasionally cases where damages are altogether refused, either on the ground that the employee's carelessness breaks any causal connection between the defendant's default and the claimant's injuries (e.g. *Norris v W Moss & Sons* [1954] 1 All ER 324, where the claimant's 'fantastically wrong' initiative resulted in injury), or where the court feels that the claimant's responsibility for the accident must be assessed at 100 per cent (*Jayes v IMI (Kynock)* [1985] ICR 155).

It should now be apparent why the decision in *McWilliams v Sir William Arrol & Co* [1962] 1 All ER 623 is regarded as so anomalous (**10.25**). Where the defendant is bound to provide safety equipment and to take reasonable steps to persuade the site workers to use it, and then the claimant is injured through failure to use the equipment, then evidence that the claimant would have refused to use it is a ground of contributory negligence. But it is curious to find a court putting *all* of the blame on the worker, by a ruling that the employers' behaviour did not 'cause' the accident. It seems a classic case of joint responsibility. If a culture had grown up in the firm in which the use of safety equipment was neglected, then the employer's duty was not satisfied by simply accepting this situation. But it is in any event hard to reconcile all these cases in this difficult area.

100 per cent contributory negligence: a problem

11.24 The Law Reform (Contributory Negligence) Act 1945 appears to have been drafted so as to give the court a free hand in apportioning liability between the claimant and the defendant. Nonetheless, it was suggested in *Pitts v Hunt* [1991] 1 QB 24 that the court cannot use it to apportion 100 per cent of the blame to the claimant. The reasoning appears to be that the Act only applies where the claimant suffers damage 'as the result partly of his own fault and partly of the fault of any other person' (s 1(1)), whereas a 100 per cent reduction implies that it is wholly the claimant's fault. This seems dubious, however. There does not seem to be any logical inconsistency in saying *both* that the claimant and the defendant are at fault *and* that it is 'just and equitable' to reduce the claimant's damages to zero. In any event, the Court of Appeal's logic seems to stop short of its proper end: if the Act does not apply, then presumably the old common law rule, defeating the claimant's claim entirely, applies, with the effect that the claim is defeated. So it should make no difference whether the Act applies or not. *Pitts v Hunt* did not refer to earlier cases which allowed a 100 per cent reduction (e.g. *Jayes v IMI (Kynock)* [1985] ICR 155) (**11.23**), and is therefore a weak authority.

'Proportionate fault'

11.25   The contributory negligence rule only reduces the claimant's damages for the claimant's own fault. It is anomalous. Generally speaking, where the defendant has been found responsible for the claimant's damage, it is no defence for the defendant to show that others too were responsible, and the risk of not being able to make out a case against any of them is on the defendant, not the claimant (**9.26**). Various critics have recently suggested that the defendant should be entitled to a reduction in damages for 'proportionate fault'. That is, that while the defendant was responsible for the claimant's loss, nonetheless the fault was by no means as grave as that of others, and accordingly the defendant should be entitled to a reduction, regardless of whether those others can be caught. This has been pleaded especially in cases where the defendant's fault was in not warning the claimant of the activities of criminals who go on to harm the claimant: the defendant's fault is not to be equated with that of the criminals, and so the defendant's liability ought not to be as great (**1.33**). This view has however found little sympathy in the courts so far.

Illegality

11.26   It is sometimes open to the defendant to argue that the claimant's claim should 'shock the conscience of the court', or that it is so undesirable that it should not be permitted. The principle is well established, but its application is vague, as are the goals the courts are attempting to pursue here. The doctrine has been summed up as being that 'bad people get less' (Weir *Casebook on Tort* (7th edn, 1992) 256). But this gives a misleadingly broad impression of the doctrine. It is certainly true that bad people get less in tort. For example, those who already have bad reputations will have a hard time convincing a court that any defamatory utterances made their reputations worse (**8.22**). But the claimant can be as bad as you like, yet still be entitled not to be run over by the defendant's car—no matter how saintly the defendant might be as a rule.

The rule is that there must be something so shocking about *the claim now being made* that it cannot be permitted. The Latin tag is *ex turpi causa non oritur actio*: 'No action arises from a disgraceful cause'. The defence is not an opportunity for the defendant to sling mud at random, but rather to show that the claimant's activities *in the case before the court* were so thoroughly tied up with serious illegality that the two cannot fairly be separated. The connection must be a close one. It has been said that if two burglars are on their way to a house they mean to steal from and one picks the other's pocket, there is no defence to an action in tort. The tort is quite distinct from the illegal plan (*National Coal Board v England* [1954] AC 403, 429, Lord Asquith). There is no necessary connection with 'illegality' in any normal sense. Workers who are guilty of offences against industrial safety legislation do not seem to be in any danger of being met by a defence of illegality if they sue for injuries suffered. And perfectly legal conduct may in some circumstances sufficiently affront the public conscience as to make recovery impossible (*Kirkham v Chief Constable of Greater Manchester* [1990] 3 All ER 246, 251, Lloyd LJ).

It is hard to disagree with the provisional conclusion of the Law Commission (*The Illegality Defence in Tort*, Law Com Consultation Paper No 160, May 2001) that the law is confused. The Commission's proposal is to restate the law as a structured discretion, giving the courts power to act as the public interest seems to require, but spelling out the considerations that should be borne in mind. As a proposal for the structure of the subject, this seems reasonable. As the Commission acknowledges, however, this would not end controversies over the application of the defence. At best, it might ensure that the inevitable arguments over its detail are conducted in a more open and rational manner than has been the case up to now.

Serious crime

11.27 Where the claimant and the defendant are jointly engaged in a serious criminal escapade, then an action in consequence of injuries sustained will fail. So the classic example given is where one burglar blows the lock off a safe so carelessly that it injures the other (*National Coal Board v England* [1954] AC 403, 429, Lord Asquith). Some judges prefer to put this on the ground that it is impossible to set an appropriate standard of care in such cases. But it is not *meaningless* to say that the careless burglar did the job badly; it is another question whether it provides a good ground for his colleague to recover damages. Examples are hard to come by, however. In *Ashton v Turner* [1981] QB 137 one participant in a drunken attempt at burglary sued the other for injuries sustained as they attempted a high-speed getaway. Illegality was one ground given for rejecting this claim, but consent to run the risk was another, and quite sufficient in itself.

Where the defendant was the victim of the crime, or was trying to prevent it, there is little sign that the defence is available. Rather, an artificially low, but nonetheless real, standard of care is applied, so that the claimant can recover, but only after producing a great deal more evidence of lack of care by the defendant than is usually required.

> **Marshall v Osmond [1983] QB 1034:** Marshall was attempting to drive off with a stolen car, but was followed by a police constable. Marshall then stopped and attempted to run away, but was knocked down by the police constable's car. Held: no defence of consent was applicable, but the duty owed by road users was relative to the circumstances in which they were placed, and by that standard the police constable was not negligent.

Extreme facts may however justify the application of the maxim.

> **Vellino v Chief Constable of Greater Manchester [2001] EWCA Civ 1249:** Vellino was frequently arrested by the police, who knew that on such occasions he would often attempt to escape by jumping from his second-floor window to the street below. In September 1994 he tried this strategy for the last time, fracturing his skull and suffering tetraplegia. Held: escaping from arrest was sufficiently serious to bring in the *ex turpi causa* maxim, and accordingly the police owed him no duty to prevent him injuring himself in this manner.

It was at one time suggested that if a householder shot a burglar then the burglar has no cause of action, even if the householder's use of force was subsequently found to be excessive, or indeed if manslaughter were established (*Murphy v Culhane* [1977] QB 94, 98, Lord Denning MR). However, it appears that this is not the law. In *Revill v Newbery* [1996] QB 567 burglars attempted to break into a garden shed. Unknown to them, the owner was hiding inside to forestall theft, and in a panic fired his 12-bore shotgun through the keyhole, causing serious injuries to one of the burglars. The civil court rejected the owner's defence of self-defence, which had been accepted by a jury on a criminal charge of wounding. Contributory negligence was assessed at 66.66 per cent; the defence of illegality was rejected entirely. The decision is a controversial one, but in line with earlier cases. So, for example, in *Farrell v Secretary of State for Defence* [1980] 1 All ER 166, where would-be robbers were shot dead by soldiers who thought they were terrorists, the issue was whether the use of deadly force was justified in the circumstances, and if it was not, there was no additional defence of illegality.

At the root of criticism of *Revill* seems to be dissatisfaction with the law on self-defence and the defence of property. If there is a problem, it lies there, and not with the law of tort. If the current law is accepted as good, so that those who use deadly force where it cannot be justified are themselves guilty of serious criminal offences (a big *if*!), then there does not seem to be anything wrong with *Revill*. Both the claimant and the defendant are criminals, and the most that the claimant is entitled to is a division of responsibility between them. Public disquiet at *Revill* and other cases, particularly that of Tony Martin, led to the enactment of Criminal Justice Act 2003, s 329. This complicated provision limits civil actions for assault or false imprisonment where the claimant has been convicted of an imprisonable offence committed on the same occasion, provided that the defendant's motivation was a lawful one.

Fights

11.28 It appears to be the law that where the claimant and the defendant fight, and the defendant injures the claimant, it is a defence if it can be shown that the claimant provoked the fight. This is sometimes put on the ground of illegality and sometimes, confusingly, on the ground of consent. So if the claimant sets out to beat up the defendant, but meets with a fiercer response than he bargained for, the claimant has no action whether or not the defendant exceeded the limits of permissible self-defence (*Murphy v Culhane* [1977] QB 94). However, this may not be so if the claimant's attack on the defendant, while unjustified, was nonetheless relatively trifling when compared to the defendant's response (*Lane v Holloway* [1968] 1 QB 379). In a case of that sort, consideration needs to be given to a reduction for the claimant's contributory negligence, though the Court of Appeal in *Lane v Holloway* declined to make one.

Tax evasion and fraud

11.29 In *Saunders v Edwards* [1987] 2 All ER 651, which concerned deceit over the sale of a flat, it appeared that both parties had engaged in a fraud on the revenue, grossly overstating the value of fixtures in the flat to reduce liability to stamp duty. This was not regarded as providing a defence to action in deceit. The case can be viewed as one where the illegality was rather peripheral to the cause of action. It was also one where the court regarded the defendant's fraud as rather more deserving of condemnation than the claimant's tax evasion. 'The moral culpability of the defendant greatly outweighs any on the part of the claimants. He cannot be allowed to keep the fruits of his fraud' ([1987] 2 All ER 651, 660, Kerr LJ).

In *Stone and Rolls v Moore Stephens* [2009] UKHL 39, a company sued their auditors for failing to notice a fraud perpetrated by the company with the knowledge of its chief executive. Obviously no such claim could succeed if the damages were to go to the benefit of the fraudster, but Langley J at first instance saw no reason why the creditors of the company (now in liquidation) should be penalized, and since they would be the beneficiaries of the action should it succeed, he rejected the defence of illegality in the circumstances. But the Court of Appeal and House of Lords disagreed. The 'controlling mind' of the company had been a fraudster; in effect, therefore, the action was being brought by a fraudulent claimant against an innocent, if negligent, defendant, and so was rightly thrown out.

Dangerous driving

11.30　In *Pitts v Hunt* [1991] 1 QB 24 the claimant (aged 18) and the defendant (aged 16) spent the evening getting drunk at a disco. They then set off home on the defendant's motorcycle, with the claimant riding pillion. With encouragement from the claimant, the defendant drove in a dangerous manner, doing his best to startle other road users. They collided with an oncoming car; at the inquest, the defendant was found to have double the legal blood-alcohol level. The claimant survived and sued. Liability was refused on the ground of illegality.

The result is not surprising, but it does not sit happily with the other material on illegality. The activity of the defendant was undoubtedly criminal in several respects, especially given that the defendant was neither licensed nor insured to drive the motorcycle, and it might have led to serious injury to other road users (though in the event it did not). But the criminality in the case is hardly in the same league as bank robbery. The real complaint against the claimant and the defendant's conduct is not so much that it was illegal as that it was crazy. The case is indeed a teenage rerun of *Morris v Murray* [1991] 2 QB 6, where the claimant and the defendant were older and had access to a more impressive vehicle, but showed a similar level of concern for their own and others' safety (**11.8**). Should the court in *Pitts* have applied the defence of contributory negligence? The court doubted whether it was possible to reduce damages for contributory negligence by 100 per cent (**11.24**); in any event, they said, when the claimant and the defendant were both engaged in an unlawful and dangerous exercise, the appropriate reduction would be 50 per cent. The case is best categorized as an application of the defence of consent, with the court being unwilling to acknowledge that it applied in the face of Road Traffic Act 1988, s 149(3), which excludes the defence in cases involving compulsory third party road insurance (**11.15**). Certainly *Pitts* is a very unsatisfactory guide to liability outside its own immediate facts.

The mentally ill claimant

11.31　Controversially, the Court of Appeal has held that where the claimant commits a serious criminal act, the claimant cannot sue a health authority for failing to treat his mental illness, even if reasonably good treatment would have avoided the claimant's later act (*Clunis v Camden and Islington Health Authority* [1998] QB 978). The criminality in the case was of the very highest sort. The claimant, who had a long history of mental illness, had stabbed another man to death, three months after his release from hospital, and was convicted of manslaughter. *Clunis* in effect contradicts earlier, similar cases where no illegality point was raised, and the claimant was allowed to succeed (e.g. *Meah v McCreamer* [1985] 1 All ER 367 (**10.38**)). The Court of Appeal stressed that the claimant's plea of insanity at his trial for murder had been rejected, and so the claimant had to be treated as an independent agent, responsible for his actions. To the same effect is *Gray v Thames Trains* [2009] UKHL 33, where a previously peaceable claimant turned violent after an accident for which the defendants were responsible, and was sentenced to indefinite detention in a mental hospital after a conviction for manslaughter. To some, a denial of liability on those facts is necessary for the consistency of the legal system—if the claimant is responsible for his own actions, he cannot blame them on the defendant. To others, this simplifies the matter too much: in both *Gray* and *Clunis*, the criminal courts had accepted pleas of diminished responsibility—in other words, had accepted that the claimant was *not* fully responsible for his own actions—and so it is hard to see how consistency requires tort law to assume otherwise.

Limitation

11.32   For a number of reasons, it is considered to be unfair to leave the defendant at risk of a legal action for too long. Accordingly, action for a tort must be brought within a certain period of time of the tort's commission. If the defendant raises the issue, it is for the claimant to prove that the action has been brought within the period. The basic period is six years (Limitation Act 1980, s 2), but there are a number of exceptions:

- actions for *defamation* must be commenced within one year, though there is a discretion to waive this period where it would cause unfairness to the claimant (Limitation Act 1980, ss 4A and 32A, as amended by Defamation Act 1996, s 5);

- actions in *negligence for personal injury* must usually be commenced within three years, though there are wide exceptions to this (**11.36**);

- special provision is made for *latent damage* by statute (**11.41**);

- a claim for *contribution* against a fellow tortfeasor must be brought within two years of the judgment or settlement which creates the claim (Limitation Act 1980, s 10);

- actions under the *Consumer Protection Act 1987* are subject to the normal time limits for the type of injury suffered, but also to an absolute ten-year long-stop from the date on which the defendant supplied the product to someone else (Limitation Act 1980, s 11A; for the precise point at which the ten-year period starts see *O'Byrne v Sanofi Pasteur MSD* [2006] 1 WLR 1606). This long-stop is absolute, with no exception for disability (**11.33**) or concealment (**11.34**). However, it has recently been held that where an action has been commenced within the period, the long-stop provisions do not necessarily prevent the substitution of a different defendant after the period has passed (*Horne-Roberts v Smithkline Beecham* [2001] EWCA Civ 2006).

There is much case law on when the period first begins to run. The usual rule is that it begins to run from the first instant when the claimant could have made a claim, whether or not the claimant knew this at the time. It will therefore sometimes be necessary to distinguish between torts, such as negligence, which are only actionable on proof of special damage, and torts which are actionable without it (see above, **10.9**). The former situation is by far the most common in practice. The basic time limit in contract is also six years, but nonetheless tort is more favourable, as in contract time usually runs from the date of the breach of contract, whereas in tort it is usually from the date of the damage, which will usually be later. A special situation is the 'continuing tort', such as a 'continuing trespass' by leaving something unwelcome on the claimant's land, or 'continuing nuisance' by allowing a state of affairs constituting a nuisance to continue for a period. A fresh tort is committed for every day that the tort is allowed to continue. Accordingly, a claim form issued too late to complain of the commencement of the tort may nonetheless complain of the portion of the tort which fell within the limitation period.

The law seems unnecessarily confused. The Law Commission has recommended that the law should be simplified, by the introduction of a 'core regime' applicable to most claims. This would involve a three-year period, to run from the first date that the claim could reasonably be made, with a ten-year long-stop (*Limitation of Actions*, Law Com Report No 270, July 2001). Any simplification of the law would be welcome. But equally there will always be many exceptions and complications relating to certain types of action, and it is unrealistic to hope for too great a simplification.

Infancy and other disabilities

11.33 If, when time would ordinarily start to run against the claimant, the claimant is under 18 or suffering from unsoundness of mind, or both, then time does not run. It begins to run when the claimant is both of age and of sound mind, or alternatively when the claimant dies (Limitation Act 1980, s 28(1)). The claimant suffers from unsoundness of mind if the claimant is incapable of managing and administering his or her affairs by reason of a mental disorder under the Mental Health Act 1983. Disability delays the start of the period, but cannot stop the clock running once it has started. So if the claimant suffered mental illness before his or her eighteenth birthday, it will stop the clock from ever starting. But a mental illness which was absent on the claimant's eighteenth birthday will not stop the clock on any cause of action arising before it.

Concealment

11.34 Where the defendant has deliberately concealed the commission of the tort or some material fact, or the action was itself based on the defendant's fraud, then time does not begin to run until the claimant could, with reasonable diligence, have been expected to discover the cause of action (Limitation Act 1980, s 32(1)). 'Deliberate concealment' is widely defined: 'deliberate commission of a breach of duty in circumstances in which it is unlikely to be discovered for some time amounts to deliberate concealment of the facts involved in that breach of duty' (s 32(2)). This requires at minimum that the defendant knew he or she was in breach of duty: *Cave v Robinson Jarvis and Rolf* [2002] UKHL 18.

There is no test of moral turpitude beyond the fact that the concealment must be deliberate.

> *Kitchen v Royal Air Force Association* **[1958] 2 All ER 241:** Solicitors negligently failed to advise a widow of her possible claim for her husband's death. Subsequently, after the period of limitation had run on that claim, the solicitors deliberately failed to pass on an offer of £100 from those responsible for the death, in case their earlier negligence was revealed. Held: their original failure to give good advice did not constitute 'concealment', but their suppression of the offer letter did.

The effect of the section is only to prevent time running in the first place. If time has already started to run, subsequent concealment by the defendant will not affect it (*Tito v Waddell (No 2)* [1977] 3 All ER 129, 245, Megarry V-C).

Personal injuries

Assault and battery

11.35 After some controversy, it has now been settled that the period for deliberate injuries is six years from their infliction, and that the special provision for personal injury caused by negligence (**11.36**) does not apply.

> *Stubbings v Webb* **[1993] AC 498:** Stubbings, over 30 at the time she made the claim, sued Webb for assaults committed between her second and fourteenth birthdays,

including rape when she was aged 11. She claimed that she had not appreciated that she might have a cause of action until she realized that there might be a link between her early experiences and her later psychiatric problems. Held: the period was six years from the end of her minority, and so she could not make a claim after her twenty-fourth birthday.

It is irrelevant whether Stubbings' action was framed as one in battery or in negligence. The question is whether it is the claimant's case that the defendant committed the tort negligently or intentionally. This unsatisfactory state of the law has however now been altered, the House of Lords ruling in *A v Hoare* [2008] UKHL 6 that such cases fall to be governed by the same principles as apply to cases of negligence, so that the period may be relaxed at the discretion of the court. Whether this proves to be any more satisfactory remains to be seen. The difficulties of resolving such disputes where many years have passed from the date of the alleged assault are obvious enough, and it is so far not clear how many additional years the claimant has under this new ruling.

Negligence: the primary period

11.36　Before 1963, the period in respect of personal injuries caused by negligence began to run as soon as the damage was suffered by the claimant. The House of Lords held that this applied even where the damage was initially undiscoverable, and only became unmistakable outside the period (*Cartledge v E Jopling & Sons* [1963] AC 758). Dissatisfaction at this result led to a change in the law, so that time will now run only from the first point when the claimant could reasonably have been expected to consider legal action. There is also a general discretion to waive the limitation period if justice would be served thereby (**11.37**). The discretion has been interpreted widely: the actions for failure to diagnose and provide for the claimants' dyslexia have been treated as claims for 'personal injuries' for this purpose (*Phelps v Hillingdon London Borough Council* [2001] 2 AC 619).

Under the modern law, time will therefore begin to run only from 'the date of knowledge' (Limitation Act 1980, s 11(4)); that is, the first date on which the claimant knew or ought reasonably to have known *all four* of the following:

• *That the injury was significant.* An injury is significant if a reasonable person in the claimant's position would think it worthwhile suing someone liable for it, at least if they admitted liability and had funds to meet the claim (Limitation Act 1980, s 14(2)). The significance or otherwise of the injury is a question about the injury itself, not about its effect on the claimant's private life or career (*McCoubrey v Ministry of Defence* [2007] EWCA Civ 17).

- *That the injury was attributable to the act or omission constituting the tort.* It is sufficient if in general terms the claimant can be said to have this knowledge, whether or not the claimant has precise knowledge of the acts or omissions concerned (*Wilkinson v Ancliff (BLT)* [1986] 3 All ER 427). It is not enough, however, if the claimant knew the injury resulted from a surgical operation, unless the claimant also knew that the operation was negligently performed (*Bentley v Bristol and Weston Health Authority* [1991] 2 Med LR 359).

- *The defendant's identity.* It sometimes happens that the claimant is initially ignorant of the identity of the appropriate defendant, as where the claimant is the victim of a hit-and-run driver. Or again, the claimant may initially have a false idea of the defendant's identity. For example, the claimant might mean to sue his employer, which is part of a group of companies, the wrong company being specified on the claimant's written contract of employment (*Simpson v Norwest Holst Southern* [1980] 2 All ER 471).

- *(Where the defendant is allegedly liable for the fault of another) the identity of the other, and the additional facts showing that the defendant is liable.*

The claimant's 'knowledge' for this purpose includes everything that a person of the claimant's age and 'with his background, his intelligence, and his disabilities' would reasonably have known (*Davis v City and Hackney Health Authority* [1991] 2 Med LR 366). It also includes things discoverable with the help of expert advice which it would have been reasonable to seek; though if the claimant does in fact act reasonably in taking professional advice, the claimant is only responsible for what the claimant *in fact* finds out (Limitation Act 1980, s 14(3)). It is unclear precisely when the claimant can be said to 'know' things of which the claimant has only a strong suspicion. The courts seem reluctant to equate knowledge with belief. Certainly in cases where there was plainly something wrong, but the claimant's beliefs fluctuated over a period, the courts seem reluctant to put the 'date of knowledge' too early, particularly as the statute does not allow the clock to be stopped once it has started. The mere fact that the claimant's solicitor has started proceedings against the defendant does not prove that the claimant 'knew' the defendant was liable; the solicitor may simply have been safeguarding the claimant's position, in case the defendant turned out to be liable (*Stephen v Riverside Health Authority* [1990] 1 Med LR 261). It has even been held that a claimant who is certain in his or her own mind that the defendant is responsible does not have 'knowledge' in a case where it is reasonable to ask for expert confirmation. The clock does not start until an expert has confirmed the claimant's suspicions (*Nash v Eli Lilly & Co* [1993] 4 All ER 383). The claimant's knowledge of the relevant law is absolutely irrelevant (Limitation Act 1980, s 14(1)).

Negligence: discretion to waive the period

11.37 Even if this primary period has run, it is still open to the claimant to argue that it would be equitable for the period of limitation to be waived (Limitation Act 1980, s 33). Various factors are taken into account under the section:

- Why did the claimant delay so long? Did the claimant act promptly and reasonably once he or she knew there might be a legal action?

- Will the evidence, on either side, still be coherent?

- How did the defendant behave after the cause of action arose? In particular, how helpful or otherwise was the defendant when responding to the claimant's reasonable requests for information?

- Was the claimant under any disability while time ran and, if so, for how long did it last?

- What steps did the claimant take to get advice, and what was that advice?

All relevant circumstances are to be taken into account, whether or not they are specifically mentioned in the 1980 Act (s 33(3)). Any delay which can be attributed to the claimant's own solicitors counts against the claimant's case, partly because it is unfair that the defendant should be prejudiced by such errors, but also because the claimant might have a remedy against the solicitors themselves. The power to waive the primary period was originally meant only for exceptional cases, but it appears that the court's discretion is in no way fettered, and the claimant does not have to demonstrate that the case is an unusual one (*Firman v Ellis* [1978] QB 886). The discretion to allow an action outside the period exists even if the claimant had commenced proceedings within the primary period which then failed for procedural reasons (*Horton v Sadler* [2006] UKHL 27, overruling *Walkley v Precision Forgings* [1979] 2 All ER 548).

Negligence: the effect of the claimant's death

11.38 Where the claimant dies, there are two types of claim which might be brought: a claim by the claimant's estate on the surviving cause of action, and (where the death was the result of the tort) a claim by the claimant's relatives for loss of their dependency (**10.66**). The limitation rules are the same for both claims. Assuming that the death occurs while the primary period is still running, then the claim on death arises automatically, with its own three-year period which runs from the death or from the claimants' 'date of knowledge', whichever is the later (Limitation Act 1980, ss 11(5) and 12(2)). The discretion to waive the primary period applies to this claim.

Property damage

Negligence: the primary period

11.39 The unfairness of holding the claimant to a six-year period, regardless of whether the claimant could possibly have discovered the damage within that period, much exercised a number of judges in the 1970s and 1980s. Indeed, the Court of Appeal was at one point prepared to say that the claimant's cause of action only really arose when the injury was reasonably discoverable by the claimant, so that time only began to run at that date (*Sparham-Souter v Town and Country Developments (Essex)* [1976] QB 858). But the Lords soon overruled this, saying that the relevant date was the date of the damage, not the date when the claimant could reasonably have discovered it (*Pirelli General Cable Works v Oscar Faber and Partners* [1983] 2 AC 1). However, what the courts took away with one hand they gave back with the other. If the foundations of a house are damaged, this may have no immediate effect on the main structure of the building, let alone the safety of the inhabitants. So damage to a particular part of a building is suffered only when *that part* is damaged, even if the problem can be traced to structural damage committed at an earlier date (*Nitrigin Eireann Teoranta v Inco Alloys* [1992] 1 All ER 854). (This is a variant of the 'complex structure' argument, on which see **5.11** above.) Confusingly, the House of Lords in *Pirelli* suggested that the matter might be different if the building was 'doomed from the start', in which case it would not be realistic to divide it up in this way. Most of the difficulties in this area have been avoided only by the *Murphy* decision, which effectively ruled out most of these claims as being claims for purely economic loss (**5.4**).

Negligent misstatement: the primary period

11.40 Where the claimant acts on the defendant's poor professional advice and the claimant comes to harm as a result, when does the claimant's claim accrue? Some cases hold that it is when the claimant first acts on the advice, others when the claimant in fact suffers harm. The cases are not easy to reconcile, but an obvious date is the last date at which the claimant (if well informed) could possibly have avoided the loss. When the claimant enters into a disadvantageous transaction, the terms of which cannot later be corrected, the loss is suffered at that time, even if the loss only becomes apparent at a later date.

> **Forster v Outred & Co [1982] 2 All ER 753:** After poor advice from her solicitors, Forster mortgaged her house to cover her son's debts. Subsequently her son went bankrupt and the mortgage company enforced its security. Held: Forster's action against her solicitors ran from the date of the mortgage.

However, no such general rule is stated in the cases, and it is impossible to reconcile it with some of them.

> **Bell v Peter Browne & Co [1990] 2 QB 495:** On their divorce, the Bells agreed that the house should be put into the name of the wife and that the husband's interest should be protected by registration. The husband's solicitors negligently failed to take this elementary precaution, and eight years later the former wife sold the property, extinguishing her former husband's interest. Held: the damage occurred at the date a competent solicitor should have effected a registration, even though this could have been done at any time before the former wife sold.

Negligence: extended period

11.41 Where the primary period has expired, there is another extended period of three years from the date on which the claimant could, with reasonable care, have discovered the loss (Limitation Act 1980, ss 14A and 14B). This is defined in similar terms to the 'primary period' for personal injury actions (**11.36**): time begins to run from the 'date of knowledge', at which the claimant ought reasonably to have realized that the defendant was liable and worth suing. The period is, however, subject to a long-stop of 15 years from the time the defendant broke his or her duty, unless the defendant is guilty of fraud or deliberate concealment. The extended period does not apply to actions which were already time-barred before this period became part of the law (18 September 1986).

Necessity

11.42 In very rare circumstances, the defendant can defeat the claim by arguing that commission of the tort against the claimant was the lesser of two evils. For a number of reasons, the courts are very reluctant to allow this plea to succeed, even in cases where the public interest was plainly served by the defendant's acting as he or she did. For one thing, defendants are not to be encouraged to take the law into their own hands in this way. For another, the question whether the community benefits from the defendant's actions is quite different from whether the claimant ought to receive compensation. So the defence may be raised to cover action taken to avoid an imminent disaster, as where the defendant destroys the claimant's property to create a fire break (*Cope v Sharpe (No 2)* [1912] 1 KB 496). But the courts have always refused to allow hunger as a defence to taking food belonging to the claimant, or homelessness as a defence to trespassing in the claimant's empty house. To allow the plea in those circumstances, it has been argued, 'would open a door which no man could shut' (*Southwark London Borough Council v Williams* [1971] Ch 734,

744, Lord Denning MR). Similarly, the defence has been refused to campaigners who tore up genetically modified crops, despite their plea that they were acting in the public's defence (*Monsanto v Tilly* [1999] NLJR 1833).

The defence is narrowly confined. Any negligence by the defendant, either in letting the emergency arise or in dealing with it, will prevent reliance on the defence. So even if the police are entitled to take extreme measures to deal with serious public disturbances, and so to that extent have a defence of necessity, that does not excuse negligence on their part.

> **Rigby v Chief Constable of Northamptonshire [1985] 2 All ER 985:** The police fired a canister of CS gas into the claimant's shop, as part of a plan to flush out a dangerous psychopath. The claimant's shop burnt out in consequence. Held: the claimant's action in trespass to land could be defeated by a plea of necessity, but action in negligence succeeded, as the police had not taken reasonable precautions to stop the spread of fire.

Indeed, some writers deny that necessity can ever be a defence to an action for negligence, as nothing can excuse carelessness in this context. But this seems to go too far, as necessity could surely in some cases justify the defendant's running a risk of injury to the claimant, which would normally count as negligence. Nonetheless, the civil law here is harsher on defendants than is the criminal law: if self-defence is relied on, it is for the defendant to prove it (rather than for the other side to negative it), and the defendant's conduct must be reasonable in the actual circumstances (not merely reasonable in the circumstances the defendant *as the defendant imagined them to be*, as the criminal law would demand) (*Ashley v Chief Constable of Sussex Police* [2006] EWCA Civ 1085).

Medical treatment

11.43 In cases where the claimant is unconscious, or for some other reason temporarily incapable of considering whether consent is appropriate, justifiable medical interventions will not be treated as batteries. This doctrine has also been applied in cases of mentally incapable claimants. In that context it has also been used to justify intervention which seems to be in their best interests and not strictly 'necessary' (*Re F* [1990] 2 AC 1). But this decision has attracted criticism, especially in so far as it relied on the *Bolam* rule, that the courts will not question doctors' views of what is reasonable (**4.46**). In some cases, statute authorizes intervention against the claimant's will (e.g. Mental Health Act 1983, s 63; see *R v Dr M* [2002] EWCA Civ 1789). Even more controversially, the House of Lords held (*R v Bournewood Community and Mental Health NHS Trust, ex p L* [1999] 1 AC 458) that detention and treatment of the mentally ill may sometimes be permitted under the common law of necessity, despite the lack of express authorization under the Act. At the very least, these cases will need to be reconsidered under the Human Rights Act 1998, particularly for conformity with Art 3 of the European Convention (prohibition of inhuman or degrading treatment) as well as Art 5 (liberty of the person). Only a few cases have however so far been resolved, and those rather controversially.

Re A (Children) (Conjoined Twins: Surgical Separation) [2001] Fam 147: Conjoined twins were born. One was capable of independent existence; the other was alive only because a common artery allowed her sister's heart to circulate blood to her. If no operation took place, both would probably die within six months; an operation to separate them would prolong the life of one but kill the other. Could the operation take place in the teeth of Art 2 (the right to life)? Held: it could. It was impermissible to deny that each life had equal value. However, where doctors had to choose between competing evils, it was permissible to have regard to issues of the quality of life.

NHS Trust A v M [2001] Fam 348: The hospital sought a declaration authorizing them to discontinue nutrition and water to M, a patient in a vegetative state believed to be permanent. Did this infringe M's right to life (Art 2)? Held: a responsible clinical decision to withhold treatment, taken in the best interests of the patient, could not be said to infringe his or her human rights. However, the court rejected the argument that withholding treatment was authorized by Art 3 (prohibition of inhuman or degrading treatment).

Simms v An NHS Trust [2002] EWHC 2734: An 18-year-old and a 16-year-old suffered from variant CJD, as a result of which both were helpless invalids with severely limited life expectancy. A declaration was sought that it was lawful to use a new treatment on them, which had never before been tested on humans. Held: any treatment had to satisfy not simply the *Bolam* test but also a requirement that the treatment be in the best interests of the patients. Here, the treatment would be approved: the possible prolongation of their lives was enough, even though no cure was possible.

Outside those cases, it is occasionally suggested that necessity can be a defence, even where the claimant is entirely capable, and has made it absolutely clear that the intervention is not being consented to. A particularly topical area is where a hospital insists on delivering a child by Caesarean section, the mother insisting that she would rather run the risks of a natural birth. Is this a battery against the mother? In *Re MB (Caesarean Section)* [1997] 2 FCR 541, the Court of Appeal held that if the mother is legally competent, she is absolutely entitled to refuse her consent. The court rejected the argument that the hospital could intervene in the interests of the child, arguing that the mother's interests could not in that situation sensibly be separated from the interests of the child. Yet, on the facts, it denied the claim. The mother agreed with the doctors that the intervention was necessary, but had refused out of a phobia of needles. She was therefore, to that extent, regarded as incapable of refusing consent. So the Court of Appeal found against her, while maintaining the basic rule. (Further consideration was given to capability to refuse consent in *Re B (Adult: Refusal of Medical Treatment)* [2002] EWHC 429 (Fam).)

This was followed by *St George's Healthcare NHS Trust v S* [1999] Fam 26, where the Court of Appeal reiterated (after S had already undergone a forced Caesarean section) that an adult of sound mind was entitled to refuse such treatment. In appropriate circumstances, consent could be dispensed with under the mental health legislation; but this legislation could not be deployed merely because the adult concerned held unusual views about her own and her child's safety. Further, someone detained under the legislation could not be forced to undergo treatment if they had adequate capacity to consent to or refuse the treatment.

The law has recently been restated by statute, in Mental Capacity Act 2005, ss 1–5, in force 1 October 2007. In most respects this simply reiterates the common law, though it is more detailed and in some respects is more demanding of those seeking a defence.

FURTHER READING

Clucas and O'Donnell 'Conjoined twins: the cutting edge' (2002) 5 Web JCLI (<http://webjcli.ncl.ac.uk/2002/issue5/clucas5.html>).

Glofcheski 'Plaintiff's illegality as a bar to recovery of personal injury damages' (1999) 19 LS 6.

Gravells 'Three heads of contributory negligence' (1977) 93 LQR 581.

Hocking and Muirhead 'Warning, warning, warning—All doctors!' (2000) 16 Prof Neg 31.

Jones 'Informed consent and other fairy stories' (1999) 7 Med Law Rev 103.

Maclean 'Caesarean sections, competence and the illusion of autonomy' (1999) 1 Web JCLI (<http://webjcli.ncl.ac.uk/1999/issue1/maclean1.html>).

Maclean 'The doctrine of informed consent: does it exist and has it crossed the Atlantic?' (2004) 24 LS 386.

O'Sullivan 'Causation and non-disclosure of medical risks—Reflections on *Chester v Afshar*' (2003) 19 Prof Neg 370.

Prime and Scanlan 'Limitation and personal injury in the House of Lords—Problem solved?' (2008) 29 SLR 111.

Stauch 'Taking the consequences of failure to warn of medical risks' (2000) 63 MLR 261.

Wicks 'The right to refuse medical treatment under the European Convention on Human Rights' (2001) 9 Med Law Rev 17.

1   What factors are relevant when, in a personal injury action, the claimant invites the court to waive the primary limitation period (**11.37**)? In what circumstances is there a similar jurisdiction to waive the period for property damage (**11.41**)?

2   Can the claimant sue his or her employer for risks which were obviously inherent in the job when the claimant took it (**11.9**)?

3   The claimant and the defendant set out to rob a house. Before they reach their intended target, they argue over the division of any goods they steal, and the defendant assaults the claimant. Can the claimant sue (**11.27**)?

4   If the claimant accepts a lift from the defendant and is then injured by the defendant's drunk driving, does the defendant have any defence to the claimant's action for negligence (**11.7, 11.22**)?

5   To which torts is contributory negligence a defence (**11.18**)?

Glossary

Italicized words have their own definitions.

Absolute privilege A defence to an action in *defamation*, by which the defendant is completely free of liability (**8.28**).

Actionable per se (of a civil wrong) Giving rise to a right of action whether or not itemizable damage can be proved (**8.19**).

Agency A legal relationship by which one party authorizes another to act, with the result that the action has legal consequences for the authorizer (or 'principal') rather than the agent (**9.18**).

Aggravated damages Damages going beyond the ordinary compensatory measure, not to punish the defendant but to reflect the claimant's injured feeling (**10.16**). Compare *exemplary damages* and *compensatory damages*.

Assault A civil wrong which consists of making another person fear immediate personal violence (**2.1**).

Battery A civil wrong which consists of inflicting force on another person (**2.4**).

Compensatory damages Damages which compensate the claimant strictly for the financial loss suffered, and no more (**10.18**). Compare *exemplary damages* and *aggravated damages*.

Concurrent liability Liability where two or more areas of law overlap, so that the claimant has a choice as to which legal ground to base the claim on (**3.7**).

Contribution Where two or more people are responsible for the same damage and one of them is held responsible for it, that one may seek to recoup part of their loss from the others. This is called 'claiming contribution' (**9.26**). Compare *contributory negligence*.

Contributory negligence Conduct by the claimant which entails that the claimant shares responsibility for any loss occurring, with the result that the amount of any claim will be reduced (**11.17**). Compare *contribution*.

Deceit A civil wrong consisting of deliberately or recklessly misinforming the claimant and thereby causing loss (**6.2**). It is also sometimes called *fraud*, though that word has a number of meanings in different contexts.

Defamation A civil wrong protecting reputation (**8.1**).

Duty of care A legal duty owed by one person to another, to take reasonable care for their safety (**1.27**). Breach of a duty of care is a necessary element in proving *negligence*.

Economic torts A set of related civil wrongs, providing remedies in some cases where a defendant deliberately inflicts economic harm on a claimant (ch 6).

Exemplary damages Damages going beyond those necessary to compensate the claimant, awarded in order to punish the defendant (**10.10**). Compare *aggravated damages* and *compensatory damages*.

False imprisonment A civil wrong which consists of depriving someone else of their freedom of movement (**2.11**).

Fraud (1) The civil wrong consisting of deliberately or recklessly misinforming the claimant and thereby causing loss. (2) Criminal liability covering the same sort of conduct. (3) Neglect of equitable duty (**6.2**).

General damages Damages for losses which cannot be itemized and proved but which are nonetheless presumed to have occurred (**10.9**). Compare *special damages*.

Genus tort A suggested civil wrong, consisting of interference with the claimant's trade interest by unlawful means (**6.27**).

Horizontal effect (of the human rights legislation) The recognition of rights which individuals have against one another; compare *vertical effect* (**1.25**).

Indemnity A right to recover certain types of losses from another person.

Injunction A court order instructing the defendant to behave in a particular way (**10.2**).

Innuendo An inference which reasonable people would draw from a particular statement, but only if they have certain special knowledge (**8.6**).

Intimidation The civil wrong of causing harm by means of an unlawful threat (**6.10**).

Joint liability A liability where two or more people took part in the same wrong and are jointly responsible for the consequences (**9.13**). Compare *several liability*.

Jus tertii A defence to a civil wrong of taking another's property, that while the claimant may have a better right to the property than the defendant, there is someone else with a still better claim (**7.4**) (Latin: 'right of a third party').

Justification This word has a number of meanings, clustering around the notion of providing a defence for what would normally be seen as indefensible conduct. In particular, (1) in the *economic torts*, pursuit of legitimate economic interests may sometimes be a defence (**6.26**); and (2) in *defamation*, the truth of the statement made may be a defence (**8.27**).

Learned Hand test A suggested test for the presence of negligence, that the defendant is responsible for a particular accident if and only if the cost of preventing it would have been less than (the probability that it would occur) multiplied by (the extent of the loss) (**1.39**).

Libel *Defamation* in cases where the offending statement was in written or otherwise permanent form (**8.20**). Compare *slander.*

Limitation Legal principle that claims must be brought within a particular time limit, usually measured as a certain number of years from the time when a claim could first have been brought (**11.32**).

Malice A word used in a number of different senses, all of them suggesting some blameworthy state of mind. (1) *Malicious falsehood* is a civil wrong consisting of harming another's interests by the deliberate circulation of false statements (**8.42**). (2) The defence of *qualified privilege* is not available if the defendant was motivated by 'malice', meaning personal spite against the claimant (**8.30**).

Malicious falsehood A civil wrong consisting of harming another's interests by the deliberate circulation of false statements (**8.42**).

Negligence (1) This word is sometimes used loosely to mean 'carelessness'. (2) More precisely, it denotes a civil wrong which is established when the claimant can prove *(i)* that the defendant owed the claimant a *duty of care*; *(ii)* that the defendant broke this duty; and *(iii)* that this breach of duty caused loss to the claimant (**1.26**).

Neighbour (1) Someone who lives next door. (2) Someone who is so closely affected by your behaviour that you ought reasonably to consider their safety before acting in a dangerous way (**1.27**).

Neighbour principle The legal principle that those who are your *neighbours* (sense 2) are likely to be owed a *duty of care* by you (**1.27**).

Nervous shock A psychiatric injury to the claimant, not amounting to a physical injury but going beyond mere distress or grief. Most examples of nervous shock would be diagnosed as Post-Traumatic Shock Disorder (PTSD) (**3.18**).

Novus actus interveniens An unexpected occurrence which disrupts causal chains, making it hard to blame those who acted before the *novus actus* for events occurring after it (Latin: 'new intervening act') (**10.41**).

Nuisance An interference with another's property right, falling short of actually taking it from its rightful owner (**7.11**). The remedies available for nuisance distinguish between a *public nuisance* and a *private nuisance.*

Objective test A test which concentrates on objective facts about the situation in which the defendant was placed rather than subjective facts about what was going through the defendant's mind (**1.41**).

Primary publisher The person with whom a particular statement originates (**8.7**). Compare *secondary publisher*.

Primary victim (of *nervous shock*) A victim of *nervous shock* who was in physical danger of personal injury (**3.21**); compare *secondary victim*.

Private nuisance A remedy for *nuisance* whereby the claimant complains simply that their own rights have been infringed, without invoking any wider public interest (**7.11**). Compare *public nuisance*.

Privilege Liberty to make statements without attracting legal consequences. In the context of defamation, it is usual to distinguish between *absolute privilege* and *qualified privilege*.

Proximate (1) Close. (2) Sufficiently closely affected by someone's conduct for that someone to owe a *duty of care* (**1.29**). Compare *remote*.

PTSD Post-Traumatic Shock Disorder. See *nervous shock*.

Public nuisance A remedy for a *nuisance* which affects a significant number of people as well as the claimant (**7.30**). Compare *private nuisance*.

Punitive damages Means the same as *exemplary damages* (**10.15**).

Pure economic loss A loss which is economic (so that it can be stated in terms of money), but does not constitute either property damage or personal injury (and so is 'purely' economic) (**5.7**).

Qualified privilege A defence to an action in *defamation*, by which the defendant is free of liability unless the claimant can establish *malice* (sense 2) (**8.28**).

Quia timet injunction An *injunction* trying to nip wrongful behaviour in the bud, by instructing the defendant not to commence a particular line of conduct (Latin: 'because [the claimant] is afraid...') (**10.3**).

Remote (1) Far away. (2) Sufficiently removed from someone's conduct for that someone not to owe a *duty of care* in respect of it (**1.29**). Compare *proximate*.

Res ipsa loquitur Legal principle that facts which strongly suggest *negligence* will be taken as proof of *negligence* unless the defendant can provide an alternative explanation of them (Latin: 'the facts speak for themselves') (**1.38**).

Secondary publisher A person who did not originate a particular statement but nonetheless aided its circulation (**8.7**). Compare *primary publisher*.

Secondary victim (of *nervous shock*) A victim of *nervous shock* who was not in physical danger of personal injury (**3.22**); compare *primary victim*.

Several liability A liability where two or more people independently commit wrongs, accidentally leading to their all being responsible in respect of the same damage (**9.13**). Compare *joint liability*.

Slander *Defamation* in cases where the offending statement was spoken and not in more permanent form (**8.20**). Compare *libel*.

Special damages Damages for losses which can be itemized and proved (**10.9**). Compare *general damages*.

Special relationship A relationship of trust which is so extraordinarily close that an especially demanding *duty of care* may be imposed to recognize it, going beyond the *duty of care* resulting from their being *neighbours* (sense 2) (**5.14**).

Strict liability Liability which involves a more demanding standard of fault than liability based on *negligence* (**1.3**).

Thin skull rule The rule that a defendant who causes personal injury is liable for the entire injury, even if its extent was unforeseeable or too *remote* (sense 2) from the defendant's conduct (**10.34**).

Tort A tort is one type of civil wrong, entitling the victim to sue the perpetrator in a civil court (**1.1**)

Tortfeasor Some who commits a *tort*.

Trespass A reference to a number of civil wrongs, with a common theme of wrongly invading the claimant's protected interest. So it may refer to (1) trespass to the person (*assault, battery* or *false imprisonment* (ch 2)); (2) trespass to land (**7.2**); or (3) trespass to chattels (not covered in this book).

Vertical effect (of the human rights legislation) The recognition of rights which individuals have against public authorities; compare *horizontal effect* (**1.23**).

Vicarious liability Liability not on the basis that the defendant committed a wrong but on the basis that someone the defendant employed committed a wrong (**9.2**).

Volenti non fit injuria Legal principle that no claimant can sue over behaviour to which he or she consented (Latin: 'No injury is suffered by one who consents') (**11.2**).

Index